Aggression
and
Violence
Throughout
the
Life Span

*This book is dedicated to Gerald R. Patterson
and the memory of Richard Haig Walters
for their inspiration and for serving
as consummate role models
of scientist-practitioner.*

Aggression
and
Violence
Throughout
the
Life Span

Ray DeV. Peters
Robert J. McMahon
Vernon L. Quinsey
editors

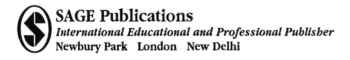

SAGE Publications
International Educational and Professional Publisher
Newbury Park   London   New Delhi

For information address:

SAGE Publications, Inc.
2455 Teller Road
Newbury Park, California 91320

SAGE Publications Ltd.
6 Bonhill Street
London EC2A 4PU
United Kingdom

SAGE Publications India Pvt. Ltd.
M-32 Market
Greater Kailash I
New Delhi 110 048 India

Printed in the United States of America

Library of Congress Cataloging-in-Publication Data

Main entry under title:

Aggression and violence throughout the life span / edited by Ray
  DeV. Peters, Robert J. McMahon, Vernon L. Quinsey.
      p. cm.
    Proceedings of the 22nd Banff International Conference on
  Behavioural Science, March, 1990.
    Includes bibliographical references and index.
    ISBN 0-8039-4550-7. — ISBN 0-8039-4551-5 (pbk.)
    1. Violence—Psychological aspects—Congresses. 2. Aggressiveness
  (Psychology)—Congressess. I. Peters, Ray DeV., 1942-
  II. McMahon, Robert J. (Robert Joseph), 1953- . III. Quinsey,
  Vernon L. IV. Banff International Conference on Behavioural Science
  (22nd: 1990: Banff, Alta.)
  RC569.5.V55A29 1992
  155.2'32—dc20   92-28264

92 93 94 95 96 10 9 8 7 6 5 4 3 2 1

Sage Production Editor: Astrid Virding

Contributors

Elaine A. Blechman, Department of Psychology, University of Colorado, Boulder, CO

Jean E. Dumas, Department of Psychological Sciences, Purdue University, West Lafayette, IN

Donald G. Dutton, Department of Psychology, University of British Columbia, Vancouver, British Columbia

Edna B. Foa, Department of Psychiatry, Medical College of Pennsylvania, Philadelphia, PA

Adelle E. Forth, Department of Psychology, Carleton University, Ottawa, Ontario

Robert D. Hare, Department of Psychology, University of British Columbia, Vancouver, British Columbia

Grant T. Harris, Research Department, Mental Health Centre, Penetanguishene, Ontario

Joseph P. Hornick, Canadian Research Institute for Law and the Family, c/o Faculty of Law, University of Calgary, Calgary, Alberta

Peter G. Jaffe, Departments of Psychology and Psychiatry, University of Western Ontario, London, Ontario

Sarah Landy, C. M. Hincks Treatment Centre, and Department of Psychiatry, University of Toronto, Toronto, Ontario

Janice K. Marques, California State Department of Mental Health, Sacramento, CA

Lynn McDonald, Faculty of Social Work, University of Calgary, Calgary, Alberta

Robin McGee, Department of Psychology, University of Western Ontario, London, Ontario

Craig Nelson, Atascadero State Hospital, Atascadero, CA

Dan Olweus, University of Bergen, Norway

Gerald R. Patterson, Oregon Social Learning Center, Eugene, OR

Ray DeV. Peters, Department of Psychology, Queen's University, Kingston, Ontario

Ronald J. Prinz, Department of Psychology, University of South Carolina, Columbia, SC

Vernon L. Quinsey, Department of Psychology, Queen's University, Kingston, Ontario

Deborah Reitzel, London Family Court Clinic, Inc., London, Ontario

Patricia A. Resick, Department of Psychology, University of Missouri-St. Louis, St. Louis, MO

Marnie E. Rice, Research Department, Mental Health Centre, Penetanguishene, Ontario

Gerald B. Robertson, Faculty of Law, University of Alberta, Edmonton, Alberta

Barbara O. Rothbaum, School of Medicine, Emory University, Atlanta, GA

Katy E. Strachan, Department of Psychology, University of British Columbia, Vancouver, British Columbia

Marlies Sudermann, London Family Court Clinic, Inc., London, Ontario

William D. Walker, Department of Psychology, Queen's University, Kingston, Ontario

Christine Wekerle, Department of Psychology, University of Western Ontario, London, Ontario

David A. Wolfe, The Institute for the Prevention of Child Abuse, and Department of Psychology, University of Western Ontario, London, Ontario

Contents

Preface

This volume is one in a continuing series of publications resulting from the Banff International Conference on Behavioural Science. These unique conferences have been held each spring since 1969 in Banff, Alberta, Canada. They serve the purpose of bringing together behavioral scientists and professionals in a forum where they can present and discuss emergent issues and topics. Thus, the Banff Conferences, as a continuing event, have served as an expressive "early indicator" of the developing nature and composition of behavioral science and scientific application.

Because distance, schedules, and restricted audience preclude wide attendance at the conferences, the resulting publications have equal status with the conferences proper. Presenters at each Banff Conference are required to write a chapter specifically for the forthcoming book, separate from their presentation and discussion at the conference itself. Consequently, this volume is not just a conference proceedings. Rather, it is an integrated volume of chapters contributed by leading researchers and practitioners who have had the unique opportunity of spending several days together presenting and discussing ideas prior to preparing their chapters.

In planning this volume, we held numerous conversations with colleagues working on the topics of aggression and violence. One issue that continually arose was the lack of integration of research and theory between the fields of childhood aggression on the one hand and adult aggression on the other. With some rare exceptions, those researchers and clinicians who deal with antisocial, externalizing problems in children and young adolescents employ different theories, concepts, and terminology than those who focus their professional attention on older adolescents and adults.

An important reason for this lack of connectedness between the study of childhood and adult aggression is that the field of developmental psychology has been dominated by those interested in children. It has been only within the past decade that theories and principles of development have begun to be extended to the analysis of human behavior throughout the entire lifespan from conception to death. This lifespan developmental perspective has come to influence many analyses of personality and cognition. However, there has been no systematic attempt to incorporate these principles into theories of aggression and violence. A major purpose of the present volume is to contribute to such an endeavor by bringing together behavioral scientists and practitioners who are concentrating their work on aggression at different points throughout the lifespan from infancy to old age. The scope of the chapters provides a unique developmental perspective on some of society's most perplexing and pernicious problems.

The volume is organized in an approximate chronological sequence. The first six chapters examine issues in the development of aggression in young children, and the progression of these behaviors to older children and adolescents. The second half of the volume concentrates on the analysis and treatment of aggression and violent behaviors in adults, ending with a review of the issues in the newest field of study in this area, elder abuse.

The book is directed toward students, practitioners, and researchers who are interested in the study and treatment of antisocial behaviors from a behavioral science perspective. It presumes a basic understanding of statistics and experimental design typical of advanced undergraduate students in the social sciences.

In bringing together an overview of the current work of several leading scientists and practitioners who are concentrating their efforts at various ages and stages of human development, we hope that this volume will help break down the isolation between those working with children and adults, and stimulate future attempts to incorporate a lifespan developmental perspective in the analysis of aggression and violence.

We would especially like to thank Philomene Kocher for her diligence in preparing the manuscript for publication, and Valerie Angus for her secretarial services. Also, we would like to acknowledge the expert guidance and support which we received from C. Terry Hendrix,

Julie Marshall, Astrid Virding, and Kristin Bergstad at Sage Publications. It has been a pleasure working with them.

While preparing this volume, Ray Peters and Vern Quinsey were on the faculty of Queen's University and Bob McMahon was on the faculty of the University of Washington. The assistance and support of these institutions is gratefully acknowledged.

RAY DeV. PETERS
ROBERT J. McMAHON
VERNON L. QUINSEY

The Banff Conferences on Behavioural Science

The Banff Conferences on Behavioural Science, held each spring since 1969 in Banff, Alberta, Canada, have pioneered the "conference of colleagues" format for professional and scientific meetings. Registration is limited and the program is designed for both formal and informal interactions among all participants. Invited addresses and workshops are presented by individuals renowned for the excellence of their research and applied acumen. Conversation hours, poster sessions, banquet, sight-seeing expeditions, and cross-country and down-hill skiing in the spectacular Canadian Rockies provide the opportunity to interact with colleagues in a relaxed atmosphere.

The original conference in 1969 had as its theme "Ideal Mental Health Services". The policy consciously adopted at that conference, and followed ever since, was to identify for the presentation of each year's theme those behavioral science researchers who could best identify the state of the art. In 1969, the conference faculty were Nathan Azrin, Ogden Lindsley, Gerald Patterson, Todd Risley, and Richard Stuart.

The conference topics for the first 21 years were as follows:

1969: I. Ideal Mental Health Services
1970: II. Services and Programs for Exceptional Children and Youth
1971: III. Implementing Behavioral Programs for Schools and Clinics
1972: IV. Behavior Change: Methodology, Concepts, and Practice

1973: V. Evaluation of Behavioral Programs in Community, Residential, and School Settings

1974: VI. Behavior Modification and Families and Behavior Modification Approaches to Parenting

1975: VII. The Behavioral Management of Anxiety, Depression, and Pain

1976: VIII. Behavioral Self-Management Strategies, Techniques, and Outcomes

1977: IX. Behavioral Systems for the Developmentally Disabled

      A. School and Family Environments

      B. Institutional, Clinic and Community Environments

1978: X. Behavioral Medicine: Changing Health Lifestyles

1979: XI. Violent Behavior: Social Learning Approaches to Prediction, Management, and Treatment

1980: XII. Adherence, Compliance, and Generalization in Behavioral Medicine

1981: XIII. Essentials of Behavioral Treatments for Families

1982: XIV. Advances in Clinical Behavior Therapy

1983: XV. Childhood Disorders: Behavioral-Developmental Approaches

1984: XVI. Education in "1984"

1985: XVII. Social Learning and Systems Approaches to Marriage and the Family

1986: XVIII. Health Enhancement, Disease Prevention and Early Intervention: Biobehavioral Perspectives

1987: XIX. Early Intervention in the Coming Decade

1988: XX. Behavior Disorders of Adolescence: Research, Intervention, and Policy in Clinical and School Settings

1989: XXI. Sports Psychology and Health Promotion

The topic for Banff XXII, held in 1990, was "Aggression and Violence Throughout the Life Span." Leading social scientists and clinicians from North America and Europe interested in the integration of empirical research with clinical application presented their current work on the study of aggressive and violent behavior.

Over the years, many people have contributed notably to the success of these conferences. Those who have attended the conferences and participated so enthusiastically in the presentations and discussions, both formally and informally, contribute enormously to their success. In particular, we would again like to express our appreciation to

Catherine Hardie-Wigram, and to Jeri Dellow of the Banff Centre for Conferences. Catherine has been extensively involved in the planning and coordination of these conferences since 1973. Her outstanding organizational skills are matched only by her patience in dealing with a revolving committee of conference planners. Jeri was a tremendous help in organizing and carrying out Banff XXII. In addition to the editors of this volume, other members of the conference Planning Committee for Banff XXII were Kenneth D. Craig and L. A. Hamerlynck.

1

Toward an Understanding of a Developmental
Paradigm for Aggressive Conduct Problems
During the Preschool Years

SARAH LANDY
RAY DeV. PETERS

The majority of publications that have discussed the early identification and treatment of conduct disorders have referred to elementary school-aged children (e.g., Farrington, Ohlin, & Wilson, 1986; Patterson, Debaryshe, & Ramsey, 1989). More recently, the aggressive conduct problems of young preschool children have become a focus of interest and research (e.g., Bates & Bayles, 1988; Greenberg & Speltz, 1988; Speltz, Greenberg, & Deklyen, 1990). This interest had primarily stemmed from a realization that current treatment strategies with older children are only successful with certain populations and often do not show transferability across situations and over time (Kazdin, 1991).

Similarly, it is widely acknowledged that treatment of many disorders identifiable in young children is more successful the earlier it is provided, before patterns of personality and interactions become entrenched and extremely resistant to change (Loeber, 1991). A number of recent surveys have identified from 14%-73% of preschoolers as having mild to severe behavioral problems (e.g.,Campbell, 1990; Hooks, Mayes, & Volkmar, 1988; Landy & Peters, 1990; Richman, Stevenson, & Tamplin, 1985), and have cited aggressive acting-out behaviors as the main manifestation. Perhaps even more significantly, several longitudinal studies have shown that chronic conduct problems beginning in early childhood later prove to be the most difficult to treat and the most intractable (Campbell, 1985; Campbell, Ewing, Breaux, & Szumowski, 1986; Olweus, 1979; Rose, Rose, & Feldman, 1989; Shamsie, 1991; White, Moffit, Earls, Robins, & Silva, 1990). As stated by Patterson et al., (1989), the stability of conduct disorders "suggests a single underlying continuum" from early childhood through adolescence to adulthood.

In spite of this growing interest in and realization of the need to treat conduct disorders at earlier ages, surprisingly little is known about the very early developmental pathways of conduct disorders from birth through the preschool years to early childhood. Yet knowledge of early etiology is essential if optimal preventative and early treatment services are to be provided. The purpose of this chapter is to review research findings that have addressed the etiology of early aggressive conduct problems and to suggest a developmental paradigm for the disorder in the preschool years.

Description of Preschoolers With
Aggressive Conduct Problems

In articles discussing aggressive conduct problems in preschoolers, researchers have typically described a collection of antisocial behavioral symptoms including extreme tantrums and aggressiveness, chronic noncompliance, argumentativeness and stubbornness, intense reactions to limit setting, and immature expression and control of emotions (e.g, Behar & Stewart, 1984; Campbell, 1990). These symptoms may or may not be accompanied by hyperactivity and/or difficulties with concentration. Although the list of symptoms noted varies among authors, all refer to strong opposition to the rules of home and/or day care and an inability to self-regulate under the stress of the arousal of intense emotions as central to the problems of these children.

Some writers have tried to go beyond external symptoms to describe the underlying conditions and deficits that may contribute to these behavioral manifestations. A number of authors have described how the excessive display of aggressive behavior may be used to ward off feelings of insecurity, aloneness, and anxiety (Greenspan, 1981; Kashani, Deuser, & Reid, 1991; Werkman, 1985). Other writers have noted difficulties and delays in the acquisition of certain capacities such as symbolization as expressed in language and pretend play; control of motor activities; attending and focusing on stimuli in the environment; and self-regulation of intense affective states (Greenspan, 1981; Santostefano, 1978, 1985). In summary, these children can be described as disorganized, fragmented, unfocused, as well as hostile, angry, and noncompliant. It appears that they have less tolerance for negative emotions than other children and that this produces not only poor control of anger, but also a lower flexibility and range of responses in stressful situations (Block & Block, 1980; Trad, 1989; Wolfson, Fields, & Rose, 1987).

The Development of Aggression and Affect Regulation

Although a considerable amount of data concerning aggression in children and disturbed behavior in the preschool years has been presented in a vast number of publications (Parke & Slaby, 1983), relatively little is known about "the developmental changes in the form and elicitors of aggression in children, as well as their relationship to earlier behavioral antecedents" (p. 569). In looking for precursors of later developmental difficulties, we need to examine and measure features of early development that are theoretically related, but not necessarily behaviorally similar, to excessive aggression. The development of affect regulation would appear to be such a capacity that can enable a child to "redirect, control, modulate, modify and bring about, adaptive functioning in emotionally arousing situations" (Cicchetti, Ganiban, & Barnett, 1990, p. 1). For it may be in the failures of adequate development of this capacity that the understanding of excessive aggression and conduct disorders may lie.

Over the last 15 years there has been very little research examining the development and regulation of aggressive behavior in preschool children. This lack has been due primarily to a shift in interest toward understanding instead the development of prosocial behavior and competence in young children (Osofsky, 1987; Parke & Slaby, 1983). The researchers who have most clearly analyzed the early developmental stages of aggression have been Parens (1979) and Szegal (1985). They have proposed stages for the development of aggressive behaviors, although Parens only studied these behaviors up to 2 years of age and Szegal to 4 years. However, observations of these authors, as well as studies by earlier researchers, enable us to identify times of increased aggression as well as periods when aggression begins to decrease. Such a developmental sequence is presented in Table 1.1. In the next sections of this chapter, we will outline the development of the display of aggression and the internal and external factors that can bring aggression under control. Such a model of normal development may contribute to the identification of children who are atypical in the nonverbal or verbal expression of aggression and delayed in acquiring other related critical capacities.

Birth to 12 Months

Development of Aggression

According to some researchers, anger can be elicited in the newborn (Campos, Barrett, Lamb, Goldsmith, & Stenberg, 1983; Parens, 1979). However, most writers limit their definition of aggressive acts to those that intend to harm or physically injure, therefore, aggression cannot be attributed to a behavior until the child has reached the stage of intentionality "when some representation of self, object and aggressive aim could exist in the mind of the child" (Edgecumbe & Sandler, 1974). The age at which intentional behavior develops has been placed at between 4 and 10 months by most writers (Harding, 1983; Kagan, 1974; Piaget, 1952).

In his observational studies, Szegal (1985) identified the first manifestations of aggression as occurring between 7 and 12 months and reported them as typically occurring in relation to somatically painful stimuli or discomfort, other experiences of tension or frustration, and particularly when the infant needed attention or comfort. Parens (1979), on the other hand, claimed that the biological upsurge of aggression begins during the separation-individuation phase at 5 months and viewed it as frequently discharged at the primary caregiver. Thus there appears to be evidence that aggressive behavior is present in the second half of the first year, although agreement about the nature of the cause and elicitors of this behavior is limited.

The Development of Affect Regulation

During this first year Greenspan (1981) comments on the importance of the infant obtaining physiological homeostasis or self-regulation in the first 3 months of life, allowing the infant to "maintain a state of equilibrium in the face of internal and external stimulation." Sander

TABLE 1.1 The Development of the Expression of Aggression and Affect Regulation

Age (months)	Aggressive Behavior	Affect Regulation
0-12	First aggressive behaviors appear at 5-7 months as a result of frustration of pleasure, pain, or an upsurge of independence.	Physiological self-regulation achieved. Self-management of tension begins. Periods of interest and interaction with environment increase. Responds in intentional way with understanding of primary cause and effect. Attachment achieved with primary caregiver. Recognizes permanence of self. Uses multiple sensory modalities and range of emotions.
12-24	Physical aggression increases, particularly over issues of possession, social issues with peers, and as the child pushes toward separation and individuation.	Child can show a full range of human emotions. Increased capacity for language and pretend play. Mental representations of self and others become organized. Develops complicated play sequences and may play reciprocally with others. Compliance increases to about 45% of the time.
24-36	Aggression in response to limit setting peaks at about 30 months. In second half of third year child gradually becomes more able to express aggression in verbal and more socially acceptable ways.	Language and pretend play become increasingly elaborate. Recovers spontaneously from temper tantrums. Emotion and cognition become increasingly integrated and anger is expressed in an organized fashion. Prosocial and empathetic behaviors increase.
36-60	By three years, a significant drop in physical expression of aggression usually takes place. Outside the family, aggression becomes limited to verbal aggression only.	Social perspective taking now possible. Understands own part in bringing about consequences. Begins to regulate own actions without external control. Develops identification with controller and sense of conscience. Responds to limits and follows rules most of the time.

(1962) has written about a similar stage of "initial adaptation," while Cicchetti, Ganiban, and Barnett (1990) refer to the capacity for "homeostatic regulation." This internal stability is achieved through the stabilization of the physiological rhythm of eating, elimination, and sleep/wake cycle. Once established, any change will cause tension within the system.

Although minimally present from birth, there is a tremendous increase during the period from 3 to 12 months in the infant's capacity and desire for social interaction, and for experiences of competence in acting on the world. Similarly, the infant develops cognitive capacities that allow for an understanding of the relationships between actions and consequences and the formation of mental representations or memories of people and events. The next critical landmark occurs between 9 and 12 months and serves to organize affect, cognition, and behavioral expression around the availability of the primary caregiver. This attachment relationship is dependent on earlier experiences with primary caregivers, and as patterns are internalized their emotional quality and synchrony will have a significant impact on the child's style of affect regulation, and ultimately on their capacity to reduce the expression of aggressive behavior under stress (Kobak & Sceery, 1988; Main, Kaplan, & Cassidy, 1985; Oppenheim, Sagi, & Lamb, 1988). At first attachment security is fragile. The capacity for object constancy, that is, the ability to remember and utilize the memory of attachment figures in times of stress and frustration, takes many months to develop and may even fail to develop adequately in many children.

Age 12-24 Months

Development of Aggression

Most researchers identify a rapid increase in the overall frequency of aggression during the second year between about 18 and 24 months (Goodenough, 1931; Montagner, Restoin, & Henry, 1982; Szegal, 1985).

Several reasons for this increase have been proffered. Parens (1979) emphasizes the infant's inability to maintain object constancy in the face of the caregiver's limit setting and refusal of the infant's immediate gratification. During these frustrating moments, the infant no longer remembers the "good" nurturing caregiver and becomes devastated and furious. This "splitting" of the "good" and "bad" caregiver may continue into the third year of life and contributes to many of the temper tantrums so typical of the "terrible twos." Similarly, Spitz (1969) and Wenar (1982) see the beginning of negativism and "no saying," and Mahler, Pine, and Bergmann (1975) describe the push toward independence as contributing to the upsurge in the degree of aggressive behaviors.

Most observational studies of toddler aggression have taken place in daycares and nursery schools, and identify possession or object acquisition as the most frequent motivators for aggressive behavior (Dawes, 1934; Goodenough, 1931; Szegal, 1985). In these studies, social difficulties with peers are also seen as major contributors.

The Development of Affect Regulation

Typically, by the end of the second year children became capable of displaying and labeling a full range of human emotions including sympathy, jealousy, and other more subtle affective experiences. They develop an increasing awareness of self as an autonomous agent and most important, change from a style of affect regulation that is primarily sensorimotor to one that relies on representational capacities. These growing symbolic capacities, which include language and pretend play, are vital in the further development of the ability to monitor, modify, and modulate behavior and emotional expression (Emde, 1985; Kopp, 1982). Play and language become more and more elaborate and are used increasingly to modulate tension and anxiety throughout the second and third years of life. Similarly, representations of pleasant experiences, objects, and attachment figures become stable and begin to sustain the child during times of stress and separation from primary caregivers. Children also become able to use negotiation in times of conflict and during separation from caregivers (Cicchetti, Cummings, Greenberg, & Marvin, 1990; Marvin, 1977).

Other important capacities that impact on the control of aggression are the inhibition of behavior in response to limits. Vaughn, Koop, and Krakow (1984) have noted self-initiated inhibition of behaviors fleetingly available to children as young as 18 months. This guiding of their own behavior without reference to the inhibiting behavior of the caregiver was found by Power and Chapieski (1986) about 45% of the time in 2-year-olds.

Finally, prosocial behavior and empathetic response to distress of others have been exhibited by children as young as 18 months (Eisenberg & Mussen, 1989; Yarrow & Waxler, 1976).

Age 24-36 Months

Development of Aggression

The frequency of aggressive behavior typically continues to increase until about 30 months and then gradually decreases (Hartup, 1974). Verbal aggression increases while biting, hitting, hair-pulling, throwing objects, and pushing are reduced (Cicchetti, Cummings et al., 1990; Goodenough, 1931; Sroufe, 1990; Stern, 1985; Szegal, 1984, 1985). Miller and Sperry (1987) found that children as young as 2½ years of age could express their anger verbally as well as justify it in a rudimentary way. They also point out that aggression toward the establishment of routine physical habits and authority conflicts may predominate in this year.

In an observational study, Fagot and Hagan (1985) noted that although physical aggressive incidents were infrequent, when they did occur, they lasted longer in older children.

The Development of Affect Regulation

During this period affect becomes much more integrated with thoughts and cognition. As language and the ability to play become more and more elaborate, by 2½ years of age children become increasingly able to describe and control their own negativism and anger through expressions in verbalizations and symbolic play (Vygotsky, 1976). Well modulated children can talk about internal states and feelings, which in turn facilitates control over nonverbal emotional expressions and enhances regulation of the emotions themselves (Bretherton, Fritz, Zahn-Waxler, & Ridgeway, 1986).

Age 36-60 Months

Development of Aggression

Most researchers report a drop in the amount of physical aggression before 3 years of age (e.g., Ammons & Ammons, 1953; Montagner et al., 1982; Szegal, 1985). Jersild and Markey (1935) and Roff and Roff (1940) both put the drop in aggression as children pass 3 years of age. At the same time, there is usually an increase in the total amount of time spent in social interactions without physical fighting. Most expression of aggression in this age period, at least outside the family, is restricted to verbal expressions of anger and is in response to conflicts with peers, particularly over possessions (Ramsey, 1987).

The Development of Affect Regulation

At this time children gradually begin to internalize standards and rules and to identify with the controller or the caregivers who have provided them with external limits for aggressive behavior and have modeled and encouraged capacities to modulate it. The development of conscience enables children to delay immediate impulses (Freud, 1968) and frees them from primary reliance on external controls and standards (Campbell, 1990; Gould, 1982; Kopp, 1982). Egocentricity starts to give way to an emerging capacity for empathetic responding and an understanding of the point of view of others (Borke, 1975; Liben, 1978; Marcus, Roke, & Bruner, 1985; Shantz, 1983). As a part of this capacity, children are able to understand their own part in bringing about consequences. A sense of personal responsibility, a "wish to please" as well as the desire to succeed, become excellent tools for early social adjustment and academic achievement in school (Campbell, 1990).

The Growth-Promoting Environment

Young children acquire the important capacities discussed in the above sections through a combination of biological maturation coupled with sensitively attuned and appropriately timed interactions with caregivers. The need for well attuned interactions with caregivers is particularly true of the development of the more complex and adaptive components of personality such as those of empathy and self-regulation (Kopp, 1982). With surveys reporting growing numbers of conduct-disordered and aggressive preschoolers, it would appear that a number of young children may not be receiving the type of interactions that are necessary in order for them to develop control of aggression. An overview of these interactional requirements, and the consequences of failing to receive them, appears in Table 1.2.

Although there is as yet no clear developmental pathway for affect regulation, a number of researchers have delineated some of the important components of parent-child interaction that are applicable to the fostering of adequate self-regulation. These principles are that:

TABLE 1.2 Interactional Needs in the Development of Affect Regulation and the Consequences of Failures in Their Provision

Age (months)	Interactional Needs	Developmental Failures
0-12	Caregiver helps the infant achieve regularity in eating, sleeping, and elimination. Provides infant with learning experiences that are stimulating but not overwhelming. Consistent caregiving allows infant to develop sense of predictability and secure attachment. Provides positive emotionality during holding and face-to-face interactions.	Extreme irritability. No predictable pattern of eating, sleeping, and elimination. Infant shows lack of organized behavior toward objects and people. Infant shows insecure attachment to primary caregivers. Display of affect unpredictable and intense in times of stress and frustration.
12-24	Caregiver encourages the development of symbolic expression of anger through play and language. Teaches child to acknowledge and label wide range of feelings. Begins to set structures and limits in consistent and calm manner. Teaches child negotiation at separation and reunions.	Continues to use only sensory-motor modes to express anger and aggression. Delayed development of pretend play and language. Lack of ability to delay gratification. Disintegration of behavior in response to limit setting. Inability to separate from caregiver without extreme anxiety or acting out.
24-36	Caregiver continues to encourage play and language. Accepts and labels a full range of affects. Provides structure and limits consistently. Positive emotionality predominates in interactions with child.	Child is still unable to control anger and physical aggression toward others. Displays short attention span and inability to play alone or with peers. Delays in impulse control and lack of self-talk evident. Inability to play with others, lack of empathy and prosocial behaviors.
36-60	Caregiver continues to model prosocial behavior and display appropriate empathy for sad and negative feelings. Child is encouraged to show independent functioning within clear structures. Supports child in efforts to control anger and aggression.	Cycle of anger and acting out and rejection evident. Child continues to disintegrate and regress in times of stress and frustration. Child shows lack of interest in symbolic play and learning new activities.

(a) The earliest interactions between the primary caregiver and infant are critically important and must provide a sufficient level of sensitive responding to the infant's needs and synchronized attunement to his or her signals and cues in order for development to proceed normally. For it is in these first interactions that physiological regulation is established and, as importantly, interactional patterns and self/other representations begin to be formed to become a foundation for later social relationships and styles of relating (Tronick, 1989).

(b) A positive emotional tone in early and subsequent interactions between infants, young children, and their caregivers is critical for emotional development and particularly for affect regulation (Emde, 1985; Giannino & Tronick, 1991; Tronick, 1989). Literature on social referencing in infancy shows clearly that not only do infants and young children mirror their caregivers' emotions, they also rely on their facial and vocal displays of affects to guide their own affective displays, their understanding of the affective meaning of events, and then to use them to guide their subsequent action and behavior (Klinnert, Campos, Sorce, Emde, & Svejda, 1983). Caregivers need to use positive, joyful, and soothing interactions to shift negative emotional states to more positive ones, especially if anger and sadness become overwhelming for the infant. It would appear that memory traces of the affective nature of early interventions may continue to resonate throughout life, and because they are inaccessible to conscious memory are difficult to change through later therapeutic intervention (Basch, 1988; Cicchetti et al., 1990; Fox & Davidson, 1984).

(c) The caregiver's interactions are critical in helping the infant and young child to tolerate negative affects and to move the child from sensorimotor expression of anger to using more mature modes such as language and pretend play (Vygotsky, 1976). While affirming the legitimacy of negative emotions and responding with empathy the caregiver needs to encourage the child to use more symbolic modes to express them. By helping the child to label his or her feelings, the child is gradually helped to develop an internal control language that can assist in gaining control of increased amounts of anxiety, tension, or frustration (Greenspan, 1981).

(d) The growth-promoting environment also facilitates the development of an early experience of a body self as separate from the caregiver. Frequent episodes of holding, rocking, verbalization, and face-to-face interaction, when provided by the caregiver, not only begin this sense of a positive self for the infant but also provide the opportunity for improving multimodal sensory perception as visual, auditory, tactile, olfactory, and kinesthetic sensations are integrated as part of the interaction.

(e) Similarly, the caregiver needs constantly to provide the infant and young child with learning experiences that can challenge, yet allow the child to return to a comfortable, already mastered, level of functioning when the child indicates a desire to do so. P. V. Trad (1990) believes this "infant previewing" may be essential for the child to feel secure and for optimal development of learning capacities. Certainly, it is critical in terms of creating a sense of efficacy and effectiveness in the young child.

(f) By the caregiver modeling understanding and empathetic reactions to the child's distress and encouraging prosocial behavior, the child is taught perspective-taking, negotiation, and to understand and to "feel" the emotions and needs of others and to use instrumental ways to relieve his or her distress. Once able to empathize with these feelings, the young child is more likely to delay and terminate aggressive behaviors that may cause pain to others.

(g) Finally, the caregiver needs to provide appropriate limit setting and behavior management techniques. This involves noticing positive behaviors and eliminating aggressive acting-out and extreme noncompliance. By providing this structure consistently, the child has an identification figure to rely on, thereby enabling him or her gradually to internalize the rules and demands of society. It is important that the caregiver both limits behaviors while at the same time supports the child's growing sense of independence and autonomy.

The Etiology of Aggressive Conduct Problems in Early Childhood

A number of excellent reviews are available describing studies that have examined the contribution of a number of variables to children's aggression (e.g., Dewit & Hartup, 1974; Feshbach, 1970; Parke & Slaby, 1983). Therefore, this chapter will emphasize factors that can be considered relevant to the development of aggressive conduct problems in very young children.

Sociocultural Factors

Earlier studies have consistently found a strong correlation between lower socioeconomic class and aggression and antisocial behavior in children (e.g., Bettelheim, 1952; Glueck & Glueck, 1950; Minuchin, Montalvio, Guerney, Rosman, & Schumer, 1966). A similarly strong link was found by Offord, Alder, and Boyle (1986) between being on welfare/living in subsidized housing and conduct disorders. However, they note that the link is probably not a direct one and likely to be mediated by family discord and disturbed family functioning. A number of studies have reported that marital conflict and dysfunction, and divorce are associated with problem preschoolers (Hetherington, 1989; Richman, Stevenson, & Graham, 1982). The association is most likely explained by the diminished ability of a depressed or angry custodial parent to provide adequate parenting when a preschooler is most vulnerable to loss of emotional availability of the caregiver and to perceived rejection (Campbell, 1990). In addition, a growing literature describes the impact of perceived lack of social support, socioeconomic distress, contextual factors like marital discord and family violence, and adverse life events on the development of children (Barocas, Seifer, & Sameroff, 1985; Lewis, Pincus, Lovely, Spitzor, & Moy, 1987). Socially isolated and stressed parents are more likely to perceive their children negatively and to engage in inappropriate child management techniques (Campbell, 1990; Farrington, 1987; Greenberg & Speltz, 1988).

Biological and Organismic Vulnerabilities

Neurological disorders, biochemical abnormalities, and temperamental factors have been implicated in the early development of conduct disorders. It is likely that a number of recent changes in prenatal and perinatal practices will make consideration of these factors increasingly important. These include the growing incidence of lack of adequate prenatal care, the high frequency of substance abuse of mothers during pregnancy (Lipsitt, 1990), and the survival of very small premature infants with serious medical sequelae and congenital defects frequently entailing neurological damage (Als, 1986).

In preschoolers and elementary school-aged children frequent minor physical anomalies (Waldrop, Pedersen, & Bell, 1968); prenatal and delivery complications; a high incidence of EEG abnormalities, particularly a pattern characteristic of a much earlier age (Harris, 1978; Hill, 1952); evidence of neurological impairment involving seizures and memory distortions (Brennan, Mednick, & Kandel, 1991; Lewis et al., 1987; Nachson & Denno, 1987); other soft neurological signs (Behar & Stewart, 1982); and a maturational lag in the CNS (Monroe, 1974) have been found more frequently in aggressive children, particularly if their aggression is characterized by explosive violence. Delinquents have also been shown to have a high threshold for arousal compared to normal controls (Brennan et al., 1991; Mednick & Hutchings, 1978). Although correlations have been found in many studies overall, results are inconclusive.

Low IQ, learning disabilities, and poor academic achievement have consistently been found with antisocial children (Lipsitt, Buka, & Lipsitt, 1990; Patterson et al., 1989). Delinquents generally have difficulty with a number of intellectual functions, particularly those requiring abstract reasoning, concept formation, sequential memory, and problem solving (Berman & Siegal, 1976). Recent classroom observational studies of antisocial children show that they spend less time paying attention to task than non-acting-out children (Shinn, Ramsey, Walker, O'Neill, & Steiber, 1987; Walker, Shinn, O'Neill, & Ramsey, 1987). Santostefano (1985) has identified a number of cognitive processes in aggressive children that are not measured on standard intelligence tests but that are seriously dysfunctional, leaving them unable to "learn about themselves by scanning, selecting, and talking about private thoughts, fantasies, and emotions, either literally or symbolically or to express themselves in pretend play" (p. 4).

A pattern of "difficult" temperament has been identified by a number of researchers (Bates & Bayles, 1988; Kagan, 1974; Thomas & Birch, 1977). In Buss and Plomin's definition, *difficulty* refers to children who are hard for caregivers to manage, while Thomas and Birch (1977) have identified a cluster of temperamental attributes, namely "irregularity of biological functions, withdrawal from the new, slow adaptability, intensity of mood and relatively frequent negative mood" (Goldsmith et al., 1987, p. 521). However, the research and concepts are controversial, as some writers, such as Rothbart (1981), do not include a difficulty construct in their definition of temperament (Goldsmith et al., 1987). Nevertheless, observational studies have shown that socialization attempts of caregivers and demands for conformity to rules of family or day care seem to cause intense difficulty from a very early age for some children, suggesting a basis in temperament style (Bates & Bayles, 1988).

Characteristics of the Parents

Having recognized the importance of the parent-child interaction, a number of studies have examined various characteristics of the primary caregivers of aggressive children in order to understand their possible contribution to the development of aggression. The father's antisocial personality has been found to be a critical variable in a number of studies, and the impact is even stronger if he is violent (Stewart & DeBlois, 1983) or alcoholic (Morris, Escoll, & Wexler, 1956). Similarly, maternal psychopathology (especially depression) has frequently been found to be an important contributing factor (Cicchetti & Aber, 1986; Lahey, Russo, Walker, & Piacentini, 1989; Tronick, Cohn, & Shea, 1985; Zahn-Waxler, Cummings, McKnew, & Radke-Yarrow, 1984).

Recently, researchers have been examining parents' "working models of attachment" (i.e., memories of their early relationships with their own parents) and their effect on both their perception of their children, on their interactional patterns with their children, and on the attachment classification and behavior patterns of their preschoolers. Using an adult attachment interview (Main et al., 1985) and preschool attachment measures and classifications (e.g., Cassidy, 1990) strong associations between adult attachment classifications and those of their children have been found (Crowell & Feldman, 1988; Main & Hesse, 1990; Main et al., 1985). Parents with secure attachment tend to have preschoolers who are similarly secure in their attachment. Moreover, similar congruence has been found between parents who have insecure-dismissing, insecure-preoccupied, and insecure-unresolved "working models" of attachment and their children's attachment classifications. Parents who are insecure-dismissing or insecure-unresolved are most likely to have children who show excessive aggression and conduct problems (Erikson, Sroufe, & Egeland, 1985; Renken, Egeland, & Marvinney, 1989). These studies are beginning to show a robust link between the way a parent was parented and the intergenerational repetition of parenting style, although the process whereby the parents' representations of attachment shape those of their child and their behavioral manifestations is still not clear (Crowell & Feldman, 1988; Grossman, Fremmer-Bombik, Rudolph, & Grossman, 1988; Main, 1990; Main et al., 1985).

In a related line of research, Bugental and her associates have been studying parental attributions of children and the relationship of these beliefs to children's "nonresponsiveness" to caretakers. A strong relationship has been found between parents' beliefs about their ability to control the world and their interactions with their children. Mothers low on the sense of "power" were affectively inconsistent and "unconvincing" in issuing of verbal commands (Bugental, 1985; Bugental & Shennum, 1984). Verbal instructions (content) were accompanied by weak vocal intonation. The same kind of messages were found to be typical of the interactions of mothers of aggressive children (Keltikangas-Jarvinen,

1990). According to Bugental (1985), younger children respond to the negative affect and vocal intonation and cannot synthesize the incompatible components of the message. This research can illustrate one way in which parents, unsure about their ability to parent, may convey this uncertainty to their children and thus perpetuate their children's negative behavior and aggression.

Parent-Child Interactions

The majority of studies that have looked at parent-child interactions of conduct-disordered children have focused on observable parent-child interactional patterns and have concentrated on the effects and perpetuation of the reciprocal reinforcement of coercive behaviors in the parent-child dyad (e.g., Patterson et al., 1989).

Other studies that have looked at the type of parental discipline in families with aggressive and conduct-disordered children have noted noncontingent discipline to be characteristic, with parents punishing not only higher numbers of deviant behaviors but also more prosocial and positive behaviors than matched parents without aggressive children (Dumas & Wahler, 1985; Patterson, 1976).

In still other studies it has been found repeatedly that lack of parental affection, actual rejection, low nurturance, love deprivation, and the caregiver's negativism toward the child result in aggressive behavior patterns (Bates & Bayles, 1988; Campbell, 1985; Campbell, Ewing, Breaux, & Szumowski, 1986; Lefkowitz, Eron, Walder, & Huesmann, 1977; Parpal & Maccoby, 1985; Walsh & Beyer, 1987). The earlier the parental rejection occurs, the more likely it is to increase aggressiveness (Kornadt, 1984).

A few attachment researchers have tried to operationalize maternal warmth and rejection in the laboratory and relate it to aggressive and noncompliant behavior in preschoolers (George & Main, 1979; J. A. Crowell, Feldman, & Ginsberg, 1988). They found support for their hypotheses that the mothers of aggressive preschoolers would be less sensitive to and supportive of their children, show more rejection of their approaches, explain the reasons for separations less to their children, and show less enthusiasm for and acknowledgement of their children's successes. Similarly, Blurton-Jones, Ferreira, Brown, and Macdonald (1979) found mothers of very aggressive preschoolers more frequently failed to respond to their children's crying. In summary, a meta-analysis of more than 100 studies showed that parent-child interactions characterized by neglect, rejection, and conflict are the variables most frequently associated with conduct problems at all ages (Loeber & Stouthamer-Loeber, 1986).

A Developmental Paradigm for the Development of Aggressive Conduct Problems in Preschoolers

There are multiple pathways to the development of hyperaggression and conduct problems that reflect the contribution of "transacting genetic, constitutional, neuropsychological, biochemical, psychological and sociological factors" (Cicchetti & Aber, 1986, p. 110). It would appear that significant numbers of children are at risk for developing early conduct problems with some at environmental risk, some primarily at risk because of intraorganismic vulnerabilities, and many at risk from both factors. By the time even very young children present in clinics, a self-perpetuating cycle of acting-out, punishment, and rejecting resulting in more acting-out has often been firmly established. The challenge of diagnosis and early intervention then becomes to determine the relative importance of the various contributory factors and thus to determine the optimal mode of intervention.

In looking for a developmental paradigm for aggressive conduct disorders in young children there is no doubt that the children's earliest and subsequent interactions with their parents are of critical importance. Both partners in those interactions are responding to a number of factors that impact on their ability to engage in mutually pleasurable and sensitive interactions. For the parents, these include their own experiences of being parented in their families of origin, and their sense of control of circumstances (Bugental, 1985). Similarly, the degree of social support and life stressors will impact significantly on the amount of energy and the emotional availability of the caregivers and may have an enormous impact on the early interactions (e.g., Tronick, 1989; Zahn-Waxler et al., 1984).

The infant for his or her part brings a number of individual characteristics into the early relationship, such as the degree of predictability, responsiveness, irritability, hypersensitivity, and the like. These characteristics may be due to a number of biochemical, neurological, or temperamental factors and can have a significant impact on the earliest interactions (Frodi et al., 1978). For the child who develops an aggressive conduct disorder it is likely that a "goodness of fit" with the principal caregivers does not exist and the infant begins to experience traumatic dyssynchronies at a very early age that start to produce significantly aberrant social, biochemical, neurological, and emotional development. To protect himself or herself from the pain of these early interactions the infant may "close himself to stimuli, thereby inhibiting the generation of information necessary for continued growth" (Basch, 1988, p. 108).

By 12 to 24 months the child will already be showing an insecure attachment and will have adopted a strategy of externalizing anxiety by exhibiting excessive crying, biting, tantrumming, and irritability in social situations with others (Matas, Arend, & Sroufe, 1978; Sroufe, 1983). The beginning of circular maladaptive responding between the child and primary caregivers has begun as the parent reacts to the aggressive behaviors and angry, defiant outbursts by further withdrawal of emotional availability, the threatening of abandonment, or by the use of physical punishment. As this cycle of rejection is continually played out, the caregivers fail to help the child develop a number of critical capacities. This style of interacting may compromise cognitive development and lead to failure of the child to resolve a number of critical developmental issues outlined above.

With increased rejection in interactions, the child soon develops a sense of her- or himself and other people as "bad," and as a result of these memorized working models of attachment begins to misinterpret social cues from others in light of these internal models (Dodge & Frame, 1982). A cycle of rejection similar to that already in motion with parents is set up in peer interactions and with teachers. The child is now at risk for failure in social and academic situations. The child's sense of inadequacy will be tragically confirmed at home, at school, and with peers. The child begins to model and to identify with parental or peer figures who use aggression or violence as their way to experience power and to overcome anxiety. The child acts out his or her "bad" self in powerful yet self-defeating ways, in a fixed pattern that soon fails to be altered by experience. As stated by Crittenden (1988) "new experiences will be encoded in terms of the old model and will be rendered useless" (p. 197). Engagement with the world, future interactional options, and even autonomy become constricted. The early pathway to conduct disorders and excessive aggression is now complete (see Figure 1.1) and later factors may be multiplicative rather than simply cumulative (Rutter, 1978). As summarized by Tronick (1989), "no single traumatic juncture or special moment separates the functional and dysfunctional pathways . . . only slowly accumulating interactive experiences with different people and events in different contexts shape the regulatory processes and representations over time" (p. 117).

Implications for Treatment

Up to this time, treatment with conduct disordered children and adolescents has concentrated on methods that have targeted the symptoms of aggression and noncompliance or the surface structure of the interaction. This has generally meant emphasis on improving behavioral interactions between parent and child and teaching parenting techniques that reinforce positive behaviors in the child (e.g., Barkley, 1987; Kennedy, 1982; Oltmanns, Broderick, & O'Leary, 1977; Pellegrini & Urbain, 1985). The deeper level of less obvious contributing factors, particularly emotional, social, and cognitive delays in the child and distorted and insecure attachment models of parents and child, have been largely ignored as targets for intervention. Seen only as the consequences of coercive interactions, they have not been considered as causing the maladaptive interactions and have been considered to be of little importance. Feelings and thoughts of the parent and child have been ignored in favor of identifiable behaviors (Greenberg & Speltz, 1988). This omission may have seriously limited the success of treatment and have contributed to the finding that short-term successes frequently disappear at longer term follow-up (Kazdin, 1987).

The pathway to conduct disorders is complex and treatment may need to target several points in the transacting system simultaneously. We need to consider a much broader conceptualization of treatment needs, to include efforts targeting the development failures of the child, as well as attempts to impact on parent and child behaviors. Dyadic training may need to address, not only discipline techniques of the parents, but also to concentrate on improving affective communication in parent-child dyads, and the parents' perception of themselves and their child (e.g., Johnson, Dowling, & Wesner, 1980; Speltz, 1990; Wesner, Dowling, & Johnson, 1982). In this way improvement in both the child's and the parents' view of self and other as "bad" can begin to be changed and the cycle of rejection described in this chapter interrupted.

We must begin to look to deeper and more extensive levels of treatment. This particularly applies to treatment of high risk and multi-problem families, which to this time have been most resistant to seeking help and least likely to respond to conventional treatment strategies.

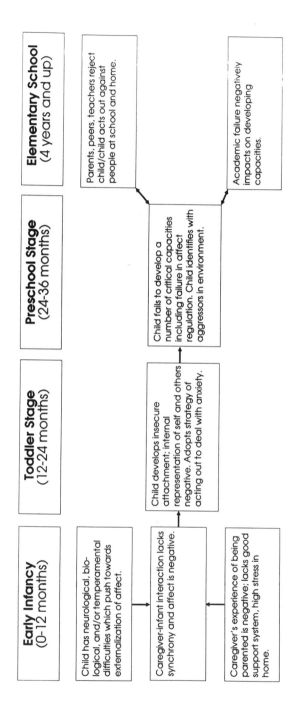

Figure 1.1. Early Developmental Pathway to Conduct Problems

Conclusions

In today's society, a high percentage of young children are at risk for developing emotional dysregulation in general and severe conduct problems in particular. A growing number of societal factors contribute to this trend including an increase in single-parent families and family breakdown, low family incomes, poor quality day care and lack of support systems, all of which contribute to the stress felt by families and caregivers of young children (Campbell, 1990). Tragically, not only are increasing numbers of infants being born at risk for neurological abnormalities and other types of long-term biological impairments, but it also appears that the lack of adequate caregiving that many infants and young children experience may result in inadequate differentiation and impoverished development of neuronal tracts and pathways (Greenough, Black, & Wallace, 1987). Once structural features of neurological development and of personality are developed, they have their own means of self-regulation that tend to maintain the current direction of development (Meyersberg & Post, 1979).

Once developed and entrenched, perceptual, cognitive, and behavioral styles determine what and how the child perceives and what is ignored, how situations are understood, and the plan and style of action chosen to deal with them. These cognitive distortions based on memories of early interactions affect memory, attention, and affect and mediate between early relationships and later personality and behavior. If the child develops negative attributional biases about the behavior of others, he makes hostile, causal inferences about another's intent even in benign circumstances (Dodge & Frame, 1982). The child may encode events so they are consistent with previous experiences. It would seem that between 18 months and 3 to 4 years of age, these models become entrenched and after that time more difficult to access and treat. In spite of a growing realization of the profound importance of the first 5 years of life on later development, less intervention for conduct problems has occurred in this period than in any other.

If we are to improve our treatment strategies, research is critical. We need to continue to improve our understanding of the normal child, how he or she gains control of aggressive behaviors, and how this is dependent and reliant upon other related developmental pathways. It is only through greater understanding of the pathways to optimal development of self-regulatory systems that we will be able to carry out diagnostic decision making enabling us to intervene early with the most at-risk populations and in the most cost effective ways. Sophisticated multi-variate research designs need to be used to articulate more clearly the pathway toward the development of conduct disorders and excessive aggressiveness and the interdependence of various contributing factors. Comparison of treatment strategies in the early years and clearer iden-tification of the critical components of each of these treatment models is also required. It would seem that researchers from a variety of theoretical positions need to come together to understand the etiology and treatment of aggressive conduct problems in the early years.

Without efforts to understand better the early development of aggres-sion and efforts to prevent or to intervene early with those identified as having difficulties, it is likely that success of treatment with conduct disordered children will continue to impact on only the less severely affected, and that the number of conduct disordered children, delin-quent adolescents, and criminal adults and the attendant misery they bring to society will continue to rise. Consequently, this mental health problem will continue to cost society more financial hardship and emotional suffering than any other single disorder.

References

Als, H. (1986). A synactive model of neonatal behavioral organization: Framework for the assessment of neurobehavioral development in the premature infant and support of infants and parents in the neonatal intensive care environment. *Physical Occupational Therapy in Pediatrics, 6,* 3-53.

Ammons, C., & Ammons, B. (1953). Aggression in doll play: Interviews of two-to-six-year-old white males. *Journal of Genetic Psychology, 82,* 205-213.

Barkley, R. A. (1987). *Defiant children: A clinician's manual.* New York: Guilford.

Barocas, R., Seifer, R., & Sameroff, A. J. (1985). Defining environmental risk: Multiple dimensions of psychological vulnerability. *American Journal of Community Psychol-ogy, 13,* 433-447.

Basch, M. F. (1988). *Understanding psychotherapy: The science behind the art.* New York: Basic Books.

Bates, J., & Bayles, K. (1988). Attachment and the development of behavior problems. In J. Belsky & T. Nezworski (Eds.), *Clinical implications of attachment* (pp. 253-299). Hillsdale, NJ: Lawrence Erlbaum.

Behar, D., & Stewart, M. (1982). Aggressive conduct disorder of children: The clinical history and direct observations. *Acta Psychiatrica Scandinavica, 65,* 210-220.

Behar, D., & Stewart, M. (1984). Aggressive conduct disorder: The influence of social class, sex and age on the clinical picture. *Journal of Child Psychology and Psychiatry, 25*(1), 119-124.

Berman, A., & Siegal, A. (1976). A neuropsychological approach to the etiology, prevention and treatment of juvenile delinquency. In A. Davids (Ed.), *Child personality and psychopathology: Current topics* (Vol. 3). New York: John Wiley.

Bettelheim, B. (1952). *Love is not enough.* Glencoe, IL: Free Press.

Block, J., & Block, J. (1980). The role of ego-control and ego-resiliency in the organization of behavior. In W. A. Collins (Ed.), *Minnesota Symposium of Child Psychology* (Vol. 13, pp. 39-101). Hillsdale, NJ: Lawrence Erlbaum.

Blurton-Jones, N., Ferreira, M., Brown, M., & Macdonald, L. (1979). Aggression, crying and physical contact in one-to-three-year-old children. *Aggressive Behavior, 5,* 121-133.

Borke, H. (1975). Piaget's mountains revisited: Changes in the egocentric landscape. *Developmental Psychology, 11,* 240-243.

Brennan, P., Mednick, S., & Kandel, E. (1991). Congenital determinants of violent and property offending. In D. J. Pepler & K. H. Rubin (Eds.), *The development and treatment of childhood aggression* (pp. 81-90). Hillsdale, NJ: Lawrence Erlbaum.

Bretherton, I., Fritz, J., Zahn-Waxler, C., & Ridgeway, D. (1986). Learning to talk about emotion: A functionalist perspective. *Child Development, 57,* 529-548.

Bugental, D. (1985). Unresponsive children and powerless adults: Cocreators of affectively uncertain caregiving environments. In M. Lewis & C. Saarni (Eds.), *The socialization of emotions* (pp. 239-261). New York: Plenum.

Bugental, D., & Shennum, W. (1984). "Difficult" children as elicitors and targets of adult communication patterns: An attributional-behavioral transactional analysis. *Monographs of the Society for Research in Child Development, 49*(Serial No. 205).

Campbell, S. (1985). *Family characteristics and child behavior as precursors of externalizing symptomatology at school entry* (Paper presented at the biennial meeting of the Society for Research in Child Development, Toronto, April 25-28, 1985). (ERIC Document Reproduction Service No. ED 262 871)

Campbell, S. (1990). *Behavior problems in preschool children: Clinical and developmental issues.* New York: Guilford.

Campbell, S., Ewing, L., Breaux, A., & Szumowski, E. (1986). Parent-referred problem three-year-olds: Follow-up at school entry. *Journal of Child Psychology and Psychiatry, 27,* 473-488.

Campos, J., Barrett, K., Lamb, M., Goldsmith, H., & Stenberg, C. (1983). Socioemotional development. In P. H. Mussen (Ed.), *Handbook of child psychology* (Vol. 11, pp. 783-916). New York: John Wiley.

Cassidy, J. (1990). Theoretical and methodological considerations in the study of attachment and the self in young children. In M. Greenberg, D. Cicchetti, & E. M. Cummings (Eds.), *Attachment in the preschool years* (pp. 87-107). Chicago: University of Chicago Press.

Cicchetti, D., & Aber, J. L. (1986). Early precursors of later depression: An organizational perspective. In L. Lipsitt & C. Rovee-Collier (Eds.), *Advances in infancy research* (Vol. 4, pp. 87-137). Norwood, NJ: Ablex.

Cicchetti, D., Cummings, E. M., Greenberg, M., & Marvin, R. (1990). An organizational perspective on attachment beyond infancy: Implications for theory, measurement and research. In M. Greenberg, D. Cicchetti, & E. M. Cummings (Eds.), *Attachment in the preschool years* (pp. 3-50). Chicago: University of Chicago Press.

Cicchetti, D., Ganiban, J., & Barnett, D. (1990). Contributions from the study of high risk populations to understanding the development of emotion regulation. In K. Dodge &

J. Garber (Eds.), *The development of emotion regulation* (pp. 1-54). New York: Cambridge University Press.

Crittenden, P. H. (1988). Relationships at risk. In J. Belsky & T. Nezworski (Eds.), *Clinical implications of attachment* (pp. 136-174). Hillsdale, NJ: Lawrence Erlbaum.

Crowell, J., & Feldman, S. (1988). Mother's internal models of relationships and children's behavioral and developmental status: A study of mother-child interaction. *Child Development, 59,* 1273-1285.

Crowell, J. A., Feldman, S., & Ginsberg, N. (1988). Assessment of mother-child interaction in preschoolers with behavior problems. *Journal of American Academy of Child and Adolescent Psychiatry, 27,* 303-311.

Dawes, H. C. (1934). An analysis of 200 quarrels of preschool children. *Child Development, 5,* 139-157.

DeWit, J., & Hartup, W. W. (Eds.). (1974). *Determinants and origins of aggressive behavior.* The Hague: Mouton.

Dodge, K. A., & Frame, C. (1982). Social cognitive biases and deficits in aggressive boys. *Child Development, 53,* 620-635.

Dumas, J. E., & Wahler, R. G. (1985). Indiscriminate mothering as a contextual factor in aggressive-oppositional child behavior: "Damned if you do and damned if you don't." *Journal of Abnormal Psychology, 13,* 1-17.

Edgecumbe, R., & Sandler, J. (1974). Some comments on "Aggression turned against the self." *International Journal of Psychoanalysis, 55,* 365-368.

Eisenberg, N., & Mussen, P. (1989). *The roots of prosocial behavior in children.* Cambridge: Cambridge University Press.

Emde, R. (1985). The prerepresentational self and its affective core. *Psychoanalytic Study of the Child, 38,* 165-192.

Erickson, M., Sroufe, L. A., & Egeland, B. (1985). The relationship between quality of attachment and behavior problems in preschoolers in a high risk population. *Monographs of the Society for Research in Child Development, 50*(1-2, Serial No. 209), 147-156.

Fagot, B., & Hagan, R. (1985). Aggression in toddlers: Response to the assertive acts of boys and girls. *Sex Roles, 12,* 341-351.

Farrington, D. P. (1987). Early precursors of frequent offenders. In J. Q. Wilson & G. C. Loury (Eds.), *From children to citizens: Vol. 3. Families, schools and delinquency prevention* (pp. 27-51). New York: Springer.

Farrington, D. P., Ohlin, L. E., & Wilson, J. Q. (1986). *Understanding and controlling crime: Toward a new research strategy.* New York: Springer.

Feshbach, S. (1970). Aggression. In P. H. Mussen (Ed.), *Carmichael's manual of child psychology* (pp. 154-260). New York: John Wiley.

Fox, N., & Davidson, R. (1984). Hemisphere substrates of affect: A developmental model. In N. A. Fox & R. J. Davidson (Eds.), *The psychobiology of affective development* (pp. 353-382). Hillsdale, NJ: Lawrence Erlbaum.

Freud, A. (1968). *Normality and pathology in childhood.* Middlesex, England: Penguin.

Frodi, A., Lamb, M., Leavitt, L., Donovan, W., Neff, C., & Sherry, D. (1978). Fathers' and mothers' responses to the faces and cries of premature infants. *Developmental Psychology, 4,* 490-498.

Giannino, A., & Tronick, E. (1991). The mutual regulation model: The infant's self and interactive regulation and coping and defensive capacities. In T. Field, P. McCabe, &

M. Schneiderman (Eds.), *Stress and coping* (pp. 47-68). Hillsdale, NJ: Lawrence Erlbaum.

Glueck, S., & Glueck, E. (1950). *Unraveling juvenile delinquency.* Cambridge, MA: Harvard University Press.

Goldsmith, H., Buss, A., Plomin, R., Rothbart, M., Thomas, A., Chess, S., Hinde, R., & McCall, M. (1987). Roundtable: What is temperament? Four approaches. *Child Development, 58,* 505-529.

Goodenough, F. L. (1931). *Anger in young children.* Westport, CT: Greenwood Press.

Gould, R. (1982). Studies of aggression in early childhood: Patterns of attachment and efficacy. *Psychoanalytic Inquiry, 2,* 21-52.

Greenberg, M. T., & Speltz, M. L. (1988). Contributions of attachment theory to the understanding of conduct problems during the preschool years. In J. Belsky & T. Nezworski (Eds.), *Clinical implications of attachment* (pp. 177-218). Hillsdale, NJ: Lawrence Erlbaum.

Greenough, W., Black, J., & Wallace, C. (1987). Experience and brain development. *Child Development, 58,* 535-559.

Greenspan, S. I. (1981). *Psychopathology and adaptation in infancy and early childhood.* New York: International Universities Press.

Grossman, K., Fremmer-Bombik, E., Rudolph, J., & Grossman, K. (1988). Maternal attachment representations as related to patterns of infant-mother attachment and maternal care during the first year. In R. A. Hinde & J. Stevenson-Hinde (Eds.), *Relationships within families* (pp. 241-260). Oxford: Clarendon Press.

Harding, C. (1983). Acting with intention: A framework for examining the development of the intention to communicate. In L. Feagans, C. Garvey, & R. Golinkoff (Eds.), *The origins and growth of communication.* Norwood, NJ: Ablex.

Harris, R. (1978). Relationship between EEG abnormality and aggressive and anti-social behavior—A critical appraisal. In L. A. Hersov & M. Berger (Eds.), *Aggression and antisocial behavior in childhood and adolescence.* Oxford: Pergamon.

Hartup, W. (1974). Aggression in childhood: Developmental perspectives. *American Psychologist, 29,* 336-341.

Hetherington, E. M. (1989). Coping with family transitions: Winners, losers, and survivors. *Child Development, 60,* 1-14.

Hill, D. (1952). EEG in episodic psychiatric and psychopathic behavior: A classification of data. *Electroencephograph Clinical Neurophysiology, 4,* 419-442.

Hooks, M., Mayes, L., & Volkmar, F. (1988). Psychiatric disorders among preschool children. *Journal of the American Academy of Child and Adolescent Psychiatry, 27,* 623-627.

Jersild, A. T., & Markey, F. V. (1935). Conflicts between preschool children. *Child Development Monographs, 21,* 169-181.

Johnson, F., Dowling, J., & Wesner, D. (1980). Notes on infant psychotherapy. *Infant Mental Health Journal, 1,* 19-33.

Kagan, J. (1974). Developmental and methodological considerations in the study of aggression. In J. deWit & W. W. Hartup (Eds.), *Determinants and origins of aggressive behavior* (pp. 107-113). The Hague: Mouton.

Kashani, J., Deuser, W., & Reid, J. (1991). Aggression and anxiety: A new look at an old notion. *Journal of the American Academy of Child and Adolescent Psychiatry, 30,* 218-223.

Kazdin, A. E. (1987). Treatment of antisocial behavior in children: Current status and future directions. *Psychological Bulletin, 102,* 187-203.

Kazdin, A. E. (1991). Aggressive behavior and conduct disorder. In T. R. Kratechwill & R. J. Morris (Eds.), *The practice of child therapy* (pp. 174-221). Elmsford, NY: Pergamon.

Keltikangas-Jarvinen, L. (1990). Attributional style of the mother as a predictor of aggressive behavior of the child. *Aggressive Behavior, 16,* 1-7.

Kennedy, R. (1982). Cognitive-behavioral approaches to the modification of aggressive behavior in children. *School Psychology Review, 11,* 47-55.

Klinnert, M., Campos, J. J., Sorce, J., Emde, R., & Svejda, M. (1983). Emotions as behavior regulators: Social referencing in infancy. In R. Plutchik & H. Kellerman (Eds.), *Emotions in early development: Vol. 2. The emotions* (pp. 57-82). New York: Academic Press.

Kobak, R. R., & Sceery, A. (1988). Attachment in late adolescence, working models, affect regulation and representations of self and others. *Child Development, 59,* 135-146.

Kopp, C. (1982). The antecedents of self-regulation. *Developmental Psychology, 18,* 199-214.

Kornadt, H. J. (1984). Development of aggressiveness: A motivation perspective. In R. Kaplan, V. Konecni, & R. Novaco (Eds.), *Aggression in children and youth* (pp. 73-87). The Hague: Martinus Nijhoff.

Lahey, B., Russo, M. F., Walker, J., & Piacentini, J. (1989). Personality characteristics of mothers of children with disruptive behavior disorders. *Journal of Consulting and Clinical Psychology, 57,* 512-515.

Landy, S., & Peters, R. DeV. (1990). Identifying and treating hyperaggressive preschoolers. *Infants and Young Children, 3*(2), 24-28.

Lefkowitz, M., Eron, L., Walder, L., & Huesmann, L. R. (1977). *Growing up to be violent: A longitudinal study of the development of aggression.* Elmsford, NY: Pergamon.

Lewis, D., Pincus, J., Lovely, R., Spitzor, E., & Moy E. (1987). Biopsychosocial characteristics of matched samples of delinquents and non-delinquents. *Journal of the American Academy of Child and Adolescent Psychiatry, 26,* 744-752.

Liben, L. (1978). Perspective taking in young children: Seeing the world through rose-coloured glasses. *Developmental Psychology, 14,* 87-92.

Lipsitt, L. (1990). Fetal development in the drug age. *Child Behavior and Development Letter, 6,* 1-3.

Lipsitt, P. D., Buka, S., & Lipsitt, L. (1990). Early intelligence scores and subsequent delinquency. *American Journal of Family Therapy, 18,* 197-208.

Loeber, R. (1991). Antisocial behavior: More endurable than changeable? *Journal of the American Academy of Child and Adolescent Psychiatry, 30,* 393-397.

Loeber R., & Stouthamer-Loeber, M. (1986). Family factors as correlates and predictors of juvenile conduct problems and delinquency. In N. Morris & M. Tonry (Eds.), *Crime and justice: An annual review of research* (Vol. 7, pp. 29-149). Chicago: University of Chicago Press.

Mahler, M., Pine, F., & Bergmann, A. (1975). *The psychological birth of the human infant.* New York: Basic Books.

Main, M. (1990). Parental aversion to infant-initiated contact is correlated with the parents' own rejection during childhood: The effects of experience on signals of security with respect to attachment. In K. Barnard & T. B. Brazelton (Eds.), *Touch* (pp. 461-495). Madison, CT: International University Press.

Main, M., & Hesse, E. (1990). Parents' unresolved traumatic expereinces are related to infant disorganised attachment status: Is frightened and/or frightening parental behavior the linking mechanism? In M. T. Greenberg, D. Cicchetti, & E. M. Cummings (Eds.), *Attachment in the preschool years.* Chicago: University of Chicago Press.

Main, M., Kaplan, N., & Cassidy, J. (1985). Security in infancy, childhood and adulthood: A move to the level of representation. In I. Bretherton & E. Waters (Eds.), *Growing points of attachment theory and research. Monographs of the Society for Research in Child Development, 50*(1-2, Serial No. 209), 66-102.

Marcus, R., Roke, E., & Bruner, C. (1985). Verbal and nonverbal empathy and prediction of social behavior of young children. *Perceptual and Motor Skills, 60,* 299-309.

Marvin, R. S. (1977). An ethological-cognitive model for the attenuation of mother-child attachment behavior. In T. M. Alloway, L. Kramer, & P. Piner (Eds.), *Advances in the study of communication and affect* (Vol 3., pp. 25-60). New York: Plenum.

Matas, L., Arend, R., & Sroufe, L. (1978). Continuity of adaptation in the second year: The relationship between quality of attachment and later competence. *Child Development, 49,* 547-556.

Mednick, S. A., & Hutchings, B. (1978). Genetic and psychophysiological factors in antisocial behavior. *Journal of the American Academy of Child Psychiatry, 17,* 209-223.

Meyersberg, H. A., & Post, R. M. (1979). A holistic developmental view of neural and psychological processes. *British Journal of Psychiatry, 135,* 139-155.

Miller, P., & Sperry, L. (1987). The socialization of anger and aggression. *Merrill Palmer Quarterly, 33,* 1-31.

Minuchin, M., Montalvio, B., Guerney, B., Rosman, B., & Schumer, R. (1966). *Families of the slums.* New York: Basic Books.

Monroe, R. R. (1974). Maturational lag in central nervous system development as a partial explanation of episodic violent behavior. In J. deWit & W. W. Hartup (Eds.), *Determinants and origins of aggressive behavior* (pp.337-344). The Hague: Mouton.

Montagner, H., Restoin, A., & Henry, J. C. (1982). Biological defense rhythms, stress, and communication in children. In W. W. Hartup (Ed.), *Review of child development research* (Vol. 6, pp. 291-319). Chicago: University of Chicago Press.

Morris, H., Escoll, P., & Wexler, R. (1956). Aggressive behavior disorders of childhood: A follow-up study. *American Journal of Psychiatry, 112,* 991-997.

Nachson, I., & Denno, D. (1987). Violent behavior and cerebral hemisphere dysfunctions. In S. A. Mednick, T. E. Moffitt, & S. A. Stack (Eds.), *The causes of crime: New biological approaches* (pp. 185-217). New York: Cambridge University Press.

Offord, D., Alder, R., & Boyle, M. (1986). Prevalence and sociodemographic correlates of conduct disorder. *American Journal of Social Psychiatry, 6,* 272-278.

Oltmanns, T., Broderick, J., & O'Leary, K. (1977). Marital adjustment and the efficacy of behavior therapy with children. *Journal of Consulting and Clinical Psychology, 45,* 724-729.

Olweus, D. (1979). Stability of aggressive reaction patterns in males: A review. *Psychological Bulletin, 86,* 852-875.

Oppenheim, D., Sagi, A., & Lamb, M. (1988). Infant-adult attachment on the kibbutz and their relation to socioemotional development 4 years later. *Developmental Psychology, 24,* 427-433.

Osofsky, J. (Ed.). (1987). *Handbook of infant development.* New York: John Wiley.

Parens, H. (1979). *The development of aggression in early childhood.* New York: Jason Aronson.

Parke, R. D., & Slaby, R. G. (1983). The development of aggression. In P. H. Mussen (Ed). *Handbook of child psychology* (4th ed.) (Vol. 4, pp. 547-642). New York: John Wiley.

Parpal, M., & Maccoby, E. E. (1985). Maternal responsiveness and subsequent child compliance. *Child Development, 56,* 1326-1334.

Patterson, G. R. (1976). The aggressive child: Victim and architect of a coercive system. In E. Mash, A. Hamerlynck, & L. Handy (Eds.), *Behavior modification and families: Theory and research* (pp. 267-316). New York: Brunner/Mazel.

Patterson, G. R., DeBaryshe, B. D., & Ramsey E. (1989). A developmental perspective on antisocial behavior. *American Psychologist, 44,* 329-335.

Pellegrini, D. S., & Urbain, E. S. (1985). An evaluation of interpersonal cognitive problem-solving training with children. *Journal of Child Psychology and Psychiatry, 26,* 17-41.

Piaget, J. (1952). *The origins of intelligence in children.* New York: International University Press.

Power, T., & Chapieski, M. (1986). Childrearing and impulse control in toddlers: A naturalistic investigation. *Developmental Psychology, 22,* 271-275.

Ramsey, P. (1987). Possession episodes in young children's social interactions. *Journal of Genetic Psychology, 148,* 315-324.

Renken, B., Egeland, B., & Marvinney, D. (1989). Early childhood antecedents of aggression and passive withdrawal in early elementary school. *Journal of Personality, 57,* 257-281.

Richman, N., Stevenson, J., & Graham, P. (1982). *Preschool to school: A behavioural study.* London: Academic Press.

Richman, N., Stevenson, J., & Tamplin, P. (1985). Prevalence of behaviour problems in three-year-old children: An epidemiological study in a London borough. *Journal of Child Psychology and Psychiatry, 16,* 222-287.

Roff, M., & Roff, L. (1940). An analysis of the variance of conflict behavior in preschool children. *Child Development, 11,* 43-50.

Rose, S., Rose, S., & Feldman, J. (1989). Stability of behavior problems in very young children. *Development and Psychopathology, 1,* 5-19.

Rothbart, M. (1981). Measurement of temperament in infancy. *Child Development, 52,* 569-578.

Rutter, M. (1978). Family, area and school influences in the genesis of conduct disorders. In L. A. Herson & M. Berger (Eds.), *Aggression and anti-social behavior in childhood and adolescence* (pp. 95-113). Oxford: Pergamon.

Sander, L. W. (1962). Adaptive relationships in early mother-child interaction. *Journal of American Academy of Child Psychiatry, 3,* 231-264.

Santostefano, S. (1978). *A bio-developmental approach to clinical child psychology.* New York: John Wiley.

Santostefano, S. (1985). *Cognitive control therapy with children and adolescents.* Elmsford, NY: Pergamon.

Shamsie, J. (1991). *Youth with conduct disorder: What is to be done?* Toronto: Ministry of Community and Social Services.

Shantz, C. (1983). Social cognition. In P. H. Mussen (Ed.), *Handbook of child psychology: Cognitive development.* New York: John Wiley.

Shinn, M. R., Ramsey, E., Walker, H. M., O'Neill, R., & Steiber, S. (1987). Antisocial behavior in school settings: Individual differences in an at-risk and normal population. *Journal of Special Education, 21,* 69-84.

Speltz, M. (1990). The treatment of preschool conduct problems. In M. Greenberg, D. Cicchetti, & E. C. Cummings (Eds.), *Attachment in the preschool years* (pp. 399-426). Chicago: University of Chicago Press.

Speltz, M., Greenberg, M., & Deklyen, M. (1990). Attachment in preschoolers with disruptive behaviors: A comparison of clinic-referred and non-problem children. *Development and Psychopathology, 2,* 31-46.

Spitz, R. (1969). Aggression and adaptation. *Journal of Nervous and Mental Disease, 149,* 81-90.

Sroufe, L. A. (1983). Infant-caregiver attachment and patterns of adaptation in preschool: The roots of maladaptation and competence. In M. Perlmutter (Ed.), *Minnesota Symposium in Child Psychology (Vol. 16, pp. 41-81). Hillsdale, NJ: Lawrence Erlbaum.*

Sroufe, L. A. (1990). An organizational perspective on the self. In D. Cicchetti & M. Beeghly (Eds.), *The self in transition: Infancy to childhood* (pp. 281-307). Chicago: University of Chicago Press.

Stern, D. (1985). *The interpersonal world of the infant.* New York: Basic Books.

Stewart, M., & DeBlois, C. (1983). Father-son resemblances in aggressive and anti-social behavior. *British Journal of Psychiatry, 142,* 78-84.

Szegal, B. (1984). *On the development of prosocial aggression in early childhood.* Unpublished Psychological Sciences dissertation, Hungarian Academy of Sciences, Budapest.

Szegal, B. (1985). Stages in the development of aggressive behaviors in early childhood. *Aggressive Behavior, 11,* 315-321.

Thomas, A., & Chess, S. (1977). *Temperament and development.* New York: Brunner/Mazel.

Trad, P. V. (1989). *The preschool child.* New York: John Wiley.

Trad, P. V. (1990). *Infant previewing.* New York: Springer-Verlag.

Tronick, E. Z. (1989). Emotions and emotional communication in infants. *American Psychologist, 44*(2), 112-119.

Tronick, E. Z., Cohn, J. F., & Shea, E. (1985). The transfer of affect between mother and infant. In M. Yogman & T. B. Brazelton (Eds.), *Affective development in infancy.* Norwood, NJ: Ablex.

Vaughn, B., Kopp, C., & Krakow, J. (1984). The emergence and consolidation of self-control from 18 to 30 months of age: Normative trends and individual differences. *Child Development, 55,* 990-1004.

Vygotsky, L. S. (1976). Play and its role in the mental development of the child. In J. S. Bruner, A. Jolly, & K. Sylva (Eds.), *Play—Its role in development and evolution* (pp. 537-554). London: Penguin.

Waldrop, M., Pedersen, F., & Bell, R. Q. (1968). Minor physical anomalies and behavior in preschool children. *Child Development, 39,* 391-400.

Walker, H., Shinn, M., O'Neill, R., & Ramsey, E. (1987). Longitudinal assessment and long-term follow-up of antisocial behavior in fourth-grade boys: Rationale, methodology, measures and results. *Remedial and Special Education, 8,* 7-16.

Walsh, A., & Beyer, J. (1987). Violent crime, sociopathy and love deprivation among adolescent delinquents. *Adolescence, 22,* 705-717.

Wenar, C. (1982). On negativism. *Human Development, 25,* 1-23.

Werkman, S. L. (1985). Anxiety disorders. In H. I. Kaplan & B. J. Sedock (Eds.), *Comprehensive textbook of psychiatry* (4th ed.) (Vol. 2, pp. 1746-1754). Baltimore, MD: Williams & Wilkins.

Wesner, D., Dowling, J., & Johnson, F. (1982). What is maternal-infant intervention? The role of infant psychotherapy. *Psychiatry, 45,* 307-315.

White, J., Moffit, T., Earls, F., Robins, L., & Silva, P. (1990). Preschool predictors of conduct disorder. *Criminology, 28,* 507-533.

Wolfson, J., Fields, J., & Rose, S. (1987). Symptoms, temperament, resiliency, and control in anxiety-disordered preschool children. *Journal of the American Academy of Child and Adolescent Psychiatry, 26,* 16-22.

Yarrow, M., & Waxler, C. (1976). Dimensions and correlates of prosocial behavior in young children. *Child Development, 47,* 118-125.

Zahn-Waxler, C., Cummings, E., McKnew, D., & Radke-Yarrow, M. (1984). Altruism, aggression and social interactions in young children with manic depressive parents. *Child Development, 55,* 112-122.

2

Developmental Disparities of Abused Children:
Directions for Prevention

DAVID A. WOLFE
CHRISTINE WEKERLE
ROBIN McGEE

Child abuse and its concomitant forms of family dysfunction have expanded in scope to include a range of caregiving behaviors that potentially can interfere with or impair a child's ongoing development. This expansion corresponded to findings indicating that physically abused children were handicapped, impaired, or different from non-abused children in ways that could not be attributed to physical injuries alone (Cicchetti & Rizley, 1981). Such children were reported to be developmentally delayed, behaviorally disordered, and recognizably different from their age peers, although no particular pattern of psychopathology was evident. Such differences could not be explained on the basis of physical injuries alone, and thus a greater emphasis emerged toward understanding the impact of maltreatment on children's psychological development. This expanded approach must be sensitive to a

AUTHORS' NOTE: Acknowledgments: Preparation of this chapter was supported in part by grants to the first author from the Institute for the Prevention of Child Abuse (Toronto) and the Medical Research Council of Canada (Ottawa).

somewhat different set of complex factors than those explored with abusive parents. Particular emphasis must be drawn to the manner in which maltreatment may interfere with or impair development of the child, which represents a less tangible and very convoluted course of events leading to diverse outcomes. This complexity began to be evident as researchers searched for psychological theories to explain the diverse and sometimes idiosyncratic developmental patterns shown by small samples of abused children.

Initially, it was presumed by many in the field that maltreatment in general, and physical abuse in particular, resulted in higher rates of externalizing disorders when compared to nonabused children. However, there has been little confirmation of the notion that child maltreatment leads to particular developmental outcomes for children across the life span (Ammerman, in press; Wolfe, 1987). Rather, more and more research findings are pointing to the conclusion that child abuse represents the visible aspect of a very major disrupting influence on the child's ongoing development. Such disruptions in normal development are of such a pronounced and significant level that the child's behavioral, emotional, and social-cognitive dimensions of development are impaired to varying degrees.

Although it is beyond the scope of this chapter to discuss in detail the theoretical reasons why children's development is disrupted by maltreatment, it is important to note that maltreatment can be considered as an "indicator" of poor socialization practices rather than the individual cause of poor developmental outcomes. That is, until we have a better understanding of the unique influence on development of particular abusive or neglectful parenting patterns, it may be more parsimonious to investigate the process of child rearing that is represented by known forms of maltreatment. For example, signs of physical abuse are usually indicative of an authoritarian parenting style that is marked by power assertive, aversive child-rearing strategies. Consequently, the child's developmental outcome is affected most dramatically by the general parenting practices that describe the child's routine and care. Thus episodes of physical abuse may be only the more visible extremes of an already aversive parent-child relationship. It can be argued, therefore, that the impact of child abuse on children's development must be considered in relation to the overall quality of care that the child is exposed to over time. Such an effect must additionally take into consideration the severity, nature, and developmental period over which forms of maltreatment are occurring.

What makes child maltreatment such an important area of study and concern is that it represents or includes many of the most prominent factors that have been confirmed to disrupt or interfere with child development. Child poverty (Gil, 1970), social isolation and environmental stress (Garbarino, 1976), aversive or inconsistent child-rearing style (Reid, Taplin, & Lorber, 1981), extrapunitiveness (Parke & Slaby, 1983), and poor child-caregiver attachment (Ainsworth, 1980) have all been linked directly or indirectly with child maltreatment, and each factor is a major influence on child development in its own right. Thus a better understanding of the process by which maltreatment affects child development can be achieved through collaborative studies that consider the interactive and multiplicative effects of these co-occurring factors.

This chapter will consider the impact of child maltreatment in terms of the child's developmental-maturational problems that emerge across childhood and adolescence. Rather than viewing the child victim's emotional and behavioral problems as signs of child psychopathology, this viewpoint acknowledges that maltreatment represents major disruptive events in the child's development that have a predictable outcome *only if considered in relation to the child's particular developmental stage and situational influences.* Because maltreatment is embedded in the parent-child relationship, it is important to consider its impact in terms of the interaction between the child's ongoing development and his or her caregiving environment (Cicchetti & Rizley, 1981). Such an understanding has important implications not only for the child's subsequent development, but increased knowledge of such developmental deviations may assist in our understanding and prevention of maltreatment by parents. This latter issue will be discussed in the final section of this chapter.

A major consideration given to the review of findings presented herein is the emergence of two general themes occurring throughout the maltreatment literature. The first theme can be described in relation to the findings linking social-cognitive and social-emotional problems in development among maltreated children to inadequate and inappropriate child-rearing methods. Ample evidence now exists to indicate that maltreated children are poorly cared for emotionally and physically from an early age, and thus show corresponding problems in attachment and relationship formation.

A second theme, very closely linked to the previous one, focuses on the child's response or adaptation to his or her environment over time. Abused and neglected children are more likely than their nonmaltreated counterparts to show signs of failure in normal adaptation. That is, how the child learns to respond to his or her environment is closely related to the level of stimulation and sensitivity provided by his or her caregivers. Maltreated children are likely to have had poor opportunities to learn appropriate adaptive skills, and thus their reported level of social competence, self-esteem, and problem-solving abilities are diminished.

These themes will be developed by reviewing the recent literature, and ways of preventing deviation or delay at various stages of development will be suggested based on these findings. Finally, the chapter concludes with a focused discussion of a rationale and suggested ways to assist children and adolescents in preventing these two major themes from re-emerging in the next generation.

The Theoretical Relationship Between Children's Development and Their Expression of Maladjustment

When studying the putative effects of maltreatment on children's development and adjustment, the manner in which the questions are asked is crucial. Initially, most researchers addressed this concern from the reasonable viewpoint that particular events or experiences (e.g., episodes of physical abuse) would be directly linked to undesirable outcomes. For example, abused children would most likely be more aggressive and emotionally insensitive as a function of their negative caregiving experiences. This linear connection approach made sense in view of existing psychological theories of personality development that stressed the role of traumatic or significant events influencing present or future behavior (e.g., social learning, psychodynamic).

Recent evidence from developmental studies indicates that the connections between negative events in childhood and later developmental outcome are often not direct or easily explainable (Sroufe & Fleeson, 1986). Clinicians and researchers, for example, began to document the small yet significant subgroups of children who seemed "resilient" to stressors in childhood (Garmezy, 1983). The logical explanation for such findings was that some factor or factors mediated the impact of maltreatment on the children's adjustment. Likely candidates for such compensatory factors are family resources, good temperament, higher intelligence, and the like, whereas candidates for destabilizing factors include parental psychopathology, prior abuse in the parent's childhood, and socioeconomic conditions (Cicchetti & Rizley, 1981).

A prominent mediator of developmental outcome that is often overlooked is the child's developmental level at the time of the ongoing maltreatment. Maltreatment alone does not account for or explain the diverse developmental outcomes being reported among its child, adolescent, and adult-survivor victims. Rather, to account for such effects more fully we must consider the particular vulnerabilities of each child. To do so with research samples of children we must define vulnerabilities (and protective mechanisms) in relation to known developmental stages and capabilities.

Thus the question of how child maltreatment affects child development in the short and long term can be restated as: What effect or effects does abuse and/or insensitive parenting have at different stages of the child's development (Shirk, 1988)? This orientation requires a somewhat different focus than that presently pursued, with special attention given to developmental limitations and abilities of children who have experienced various forms of maltreatment. Rather than a linear relationship, one should expect to find a number of influencing factors that can account for the differences seen among samples of maltreated children. Of particular concern throughout this endeavor is the connection between children's exposure to abusive caregiving and their subsequent experience of and behavior in interpersonal relationships. The manner in which developmental level can mediate the impact of abusive experiences is discussed below, based on three possibilities outlined by Shirk (1988).

First, developmental level may dictate how the child actually experiences the abusive situations. A major tenet of social-cognitive theories of development is that children at different levels of development will qualitatively differ in how they experience (negative) events. Thus they will reconstruct their experience of the abuse in distinctive ways. Toddlers and preschoolers, for example, are more likely to perceive their own abuse as being "justified" because they blame themselves for adult anger and actions (Covell & Abramovitch, in press). The older child, in contrast, is able to draw upon situational factors to decipher a conflict situation, or may project undue blame to persons or situations that are not directly responsible (e.g., a sibling) in an effort to protect his or her ideal view of a parent. Most importantly, these different cognitive constructions or interpretations will, in turn, produce different emotional reactions. When attributions of blame (either to self or the perpetrator) result from the maltreatment, then emotional reactions of sadness, guilt, or anger will be more likely to result (Fincham, Beach, & Nelson, 1987). A second possibility noted by Shirk (1988) of how developmental level mediates the impact of abuse emphasizes that differential outcomes may result from developmental differences at the time of abuse. As well as qualitative differences (i.e., how abuse is experienced by the child), maltreatment may affect major developmental tasks directly. This notion relies on the evidence that later maladaptation is linked to incomplete mastery of important developmental accomplishments in early childhood (Paterson & Moran, 1988; Sroufe & Fleeson, 1986). These tasks are generally described in terms of forming attachments, communicative development, self-autonomy, and peer relations (e.g., Cicchetti & Olsen, 1990; Shirk, 1988). It is believed, therefore, that maltreatment disrupts the normal course of development in which these tasks are mastered by the child. Moreover, this disruption sets into motion a sequence of developmental alterations that continues to impair adaptation well into the future.

It is crucial to consider another, more clinically significant, implication that this second factor may have for the abused child's course of development. Shirk (1988) notes that this model of developmental psychopathology assumes that individuals possess "sensitive periods" during which specific behaviors are more susceptible to environmental influences. That is, behaviors that are associated with an age period's most pivotal task, such as attachment, should be most susceptible to insensitive caregiving or maltreatment or other environmental influences. Moreover, this viewpoint assumes that disruptions of different developmental tasks (e.g., attachment, peer relations) should lead to different developmental outcomes for the child. Therefore, an understanding of how abuse may affect a child's development and adjustment must take into full account the developmental task or tasks that were disrupted by the trauma. In presenting some of the findings from studies of different ages of abused children, we will see that their expressions of adjustment difficulties are closely linked to the type and extent of developmental disruption that was documented.

Finally, Shirk (1988) notes that developmental level can mediate the impact of abuse in terms of developmental expressions of enduring distress resulting from the abuse. Children typically do not express or exhibit their distress in ways that are easily interpreted or causally linked to prior events (Cicchetti, 1984). Such expressions of trauma or distress are influenced by developmental level, and thus are not simply a function of the type of trauma experienced. Shirk (1988) points out that children who are more advanced in social-emotional development are more likely to express their distress as "thought symptoms" than are their less advanced peers, who do so in "action symptoms." Thus clinicians often report that disturbed children "act out" their problems by displaying symptoms of maladjustment, although the children themselves cannot vocalize their distress. The manner in which distress is expressed, moreover, can and does change over the course of development as well, so that the problems being observed in early childhood (e.g., aggression, peer rejection) may transform into other forms of expression later on (e.g., stealing, firesetting, delinquent behavior). As Shirk concludes, "Each developmental period introduces a new challenge for which the physically abused child has been compromised. Early trauma reduces the child's ability to master developmental tasks and is expressed in a predictable sequence of symptoms" (p. 62).

We now turn our attention to some of the empirical findings relating to maltreated children, which can be more readily interpreted in reference to the developmental framework noted above.

Problems Relating to Affective and Social-Emotional Development

Early experiences with the caregiver are most important in terms of the child's development of positive relationships with others and contentment in his or her social environment. In this section, we look at two major developmental tasks: attachment to the caregiver, and the emergence of early self-concept and affective expression, and make reference to observed problems found among samples of maltreated infants and toddlers. It is the failure to master these critical tasks that is believed to set the stage for the wide range of adjustment problems found later on in the life-span development of these youngsters.

Attachment

The consequences of early attachment problems in the parent/child relationship (6-12 months of age) have been linked to enduring and diffuse child adjustment problems later on (Ainsworth, Blehar, & Waters, 1978). In the field of child maltreatment, the attachment construct has been theoretically linked to the perpetuation of maltreatment across generations (Kaufman & Zigler, 1989), the failure of these children to form subsequent relationships with others (Erickson, Sroufe, & Egeland, 1985), and their vulnerability to additional developmental failures that rely to some extent on early attachment success (Aber & Allen, 1987).

The theory linking the importance of attachment to future development is relatively straightforward. As presented by Bowlby (1969) and

Sroufe and Fleeson (1986), the infant develops an "internal working model" of self and others through repeated interactions with the attachment figures. Positive interactions lead to self-efficacy and successful future relationships with others. Insecure attachment, on the other hand, leads to a negative view of self, which is associated with low social competence, poor adaptive ability, and long-term problems in relationship formation (Paterson & Moran, 1989).

The quality of the attachment relationship has been tied most closely to early patterns of parent/child interactions that can be distinguished by the degree of "sensitive responsiveness" to the infant's needs and signals for proximity and contact (Ainsworth et al., 1978). Sensitivity involves an "openness to signals" (Pederson et al., in press) in the context of the need to attend to other competing stimuli. As summarized by Paterson and Moran (1989):

> The parent must be readily available to the child, responsive to its needs, and accepting of the child as a person. The child should not be subjected to threats of withdrawal of love or caring, or threats to abandon the family. Finally, the child should not be made to feel responsible for the parent's illnesses or death. (p. 615)

The maltreating parent often displays such insensitivity in addition to overt acts of violence (see, e.g., Crittenden & Bonvillian, 1984; Oldershaw, Walters, & Hall, 1986).

It is not surprising therefore, in light of the importance of maternal sensitivity to infant attachment, that mothers suffering from forms of mental illness that impair daily functioning (e.g., depression; Zahn-Waxler, Cummings, McKnew, & Radke-Yarrow, 1984) as well as those who abuse or neglect their children (e.g., Schneider-Rosen & Cicchetti, 1984) tend to have insecurely attached infants. Cicchetti, Toth, and Bush (1988), in fact, found that the vast majority of maltreated infants form insecure attachments with caregivers (70% to 100% across studies), which over time have a strong tendency to become anxious-avoidant patterns of attachment. Because in any relationship the interactants learn not only their own role but also the role of the other person (Sroufe & Fleeson, 1986), the significance of this poor resolution of attachment may continue to influence the child's relationship formation with peers, future partners, and future offspring (e.g., Main, Kaplan, & Cassidy, 1985).

Early Self-Concept and Affective Expression

Closely related to the important task of attachment formation is the issue of the development of the autonomous self (18-24 months). Cicchetti et al. (1988) note that during this stage the infant should gain a well-differentiated sense of functioning as an independent entity. They report that nearly 80% of maltreated toddlers show neutral to negative affect during visual self-recognition experiences. As well, such toddlers are more aggressive, frustrated, and noncompliant than comparison children in problem-solving tasks that require autonomy. From a developmental perspective, this finding supports the previous arguments detailing the insensitivity of their caregiving environment and, furthermore, extends the impact of this insensitivity to the important task of independence.

Early relationships shape what the child knows how to do and what he or she understands (Sroufe & Fleeson, 1986), and thus are crucial to the ongoing development of self-concept. Bowlby (1969) has argued that working models of the self (which are connected later on to self-esteem and self-concept) develop in parallel with working models of attachment figures. Accordingly, children with sensitive caregivers view themselves as worthy of care and develop the beginnings of a healthy self-image.

The self-perceptions of abused children reflect a distorted view of themselves in relation to others, which is the precursor to low self-esteem and poor self-control (Cicchetti et al., 1988). According to developmentalists, self-perceptions of competence emerge from the parents' beliefs about their children's abilities. The child's perceived competence, in turn, influences his or her affect and behavior (Harter, 1983). It is typical for young children to overrate their competence and then adjust their self-ratings (downward) as they mature. Children who underrate their competence, however, are overly represented in clinical populations (Boivin & Begin, 1989; Garrison, Earls, & Kindlon, 1983). This latter concern has been initially documented in two very recent studies of abused children. Vondra, Barnett, and Cicchetti (1989, in press) found that both preschool and school-aged (1st through 3rd grades) samples of maltreated children rated themselves as significantly higher on peer acceptance than lower or middle income age-mates. These children were also found to have more exaggerated perceptions of their physical competence, relative to teacher reports. Interestingly, this pattern shifted among older youngsters (Grades 4-6), where the maltreated sample described themselves as *less competent and less accepted* than their age-mates. The researchers argue that an exaggerated positive self-concept may be a sign of disturbance as much as an unrealistically low self-concept, in that the child may be masking any underlying feelings of self-doubt and inadequacy. Maltreated children, according to this argument, fail to develop an independent, undistorted view of themselves, and this failure sets the stage for subsequent problems in relationship development and peer interaction.

Other than early self-concept formation, children begin to learn the importance of emotions for communication and regulation in the first year of life. Recent evidence suggests that they begin to develop rudimentary attempts to attribute cause to emotional expression by their second year (Bretherton, Fritz, Zahn-Waxler, & Ridgeway, 1986). Of most significance to maltreatment is the manner in which children's emotional expression and behavior can be influenced by adult reactions to the child or ambient adult expressions. Young children look to the emotional expression and cues of their caregivers to help them understand a novel or startling event (e.g., Cummings, Zahn-Waxler, & Radke-Yarrow, 1981). For the nonmaltreated child, this social-referencing process implies that he or she will learn to manage fearful or novel situations (e.g., learning to walk) by looking to the parent for appropriate cues of fear, encouragement, pleasure, and so on. For the maltreated child, however, this process may be considerably less adaptive and more emotionally arousing. When faced with a novel situation, the child with an insensitive, demanding parent may not receive the necessary reassurance or appropriate emotional expression to assist him or her in managing arousal. When they look to their parents for an explanation of how to respond to a fearful situation, they are likely to see expressions of anger, impatience, or dissatisfaction. Thus the emotional atmosphere that these children frequently encounter poses a dilemma to their coping and adaptational abilities in early to middle childhood, as shown below.

Problems Relating to Social-Cognitive Development

We now turn our attention to the manner in which children learn to acquire social knowledge, a critical aspect of learning to adapt to the social world. Developmental theorists posit that this is an ongoing process in which the child constructs and tests social conceptions in relation to personal and social encounters (e.g., Shirk, 1988). This process of acquiring social knowledge takes place in the context of everyday social interaction, in which the child experiences the nuances of interpersonal behavior.

Again, we find that maltreated children are at a significant developmental risk due in part to the negative, dysfunctional social interactions that they experience on an everyday basis in their own families. Because their family members are more likely to be coercive, to make fewer positive or neutral expressions to one another, and to engage in proportionately more negative than positive interchanges (Wolfe, 1985), they will have a greater likelihood of learning distorted, maladaptive beliefs about the social world (Smetana, Kelly, & Twentyman, 1984). The development of social sensitivity, empathy, and peer relations among maltreated children is discussed below.

Social Sensitivity and Empathy

Due to the significance of relationship development, researchers have turned their attention to initial manifestations of sensitivity to others' emotions and early prosocial behavior among maltreated children. *Social sensitivity* refers to a developmental achievement that is defined as the ability to perceive and comprehend the feelings and motives of others accurately (Rotenburg, 1980). It is well established that a number of family factors correlate with the development of moral reasoning and social sensitivity, and these factors by and large are descriptive of maltreating families. They include, for example, a warm, accepting relationship of mutual trust and esteem between parent and child, the type and degree of discipline used (Parke & Slaby, 1983), the role model parents offer the child (Bandura, 1973), and independence opportunities that parents provide (Maccoby & Martin, 1983).

For example, Main and George (1985) observed abused children on the playground, where they could observe their reactions to distress in playmates. They found that the target children not only failed to show concern toward others, they actively responded to distress in others with fear, physical attack, or anger. Similarly, Barahal, Waterman, and Martin (1981) compared 6- to 8-year-old abused and control children on measures of locus of control, social sensitivity, cognitive perspective taking, and moral judgment. After adjusting for IQ level, they found that abused children displayed greater external locus of control and less comprehension of social roles than comparisons. These results suggest that the experience of abuse has a major effect on children's ability to discriminate and identify emotions, an ability that acts as an important precursor to social competence (see also Camras, Grow, & Ribardy, 1983; George & Main, 1979; Howes & Espinosa, 1985).

Because abused children have been raised in an atmosphere of power-assertion and external control, it has also been suspected that their level of moral reasoning may be significantly below their peers. The maltreating parent typically fails to invoke in his or her child concern for the welfare of others, especially in a manner that the child will internalize and imitate (Maccoby & Martin, 1983). In one of the few well-designed studies of this issue, Smetana et al. (1984) compared 12 abused, 16 neglected, and 16 matched control children of preschool age in their judgments regarding the dimensions of seriousness, deserved punishment, rule contingency (the permissibility of actions in the absence of rules) and generalizability of familiar moral and conventional nursery school transgressions (i.e., physical harm to another, psychological distress, and resource distribution). Interestingly, the results discriminated primarily between the two maltreated groups. Abused children considered transgressions entailing psychological distress to be more universally wrong for others (but not for themselves), whereas neglected children considered the unfair distribution of resources to be more universally wrong for themselves (but not for others). These findings are consistent with the type of chronic maltreatment each group of children had experienced. The findings are also consistent with the assertion that children's moral and social judgments are actively constructed from social experiences that, in this case, may involve the internalization of standards of behavior that reflect their victimization experiences (Wolfe, 1987).

Attributional Bias and Peer Relations

Closely related to the social-cognitive development of social sensitivity and empathy is how the child manifests such changes in his or her encounters with peers. Because child maltreatment represents a stressful event that requires attribution and appraisal on the part of the child, the child's interpretation of traumatic life events are presumed to influence his or her adaptive or maladaptive coping responses (Mueller & Silverman, 1989). For example, several authors (Dodge & Richard, 1985; Parke & Slaby, 1983; Rubin & Krasnor, 1986) have suggested that behavior problems in children may develop as a function of the ways in which children process social information.

Studies have often found the theme of aggressive behavior and poor self-control throughout the developmental stages of a significant proportion of abused children. Beginning with preschool age subjects, studies have shown that abused children direct significantly more aggression toward peers than do nonabused children (Egeland & Sroufe, 1981; George & Main, 1979; Hoffman-Plotkin & Twentyman, 1984). By the time these children reach school age, problems with aggression and peer relations are widely reported at home and school. Such problems with aggression and self-control continue in a linear fashion well into adolescence, during which time these youth are more likely to be convicted of serious and/or violent crimes (e.g., Lewis, Pincus, & Glaser, 1984; McCord, 1983; Tarter, Hegedus, Winston, & Alterman, 1984).

Current theory in adult conflict and problem solving posits that attribution of blame instigates an immediate affective reaction (e.g., anger, sadness) that, in turn, may influence the individual's response (Fincham et al., 1987). Specifically, aggressive behavior is potentiated by anger, whereas withdrawal is potentiated by sadness. Dodge and his colleagues have demonstrated that aggressive, rejected children are biased in their attributions of others' intentions, and that this attributional pattern is directly related to their decision to retaliate aggressively (Dodge, 1980; Dodge & Frame, 1982; Dodge, Murphy, & Buschbaum, 1984). Dodge and Richard (1985) have speculated on the origins of attributional biases and problem-solving deficits found among maladjusted children, such as victims of abuse and neglect. Events such as early trauma "may leave a lasting impression on a child by shaping the child's perception of future events . . . [and] may increase the probability that the child will be perceptually ready to interpret hostility and aggression in his or her world in the future" (p. 53). How the child comes to attribute the behavior of his or her parents, therefore, may generalize to peer situations and result in aggression, rejection, and low social competence (Shirk, 1988).

Implications for Primary and Secondary Prevention

The Case for Prevention

From the above discussion of recent findings relating child maltreatment to developmental differences, we see that critical advances in our thinking and understanding of this problem have occurred. Our explanation of how maltreatment affects children has grown from a reliance on major, visible signs of trauma (e.g., injuries or overt behavior problems) to a recognition of the large number of subtle, yet crucial, ways by which the impact of maltreatment is mediated by the child's course of development.

A prominent theme throughout the above studies linking maltreatment to developmental deviation is that the effects are cumulative over time, creating somewhat of a domino effect on subsequent development. Associated with this theme is the notion that maltreatment itself encompasses more than visible, distinct actions toward a child that exceed a community standard. From a socialization perspective, maltreatment refers to the everyday experiences of a child that are unhealthy or inappropriate for his or her psychological growth and development. The child's development may be delayed or disrupted by these everyday actions taken by a parent who is not sensitive to the child's needs and abilities. It is not the isolated episodes of violence or rejection that set in motion the developmental disparities; rather, this perspective maintains that such episodes are just visible markers of a more pervasively disturbed parent-child relationship.

What impact does this view have on treatment and prevention directions? This theme departs from most current efforts to treat child victims of maltreatment and to prevent its recurrence, in that most forms of treatment for child abuse (the most studied form of maltreatment) have been directed at parents, once the abuse has been identified. Treatment of such parents and their children is a critical and necessary part of comprehensive services, yet we need to be aware of the limitations of interventions that take place after maltreatment has become commonplace.

Treatments based on a behavioral or social learning model, for example, are designed to assist parents in managing difficult child behavior without resorting to violence or coercion, while at the same time trying to encourage abusive parents to initiate more positive strategies of child rearing. By and large, this intervention approach has met with promising success in altering identified negative parenting behaviors, such as physical punishment or harsh criticism (Azar & Wolfe, 1989). A difficulty with this approach is that it rests on the assumption that the parent's new behavior will be maintained by the child's positive improvements, and that the parent's gains in skill will generalize to new and less familiar situations. Simultaneously, this approach to treatment must deal with the reality that the parent-child relationship has been in formation for some time, and thus many factors are in place that serve to maintain its aversiveness and coercive style (Patterson, 1982). By the time treatment has begun, the family patterns associated with abuse and inappropriate interactions (e.g., coercive exchanges) have often become well established (Wolfe, 1987). Family members and therapists face a major challenge in reversing the patterns that have formed. Moreover, the child's developmental impairments (e.g., language delay, peer problems, social-cognitive deficits resulting in behavior disorders) may be of such a level that they pose a further threat to the deterioration of the parent-child relationship.

Similar criticisms can be directed to insight-oriented treatment approaches based on a psychodynamic "trauma" model, whereby the parent's symptoms represent conversions of past traumatic experiences that have not been resolved (cf. Azar & Wolfe, 1989). Such strategies attempt to reduce parent-child conflict by recovering and understanding past traumatic events experienced by the parent and/or child. Because previously experienced events form part of the present repertoire of child-rearing methods, it is not surprising that this approach has some appeal to therapists and clients who wish to deal with internalized conflicts. Yet, as Shirk (1988) points out, the dangers of reembracing the trauma model of treatment is that it assumes a linear relationship between past traumatic events and present symptoms. The child's behavior disorder, according to this view, would be a direct expression of his or her unresolved anger or similar, unconsciously held, feelings toward the parent. It may fail to recognize the indirect, mediating influence of development on the expression of such symptoms, in which the child's behavior problem occurs as a function of developmental deficits linked to poor child rearing.

If we accept the theoretical and philosophical argument that maltreatment is indirectly responsible for a myriad of developmental problems, then our understanding of the behavioral and emotional adjustment problems shown by maltreated children will rest on such developmental deficits in addition to some direct effects of maltreatment (trauma) or insensitive parenting. Such a position carries with it important implications for establishing intervention and prevention goals.

First, we need to learn to recognize the developmental differences that may emerge as a function of maltreatment. A child's symptoms would be seen as an understandable result of his or her efforts to learn social behaviors without the benefit of sensitive parenting or careful guidance. The identified "referral concern," therefore, shifts from one that assesses current problematic behavior alone toward one that identifies the developmental concerns that underlie such expressions. This premise directs intervention to the strengthening of developmentally relevant tasks or skills, in addition to specific presenting complaints.

Second, we can take advantage of this organizational perspective by seeking to enlist greater cooperation from parents in developing desirable, effective strategies of child rearing. That is, intervention (and, most importantly, prevention) can be planned from an earlier point in time in such a way that undesirable (and potentially problematic) developmental deficits can be minimized. Rather than relying on aversive contingencies (i.e., detecting abuse and neglect and imposing changes on the family), a developmentally guided intervention/prevention strategy works on the principle of providing the least intrusive, earliest assistance possible. The focus can be shifted away from identifying misdeeds of the parent, and more toward promoting an optimal balance between the needs of the child and the abilities of the parent.

Finally, we should apply some existing methods and formulate new ways to structure experiences that help children to succeed in the two prominent areas of development that were noted previously: the social-emotional basis of relationship formation, and social competence (skill development, social sensitivity). The objectives of this goal would be: (a) to strengthen the child's self-identity and self-differentiation from an early age, either through improved parent-child relations (the preferred method) and/or through extrafamilial opportunities (e.g., counseling, therapeutic nurseries, structured day care, out-of-home placements); (b) to teach social sensitivity and perspective taking in a manner commensurate with his or her level of development (e.g., Kendall, Lerner, & Craighead, 1984); and (c) to provide successful opportunities for slightly older children to develop and expand their interpersonal skills to relationships outside of the immediate family (e.g., peers, social or sports activities).

This logic of intervention/prevention reflects the growing recognition that child abuse and related forms of maltreatment are seldom caused by intrinsic personality characteristics of the parent. Instead, it presumes that maltreatment is the product of the interaction between the parent's abilities and resources and the child's emerging behavioral and emotional characteristics (i.e., the parent-child relationship). Ways to strengthen this relationship offer considerably more promise than those aimed at correcting only one component (i.e., the parent) or treating only the visible symptoms of conflict.

In addition, this reasoning fits well with a "Life Transitions" model of child adjustment (Felner, Farber, & Primavera, 1983), which states that most significant life events are markers of change and require additional adaptive effort. A primary prevention framework considers the entire transitional period of the individual as he or she adapts to changes, rather than viewing stressful occurrences (e.g., abuse and neglect experiences) as unitary events. Thus the goal of preventing psychopathology among maltreated children becomes one of reducing and understanding vulnerability, while allowing for developmental enhancement. This approach turns us away from a primary emphasis on negative (stressful) life experiences and their pathogenic consequences, to the nature of the changes that characterize such transitions and the process of adapting to them. Our prevention/intervention question thus can be reworded to fit this life transitions framework: Rather than asking what specific effect maltreatment may have, we should determine what personal and situational factors may be associated with differing levels of adaptive success. In this manner we can formulate methods for enhancing growth and reducing vulnerability among this population.

Child maltreatment is a complex phenomenon that appears to respond better to prevention than to treatment after the fact (both in terms of empirical findings as well as moral preference; see Daro, 1988; Fink & McCloskey, 1990; Wekerle & Wolfe, 1991). When prevention efforts are phrased more in terms of what can be improved upon, rather than what can be stopped from happening, we are turning more in the direction of true family support and the encouragement of personal self-efficacy. Our knowledge of the effects of child maltreatment brings us closer and closer to the realization that it reflects core problems in our socialization patterns (rather than extreme deviation from the norm). In parallel, we are obligated to take a dedicated look at what our cultural and community agents are doing or not doing to foster development of children and families in future generations.

References

Aber, J. L., & Allen, J. P. (1987). Effects of maltreatment on young children's socioemotional development: An attachment theory perspective. *Developmental Psychology, 23,* 406-414.

Ainsworth, M. D. S. (1980). Attachment and child abuse. In G. Gerbner, C. J. Ross, & E. Zigler (Eds.), *Child abuse: An agenda for action* (pp. 35-47). New York: Oxford University Press.

Ainsworth, M. D. S., Blehar, M. C., Waters, E., & Wall, S. (1978). *Patterns of attachment: A psychological study of the strange situation.* Hillsdale, NJ: Lawrence Erlbaum.

Ammerman, R. T. (in press). The role of the child in physical abuse: A reappraisal. *Victims and Violence.*

Azar, S. T., & Wolfe, D. A. (1989). Behavioral intervention with abusive families. In E. J. Mash & R. A. Barkley (Eds.), *Behavioral treatment of childhood disorders* (pp. 451-489). New York: Guilford.

Bandura, A. (1973). *Aggression: A social learning analysis.* Englewood Cliffs, NJ: Prentice-Hall.

Barahal, R. M., Waterman, J., & Martin, H. P. (1981). The social cognitive development of abused children. *Journal of Consulting and Clinical Psychology, 49,* 508-516.

Boivin, M., & Begin, G. (1989). Peer status and self-perception among early elementary school children: The case of the rejected children. *Child Development, 60,* 591-596.

Bowlby, J. (1969). *Attachment and loss* (Vol. 1). New York: Basic Books.

Bretherton, I., Fritz, J., Zahn-Waxler, C., & Ridgeway, D. (1986). Learning to talk about emotions: A functionalist perspective. *Child Development, 57,* 529-548.

Camras, L., Grow, G., & Ribardy, S. (1983). Recognition of emotional expression by abused children. *Journal of Clinical Child Psychology, 12,* 325-328.

Cicchetti, D. (1984). The emergence of developmental psychopathology. *Child Development, 55,* 1-7.

Cicchetti, D., & Olsen, K. (1990). The developmental psychopathology of child maltreatment. In M. Lewis & S. M. Miller (Eds.), *Handbook of developmental psychopathology* (pp. 261-279). New York: Plenum.

Cicchetti, D., & Rizley, R. (1981). Developmental perspectives on the etiology, intergenerational transmission, and sequelae of child maltreatment. In D. Cicchetti & R. Rizley (Eds.), *New directions for child development: Developmental perspectives on child maltreatment* (pp. 31-55). San Francisco: Jossey-Bass.

Cicchetti, D., Toth, S., & Bush, M. (1988). Developmental psychopathology and incompetence in childhood: Suggestions for intervention. In B. B. Lahey & A. E. Kazdin (Eds.), *Advances in clinical child psychology* (Vol. 11, pp. 1-77). New York: Plenum.

Covell, K., & Abramovitch, R. (in press). Children's understanding of maternal anger: Age and source of anger differences. *Merrill-Palmer Quarterly.*

Crittenden, P. M., & Bonvillian, J. D. (1984). The relationship between maternal risk status and maternal sensitivity. *American Journal of Orthopsychiatry, 54,* 250-262.

Cummings, E. M., Zahn-Waxler, C., & Radke-Yarrow, M. (1981). Young children's responses to expressions of anger and affection by others in the family. *Child Development, 52,* 1274-1282.

Daro, D. (1988). *Confronting child abuse: Research for effective program design.* New York: Free Press.

Dodge, K. A. (1980). Social cognition and children's aggressive behavior. *Child Development, 51,* 162-170.

Dodge, K. A., & Frame, C. L. (1982). Social cognitive biases and deficits in aggressive boys. *Child Development, 53,* 620-635.

Dodge, K. A., Murphy, R. R., & Buschbaum, K. (1984). The assessment of intention-cue detection skills in children: Implications for developmental psychopathology. *Child Development, 55,* 163-173.

Dodge, K. A., & Richard, B. A. (1985). Peer perceptions, aggression, and the development of peer relations. In J. B. Pryor & J. D. Day (Eds.), *The development of social cognition* (pp. 35-58). New York: Springer.

Egeland, B., & Sroufe, L. A. (1981). Attachment and early maltreatment. *Child Development, 52,* 44-52.

Erickson, M. F., Sroufe, L. A., & Egeland, B. (1985). The relationship between quality of attachment and relationship problems in preschool in a high-risk sample. *Monographs of the Society for Research in Child Development, 50*(Serial No. 209).

Felner, R. D., Farber, S. S., & Primavera, J. (1983). Transitions and stressful life events: A model for primary prevention. In R. D. Felner, L. A. Jason, J. N. Moritsugu, & S. S. Farber (Eds.), *Preventive psychology: Theory, research, and practice*. Elmsford, NY: Pergamon.

Fincham, F. D., Beach, S., & Nelson, G. (1987). Attribution processes in distressed and nondistressed couples: III. Causal responsibility attribution for spouse behavior. *Cognitive Therapy and Research, 11*, 71-86.

Fink, A., & McCloskey, L. (1990). Moving child abuse and neglect prevention programs forward: Improving program evaluations. *Child Abuse & Neglect, 14*, 187-206.

Garbarino, J. (1976). A preliminary study of some ecological correlates of child abuse: The impact of socioeconomic stress on mothers. *Child Development, 47*, 178-185.

Garmezy, N. (1983). Stressors of childhood. In N. Garmezy & M. Rutter (Eds.), *Stress, coping, and development in children* (pp. 43-84). New York: McGraw-Hill.

Garrison, W., Earls, F., & Kindlon, D. (1983). An application of the Pictorial Scale of Perceived Competence and Acceptance within an epidemiological survey. *Journal of Abnormal Child Psychology, 11*, 367-377.

George, C., & Main, M. (1979). Social interactions of young abused children: Approach, avoidance, and aggression. *Child Development, 50*, 306-318.

Gil, D. G. (1970). *Violence against children: Physical child abuse in the United States.* Cambridge, MA: Harvard University Press.

Harter, S. (1983). Developmental perspectives on the self-system. In P. H. Mussen (Ed.), *Handbook of child development* (Vol. 4, pp. 275-385). New York: John Wiley.

Hoffman-Plotkin, D., & Twentyman, C. T. (1984). A multimodal assessment of behavioral and cognitive deficits in abused and neglected preschoolers. *Child Development, 55*, 794-802.

Howes, C., & Espinosa, M. (1985). The consequences of child abuse for the formation of relationships with peers. *Child Abuse & Neglect, 9*, 397-404.

Kaufman, J., & Zigler, E. (1989). The intergenerational transmission of child abuse and the prospect of predicting future abusers. In D. Cicchetti & V. Carlson (Eds.), *Child maltreatment: Research and theory on the causes and consequences of child abuse and neglect* (pp. 129-150). New York: Cambridge University Press.

Kendall, P., Lerner, R., & Craighead, W. (1984). Human development and intervention in childhood psychopathology. *Child Development, 55*, 71-82.

Lewis, D. O., Pincus, J. H., & Glaser, G. H. (1979). Violent juvenile delinquents: Psychiatric, neurological, psychological, and abuse factors. *Journal of the American Academy of Child Psychiatry, 18*, 307-319.

Maccoby, E. E., & Martin, J. A. (1983). Socialization in the context of the family: Parent-child interaction. In P. H. Mussen (Ed.), *Handbook of child psychology* (Vol. 4, pp. 1-101). New York: John Wiley.

Main, M., & George, C. (1985). Responses of abused and disadvantaged toddlers to distress in agemates: A study in the day care setting. *Developmental Psychology, 21*, 407-412.

Main, M., Kaplan, R., & Cassidy, J. (1985). Security in infancy, childhood, and adulthood: A move to the level of representation. In I. Bretherton & E. Waters (Eds.), Growing points of attachment theory and research. *Monographs of the Society for Research in Child Development, 50*(1-2, Serial No. 209).

McCord, J. (1983). A forty year perspective on effects of child abuse and neglect. *Child Abuse & Neglect, 7,* 265-270.

Mueller, E., & Silverman, N. (1989). Peer relations in maltreated children. In D. Cicchetti & V. Carlson (Eds.), *Child maltreatment: Theory and research on the causes and consequences of child abuse and neglect* (pp. 529-578). New York: Cambridge University Press.

Oldershaw, L., Walters, G. C., & Hall D. K. (1986). Control strategies and noncompliance in abusive mother-child dyads: An observational study. *Child Development, 57,* 722-732.

Parke, R. D., & Slaby, R. G. (1983). The development of aggression. In P. H. Mussen (Ed.), *Handbook of child psychology* (Vol. 4, pp. 547-641). New York: John Wiley.

Paterson, R. J., & Moran, G. (1988). Attachment theory, personality development, and psychotherapy. *Clinical Psychology Review, 8,* 611-636.

Patterson, G. R. (1982). *Coercive family process.* Eugene, OR: Castalia.

Pederson, D., Moran, G., Sitko, C., Campbell, K., Ghesquire, K., & Acton, H. (in press). Maternal sensitivity and the security of mother-infant attachment: A Q-sort study. *Child Development.*

Reid, J. B., Taplin, P., & Lorber, R. (1981). A social interactional approach to the treatment of abusive families. In R. B. Stuart (Ed.), *Violent behavior: Social learning approaches to prediction, management, and treatment* (pp. 83-101). New York: Brunner/Mazel.

Rotenburg, K. J. (1980). Children's use of intentionality in judgments of character and disposition. *Child Development, 51,* 282-284.

Rubin, K. H., & Krasnor, L. R. (1986). Social-cognitive and social behavioral perspectives on problem solving. In M. Perlmutter (Ed.), *The Minnesota Symposia on Child Psychology* (Vol. 18, pp. 1-68). Hillsdale, NJ: Lawrence Erlbaum.

Schneider-Rosen, K., & Cicchetti, D. (1984). The relationship between affect and cognition in maltreated infants: Quality of attachment and the development of visual self-recognition. *Child Development, 55,* 648-658.

Shirk, S. R. (1988). The interpersonal legacy of physical abuse of children. In M. Straus (Ed.), *Abuse and victimization across the lifespan* (pp. 57-91). Baltimore, MD: Johns Hopkins University Press.

Smetana, J., Kelly, M., & Twentyman, C. (1984). Abused, neglected, and nonmaltreated children's judgments of moral and social transgressions. *Child Development, 55,* 277-287.

Sroufe, L. A., & Fleeson, J. (1986). Attachment and the construction of relationships. In W. W. Hartup & Z. Rubin (Eds.), *Relationships and development* (pp. 51-71). Hillsdale, NJ: Lawrence Erlbaum.

Tarter, R. E., Hegedus, A. E., Winston, N. E., & Alterman, A. I. (1984). Neuropsychological, personality, and familial characteristics of physically abused delinquents. *Journal of the American Academy of Child Psychiatry, 23,* 668-674.

Vondra, J., Barnett, D., & Cicchetti, D. (1989). Perceived and actual competence among maltreated and comparison school children. *Development and Psychopathology, 1,* 237-255.

Vondra, J., Barnett, D., & Cicchetti, D. (in press). Self-concept, motivation, and competence among preschoolers from maltreating and comparison families. *Child Abuse & Neglect.*

Wekerle, C., & Wolfe, D. A. (1991). *An empirical review of prevention strategies for child abuse and neglect.* Manuscript under review.

Wolfe, D. A. (1985). Child abusive parents: An empirical review and analysis. *Psychological Bulletin, 97,* 462-482.

Wolfe, D. A. (1987). *Child abuse: Implications for child development and psychopathology.* Newbury Park, CA: Sage.

Zahn-Waxler, C., Cummings, E. M., McKnew, D. H., & Radke-Yarrow, M. (1984). Altruism, aggression, and social interactions in young children with a manic-depressive parent. *Child Development, 55,* 112-122.

3

Developmental Changes in Antisocial Behavior

GERALD R. PATTERSON

The idea that measures of children's antisocial behavior are highly stable over extended periods of time is now a part of the conventional wisdom (Loeber, 1982; Olweus, 1979). In this report I examine the concept of stability from two very different perspectives. On the one hand, the data will show that during preadolescence the individual difference rankings are highly stable over time. The data will also show that the mean level for the cohort is also quite stable during this same interval (i.e., as a group, preadolescents are not becoming increasingly antisocial).

These manifestations of stability mask dramatic shifts in the underlying process of the antisocial trait. There are three kinds of changes. On the one hand, there is evidence that the process is nonstationary. The stationarity assumption requires that the relation between variables A and B remains constant throughout the time interval. In the present

AUTHOR'S NOTES: Support for this project was provided by Grant No. MH 37940 from the Center for Studies of Antisocial and Violent Behavior, NIMH, U.S. PHS, and Grant No. MH 37911 from the Behavioral Sciences Research Branch, Family Processes Division, NIMH, U.S. PHS.

I wish to thank Mike Stoolmiller for his contributions to the statistical analyses, particularly the material concerned with LGM, and Terry Duncan for his meticulous development of the toddler progression data.

instance, the data will show significant changes over time in the relation between parental monitoring and child antisocial behavior. The second important change is in the *form* (i.e., kind) and the intensity of the antisocial acts themselves. Although the general outlines of the antisocial trait are highly stable over time, new forms of antisocial behavior are constantly being added (and deleted). The third shift is in the setting in which antisocial acts occur. It is assumed that the problem child is one of the first to be out on the street and unsupervised by adults. In that setting, he is in the company of deviant peers. This street-deviant peer setting actually defines an important boundary area for the antisocial process. It defines a new state in the process—one that has profound implications for the future trajectory in the life course of the problem child.

This chapter constitutes an empirical exploration of process. This type of analysis requires a longitudinal data set; it also requires a profound change in how one thinks about data analysis. The preoccupation in the social sciences with correlational analysis often leads to its inappropriate application to longitudinal data sets. The immediate effect of calculating a correlation is to remove differences in mean level; in effect, we discard what may be of greatest interest for developmental analyses. We need to continue analyzing differences in ordinal ranks, but maintain a balance by carefully examining intraindividual growth curves that may signal important changes for a subset of the cohort. This alternative perspective was detailed by D. R. Rogosa, Brandt, and Zimowski (1982) and McArdle (1988). Several examples of this perspective are presented in a section that follows.

There is another change in perspective about data analysis that seems particularly relevant for developmental models. The metaphor for this perspective would be a kind of progression. For example, children's behavior problems may move in an orderly way from relatively trivial juvenile forms of aggression to the more severe acts of burglary or assault. Examples are presented in the context of Guttman-like (1944) progressions in which boys move from disobedience, a relatively trivial problem that characterizes many toddlers, to frequent hitting, which describes only a few. The idea is that all of the boys with the infrequent (but severe) problems will also have moved through each of the more frequent (but less severe) problems.

The analyses of developmental changes also focus our attention on the importance of time as a variable. The timing of shifts from one developmental state to another is often a critical determinant for future life-course trajectories. For example, the coercion model holds that the more extreme the level of problem behaviors, the more likely the child is to move on to the next stage (i.e., *state*) in the deviancy process. Another assumption of the coercion model is that the earlier the onset, the longer the duration in the process. In the present chapter, age at first arrest signifies such a change in state. Event history analysis seems ideally suited to problems involving the duration of time for a shift from one state to another (Allison, 1984; Singer & Willett, 1991); it makes it possible to specify precisely what the relation is between age of the youth and risk for first arrest. Multiple regression analysis can be used to evaluate the contribution of variables such as social disadvantage to changes in risk (i.e., which variables determine the time interval until first arrest).

In the discussion that follows, each of the perspectives on data analysis are applied to address the question of how the process is changing while the antisocial trait remains stable over time.

Two Forms of Stability in Antisocial Behavior

The hypothesis is that during pre- to early adolescence, the process that produces antisocial behavior is well stabilized. What this means is that over a period of four or five years, there is very little change in the ordinal rankings that describe individual differences in this trait. Correlations of scores assessed at one point in time with those assessed later on will be used to assess this aspect of stability.

Hirschi and Gottfredson (1983) demonstrated the universality of the age-crime frequency curve across time and cultures. The data demonstrated that for both boys and girls there is a marked increase in the frequency of arrests between the ages of 10 and 15, followed by a dramatic decrease from early adulthood on. As they noted, this could reflect the fact that increasing numbers of adolescents become antisocial during this interval and/or that those who are antisocial increase the frequency of their delinquent acts. In this chapter, the hypothesis is tested that the change in mean level of antisocial behavior is not isomorphic with the distribution for age-crime frequency (i.e., the police arrest data do not reflect an increase in the number of antisocial adolescents).

Stabilities in Individual Differences

Various reviews of the empirical literature strongly support the idea that measures of the antisocial trait for children tend to be quite stable as early as age 5 or 6 (Loeber, 1982; Olweus, 1979). Olweus noted that measures of the antisocial trait are at least as stable as are measures of intelligence. For example, Martin (1981) used observation data to show a correlation of .49 between rates of coercive behavior at age 18 months and scores obtained at age 49 months. In our own work, we have assumed that using multiagent, multimethod definitions for the trait would significantly enhance stability estimates (Patterson & Bank, 1986, 1987).

The literature implies that early forms of juvenile antisocial behavior, such as temper tantrums or grade-school troublesomeness, significantly predict adolescent delinquency or adult criminality. If they are indeed the forerunners of later criminal acts, then the task for developmental psychologists is to identify the mechanisms that explain how stability might hold even when the topography is changing. We will return to this question in a section that follows.

The data used to test the stability hypothesis were based on families from the Oregon Youth Study (OYS) who lived in high-risk crime areas. The families were intensively assessed when the boys were in Grades 4, 6, and 8. Antisocial behavior was defined at each grade by indicators based on parent and teacher ratings and six telephone interviews with the child. The demographic information for this sample was reported by Capaldi and Patterson (1987), and the details of the psychometric analyses of the indicators for the construct were presented by Capaldi and Patterson (1989). The findings are summarized in Figure 3.1.

The stability coefficient of .92 for the trait assessed at Grades 4 and 6 was comparable to the stability between Grades 6 and 8. The findings offer strong support for the hypothesis. As might be expected, the use of multimethod, multiagent definitions results in higher stability coefficients than is ordinarily found in the literature. Nevertheless, the figure represents a kind of idealized statement, somewhat analogous to a correction for attenuation.

The data also show an acceptable fit of the a priori model to the data set, as shown by the nonsignificant chi-square values. In that each of them was used at both points in time, it seems reasonable to conclude that the error terms must be correlated. Introducing these covariances into the model resulted in a significantly better fit and led to an acceptable overall fit for the model.

The disturbance terms for the Time 2 measures showed that the prior measures accounted for about 61% of the variance for the first model and 60% of the variance for the second. It seems reasonable to conclude that the ordinal rankings for this trait are quite stable from Grade 4 to Grade 8.

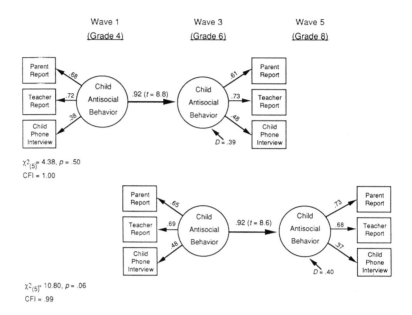

Figure 3.1. The Stability for the Latent Antisocial Behavior Construct ($N =$ 206)

Two Cohort Changes in Mean Level

As noted earlier, Hirschi and Gottfredson (1983) reviewed the extensive literature for a variety of crimes and noted that the distribution of crimes by age seemed to be invariant. Data collected over the last century showed the same characteristics. There is a dramatic surge in frequency from age 10 through age 15 and an equally dramatic decrease starting in late adolescence and continuing through adulthood. The distribution in Figure 3.2 is a record of violent crimes reported by Cairns (1979).

The changes in crime frequency have enormous implications for social policy. Obviously, a theory about crime must explain both the *increase* in frequency during early adolescence and the *decrease* in frequency that begins in late adolescence. Patterson and Yoerger (1991) have taken the position that the crime frequency age distribution is the result of two invariances and does *not* represent an increase in the number of adolescents who are antisocial.

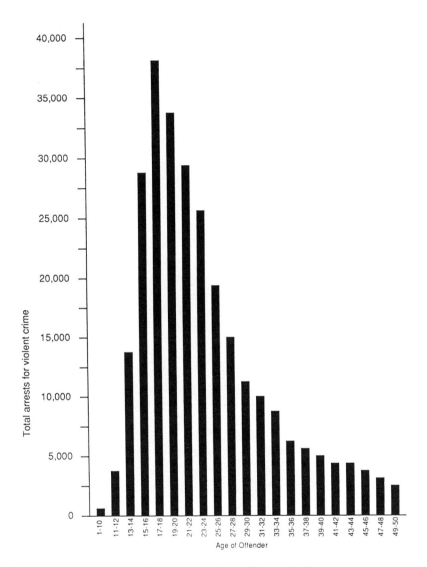

Figure 3.2. Arrests for Violent Crime (from Cairns, 1979)

Data presented here were designed to test the alternative hypothesis that the crime-age frequency distribution is really a reflection of increases in antisocial behavior for the adolescent cohort as a whole. Support for this hypothesis would require that teacher, parent, or child self-reports of antisocial behavior show an increase in mean level over time that would correspond roughly with the crime-frequency data. It is important to note that the empirical findings now available in the literature do not seem to support this hypothesis. Cairns, Cairns, Neckerman, Ferguson, and Gariepy (1989) found a significant decrease in teachers' ratings of fighting, arguing, and trouble-making. In keeping with the data of Cairns et al., Achenbach and Edelbrock (1979b) found no age-related changes in arguing and only moderate decreases in fighting for teachers' ratings for boys aged 10 through 16.

To test this hypothesis with the longitudinal data from the OYS, Stoolmiller (1990) developed a priori scales for covert and overt antisocial acts from teacher reports on the Child Behavior Checklist (CBC) (Achenbach & Edelbrock, 1979a). Itemetric studies were completed separately for each age level and each type of antisocial behavior. Covert and overt acts showed the same frequency curve when plotted as a function of age. The data from the two scales were combined to form an 18-item scale. The frequency curve by age is summarized in Figure 3.3. It can be seen that there was a slight increase between ages 10 and 11 in mean level of antisocial behavior reported by teachers. In no way is this commensurate with the dramatic year-by-year increases shown in Figure 3.2, however. The most parsimonious conclusion would be that there is a good deal of stability in mean level for the at-risk cohorts over this time interval. Aside from the rather modest increase at ages 10 to 11, the amount of aggressivity perceived by teachers remains quite steady, as do the ordinal rankings for individual differences.

At this point, we could use an analysis of variance for repeated measures to test for the significance of the one increase that was noted in the teachers' ratings and then move on to the next problem in the discussion. In doing so, however, we would be overlooking the very interesting question of whether the five-years' worth of ratings by different sets of teachers are really measuring the same thing. A new alternative has become available in the last decade; *latent growth modeling* (LGM) provides a basis for simultaneously addressing this and several other complex questions. In the LGM, the intraindividual growth pattern is the focus for the analyses (D. R. Rogosa et al., 1982). McArdle (1988) and McArdle and Epstein (1987) described this extension of structural equation modeling (SEM); it seems ideally suited to the study of developmental issues.

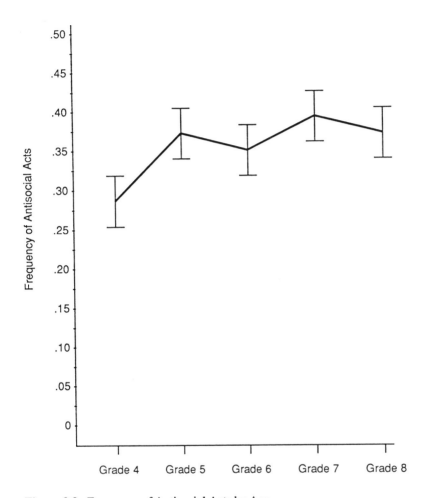

Figure 3.3. Frequency of Antisocial Acts by Age

The first question to be addressed in such an analysis concerns the fit of the intraindividual growth curves for antisocial acts to the group curve portrayed in Figure 3.4. As shown there, the latent construct for antisocial behavior loaded significantly on the ratings collected at each of the five points in time. Even though the ratings were provided by five different sets of teachers for five different age groups, the general fit of the model showed that they were basically talking about the same thing.

The overall fit of the model to the data set was excellent, chi-square (13) = 11.28, $p < .50$. Other estimates of goodness-of-fit indices (GFI = .982, AGFI = .974) were also in agreement with this conclusion. In effect, the intraindividual growth curves were described by the group curve.

Note that, in order to identify the model, one loading must be constrained to a value other than zero. We chose "1" as a loading for the Wave 1 indicator not only for the sake of convenience, but also because it demonstrated the amount of growth (or lack of it). It can be compared to the loading for Wave 2 (1.25) and the other loadings that followed as an index of change.

The largest amount of growth seemed to have occurred from Grades 4 to 5. To determine whether these changes were significant, several alternative models of growth were examined. For example, one model stipulated that no growth occurred at any point. To test this model, all factor loadings were constrained to 1.0, but this model did not fit when tested against the data set. The next model stipulated that there was linear growth each year, but this model did not fit either. The only model that did provide an acceptable fit to the data stipulated that there was growth only from Grade 4 to Grade 5, chi-squared (3) = 3.74, $p < .50$.

For the cohort as a whole, there was a significant increase in antisocial acts accompanying the transition to middle school. Nevertheless, one might ask whether the individual growth curves for the more disturbed boys were the same as those for the less disturbed boys. To find the answer to this question, the sample was split into three subgroups based on child antisocial scores for Wave 1. To keep group sizes approximately even, the cohort was split into low, medium, and high levels of child antisocial at the 33rd and 67th percentiles. As we expected, the three groups differed significantly on their mean scores (factor scores) for the teacher ratings. The general growth patterns were similar for the three groups, however. The differences among the subgroups in slope (i.e., shape of factor loadings) was nonsignificant. Whatever is happening to that age cohort seems to effect all three groups in a similar fashion, even though they start at different levels.

The findings showed high levels of stability in antisocial behavior between the ages of about 10 and 15. Prior measures of the antisocial trait accounted for more than 60% of the variance in later measures of the trait for two-year intervals. Boys of this age seem to maintain their individual difference rankings for this trait. The data also showed that during early adolescence there are only minor increases in the mean level for antisocial behavior as perceived by teachers.

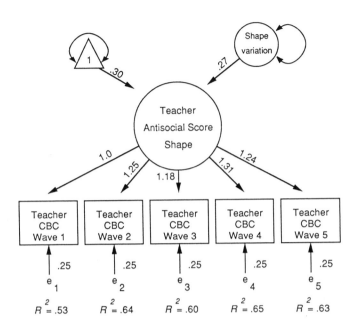

Figure 3.4. Basic Model: Latent Growth Curve for Teacher CBC Antisocial

The sections that follow identify underlying changes that occur in the process during this same interval. The changes have major implications for the long-term adjustment of these boys.

Nonstationarity: Changes in Causes

The hypothesis to be examined in this section is that the process that underlies antisocial behavior may not be stationary during the interval from age 10 through age 15. We can specify the relation between two variables as $p(A/B)$. If this value changes during a series of trials, then the process is said to be nonstationary. In the present context, we assume that parenting practices such as monitoring and discipline are both structurally related to measures of child antisocial behavior. If the relation between parenting practices and child outcomes changes significantly as a function of age of the child, then it might be said that this process is also nonstationary. The implication is that even though the measures of child adjustment might be highly stable during the interval, there are changes in process under way that portend changes in adjustment.

Stability and Parallel Continuities

Reviewers of empirical studies have typically concluded that parents of antisocial children tend to practice harsh and inconsistent discipline, show little positive involvement with the child, and demonstrate poor monitoring and supervisory skills (Loeber & Dishion, 1983; McCord, McCord, & Howard, 1963). The social-interactional perspective takes the position that family members directly train the child to perform antisocial behaviors (Forehand, King, Peed, & Yoder, 1975; Patterson, 1982; Snyder, 1977; Wahler & Dumas, 1984). The parents tend to be noncontingent in their use of positive reinforcers for prosocial behavior and in their use of effective punishment for deviant behavior. The noncontingent parent permits dozens of daily interactions in which coercive child behaviors are directly reinforced by family members (Snyder & Patterson, 1986). Some of the reinforcement is positive (e.g., attend, laugh, approve), but most important contingencies for coercive behavior are escape-conditioning contingencies. The child uses aversive behavior as an effective means of terminating aversive intrusions by other family members. These behaviors make it possible for the child to survive in a highly aversive social system.

The training for deviant behaviors is paralleled by a lack of training for many prosocial skills. Observations in the homes of distressed families have shown that children's prosocial acts are often ignored or responded to inappropriately (Patterson, 1982; Patterson, Reid, & Dishion, 1992; Snyder, 1977). It seems that some families produce children characterized by not one problem, but two: They have antisocial symptoms, and they are socially unskilled.

The formulation presupposes a significant correlation between parental discipline and monitoring on the one hand, and child antisocial behavior on the other. Forgatch (1991) summarized the findings from three samples that showed such a pattern. She also used a quasi-experimental design based on data from families with antisocial boys referred for treatment to test for the causal status of parenting practices. The data showed that changes during treatment in parental discipline and monitoring were accompanied by significant reductions in child antisocial behavior. If the parents' discipline and monitoring skills showed no change, the boy's antisocial behavior tended to remain the same.

Forgatch and Toobert (1979) used a random-assignment design to demonstrate the effectiveness of a brief audiotape outlining more effective discipline procedures for normal preschool children. A comparison of the baseline, termination, and follow-up data for both groups showed a significant experimental effect for the discipline tape. Dishion, Patterson, and Kavanagh (in press) described a random-assignment design applied to adolescents at risk for substance abuse. The analyses showed families assigned to parent training significantly changed their discipline practices, and those assigned to peer training or media alone did not. Structural equation modeling (SEM) showed that discipline measured at termination made a significant contribution to changes in antisocial behavior after antisocial behavior assessed at baseline had been partialled out.

The findings from all three studies support the hypothesized causal status of parental discipline practices for antisocial child behavior.

Parallel Continuity

The hypothesis is that the stabilities for parenting practices parallel those for antisocial behavior. Patterson and Bank (1989) tested this hypothesis using data from the OYS samples assessed at Grades 4 and 6. The stability (i.e., path) coefficients for the multiagent, multimethod definitions of parental monitoring and discipline were .75 and .82 respectively. These findings closely parallel the stabilities found for antisocial behaviors in this chapter.

Subsequent studies revealed one of the reasons for the parallel in stabilities. The relation between child adjustment and parenting practices seems to be bidirectional. The complex relation is considered in the section that follows.

Bidirectional Relation Between Parent and Child Behaviors

Clinical experience would suggest that the child's increased deviancy functions as a feedback loop to further disrupt already ineffective parenting efforts. Patterson, Bank, and Stoolmiller (1990) tested the hypothesis using data from the OYS collected at Grades 4 and 6. The analyses showed a significant contribution of the earlier measure of child antisocial behavior with later measures of parenting practices. The contribution was significant even after the contribution of prior parenting practices had been partialled out. The more extreme the child's antisocial behavior was at Time 1, the more likely parental monitoring and discipline practices were to change for the worse. The relative contributions of prior monitoring measures and prior child antisocial behavior measures to monitoring at Time 2 were .42 and −.29 ($p < .05$) respectively. The comparable figures for parental discipline measures were .46 and −.36 respectively.

Vuchinich, Bank, and Patterson (1991) used longitudinal data from the OYS to demonstrate a bidirectional relation between child antisocial behavior and parental discipline. The data were used first to demonstrate a cross-lagged effect of prior child antisocial behavior on later measures of parental discipline. The bidirectional effect was contemporaneous during Grade 5.

The findings are consistent with the hypothesis that high levels of child deviant behavior may bring about increased disruptions in parenting practices. The bidirectional effects describe a situation in which there could be rapid changes in *both* parenting practices and child behaviors in a relatively short period of time. One implication of a bidirectional relation would be that the path coefficient describing the relation between parenting practices and child adjustment should *increase* over time. The simplest way to demonstrate such an effect would be to model the relation between the two constructs at Grade 4 and again at Grades 6 and 8. The magnitude of the path coefficients should increase over time.

In the structural equation model, only the data from parental monitoring were included because it was measured with exactly the same instruments at all three points in time. As shown in Figure 3.5, the path coefficient relating Parental Monitoring to Child Antisocial at Grade 4 was −.45, and the fit of the model to the data was quite good. Two years later, the coefficient was −.59. There was a further increase in the magnitude of the path coefficient at Grade 8 (−.67).

As the boys grow older, the correlations between the residual error terms increase for both parent reports and child reports. If we had relaxed the constraints on the models, then the fit would have been acceptable for the last two models. In order to facilitate the comparisons of the path coefficients between the models, however, the modifications were not made.

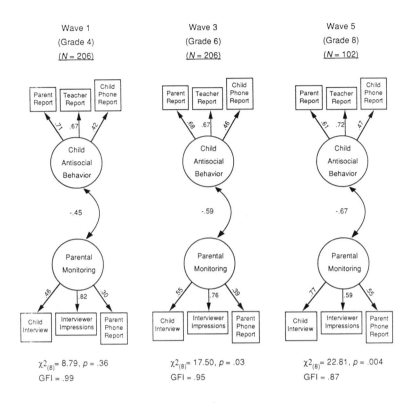

Figure 3.5. Nonstationarity in the Parental Monitoring Construct

The findings emphasize the fact that the relation between parenting practices and child outcome is changing over time. Because we did not have exactly the same measure of parental discipline at each of the three points in time, we could not analyze the changes taking place in that practice. As we shall see later in this chapter, however, the fact that the contribution of parental monitoring is becoming increasingly important takes on added significance when we examine the findings in the next section. If the parents cannot, or do not, maintain adequate supervision of the older child, the child is at grave risk for early arrest. This, in turn, implies a profound change in state that has implications for the child's future life course.

A Shift in Setting and in State

Most child antisocial acts are committed in the home and in the school. In those settings the concerned adults are, of course, the parent(s) and the school staff. By Grade 4, however, a significant number of problem children are performing antisocial behaviors in a much broader arena. The setting that assumes increasing importance is the larger community (i.e., the streets). In that setting, childhood antisocial acts begin to take on slightly altered forms. For example, stealing from mother's purse is replaced by theft from the local store, and a school-yard fight might be replaced by an assault while mugging. I discuss in the section that follows how some of these changes come about and how they might be studied. Let us assume for the moment that these changes are understandable shifts in the process.

The key assumption is that some interaction between the parents' level of monitoring skill and the child's level of deviancy determines how quickly he or she will be out on the streets. The more deviant the child and the less effective the parent at supervising, the sooner he or she will be on the streets. In a very important sense, the childhood level of deviancy determines the time interval for first arrest. As we shall see, the earlier the age of onset, the greater the risk for chronic juvenile offending and adult offending, as well.

By itself, just being arrested is probably of little moment. According to Patterson, Capaldi, and Bank (1991) and Patterson, DeBaryshe, and Ramsey (1989), being arrested before the age of 15 is quite a different matter. In a sense, it represents a kind of marker variable for the coercion model. Once this rite of passage has been accomplished, the youth is on a predictable trajectory—one that is accompanied by very negative outcomes during the adult years (e.g., poor work history, risk for institutionalization, alcoholism, drug abuse, divorce, and high rates of accidents and disease). It is for these reasons that we consider an early police arrest as symbolizing a change of state in the coercion model. It is a fundamental shift in that the kind of consequences provided by the community for antisocial acts are quite different from what had been provided by parents, peers, and teachers. The new state includes a clearly labeled social niche and legal definitions for both the acts and the consequences.

Wandering and Street Time

Patterson and Stouthamer-Loeber (1984) presented data from a sample of normal families that showed marked decreases in adult supervision during the interval from preadolescence to early adolescence. What this means is that with increasing age, these young people are spending increasing amounts of time on the streets. Elliott and Menard (1990) showed that during this same interval there is increasing contact with deviant peers for all adolescents. Presumably, the more antisocial the youth the greater the frequency of contact with members of the deviant peer group. The combination of increasing amounts of unsupervised time and increasing contacts with deviant peers provides a vehicle for the rapid increases in the performance of delinquent acts (Elliott, Huizinga, & Ageton, 1985).

Stoolmiller (1990) has used the longitudinal data from the OYS for a sophisticated test of the hypothesis that wandering or unsupervised street time increases as a function of age. The multiagent data showed significant increases in mean level between Grades 4 and 8. The findings replicated the earlier study by Patterson and Stouthamer-Loeber (1984). Stoolmiller also showed that the intraindividual growth curves for wandering covaried significantly with intraindividual growth curves for antisocial acts. Teachers' ratings provided the data for the antisocial acts. Stoolmiller's analyses also showed that boys who were heavily involved in wandering during Grade 4 made the largest increases in antisocial acts perceived by teachers over the ensuing four years.

We are currently examining the contribution of parental monitoring and child antisocial behavior as potential determinants for both early onset and marked increases in slope (growth) for wandering.

The Time Interval to Change in State

The timing hypothesis has three parts. First, it is assumed that the more antisocial the child, the earlier the age of onset (first arrest). Second, it is assumed that the earlier the start, the greater the risk for repeated arrests in the immediate future. Third, the earlier the age of onset, the longer the duration for remaining in the process. If one can accurately predict an early age for first arrest, then the other two assumptions follow as a matter of course. Therefore, the main focus will be to predict the length of the time interval from Grade 4 to first arrest.

Given that the time interval to first arrest is the dependent variable, then event history analysis would seem to be the analysis of choice (Allison, 1984; Singer & Willett, 1991). At each age level, we can calculate the likelihood of a first arrest for all boys who remain at risk. The format also includes a provision for taking into account individual differences that would make one child a greater risk than another child. We hypothesized that extremely antisocial children are at greatest risk for early arrest. In a test of this hypothesis, we used the Antisocial construct assessed at Grade 4 as a covariate in a continuous-time regression analysis to predict changes in risk status for first arrest (Patterson, Crosby, & Vuchinich, 1991).

We used the data from juvenile court files to determine the age of first arrest for the two OYS cohorts. The cumulative proportion of the OYS sample involved in a first arrest is plotted in Figure 3.6. There appeared to be a definite developmental shift as a function of age. In other words, the risk for first arrest seemed to increase as the child grew older, with a marked surge around age 12 or 13. Before proceeding with a formal analysis, we were interested in determining just how generalizable these findings might be. It is not at all clear that findings from a small metropolitan center such as Eugene, OR, would fit a sample of boys from a larger metropolitan area. Farrington (1987) collected longitudinal data from inner-city London for first arrests by age for 378 boys; those data are also summarized in Figure 3.6. The slopes for the two samples are quite similar; both show an increase in prevalence between ages 12 and 13. It seems, then, that the data from the OYS are quite similar to what obtains in other settings.

Data from official records collected for the OYS in December 1990 showed that by age 15 years 11 months, 80 boys had been arrested at least once. It can be seen in Table 3.1 that 10% of the sample had already been arrested by age 11 years 11 months. In that only 8 boys have not yet reached the early starter threshold (15 years 11 months), the hazard rates are a fairly good estimate of the risks for the OYS.

The last column in Table 3.1 summarizes the changes in risk for first arrest as a function of age. At each year, the number of boys arrested is divided by the number of boys still at risk. For example, at age 11-12 there were five first arrests and a subset of 191 boys at risk (15 had previously been arrested). The hazard rate at age 11 was .025. Examination of the hazard rates shows a substantial increase in risk between ages 12 and 13. This suggests the possibility of a kind of developmental spurt in risk for that interval. The analyses by Patterson, Crosby, and Vuchinich (1991) are in keeping with this idea. They showed that the

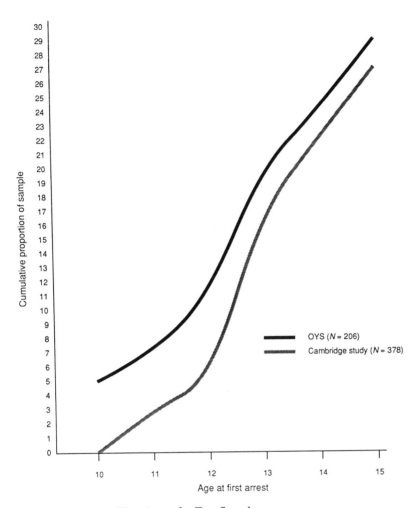

Figure 3.6. Age at First Arrest for Two Samples

model that specified a change in hazard rate as a function of time provided the best fit to the distribution of hazard rates.

Is it true that the most deviant boys start first? This hypothesis was tested in two ways. The most straightforward test would be simply to correlate age of first arrest with the composite antisocial trait score assessed at Grade 4. When this was done with the present data set, the

TABLE 3.1 Life Table and Hazard Rates for Age at First Arrest

Age Interval	Number at Risk	Number Having Contact	Hazard Rate	Number Censored on 12/4/1990
6-7 years	206	2	.0097	0
7-8	204	2	.0098	0
8-9	202	1	.0050	0
9-10	201	5	.0249	0
10-11	196	5	.0255	0
11-12	191	5	.0262	0
12-13	186	13	.0699	0
13-14	173	19	.1098	0
14-15	154	13	.0844	0
15-16	141	15	.1064	8
16-17	118	11	.0932	60
17-18	47	2	.0425	45

NOTE: The hazard rate is the number of subjects having first police contact divided by the number at risk of having such a contact.

multiple correlation was .572 ($p < .001$). In keeping with the hypothesis, the standard partial beta for the antisocial trait made the largest contribution, $-.4232$ ($t = -4.27, p < .001$). Adding a measure of social disadvantage (parent occupation and education) significantly increased our ability to predict age of onset. The standard partial beta was .240 ($t = 2.98, p < .005$). The more antisocial the child and the more socially disadvantaged the family, the greater the risk for an early arrest.

Again, the problem with this analysis is that a substantial number of boys have not reached the cutoff age (15 years, 11 months). These boys constitute "noise" for the multiple regression analyses. Continuous-time regression analyses are a part of event history analysis designed to address problems of this kind. Such an analysis showed essentially the same outcome as that obtained for the multiple regression findings (Patterson, Crosby, & Vuchinich, 1991). The findings support the idea that the more deviant (more antisocial and more disadvantaged) the child, the greater the risk for an early start.

Are boys who start early really at greatest risk for immediate rearrests? Blumstein, Cohen, Roth, and Visher (1986) summarized the findings from three longitudinal studies. They showed in each case that the earlier the age of first arrest, the greater the average annual arrest frequency. Patterson, Crosby, and Vuchinich (1991) made a similar analysis of the OYS data set. They found that given an arrest by age 15, the expected rearrest was on the average about once every 14 months. The findings from the OYS and those of Blumstein and his colleagues all provide strong support for the hypothesis that early starters are at grave risk for immediate rearrest.

Blumstein et al. (1986) analyzed the data from three studies that included data from adult arrests. The data showed a strong relation between the number of juvenile arrests and the risk for offending as an adult.

Some Metamorphoses for Antisocial Acts

We have established that individual differences in antisocial behavior remain highly stable during early adolescence, as does the mean level of antisocial behavior for the cohort. During the same interval, there are profound changes in the kind of contribution made by the parent to this process. There is also significant expansion in the settings in which antisocial acts occur; the street scene becomes increasingly important in teaching new forms of antisocial behavior. This raises the question of just how some new forms of antisocial behavior get introduced over time.

Changes in form for deviant behaviors can come about in a number of ways. Subtle differences in the contingencies presented within a setting can produce such changes. For example, if trial efforts to increase the amplitude of the aggression pay off, then there is likely to be a shift toward increasing severity over time. On the other hand, the child's behavior may place him at risk for entering a new setting (e.g., the street). In that setting, he is interacting with a new set of social agents, the deviant peer group. Under their aegis, he could make rapid progress in learning new forms of antisocial behavior.

New Forms of Antisocial Behavior

There are several elements to the idea that new forms of antisocial behavior may be added during early adolescence. One assumption is that the street scene represents a new training ground for the acquisition of new forms. The second assumption is that the parents' monitoring practices are simply overwhelmed by the extremely deviant youth who demands to be out on the street. The third idea is that over time, for a subset of youth, there will be increases in mean level for certain new forms of antisocial behavior. Each of these hypotheses has been explored in detail by Patterson, Bank, and Stoolmiller (1990).

The key problem is to find a means for describing intraindividual growth for changes in social behavior. As noted earlier, the mathematics were worked out some time ago (D. Rogosa, 1980), and some initial applications have been made to social science (e.g., McArdle, 1985). The assumption is that the same trait measured at different points in time can be shown to form a latent construct for that trait. The second, and perhaps more interesting, assumption is that various covariates can be introduced that will account for significant amounts of variance in the latent construct (i.e., both growth and the variables that effect it can be modeled).

In the present case, we are interested in searching for not just one thing changing over time, but the possibility that *several* forms of antisocial behavior may be increasing during the same time interval. This means building a latent construct comprised of different forms of antisocial behavior that are all changing over time in the same way (i.e., a latent construct for change). To explore this possibility, Patterson, Bank, and Stoolmiller (1990) used the OYS data collected from teachers' ratings at Grades 4, 6, and 9.

Inspection of normative data from Achenbach and Edelbrock (1979b) suggested several behaviors that might be candidates for such an analysis. His data suggested that both truancy and substance use showed gradual changes in mean level over time. We selected these behaviors together with two others that we thought would not show this kind of growth (e.g., fighting should decrease, lying and cheating should show no change). A shape index was calculated for each individual child for each of the four problem behaviors. The index described the rate of growth from Grade 4 through Grade 9. If truancy and substance abuse are to be thought of as defining a latent construct for change, then the shape indices should be significantly correlated. As predicted, the correlation was .90; the correlations with fighting and lying/cheating were close to zero. It is reasonable to conclude that truancy and substance abuse are changing in similar ways over time.

At the time of this writing, we are building a latent growth model to test the idea that wandering and deviant peer involvement measured at Grade 4 will account for intraindividual growth in this new latent construct for change. If, as expected, they do make a significant contribution, then we have provided important support for the general idea of how changes in settings and agents might precede changes in form.

Escalation: Changes in Intensity

The assumption is that the longer a child is involved in the coercion process, the greater the risk for movement toward increasing amplitude or severity of the behavior. We believe that this shift toward increasing severity characterizes both the toddler and the adolescent. In general, it would be characterized by a movement from relatively trivial acts to more severe crimes. In keeping with this idea, Loeber and LeBlanc (1991) cited studies based on self-report and official records (and one negative finding) that show early starters are at greater risk than late starters for more severe crimes. They also cited three studies showing a progression from less severe to more severe crimes for delinquents in general, and they make a claim for extensive qualitative and quantitative changes as a function of continued time in process.

Within the coercion model, the explanation offered for this shift over time is based on the escalation mechanism. The idea is that quite often, when one member of a dyad escalates the intensity of his or her aversive behavior, it pays off (i.e., the other member of the dyad submits, withdraws, or reacts in a neutral to positive manner) (Patterson, 1982). Do individuals in fact escalate in intensity during aversive exchanges? The analyses of extended coercive chains showed that the aggressive child was more likely to escalate in intensity very early during the interchange, and siblings and mothers tended not to escalate until the second or third reaction in sequence (Patterson, 1980). Snyder (1991) showed that escalation was more likely to occur in clinical samples than in normal samples. Most of the increase in intensity for both samples was during the second or third reaction in an episode. Reid, Taplin, and Lorber (1981) compared three studies and demonstrated that, for clinical and normal samples alike, there was a significant increase in the risk for high-amplitude aggression as the duration of the conflict extended. Chains longer than 23 seconds seemed particularly at risk.

Are those increases in intensity more likely to be reinforced? To date, most of the studies on the reinforcement for escalation have been confined to laboratory studies of fighting mice. These studies were reviewed by Patterson (1982). The fact that such studies have not been done with families in natural settings is a critical omission and means that the escalation mechanism must be entertained with a good deal of caution.

According to the coercion model, an increase in amplitude is likely to prove functional (i.e., the other person is apt to withdraw from the exchange). In the short run the person who withdraws reduces the pain he or she experiences; in the long run, however, he or she has increased the risk that the other person will use high-amplitude coercive behaviors in future bouts. The reciprocal escalation is thought to be most likely if the "power" is relatively equal for both parties.

Other forms of antisocial behavior may escalate because they produce positive reinforcing outcomes, or they are reinforcing because they produce a means of avoiding unpleasant experiences. Skipping school is more reinforcing than simply being tardy. Stealing a car is more reinforcing than stealing a T-shirt. The longer a child is in the coercive process and the higher his rate of performance, the greater the risk for engaging in more severe forms of antisocial acts. It is hypothesized that all boys who remain in a coercive process are moving steadily toward greater severity of antisocial acts.

It is hypothesized that antisocial acts fall on a continuum from trivial to extremely aversive (e.g., from whining to teasing, hitting, assault, and homicide). The review of studies by Patterson (1982) showed that trivial acts occurred much more frequently than did more serious acts. If there is a progression over time from trivial to severe acts, this implies that a child who engages in firesetting has passed through all of the previous, less severe antisocial acts in the progression. In a cross-sectional design, Patterson and Dawes (1975) examined the transitivity hypothesis for a progression of observed child coercive behaviors. The data were consistent with the hypothesis that all children who performed a low-rate serious behavior also performed the higher rate behaviors that preceded it in the progression. In an examination of child referral symptoms, Patterson (1982) also found a progression from disobedience to lying, stealing, and firesetting. In keeping with the transitivity hypothesis, 78% of the firesetters were said to be stealers, and 86% of the stealers were thought to be liars.

A progression for antisocial acts involving children might be visualized as a set of nested Venn diagrams, as shown in Figure 3.7. In this perfect progression, all boys who attack other children with an object would also be observed hitting others, having temper tantrums, and being disobedient. On the other hand, not all children who hit have moved on to attacking others with an object. If we intercorrelated all of these variables, we would find that all of the correlations are positive and tend to be higher among adjacent variables. So, although noncompliance correlates with attacking with an object, the correlation is much higher between fighting and attacking with an object. Notice that the

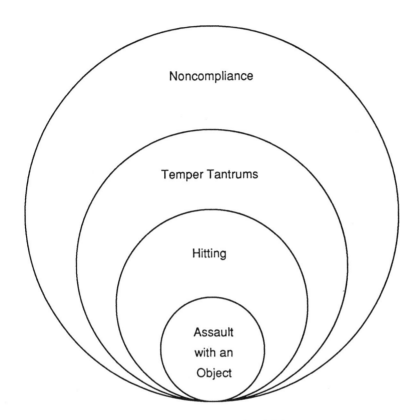

Figure 3.7. A Transitive Progression for Antisocial Acts

progression begins with noncompliance, a problem that characterizes at least half of all normal toddlers.

At this time there is no single index that summarizes all of the information in a progression. The most promising format seems to be the Longitudinal Guttman Simplex (LGS) outlined by Collins and Cliff (1990). Our own approach has been to begin with a simple descriptive analysis of progressions over time. To illustrate, the data base consists of 77 boys and 65 girls from the longitudinal study of normal families by Eddy and Fagot (1991). The present chapter examines some of the maternal CBC ratings for boys from that study. The mothers' ratings for boys were collected at 18 months of age and again at 24 to 36 months and 48 to 60 months of age. Do coercive behaviors change over time in such a way as predicted by the idea of a progression in severity?

Patterson and Duncan (1991) studied comparable data for boys and girls based on ratings by mothers and fathers, but only the subset of data from mothers' ratings of sons will be considered here. Three child traits were selected that illustrate the transitive progression expected during the toddler-to-preschool interval. Behaviors such as disobedience, temper tantrums, and physical attacks certainly occur for all children at some time, but the mothers in this study implied that they occur frequently enough to be perceived as a problem. The three child problem behaviors were ordered from most to least frequently occurring.

It can be seen in Figure 3.8 that the same progression held at each age. Disobedience characterized the majority of the boys, temper tantrums were second in the progression, and physical attacks characterized very few of the boys. One might expect that as the socialization process gets under way, many of the boys will drop out of the coercive process. In fact, as reflected in the mothers' ratings, five dropped out at Wave 2 and three dropped out at Wave 3.

In what sense do these static data define a progression? One characteristic that is of immediate interest would be the conditionals that describe transitive relationships (e.g., are all subjects classified as being at one step in the progression also classified as having been in the prior one). It can be seen in Figure 3.8 that 75% of the toddlers who physically attack also engage in temper tantrums and 88% of those with frequent temper tantrums are also described as disobedient. Similar support for the transitivity hypothesis is given by the data collected at Wave 2 and moderate support is given by Wave 3 data. Generally speaking, the vast majority of boys classified as engaging in an extreme act were also described as engaging in the immediately prior, less extreme act.

The escalation in intensity hypothesis requires that the effect occurs *over time*. Longitudinal data based on mothers' ratings of their sons at two points in time were used to test this hypothesis. These data for toddlers presumably describe a very early stage in the coercion process. It would be expected, therefore, that the stability across time would be only moderate as compared to the data for adolescent samples. While the mothers' ratings may reflect shifts toward greater or fewer problems over time, it is assumed that the changes in either direction will follow the pattern that describes the coercion progression: disobedience/temper tantrum/physical attack.

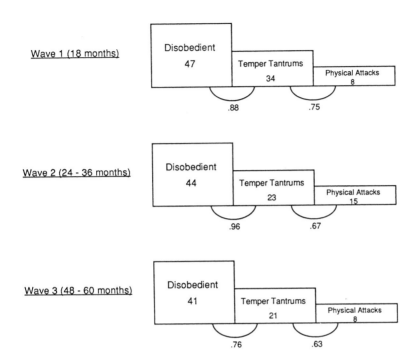

Figure 3.8. Coercive Progressions at Three Waves: Boys (N = 56)

To examine this hypothesis, we focused our attention primarily on the temper-tantrum category because it can serve as a base for detecting shifts in maternal ratings either toward worsening or improving, as defined by the progression. The findings are summarized in Figure 3.9. It can be seen that 34 mothers perceived temper tantrums as a problem for their toddler sons at Wave 1. By Wave 2, 10 of them had maintained this particular concern. Their ratings at Wave 2 also showed that 9 of the original 34 felt that their sons had moved further in the progression (i.e., they now had temper tantrums *and* they engaged in physical attacks). These 9 cases would be thought of as support for the escalation hypothesis.

Fifteen of the original 34 mothers now felt that things were going better for their sons. Five thought that things were much better and that the boys no longer were involved in the coercion progression. Ten were

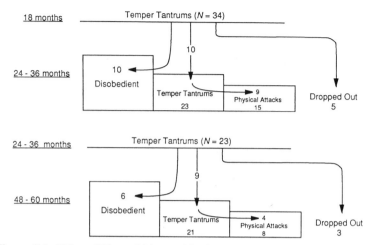

Figure 3.9. Ebb and Flow of Maternal Ratings from the Coercion Progression

no longer engaged in temper tantrums, but they did remain somewhat disobedient. The shifts from Wave 2 to Wave 3 show a similar pattern.

Descriptively, it seems that much of the ebb and flow of the maternal ratings can be nicely described by single-step shifts within the coercion progression. Over time, some boys are perceived as improving; others become worse. Those that drop out are not following an orderly pattern, at least as measured by this time interval (i.e., they moved two categories instead of one).

The most surprising finding in the Patterson and Duncan (1991) report was the fact that almost no new cases were added after the toddler assessment. This could be because we set the cut-off score for being in the process so high (47 of 56 cases). During the ensuing three or more years, however, only one of the nine toddlers previously not in the process was added. At ages 4 and 5, the vast majority of boys and girls in the coercion progression had been there all along, at one level or another. If these findings stand, they would provide powerful support for believing that the future problem child might be identifiable at some time after the first 12 to 18 months. This is very much in keeping with the findings from the longitudinal study by Martin (1981), which showed a correlation of .49 between coercive behaviors observed at 22 months and again 42 months later. One might ask why a process that begins so early is so stable. We suspect some interaction between an irritable and unskilled mother and an infant with difficult temperament, but at this time it is simply not clear which variable is causal; perhaps they are both interactive.

Our prediction is that the child who is at the extreme in the coercion progression at age 4 or 5 will be at risk for identification as Oppositional Defiant Disordered at age 7 or 8. We are currently testing this hypothesis. These simple descriptive analyses of maternal ratings seem to tell us a great deal about how the escalation in coercive behaviors might operate during the preschool years. Given that the patterns are similar for data from mothers and fathers, we have some degree of confidence that this is the proper way to proceed. The background problem lies in our doubts concerning the nature of parent ratings at this early stage in development. For example, Eddy, Fagot, and Patterson (1991) found a correlation of only .42 between mother and father ratings of toddlers and .33 for ratings at kindergarten. Perhaps both mother and father ratings could be used to obtain a more robust definition of the coercion categories.

Implications

The findings provided strong support for the idea that a multiple indicator measure of the childhood trait for antisocial behavior is highly stable over a five-year interval. The mean level of the antisocial score was also shown to be quite stable over time in that only a moderate increase in teacher ratings was detected after one year. Not only did the trait ratings predict later delinquency, they also predicted the time of *onset* of the youth's delinquent career. The more extreme the childhood trait score, the greater the risk for an early arrest. Early onset also placed the child at risk for chronic juvenile offending.

It seems that by Grade 4, the most salient feature of the antisocial behavior is its stability over time. However, it was shown that behind the stability, several important shifts occur. Data were presented that were consistent with the idea that during this time interval, antisocial acts may change both their form and their intensity.

The second shift that is of interest concerned the apparent non-stationarity for one of the main sets of variables serving as determinants for antisocial behavior. The data showed a strong nonstationarity in the contribution of parental monitoring as it related to antisocial behavior at pre- to midadolescence. Presumably, as the antisocial behavior of the adolescent increases, it may disrupt parental efforts to monitor, thus defining a bidirectional relation.

At all ages, children's antisocial behavior may most profitably be studied
from a developmental perspective. If we restrict our vision to individual
differences, we will most certainly miss the mark. As shown here, individual
differences may be shown to be highly stable; nevertheless, there are shifts
within the process that have profound implications for the individual's
adjustment 5 or 10 years hence. It is time to include the concept of time in
our studies of children's behavior. In doing so, we will begin the construction of a genuinely developmental perspective.

References

Achenbach, T. M., & Edelbrock, C. S. (1979a). *Child Behavior Checklist.* Bethesda, MD:
National Institute of Mental Health.

Achenbach, T. M., & Edelbrock, C. S. (1979b). The child behavior profile: II. Boys ages
12-16 and girls aged 6-11 and 12-16. *Journal of Consulting and Clinical Psychology,
4,* 223-233.

Allison, P. D. (1984). *Event history analysis: Regression for longitudinal event data.*
Beverly Hills, CA: Sage.

Blumstein, A., Cohen, J., Roth, J. A., & Visher, C. A. (Eds.). (1986). *Criminal careers
and career criminals* (Vols. 1 & 2). Washington DC: National Academy Press.

Cairns, R. B. (1979). *Social development: The origins and plasticity of interchanges.* San
Francisco: Freeman.

Cairns, R. B., Cairns, B. D., Neckerman, H. J., Ferguson, L. L., & Gariepy, J. L. (1989).
Growth and aggression: I. Childhood to early adolescence. *Developmental Psychology,
25,* 320-330.

Capaldi, D. M., & Patterson, G. R. (1987). An approach to the problem of recruitment
and retention rates for longitudinal research. *Behavioral Assessment, 9,* 169-177.

Capaldi, D. M., & Patterson, G. R. (1989). *Psychometric properties of fourteen latent
constructs from the Oregon Youth Study.* New York: Springer.

Collins, L. M., & Cliff, N. (1990). Using the longitudinal Guttman simplex as a basis for
measuring growth. *Psychological Bulletin, 108,* 128-134.

Dishion, T. J., Patterson, G. R., & Kavanagh, K. (in press). An experimental test of the
coercion model: Linking theory, measurement, and intervention. In J. McCord & R.
Tremblay (Eds.), *The interaction of theory and practice: Experimental studies of
intervention.* New York: Guilford.

Eddy, J. M., & Fagot, B. I. (1991, April). *The coercion model of antisocial behavior:
Generalization to 5-year-old boys and girls and their parents.* Paper presented at the
meeting of the Society for Research in Child Development, Seattle, WA.

Eddy, J. M., Fagot, B. I., & Patterson, G. R. (1991, November). *Parent agreement on
Child Behavior Checklist items: Eighteen months to eighth grade.* Paper presented at
the conference of the Association for Advancement of Behavior Therapy, New York.

Elliott, D. S., Huizinga, D., & Ageton, S. S. (1985). *Explaining delinquency and drug use.*
Beverly Hills, CA: Sage.

Elliott, D. S., & Menard, S. (1990). *Delinquent behavior and delinquent peers: Temporal and developmental patterns*. Unpublished manuscript.

Farrington, D. P. (1987). Early precursors of frequent offending. In J. Q. Wilson & G. C. Loury (Eds.), *From children to citizens: Vol. 3. Families, schools, and delinquency prevention* (pp. 27-51). New York: Springer.

Forehand, R., King, H. E., Peed, S., & Yoder, P. (1975). Mother-child interactions: Comparison of a noncompliant clinic group and a nonclinic group. *Behavior Research and Therapy, 13*, 79-85.

Forgatch, M. S. (1991). The clinical science vortex: A developing theory of antisocial behavior. In D. Pepler & K. H. Rubin (Eds.), *The development and treatment of childhood aggression* (pp. 291-315). Hillsdale, NJ: Lawrence Erlbaum.

Forgatch, M. S., & Toobert, D. (1979). A cost-effective parent training program for use with normal preschool children. *Journal of Pediatric Psychology, 4*, 129-143.

Guttman, L. A. (1944). A basis for scaling qualitative data. *American Sociological Review, 9*, 139-150.

Hirschi, T., & Gottfredson, M. (1983). Age and the explanation of crime. *American Journal of Sociology, 89*(3), 552-584.

Loeber, R. (1982). The stability of antisocial and delinquent child behavior: A review. *Child Development, 53*, 1431-1446.

Loeber, R., & Dishion, T. J. (1983). Early predictors of male delinquency: A review. *Psychological Bulletin, 94*, 68-99.

Loeber, R., & LeBlanc, M. (1991). Toward a developmental criminology. In N. Morris & M. Tonry (Eds.), *Crime and justice* (Vol. 12, pp. 375-473). Chicago: University of Chicago Press.

Martin, J. A. (1981). A longitudinal study of the consequences of early mother-infant interaction: A microanalytic approach. *Monographs of the Society for Research in Child Development, 46*(3, Serial No. 190).

McArdle, J. J. (1988). Dynamic but structural equation modeling of repeated measures data. In J. R. Nesselroade & R. B. Cattell (Eds.), *Handbook of multivariate experimental psychology* (2nd ed.) (pp. 561-614). New York: Plenum.

McArdle, J. J., & Epstein, D. (1987). Latent growth curves within developmental structural equation models. *Child Development, 58*, 110-133.

McCord, W., McCord, J., & Howard, A. (1963). Familial correlates of aggression in nondelinquent male children. *Journal of Abnormal and Social Psychology, 62*, 79-93.

Olweus, D. (1979). Stability of aggressive reaction patterns in males: A review. *Psychological Bulletin, 86*, 852-875.

Patterson, G. R. (1980). Mothers: The unacknowledged victims. *Monographs of the Society for Research in Child Development, 45*(5, Serial No. 186), 1-64.

Patterson, G. R. (1982). *A social learning approach to family intervention: III. Coercive family process*. Eugene, OR: Castalia.

Patterson, G. R., & Bank, L. (1986). Bootstrapping your way in the nomological thicket. *Behavioral Assessment, 8*, 49-73.

Patterson, G. R., & Bank, L. (1987). When is a nomological network a construct? In D. R. Peterson & D. B. Fishman (Eds.), *Assessment for decision* (pp. 249-279). New Brunswick, NJ: Rutgers University Press.

Patterson, G. R., & Bank, L. (1989). Some amplifying mechanisms for pathologic processes in families. In M. R. Gunnar & E. Thelen (Eds.), *Systems and development: Minnesota Symposia on Child Psychology* (Vol. 22, pp. 167-210). Hillsdale, NJ: Lawrence Erlbaum.

Patterson, G. R., Bank, L., & Stoolmiller, M. (1990). The preadolescent's contributions to disrupted family process. In R. Montemayor, G. R. Adams, & T. P. Gullotta (Eds.), *From childhood to adolescence: A transitional period?* (pp. 107-133). Newbury Park, CA: Sage.

Patterson, G. R., Capaldi, D. M., & Bank, L. (1991). An early starter model for predicting delinquency. In D. Pepler & K. H. Rubin (Eds.), *The development and treatment of childhood aggression* (pp. 139-168). Hillsdale, NJ: Lawrence Erlbaum.

Patterson, G. R., Crosby, L., & Vuchinich, S. (1991). *Predicting risk for early police arrest.* Manuscript submitted for publication.

Patterson, G. R., & Dawes, R. M. (1975). A Guttman scale of children's coercive behaviors. *Journal of Consulting and Clinical Psychology, 43,* 594.

Patterson, G. R., DeBaryshe, B. D., & Ramsey, E. (1989). A developmental perspective on antisocial behavior. *American Psychologist, 44,* 329-335.

Patterson, G. R., & Duncan, T. (1991). *Toddler progressions to deviancy.* Unpublished technical report (available from Oregon Social Learning Center, 207 E. 5th Ave., # 202, Eugene, OR 97401).

Patterson, G. R., Reid, J. B., & Dishion, T. J. (1992). *A social interactional approach: IV. Antisocial boys.* Eugene, OR: Castalia.

Patterson, G. R., & Stouthamer-Loeber, M. (1984). The correlation of family management practices and delinquency. *Child Development, 55,* 1299-1307.

Patterson, G. R., & Yoerger, K. (1991, April). *A model for general parenting skill is too simple: Mediation models work better.* Paper presented at the meeting of the Society for Research in Child Development, Seattle, WA.

Reid, J. B., Taplin, P. S., & Lorber, R. (1981). A social interactional approach to the treatment of abusive families. In R. Stuart (Ed.), *Violent behavior: Social learning approaches to prediction, management, and treatment* (pp. 83-101). New York: Brunner/Mazel.

Rogosa, D. (1980). A critique of cross-lagged correlation. *Psychological Bulletin, 88,* 245-258.

Rogosa, D. R., Brandt, D., & Zimowski, M. (1982). A growth curve approach to the measurement of change. *Psychological Bulletin, 92,* 726-748.

Singer, J. D., & Willett, J. B. (1991). Modeling the days of our lives: Using survival analysis when designing and analyzing longitudinal studies of duration and the timing of events. *Psychological Bulletin, 110,* 268-290.

Snyder, J. J. (1977). Reinforcement analysis of interaction in problem and nonproblem families. *Journal of Abnormal Psychology, 86,* 528-535.

Snyder, J. J. (1991, July). *Studies in escalation.* Seminar conducted at the Oregon Social Learning Center, Eugene.

Snyder, J. J., & Patterson, G. R. (1986). The effects of consequences on patterns of social interaction: A quasiexperimental approach to reinforcement in natural interaction. *Child Development, 57,* 1257-1262.

Stoolmiller, M. (1990). *Latent growth model analysis of the relation between antisocial behavior and wandering.* Unpublished doctoral dissertation, University of Oregon, Eugene.

Vuchinich, S., Bank, L., & Patterson, G. R. (1991). Parenting, peers, and the stability of antisocial behavior in preadolescent boys. *Developmental Psychology, 28,* 510-521.

Wahler, R. G., & Dumas, J. E. (1984). Family factors in childhood psychopathology: Toward a coercion neglect model. In T. Jacob (Ed.), *Family interaction and psychopathology* (pp. 115-132). New York: Plenum.

4

Working With Children and Adolescents to End the Cycle of Violence: A Social Learning Approach to Intervention and Prevention Programs

PETER G. JAFFE

MARLIES SUDERMANN

DEBORAH REITZEL

The issue of wife assault has evolved from a hidden problem or family secret to a major social issue that demands the attention of the public and government organizations. The 1980s have represented a decade of significant developments in research, programs, and policy in this field. For example, social scientists and women's organizations have confirmed the significant number of men that physically, sexually, and emotionally abuse their partners (Dutton, 1988). Numerous studies have pointed to the fact that this violence accounts for a large proportion of homicides as well as serious physical injuries and emotional trauma in the lives of victims (Jaffe, Wolfe, & Wilson, 1990).

AUTHORS' NOTE: The preparation of this chapter and the research project in the London Board of Education was supported in part by a grant from the Ontario Ministry of Community and Social Services.

During the 1980s the major advances in this field centered on the consolidation of shelters for battered women and their children. Increased sensitivity of social service and mental health professionals to victims of violence was encouraged. Attempts have been made to make the criminal justice system responsive to the plight of battered women. Police forces throughout North America have begun to treat wife assault as a crime rather than a "family disturbance." In most jurisdictions, policy directives call for the laying of charges when officers have reasonable and probable grounds that an assault took place (e.g., Jaffe, Wolfe, Telford, & Austin, 1986). Since the majority of victims seek safety first and then a change of their husband's (partner's) behavior (Jaffe & Burris, 1984), many programs have emerged to provide counseling for the batterer. These programs are usually a form of group treatment that requires men to accept responsibility for the violence and explore new attitudes and behaviors that enable them to relate to women and resolve interpersonal conflict (Sonkin, Martin, & Walker, 1985).

Until recently, children who observe this violence have been ignored. Child abuse awareness programs focus on the dramatic incidents of physical or sexual abuse where the trauma is obvious. Children who witness violence face a form of emotional or psychological abuse (Hart & Brassard, 1987). Witnessing violence not only creates the fear and anxiety of an overwhelming life event, but also may damage children's social, emotional, and behavioral development. Violence against women is modeled as acceptable behavior irrespective of whether it reflects a maintenance of power and control in relationships, resolution of conflicts, or gender inequality.

Attention to the needs of children who witness violence is essential for both immediate and long-term consequences. As discussed later in this chapter, witnessing violence may be a significant factor in childhood adjustment problems. On a long-term basis, these children may be at risk of becoming the next generation of male batterers and female victims of violence. Significant implications are apparent for the development of prevention programs in this area.

The purpose of this chapter is to review the current literature on the impact of witnessing violence on children. This review will lend itself to a social learning perspective on understanding how violence affects child observers and can be transmitted to future generations. The implications of early intervention programs and prevention strategies will be outlined. The essential role of school systems in this area will be discussed in the concluding section.

Children Who Witness Abuse

Current research on the psychological effects of witnessing family violence on children was preceded by several important developments. Early research on battered women provided dramatic case studies demonstrating the dangerous and chaotic conditions to which their children were exposed (Straus, Gelles, & Steinmetz, 1980). Retrospective accounts of battered women, as well as of male batterers, pointed to the concern that witnessing violence in one's family of origin predisposes women to be imprisoned in their own battering relationship or, for men, to batter their spouses (Brassard, Germain, & Hart, 1987; Roy, 1977). Research by Straus and his colleagues at the University of New Hampshire discovered that the rate of wife beating was 1,000% higher for men who observed family violence in childhood, in comparison to men without such experiences (Straus et al., 1980).

The initial descriptive studies of children who witness family violence were focused on children who accompany their mothers to battered women's shelters, and these children were found to be suffering from a host of serious emotional and behavioral problems (Hughes, 1988; Layzer, Goodson, & deLange, 1985). Studies by Jaffe, Wolfe, and Wilson have provided a more clear and in-depth view of the problems experienced by children who witness family violence, through use of standardized measures and the use of matched comparison groups who have not witnessed violence. Sex differences and exploration of maternal stress and health as a mediating variable in the effect on children were also addressed in this research program.

One of the first studies in this program (Wolfe, Jaffe, Wilson, & Zak, 1985) compared 102 children from transition homes (battered women's shelters) and their mothers to 96 community children who had not witnessed violence, together with their mothers. Child problems were assessed through the Achenbach Child Behavior Checklist (CBCL) (Achenbach & Edelbrock, 1983), while maternal stress and health were assessed by means of the General Health Questionnaire (Goldberg & Hillier, 1979), Life Experiences Survey (Sarason, Johnson, & Siegel, 1979), and an index of family crisis. Results showed that even though the comparison group was far from problem free, the children who had witnessed violence had 2.5 times greater prevalence of clinical level (70+) behavior and adjustment problems as measured by the Achenbach CBCL sum t score. The violence-exposed group had 34% of boys and 20% of girls with CBCL sum t scores greater or equal to 70, which compares very unfavorably to an expected population rate of 2% of such high scores. Furthermore, for the violence-exposed group, only 26.5% of children fell into a low-problem group (CBCL sum t score lower than 55) while 49% of comparison group children not exposed to violence fell into this range. In this study, level of physical violence in the family (measured by maternal report on the Straus Conflict Tactics Scale) significantly predicted both child social competence and child behavior problems. However, maternal stress levels accounted for more of the variance in child behavior problems than actual physical violence level.

These findings suggest that some of the negative effects on children witnessing family violence are mediated by means of the deleterious effect of the violence on their mother. As well, direct effects on children are also present.

Further issues in studying children who reside in women's shelters include investigations regarding what role the disruption of moving to a shelter has on children's behavioral and emotional problems, and whether negative effects on children and mothers diminish over time, if the violence has ended. A study by Wolfe, Zak, Wilson, and Jaffe (1986) addressed these issues by comparing a group of children and mothers currently in shelters, who had experienced violence within the past six weeks, with a group who had left the shelter but had not reexperienced violent situations for at least six months. A matched community comparison group was also employed. The findings, while based on a relatively small sample, were very interesting. The former resident group, although experiencing less maternal stress than the current resident group, had the worst family disadvantage on a scale that encompasses socioeconomic and other related variables. There were also some interesting trends in child behavior problems indicating that while child internalizing problems were highest in the current shelter group, the former resident group tended to have higher externalizing child behavior problems.

A third study compared the social and behavioral adjustment of boys who had witnessed violence, but not been physically abused, with those who had been physically abused themselves, but had not witnessed violence, as well as to a nonabused, nonexposed comparison group (Jaffe, Wolfe, Wilson, & Slusczarzck, 1986).

Results showed that both the abused and exposed groups had significantly higher internalizing *and* externalizing scores than the comparison group. Ninety per cent of the abused boys, and 74% of the exposed boys had total Achenbach CBCL behavior problem scores greater than one standard deviation from the mean of the standardization sample of the scale, while only 13% of the comparison group fell in this range. Conclusions from this study were that boys who had recently been exposed to family violence/wife assault had a level of emotional and behavioral problems that resembled that of boys who had themselves been physically abused, and that significantly differentiated them from comparison boys not exposed to violence.

Findings in regard to sex differences have also been of interest. Jaffe, Wolfe, Wilson, and Zak (1986) found that for children aged 6 to 11 years, there were very significant sex differences in boys and girls exposed to violence. While boys showed negative effects in internalizing, social competence, and externalizing areas, girls showed effects only in internalizing and social competence areas. Also, total behavior problems on the Achenbach CBCL were predicted much more by amount of physical aggression by fathers (maternal report) for boys (Pearson $r = 0.47$) than for girls (Pearson $r = 0.13$).

In reviewing the studies on children exposed to family violence, one is struck by the fact that research in this area is still in its infancy. Many more studies will be needed to replicate the present findings, to extend them to exposed children never residing in shelters, and to disentangle the direct effects of witnessing violence from effects mediated through the distress of mothers, to name but a few future directions. However, several clear and important findings do emerge. In the above samples, 34% of boys and 20% of girls who witness violence demonstrate a level of adjustment problems that would warrant a significant clinical intervention according to the norms of the Achenbach Child Behavior Checklist. Boys demonstrate a high level of externalizing (e.g., fighting, destruction of property) and internalizing (e.g., withdrawal, anxiety) behavior problems as well as deficits in social competence (e.g., school achievement, peer difficulties) in comparison to boys from nonviolent homes. Girls who observe violence are more likely to experience significant internalizing behavior problems related to anxiety and depression, than externalizing problems.

Children who observe wife assault also are affected in ways not measured by standard mental health assessment procedures. A specific child interview guide, the *Child Witness to Violence Interview* (Jaffe, Wolfe, & Wilson, 1990) was developed to assess such effects. Findings using this interview show that children exposed to family violence have inappropriate views on the acceptability and utility of violence as a means to conflict resolution. Furthermore, these children blame themselves for the onset of family violence. They also feel worry and responsibility for protecting their younger siblings and their mother from the violence.

Formulation

In considering theoretical perspectives on how witnessing family violence affects children, two models have frequently been suggested. One is the social learning model, which suggests that children who see their father hit their mother are given the message that this is a normative or acceptable behavior, and learn violence is a valid conflict-resolution strategy. Bandura (1973) has suggested that children are more likely to imitate violence if they strongly identify with the perpetrator, and if the violence is successful in gaining power and control. Both of these conditions are present in many family violence episodes, especially for boys. The social learning model would seem to be a good explanation of the much higher incidence of wife beating in boys who have witnessed family violence. However, the social learning model does not seem to address the issue of emotional disturbance (internalizing problems) nor does it explain all social competence effects, or all behavior problem (externalizing) effects.

A second model is the family disruption hypothesis (Widom, 1989). According to this model, children are affected by the "fall out" from family violence, in terms of decreased parental effectiveness, changes in family residence, sibling distress, and anticipatory fear of new episodes of violence. Certainly this model has much face validity and is supported by the findings on the important role of maternal health/stress as a mediating factor for the effects on children (Wolfe et al,. 1985). Extensive research on children of divorce (R. E. Emery, 1982) and on children of depressed mothers (Beardslee, Bemporad, Keller, & Klerman, 1983; Biglan, Hops, & Sherman, 1988; R. Emery, Weintraub, & Neale, 1982) would add supporting, although indirect, evidence in support of the family disruption hypothesis.

Although a more descriptive than theoretical model at present, the Post-Traumatic Stress Disorder (American Psychiatric Association, 1987) formulation also has applicability especially for children who have witnessed severe episodes of wife assault. Criteria for Post-Traumatic Stress Disorder (PTSD) include the presence of a traumatic event, reexperiencing of the traumatic event by means of recurrent nightmares, waking flashbacks, or intrusive thoughts about the event, dulling of emotional responsiveness to current environmental stimuli, sleep disturbance, memory impairment, concentration difficulties, and avoidance of activities that trigger memories of the traumatic event(s). Although systematic study of PTSD symptoms in children exposed to wife assault is just beginning, clinical observation indicates that exposed children do often exhibit some or many symptoms of the PTSD syndrome.

Witnessing family violence/wife assault appears to have multifaceted and wide-ranging effects on children's cognitive, behavioral, and emotional development. No one model at present serves to capture all the actual and potential effects observed in research, and a comprehensive model of the effects of witnessing family violence needs to incorporate all of the above theoretical formulations, in order to represent adequately the emerging research findings, and point the way to intervention.

Intervention

Knowledge of the effects on children of witnessing family violence is so new as to be relatively unknown to child mental health practitioners. Children's mental health practitioners, family doctors, and other providers of services to children and families need to take steps to include questions about family violence in their routine assessment of children and families. In regard to intervention, stopping the violence is obviously the first line of intervention. In this regard, the growing provision of services for housing and support of battered women and their children has served as an intervention for children. Specific treatment approaches for children are only now being developed (Grusznski, Brink, & Edelson, 1988; Hughes, 1988; Wilson, Cameron, Jaffe, & Wolfe, 1989). Group approaches have been developed as a useful adjunct to individual attention. Groups allow children to learn they are not alone in their experiences, and to learn about new approaches to conflict resolution. Components that have been found useful in group treatment include labeling of feelings, dealing with anger, safety skills, social support, responsibility for family violence, and understanding family violence (Alessi & Hearn, 1984; Jaffe et al., Wilson, & Wolfe, 1990). However, evaluation of group counseling approaches have shown that group counseling may be most useful with mild to moderate level exposure to family violence. Children who have experienced severe, repeated violence require much individual treatment, in addition to the assistance of group intervention (Jaffe et al., Wilson, & Wolfe, 1990). Also, further evaluation of group treatment is needed with regard to outcome compared to nontreated controls and the relative importance of difference components of group treatment.

Adolescents At Risk

Many of the childhood adjustment problems that are associated with witnessing violence become magnified through the demands and stresses of adolescence. Dramatic symptoms such as increasing assaultive and violent behavior as well as suicide attempts are reported in the literature (Grusznski et al., 1988). Many adolescents may seek to escape from the violence and end up in police statistics as "missing persons" or "runaways" (Jaffe, Wolfe, & Wilson, 1990).

Although the symptoms are dramatic and the needs more apparent for adolescents than for latency-age children, adolescents present themselves as more resistant to intervention programs. By the very nature of adolescence, these youngsters will look to their peers for direction rather than adult advice, especially when it is linked to the stigma of consultation with a mental health professional. As well, adolescents may have a more pronounced problem because of the many socialization influences that promote violence against women. Aside from what they have witnessed at home, adolescents have a high probability of viewing a significant amount of violence on TV, in movies, and through rock videos. The challenge to change their attitudes is enormous.

However, adolescence presents unique opportunities for change aside from the risk factors and likely resistance. Foremost is the fact that adolescents are becoming involved in their first intimate relationships outside their family. Recent research suggests that the reported incidence and pattern of assaultive behaviors in dating violence is similar to wife assault. It comes as no surprise that dating violence has been linked to witnessing violence at home (Mercer, 1987). Research in this area is just beginning, but two recent findings are of note. Research with adjudicated young offenders has found that a history of witnessing family violence is associated with significantly increased reoffending risk (Leschied, Jaffe, Sudermann, Austin, & Willis, 1988). A recent study of high school students found that male students from homes where adults sometimes used physical force on one another were four times more likely (30% vs. 7.2% for all males) to report using physical force with a dating partner (Head, 1988). Another relevant finding from this study was that male adolescents from homes where *no* type of physical force was reported (either between adults or adult to children) were much less likely to use force in order to have intercourse with their dating partners (2.9%), compared to the male sample as a whole (14.9%). These findings provide one of the first empirical links between witnessing family violence and both physical violence and attempted rape in adolescent dating relationships. There were also some indications in this study that female adolescents were more likely to be victims of force and attempts at coerced sexual acts in dating relationships if they witnessed family violence. For example, girls from homes where adults sometimes used physical force with one another were about 33% more likely to be victims of physical violence in dating relationships than the total sample, and about 25% more likely to report being pressured for intercourse by their dating partner.

The results of these studies on adolescents highlights the need for early preventative efforts with witnesses to family violence, before these children become adolescents and begin acting out in the community and, especially for boys, begin victimizing others in terms of dating violence and delinquent reoffending.

A second salient opportunity for intervention with adolescent populations comes from peer influences that may be channeled in a positive and nonviolent manner. If peer groups can be sensitive to the existence of abuse, not condone the violence in dating relationships with silence, and support victims of abuse, then significant social change is possible.

The views of adolescents about this topic would give rise to considerable optimism. Recently, several workshops on the topic of wife assault and the prevention of violence in intimate relationships have been implemented with secondary school students from Toronto, London, and other regions in Southwestern Ontario. The adolescents seemed open to information about family violence and expressed a desire to see more educational and preventive initiatives implemented within the school system. When student discussion groups were asked to propose an intervention plan at a workshop in Toronto, it was found that the students viewed education as the most pressing need regarding this issue with the school system being chosen as the best forum for intervention (Jaffe & Reitzel, 1990). Furthermore, students at the Toronto and London workshops frequently expressed the view that educators should be implementing prevention programs at the elementary school level, when dysfunctional attitudes and stereotypes are less likely to be fully formed or as firmly entrenched. Students acknowledged the role that current social values and stereotypes play in perpetuating violence. A considerable number of students expressed deep concern over the issue, and suggested ways in which students themselves could play an active role in the prevention of violence.

As described above, the apparent interest and enthusiasm of students in the issue of preventing violence in intimate relationships as well as students' interest in dating that typically commences with adolescence, make the secondary school system a fertile environment for the implementation of violence prevention programs. Some innovative prevention plans that have recognized this opportunity and piloted programs with secondary schools will be described below.

Prevention Programs

Given the documented wide gap between children and adolescents in need of mental health treatment services and the availability of such services (Ontario Ministry of Community and Social Services, 1988), as well as the difficulty in treating the multifaceted social, emotional, cognitive, and behavioral sequelae of witnessing family violence/wife assault, primary prevention is an important focus for mental health researchers in this field. School systems are a natural forum for primary prevention efforts, due to the nearly universal availability of all children and a majority of adolescents in this system. Both elementary and high school ages are considered good targets for primary prevention efforts.

In our province, the Ontario Ministry of Education has set the stage for innovative awareness and prevention programs concerning family violence. This ministry has articulated that awareness of family violence and the impact of witnessing violence on children are important goals for teachers in the 1990s. Professional development programs for educators on this topic have been implemented in at least one half of Ontario school boards to date. Programs have targeted issues of wife assault, impact on child witnesses, suggested guidelines for teachers to follow upon disclosure, and referral of children to community agencies. Another, related development is the creation of new curriculum materials integrating information and resources on this topic.

The present authors have recently undertaken a primary prevention program designed for use with school students. The goals of the London Secondary School Intervention Project on Family Violence in Intimate Relationships project were to provide knowledge about the incidence and causes of family and dating violence, to shape more prosocial attitudes in these areas, to offer knowledge of community agency resources for those currently affected by the problem, and to generate ideas by students as to ways students can ameliorate such problems. Physical, sexual, and verbal abuse were all issues that were targeted, and the role of violence in the media and in sports perpetuating acceptance of violence was also addressed.

Initial phases of this project involved the development of an administration-based planning committee (including representatives from the London Board of Education, the London Family Court Clinic, and elementary and secondary school officials) and school-based planning committees (consisting of keen teachers, students, and administrators), as well as a number of information presentations and workshops to parties interested in or affected by the high school intervention program. Included among those receiving presentations or workshops were the following: all principals in London, staff delegates from every school (at the elementary and secondary level) in London, all staff at each of the five high schools receiving the program, the London Home and School Association, parents of students at the five target high schools, and finally, community resource personnel who participated in the workshops as speakers and discussion group facilitators.

The format of intervention varied slightly from school to school, but in each case included information presentations to large groups of students, followed by small classroom discussions of the information presented. Of the initial group of five high schools participating, three devoted an entire school day to the family violence day-long interventions. Topics typically covered by speakers in the large group presentations included the prevalence of violence in current adolescent-oriented media and news stories on family violence in the national and local area, the prevalence of wife assault in our society, myths about wife assault in our society, reasons why some men are disposed to abuse their partners, why women appear to accept such violence, police responses to family violence, and availability of community agencies to assist families experiencing abusive relationships. Excerpts from several education videos were also employed, relating to experiences of teenagers in families affected by wife assault as well as to teenagers' experiences of power, control, and violence issues in their own dating relationships.

Small-group discussions were led by facilitators from community agencies and teaching staff with an interest in the topic. All facilitators attended a day-long training workshop.

The group discussion periods were divided into two major themes, processing the information presented during the large-group presentation, and developing student and school-based action plans for the prevention of violence. Specific topics covered within these guidelines varied somewhat from one group to another dependent primarily upon student responses to the presentation. However, most discussion groups included discussions of societal attitudes that condone and promote the use of violence, male and female stereotypes perpetuated by society and the media, violence in sports and the media, violence in students' own families and dating relationships, victim blaming, increasing communication skills, feelings, finding alternatives to violence, relevant community and school resources that are available, and the development of prevention and intervention strategies. It should also be noted that specific group exercises varied somewhat in accordance with both group cohesiveness and comfort level, and the facilitators' individual strengths and orientation. Some of the most common group exercises included informal discussions, group debates, pen-and-paper exercises, brainstorming ideas, and role-playing conflict resolution or problem-solving strategies.

Other features of the interventions that were school specific included student theater presentations, a professional theater presentation, and talks by an adult survivor of partner abuse who recounted her high school dating experiences with her abusive partner. School-based counseling and referral services were made available for students who made personal disclosures or appeared distressed. Initial participation included five high schools, and more than 7,000 students, their teachers, and administrators.

A research and evaluation component involved administration of a 48-item questionnaire on violence in intimate relationships that was developed by the present authors. Attitudes, knowledge about family and dating violence were assessed, as well as awareness of abuse in the students' own relationships. The questionnaire was administered one week prior to the intervention, one week after the intervention, and at three schools, six to eight weeks after the intervention. The questionnaire included several items from previous investigations of students' attitudes regarding family and dating violence (Head, 1988; Giarusso, Johnson, Goodchilds, & Zellman, 1979), in order to allow comparison of knowledge and attitudes expressed by students in the present study to those revealed in these previous studies.

Preliminary results from the pretest phase of the intervention included several interesting findings. A very high proportion of students (61%) were aware of physical, sexual, or verbal violence or abuse in dating relationships of their own or those of their friends and acquaintances. Also, 64% of students knew someone who had experienced physical, sexual, or verbal abuse in a family context.

A high proportion (84%) believed that the school system was an appropriate venue for prevention and education efforts with regard to family violence. Also, far more students reported they would talk to peers (41%) rather than teachers (9%) if they had a problem with family or dating violence. These findings emphasize the importance of education and prevention efforts aimed at high school students.

System-level results have included an enthusiastic response by many school system administrators, principals, and teachers. A substantial number of new initiatives in terms of repeated high school intervention, increased training on family violence for newly promoted high school principals and department heads, increased in-service training for teachers on the issue, including how to respond to disclosure, and a spread of intervention to the elementary grade schools are under way.

Another outcome of this program worth noting was the response of community agencies. One of community agencies that directly served battered women reported an approximately 40% increase in referrals after the program was run, with quite a few clients mentioning that their children had participated in the school prevention program. The group facilitators, 93 social service and mental health professionals from 25 different community agencies, reported very positive feedback on the program.

They felt that their involvement in the group discussions provided them with an opportunity to have a greater impact on the prevention of violence than can normally be attained in their daily work with children and adolescents who are already in crises. They welcomed the opportunity to exercise their skills and expertise with a primarily non-clinical, normative population.

While school-based efforts at primary prevention await refinement through evaluation, development of valid measures of outcome, and long-term follow-up, the potential for challenging students' basic attitudes and social beliefs appears to be high through programs such as the present one.

Future Issues

Although our preliminary primary prevention efforts could be strengthened through replication and hopefully expansion, they do represent small steps toward a violence-free society. Radical societal change is required to address the growing concern about violence firmly integrated in North American culture. In addressing the goal of terminating violence against women and children, the school system becomes an important vehicle for program development.

The school system holds the key to prevention because the existing justice, mental health, and social service systems will never have the funding or comprehensive mandate to meet the challenge. Even if one were to consider 1 in 10 women and children suddenly identifying themselves as victims and witnesses to violence, these systems would be totally bogged down within several weeks. Although many educators may debate the proposal to expand the school system's mandate, the reality is that most schools already struggle with the aftermath of student and parental violence and need to play a central role in an integrated community response to this issue. The current trend of hiring security guards in itself is not an answer. We would like to suggest several areas that need to be considered in the next decade to help schools become more responsive.

Teacher training is an important avenue to explore. Teachers need to become more aware of violence in relationships and how this violence affects their students. In Ontario, the Ministry of Education has offered incentive funding to each school district to organize workshops for teachers on the impact of witnessing wife assault on students. Increasing teachers' knowledge of community resources that offer services to battered women, their partners, and their children is also a part of these programs.

Another important area relates to curriculum development. There needs to be a learning opportunity at all grade levels to make students more aware of violence and alternative conflict resolution techniques. Whether students are in primary grades and exposed to violence on Saturday morning cartoons or whether they are teenagers involved in dating violence, they need to discuss alternatives to violence in our society. Excellent programs have been developed by several states to help students consider these issues (e.g., Jones, 1987; Levy, 1984). These programs need to have a broader base of support in other jurisdictions and expand to younger students in the primary grades.

In many ways, school systems already struggle with some of these issues in other endeavors. There may be no need to reinvent the wheel, but rather refocus energy and creativity in these areas. For example, many school systems have excellent social skills development programs for high risk students or students with serious behavior problems. These programs can be expanded to offer more comprehensive learning experiences for all children irrespective of whether they are a perpetrator, victim, or witness to violence.

All schools try to create ideal learning environments where teachers express a clear commitment and concern for their students and students are encouraged to be responsible and caring citizens. School climates that facilitate these kinds of feelings and behaviors represent the cornerstone of any prevention program. Ultimately the goals of primary prevention of violence can only be achieved when schools play a leadership role in this area.

References

Achenbach, T. M., & Edelbrock, C. S. (1983). *Manual for the child behavior checklist and revised child behavior profile.* Burlington, VT: University Associates in Psychiatry.

Alessi, J. J., & Hearn, K., (1984). Group treatment of children in shelters for battered women. In A. R. Roberts (Ed.), *Battered women and their families* (pp. 49-61). New York: Springer.

American Psychiatric Association. (1987). *Diagnostic and statistical manual of mental disorders* (3rd. ed., rev.). Washington, DC: Author.

Bandura, A. (1973). *Aggression: A social learning analysis.* Englewood Cliffs, NJ: Prentice-Hall.

Beardslee, W. R., Bemporad, K., Keller, M. B., & Klerman, G. L. (1983). Children of parents with major affective disorder: A review. *American Journal of Psychiatry, 140,* 825-832.

Biglan, A., Hops, H., & Sherman, L., (1988). Coercive family processes and maternal depression. In R. DeV. Peters & R. J. McMahon (Eds.), *Social learning and system approaches to marriage and the family.* New York: Brunner/Mazel.

Brassard, M. R., Germain, R., & Hart, S. N. (1987). The challenge: To better understand and combat psychological maltreatment of children and youth. In M. R. Brassard, R. Germain, & S. N. Hart (Eds.), *Psychological maltreatment of children and youth* (pp. 3-24). Elmsford, NY: Pergamon.

Dutton, D. G. (1988). *The domestic assault of women: Psychological and criminal justice perspectives.* Toronto: Allyn & Bacon.

Emery, R., Weintraub, S., Neale, J. M. (1982). Effects of marital discord on the school behavior of children of schizophrenic, affectively disordered, and normal parents. *Journal of Abnormal Child Psychology, 16,* 215-228.

Emery, R. E. (1982). Interparental conflict and the children of discord and divorce. *Psychological Bulletin, 92,* 310-330.

Giarusso, R., Johnson, P., Goodchilds, J., & Zellman, G. (1979). Adolescents' cues and signals: Sex and assault. In P. Johnson (Chair), *Acquaintance rape and adolescent sexuality.* Symposium conducted at the meeting of the Western Psychological Association, San Diego, CA.

Goldberg, D. P., & Hillier, V. F. (1979). A scaled version of the General Health Questionnaire. *Psychological Medicine, 9,* 139-145.

Grusznski, R. J., Brink, J. C., & Edelson, J. L. (1988). Support and education groups for children of battered women. *Child Welfare, 67*(5), 431-444.

Hart, S. N., & Brassard, M. R. (1987). A major threat to children's mental health: Psychological maltreatment. *American Psychologist, 42,* 160-165.

Head, S. (1988). *A study of attitudes and behaviour in dating relationships with special reference to the use of force.* Unpublished report, Board of Education for the City of Scarborough.

Hughes, H. M. (1988). Psychological and behavioral correlates of family violence in child witnesses and victims. *American Journal of Orthopsychiatry, 18,* 77-90.

Jaffe, P., & Burris, C. A. (1984). *An integrated response to wife assault: A community model* (Working Paper No. 1984-27). Ottawa: Solicitor General of Canada.

Jaffe, P., & Reitzel, D. (1990). Adolescents' views on how to reduce family violence: An analysis of responses to a community workshop. In R. Roesch, D. G. Dutton, & V. S. Sacco, *Family Violence: Perspectives on treatment, research and policy.* Burnaby, British Columbia: Simon Fraser University.

Jaffe, P., Wilson, S. K., & Wolfe, D. (1989). Specific assessment and intervention strategies for children exposed to wife battering: Preliminary empirical investigation. *Canadian Journal of Community Mental Health, 7,* 157-163.

Jaffe, P., Wolfe, D., Telford, A., & Austin, G. (1986). The impact of police charges in incidents of wife abuse. *Journal of Family Violence, 1*(1), 37-49.

Jaffe, P., Wolfe, D. A., & Wilson, S. K. (1990). *Children of battered women.* Newbury Park, CA: Sage.

Jaffe, P., Wolfe, D., Wilson, S., & Slusczarzck, M. (1986). Family violence and child adjustment: A comparative analysis of girls' and boys' behavioral symptoms. *American Journal of Psychiatry, 143*(1), 74-77.

Jaffe, P., Wolfe, D., Wilson, S., & Zak, L. (1986). Similarities in behavior and social maladjustment among child victims and witnesses to family violence. *American Journal of Orthopsychiatry, 56,* 142-146.

Jaffe, P., Wolfe, D. A., Wilson. S., & Zak, L. (1985). Critical issues in the assessment of children's adjustment to witnessing family violence. Canada's Mental Health, 33(4), 15-19.

Jones, L. E. (1987). *Minnesota coalition for battered women school curriculum project evaluation report.* Unpublished manuscript, University of Minnesota, School of Social Work, Minneapolis.

Layzer, J. I., Goodson, B. D., & deLange, C. (1985). Children in shelters. *Response, 9*(2), 2-5.

Leschied, A., Jaffe, P., Sudermann, M., Austin, G., & Willis, W. (1988). *The changing profiles of young offenders with special needs: Trends and critical issues.* Unpublished research report for the Ontario Ministry of Community and Social Services.

Levy, B. (1984). *Skills for violence-free relationships.* Santa Monica: Southern California Coalition for Battered Women.

Mercer, S. L. (1987). *Not a pretty picture: An exploratory study of violence against women in high school dating relationships.* Unpublished data available from Education Wife Assault, Toronto.

Ontario Ministry of Community and Social Services. (1988). *Investing in Children.* Toronto: Ontario Ministry of Community and Social Services.

Roy, M. (1977). *Battered women: A psychological study of domestic violence.* New York: Van Nostrand.

Sarason, I. G., Johnson, J. H., & Siegel, J. M. (1979). Assessing the impact of life changes: Development of the Life Experiences Survey. *Series in Clinical and Community Psychiatry, 6,* 131-149.

Sonkin, D. J., Martin, D., & Walker, L. E. (1985). *The male batterer: A treatment approach.* New York: Springer.

Straus, M. A., Gelles, R. J., & Steinmetz, S. (1980). *Behind closed doors.* Garden City, NY: Doubleday.

Widom, C. S. (1989). Does violence beget violence? A critical examination of the literature. *Psychological Bulletin, 106,* 3-28.

Wilson, S., Cameron, S., Jaffe, P., & Wolfe, D. (1989). Children exposed to wife abuse: An intervention model. *Social Casework: The Journal of Contemporary Social Work, 70,* 180-184.

Wolfe, D. A., Jaffe, P., Wilson, S., & Zak, L. (1985). Children of battered women: The relation of child behavior to family violence and maternal stress. *Journal of Consulting and Clinical Psychology, 53,* 657-665.

Wolfe, D. A., Zak, L., Wilson, S., & Jaffe, P. (1986). Child witnesses to violence between parents: Critical issues in behavioral and social adjustment. *Journal of Abnormal Child Psychology, 14*(1), 95-104.

5

Bullying Among Schoolchildren: Intervention and Prevention

DAN OLWEUS

Bullying among schoolchildren is certainly a very old phenomenon. The fact that some children are frequently and systematically harassed and attacked by other children has been described in literary works and many adults have personal experience of it from their own school days. Although many are acquainted with the bully/victim problem, it was not until fairly recently—in the early 1970s—that efforts were made to study it systematically. So far, these attempts have largely been confined to Scandinavia. In the 1980s, however, bullying among school children also received some public attention in other countries, such as Japan, England, Australia and the United States. There are now clear indications of an increasing societal as well as research interest into bully/victim problems in several parts of the world.

AUTHOR'S NOTE: The research reported was supported by grants from the William T. Grant Foundation, the Norwegian Research Council for Social Research, the Swedish Delegation for Social Research (DSF), and in earlier phases, from the Norwegian Ministry of Education. Several of the ideas presented were developed while the author was a Fellow at the Center for Advanced Study in the Behavioral Sciences, Stanford, USA. He is indebted to the University of Bergen, the Spencer Foundation, the Norwegian Research Council for Social Research, and the Center for Advanced Study in the Behavioral Sciences for financial support of his year at the Center.

This chapter gives an overview of some recent research findings on bullying or victimization among schoolchildren in Scandinavia. I will confine myself mainly to the effects of a large-scale intervention program against bully/victim problems that has been evaluated in 42 schools in Bergen, Norway (Olweus, 1991). I will also briefly describe the content of the program and some of the principles on which it was based.

A number of findings concerning developmental antecedents of bullying problems, characteristics of typical bullies and victims, and the veracity of some popular conceptions of the causes of these problems are presented only briefly or not at all in this context, since these results have been described in detail in previous publications (e.g., Olweus, 1973a, 1978, 1979, 1980, 1981, 1983, 1984, 1986, 1987, 1991). It should be mentioned, however, that the findings from this earlier research have generally been replicated in several different samples and were obtained with a number of different methods, including peer ratings, teacher nominations, self-reports, grades, projective techniques, hormonal assays, and mother/father interviews about child-rearing practices. Most of these results were derived from my ongoing Swedish longitudinal project (comprising approximately 900 boys), started in the early 1970s.

Before embarking on the main theme of the chapter, I will give a brief definition of what I mean by *bullying* or *victimization*. In addition, I will sketch a portrait of typical victims and bullies as background for the intervention program. (For a more comprehensive overview, see e.g., Olweus, 1984, 1991.)

Definition of *Bullying*

I define *bullying* or *victimization* in the following general way: A person is being bullied or victimized when he or she is exposed, repeatedly and over time, to negative actions on the part of one or more other persons.

The meaning of the expression *negative actions* must be specified further. It is a negative action when someone intentionally inflicts, or attempts to inflict, injury or discomfort upon another—basically what is implied in the definition of aggressive behavior (Olweus, 1973b). Negative actions can be carried out by physical contact, by words, or in other ways, such as making faces or "dirty" gestures or refusing to comply with another person's wishes.

It must be stressed that the term *bullying* or *victimization* is not (or should not be) used when two persons of approximately the same strength (physical or psychological) are fighting or quarreling. In order to use the term *bullying,* there should be an imbalance in strength (an asymmetric power relationship): The person who is exposed to the negative actions has difficulty in defending him- or herself and is somewhat helpless against the person or persons who harass.

It is useful to distinguish between *direct bullying/victimization*— with relatively open attacks on the victim—and *indirect bullying/victimization* in the form of social isolation and exclusion from a group. It is important to pay attention also to the second, less visible form of victimization.

In the present chapter the expressions *bullying, victimization,* and *bully/victim problems* are used synonymously.

Prevalence

In connection with a nationwide campaign against bully/victim problems in Norwegian comprehensive schools (all primary and junior high schools in Norway), launched by the Ministry of Education in 1983, data were collected with my Bullying Questionnaire[1] from more than 700 schools from all over Norway (Olweus, 1985, 1986, 1991).

On the basis of this survey, one can estimate that some 84,000 students, or 15% of the total in the Norwegian comprehensive schools (568,000 in 1983-1984), were involved in bully/victim problems "now and then" or more frequently—as bullies or victims (Autumn 1983). This percentage represents one student out of seven. Approximately 9%, or 52,000 students, were victims, and 41,000, or 7%, bullied other students "now and then" or more frequently. Some 9,000 students were both victims and bullies.

It can thus be stated that bullying is a considerable problem in Norwegian comprehensive schools, a problem that affects a very large number of students. Data from other countries such as Sweden (Olweus, 1986), Finland (Lagerspetz, Björkqvist, Berts, & King, 1982), England (Smith, 1989), and the United States (Perry, Kusel, & Perry, 1988) indicate that this problem exists outside Norway as well, and with similar or even higher prevalence rates.

Characteristics of Typical Victims and Bullies

The picture of the typical victim that emerges from the research literature is relatively unambiguous (see Olweus, 1978, 1986). Victims of bullying are more anxious and insecure than students in general. They are often cautious, sensitive, and quiet. When attacked by other students, they commonly react with crying (at least in the lower grades) and withdrawal. They have a negative view of themselves and their situation. They often look upon themselves as failures and feel stupid, ashamed, and unattractive.

Further, the victims are lonely and abandoned at school. As a rule, they do not have a single good friend in their class. They are not aggressive or teasing in their behavior; accordingly, one cannot explain the bullying as a consequence of the victims themselves being provocative to their peers (see below). If they are boys, they are likely to be physically weaker than boys in general.

In summary, the behavior and attitude of the victims seem to signal to others that they are insecure and worthless individuals who will not retaliate if they are attacked or insulted. A slightly different way of describing typical victims is to say that they are characterized by *an anxious reaction pattern combined* (in the case of boys) *with physical weakness.*

This is a sketch of the most common type of victim, whom I have called *the passive* or *withdrawn victim.* There is also another, smaller group of victims, *the provocative victims,* who are characterized by a combination of both anxious and aggressive behavior patterns (see Olweus, 1973a, 1978, for more information about this kind of victim).

A distinctive characteristic of typical bullies is their aggression toward peers; this is implied in the definition of a bully. They are, however, often also aggressive toward teachers, parents, and siblings. Generally, they have a more positive attitude to violence and use of violent means than students in general. They are often characterized by impulsivity and strong needs to dominate others. They have little empathy with victims of bullying. If they are boys, they are likely to be physically stronger than boys in general and victims in particular.

In contrast to a fairly common assumption among psychologists and psychiatrists, we have found no indications that the aggressive bullies (boys) are anxious and insecure under a tough surface. Data based on several samples and using both direct and indirect methods such as projective techniques and hormonal assays all pointed in the same direction: The bullies had unusually little anxiety and insecurity or were roughly average on such dimensions (Olweus, 1981, 1984). And they did not suffer from poor self-esteem.

In summary, typical bullies can be described as having *an aggressive reaction pattern combined* (in the case of boys) *with physical strength.*

Bullying can also be viewed as a *component of a more general conduct-disordered, antisocial, and rule-breaking behavior pattern.* From this perspective, it is natural to predict that youngsters who are aggressive and bully others in school run a clearly increased risk of later engaging in other problem behaviors such as criminality and alcohol abuse. Several recent studies confirm this general prediction (Loeber & Dishion, 1983; Magnusson, Stattin, & Dunér, 1983).

In our own follow-up studies we have also found strong support for this view. Approximately 60% of boys who were characterized as bullies in Grade 6 through Grade 9 had at least one conviction by the age of 24. Even more dramatically, as many as 35%-40% of the former bullies had three or more convictions at this age, while this was true of only 10% of the control boys (those who were neither bullies nor victims) in Grades 6-9. Thus as young adults the former school bullies had a fourfold increase in the level of relatively serious, recidivist criminality.

It should be mentioned that the former victims had an average or somewhat below average level of criminality in young adulthood.

A Question of Fundamental Democratic Rights

The results obtained in my research demonstrate convincingly that bullying is a considerable problem in Scandinavian elementary and junior high schools, that the teachers (in 1983) did relatively little to counteract it, and that the parents knew too little about what their children were exposed to or engaged in. The *victims* of bullying are a large group of students who are to a great extent neglected by the school. We know that many of these youngsters are the targets of harassment for long periods of time, often for many years (Olweus, 1977, 1978). It does not require much imagination to understand what it is to go through the school years in a state of more or less permanent anxiety and insecurity, and with poor self-esteem. It is not surprising that the victims' devaluation of themselves sometimes becomes so overwhelming that they see suicide as the only possible solution.

Bully/victim problems have even broader implications than those suggested above. They really concern some of our fundamental democratic principles: Every individual should have the right to be spared oppression and repeated, intentional humiliation, in school as in society at large. No student should be afraid of going to school for fear of being harassed or degraded, and no parent should need to worry about such things happening to his or her child!

Bully/victim problems also relate to a society's general attitude to violence and oppression. What kind of view of societal values will a student acquire who is repeatedly bullied by other students without interference from adults? The same question can be asked with regard to students who, for long periods of time, are allowed to harass others without hindrance from adults. To refrain from actively counteracting bully/victim problems in school implies a tacit acceptance of them.

In this context, it should be emphasized that it is of great importance to counteract these problems for the sake of the aggressive students, as well. As reported above, school bullies are much more likely than other students to follow an antisocial path. Accordingly, it is essential to try to redirect their activities into more socially acceptable channels. And there is no evidence to suggest that a generally "tolerant" and permissive attitude on the part of adults will help bullies outgrow their antisocial behavior pattern.

Main Goals and Components of Intervention Program

Against this background, it is now appropriate to describe briefly the effects of the intervention program that we developed in connection with the campaign against bully/victim problems in Norwegian schools.

The major goals of the program were to reduce as much as possible existing bully/victim problems and to prevent the development of new problems.

The main components of the program, which was aimed at teachers and parents as well as students, were the following:

(1) A 32-page booklet for school personnel describing what is known about bully/victim problems (or rather, what was known in 1983) and giving detailed suggestions about what teachers and the school can do to counteract and prevent the problems (Olweus & Roland, 1983). Efforts were also made to dispel common myths about the nature and causes of bully/victim

problems that might interfere with an adequate handling of them. This booklet was distributed free of charge to all primary and junior high schools in Norway.

(2) A four-page folder with information and advice to parents of victims and bullies as well as "ordinary" children. This folder was distributed by the schools to all families in Norway with school-age children (also free of charge).

(3) A 20-minute video cassette showing episodes from the everyday lives of two bullied children, a 10-year-old boy and a 14-year-old girl. This cassette could be bought or rented at a highly subsidized price.

(4) A short questionnaire designed to obtain information about different aspects of bully/victim problems in the school, including frequency and the readiness of teachers and students to interfere with the problems. The questionnaire was completed by the students individually (in class) and anonymously. Registration of the level and nature of bully/victim problems in the school was thought to serve as a basis and starting point for active interventions on the part of the school and the parents. A number of the results presented earlier in this chapter were based on information collected with this questionnaire.[2]

Another "component" was added to the program as used in Bergen, the city in which the evaluation of the effects of the intervention program took place. Approximately 15 months after the program was first offered to the schools (in early October, 1983) we gave, in a two-hour meeting with the staff, individual feedback information to each of the 42 schools participating in the study (Manger & Olweus, 1985). This information, derived from the students' responses to the questionnaire in 1983, focused on the level of problems and the social environment's reactions to the problems in the particular school as related to data from comparable schools obtained in the nationwide survey (October, 1983). At the same time, the main principles of the program and the major procedures suggested for intervention were presented and discussed with the staff. Since we know from experience that many (Norwegian) teachers have somewhat distorted views of the characteristics of bullying students, particular emphasis was placed on a discussion of this topic and on appropriate ways of handling bullying behavior. Finally, the teachers rated different aspects of the program, in particular its feasibility and potential efficacy. Generally, this addition to the program, as well as the program itself, was quite favorably received by the teachers, as expressed in their ratings.

Subjects and Design

Space limitations prevent detailed presentation of methodological information including sampling scheme, definition of measuring instruments and variables, and significance tests. Only summary descriptions and main results will be provided in this chapter.

Evaluation of the effects of the intervention program is based on data from approximately 2,500 students originally belonging to 112 classes, Grades 4 through 7, in 42 primary and junior high schools in Bergen (modal ages at Time 1 were 11, 12, 13, and 14 years, respectively). Each of the four grade/age cohorts consisted of 600-700 subjects with a roughly equal distribution of boys and girls. The first time of data collection (Time 1) was in late May (and early June) 1983, approximately four months before the initiation of the campaign. New measurements were taken in May 1984 (Time 2) and May 1985 (Time 3).

Since the campaign was nationwide, it was not possible to set up a strictly experimental study with random allocation of schools or classes to treatment and control conditions. Instead, a quasi-experimental design (sometimes called an age cohort or selection cohort design, see Cook & Campbell, 1979) was chosen, making use of "time-lagged contrasts between age-equivalent groups." In particular, for three of the cohorts data collected at Time 1 (see Figure 5.1) were used as a baseline with which data for age-equivalent cohorts at Time 2 could be compared. The latter groups had then been exposed to the intervention program for about eight months. To exemplify, the data for the Grade 5 cohort at Time 1 (modal age 12 years) were compared with the Time 2 data for the Grade 4 cohort, which at that time had reached the same age as the baseline group. The same kind of comparisons were made between the Grade 6 cohort at Time 1 and the Grade 5 cohort at Time 2, and between the Grade 7 cohort at Time 1 and the Grade 6 cohort at Time 2.

Comparisons of data collected at Time 1 and Time 3 permit an assessment of the persistence or possible decline or enhancement of the effects over a longer time span. For these comparisons data for only two of the cohorts could be used as a baseline, those of the Grade 6 and Grade 7 cohorts, which were contrasted with data collected at Time 3 on the Grade 4 and Grade 5 cohorts respectively. The latter groups had been exposed to the intervention program for approximately 20 months at that time.

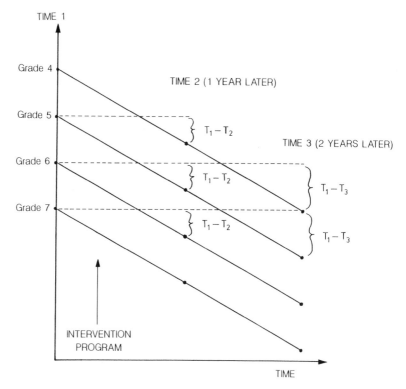

Figure 5.1. Design for Evaluation of Effects of Intervention Program. Fictitious Data (that to some extent reflect the general trend of the empirical findings).

An attractive feature of the design is the fact that two of the cohorts serve as a baseline group in one set of comparisons and as a treatment group in another. This is the case with the Grade 5 cohort at Time 1, the data for which are used as a baseline in comparison with the Grade 4 cohort data collected at Time 2 (after 8 months of intervention). In addition, the Grade 5 cohort data obtained at Time 2 serve to evaluate the possible effects of eight months of intervention when they are compared with the data for the Grade 6 cohort at Time 1. The same situation applies to the Grade 6 cohort in comparisons with the Grade 5 and Grade 7 cohorts respectively.

The advantage of this aspect of the design is that a possible bias in the sampling of the cohorts (selection bias) would operate in opposite directions in the two sets of comparisons, thus making it much more difficult to obtain consistent (apparent) intervention effects across cohorts as a consequence of such bias. There are, however, no grounds for expecting such bias since the classes/schools were distributed on the different cohorts by a basically random procedure. Accordingly, the cohorts should be essentially equivalent in important respects at Time 1. This aspect of the design would provide the same kind of protection against faulty conclusions in case the baseline data for one or both of these cohorts were unusually high or low simply as a function of chance.

To avoid erroneous conclusions due to possible selective attrition (more extreme or deviant individuals may be more likely to drop out in longitudinal studies), analyses were restricted to students for whom there were valid data at both time points in a particular comparison (both for the baseline and the intervention groups). In the present research, however, the results were basically the same whether we controlled or did not control for such attrition.

It should also be noted that since selection of the subjects was not based on some kind of "extreme score" criterion, the problem with regression toward the mean, which looms large in many evaluation studies, is not at issue in the present research. In the present design, the common and serious problem of attempting to adjust statistically for initial differences between nonequivalent groups is also avoided.

Statistical Analyses

Since classes rather than students were the basic sampling units (with students nested within classes), it was considered important to choose a data analytic strategy that reflected the basic features of the design. Accordingly, data were analyzed with ANOVA (analysis of variance) with students nested within classes nested within schools nested within times/occasions (Time 1 vs. Time 2, Time 1 vs. Time 3). Sex of the subjects was crossed with times, schools (within times), and classes (within schools). Since several of the cohorts figured in two comparisons, the analyses had to be conducted separately for each combination of cohorts (for further information, see Olweus & Alsaker, in press).

For several of the variables (or derivatives of them such as percentages), less refined (and in some respects, less informative) analyses with chi-squared and t tests were also carried out. The findings from these analyses were in general agreement with those obtained in the ANOVAs.

Properties of the outcome variables analyzed are discussed in Olweus (1991) in some detail. Generally, it was concluded that the evidence available attests to the adequacy and validity of the data employed.

Results

Results for the self-report variables "Being exposed to direct bullying" and "Bullying other students" are presented separately for boys and girls in Figure 5.2 through Figure 5.5. (Due to space limitations, only the results for these two variables are shown graphically. See Olweus, 1991, for a more complete presentation.) Since the design of the study is relatively complex, a few words about how to read the figures are in order.

The left-hand panel shows the effects after 8 months of intervention, while the right-hand panel displays the results after 20 months. The upper curves (designated Before) show the baseline data (Time 1) for the relevant cohorts (the Grade 5, Grade 6, and Grade 7 cohorts in the left-hand panel and the Grade 6 and Grade 7 cohorts on the right). The lower curves (designated After) display data collected at Time 2 (after 8 months of intervention) in the panel to the left and at Time 3 (after 20 months of intervention) in the right-hand panel for the age-equivalent cohorts (the Grade 4, Grade 5, and Grade 6 cohorts at Time 2 and the Grade 4 and Grade 5 cohorts at Time 3).

It should be noted that there are minor differences in the baseline data (Before) for the Grade 6 and Grade 7 cohorts when presented in the left- and right-hand panels respectively. This is a consequence of the restriction of the analyses to subjects who had valid data at both time points; accordingly, not exactly the same subjects entered the two sets of analyses.

The main findings of the analyses can be summarized as follows:

- There were marked reductions in the levels of bully/victim problems for the periods studied, 8 and 20 months of intervention respectively. By and large, reductions were obtained for both boys and girls and across all cohorts compared. For the longer time period the effects persisted in the case of "Being exposed to direct bullying" and "Being exposed to indirect bullying" and were strengthened for the variable "Bullying other students."
- Similar reductions were obtained for the aggregated peer rating variables "Number of students being bullied in the class" and "Number of students in the class bullying other students." There was thus consensual agreement

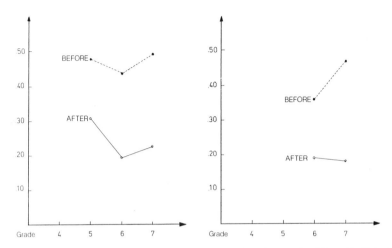

Figure 5.2. Effects of Intervention Program on "Being Exposed to Direct Bullying" for Boys.

NOTE: Left-hand panel shows effects after 8 months of intervention, and right-hand panel displays results after 20 months of intervention. Upper curves (designated Before) show baseline date (Time 1), and the lower curves (designated After) display data collected at Time 2 in the left-hand panel and at Time 3 in the right-hand panel.

in the classes that bully/victim problems had decreased during the periods studied.

- In terms of percentages of students reporting being bullied or bullying others "now and then" or more frequently, the reductions amounted to approximately 50% or more in most comparisons.
- There was no displacement of bullying from the school itself on the way to and from school. There were reductions or no changes on (self-report) items measuring bully/victim problems on the way to and from school.
- There was also a reduction in general antisocial behavior such as vandalism, theft, and truancy. (For the Grade 6 comparisons the effects were marginal for both time periods.)
- In addition we could observe marked improvement as regards various aspects of the "social climate" of the class: improved order and discipline, more positive social relationships, and a more positive attitude to schoolwork and the school.
- At the same time, there was an increase in student satisfaction with school life as reflected in "liking recess time."

In the majority of comparisons for which reductions were reported above, the differences between baseline and intervention groups were

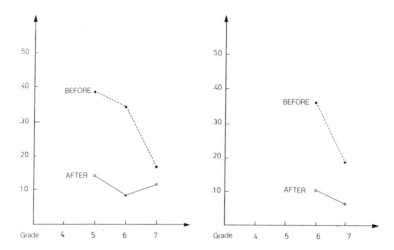

Figure 5.3. Effects of Intervention Program "Being Exposed to Direct Bully-ing" for Girls.

NOTE: Left-hand panel shows effects after 8 months of intervention, and right-hand panel displays results after 20 months of intervention. Upper curves (designated Before) show baseline date (Time 1), and the lower curves (designated After) display data collected at Time 2 in the left-hand panel and at Time 3 in the right-hand panel.

highly significant or significant (in spite of the fact that many of them were based on single items).

Prevention of New Cases of Victimization

By combining information from two questionnaire items—"How often have you been bullied in school (this spring term)?" and, "Have you been bullied more or less this spring term as compared with the spring term a year ago?"—it was possible, given certain reasonable assumptions, to estimate which victimized individuals at a certain time point were "new cases" and which were not. In this way, incidence rates (number and percentage of new cases, see Olweus, 1989) could be calculated for each cohort and time point, to be related to incidence data from the relevant comparison cohort.

At baseline (Time 1 in Figure 5.1)—before the intervention—the percentage of new victimization cases (out of the total number of subjects) was estimated at 2.6% for the boys and 1.7% for the girls.

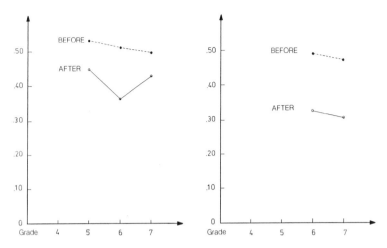

Figure 5.4. Effects of Intervention Program on "Bullying Other Students" for Boys.

NOTE: Left-hand panel shows effects after 8 months of intervention, and right-hand panel displays results after 20 months of intervention. Upper curves (designated Before) show baseline date (Time 1), and the lower curves (designated After) display data collected at Time 2 in the left-hand panel and at Time 3 in the right-hand panel.

After the intervention program (Times 2 and 3 in Figure 5.1), corresponding figures were considerably lower, approximately 0.6% for the boys and 0.5% for the girls. These results indicate that the intervention program not only affected already existing victimization problems, but also reduced considerably the number/percentage of new cases. On the basis of these analyses it can be concluded that the intervention program had both primary and secondary prevention effects (Cowen, 1984).

It should be mentioned that at Time 1 the new cases estimated in this way constituted approximately 20% of the total number of victimized children.

Quality of Data and Possible Alternative Interpretations

It is beyond the scope of this chapter to discuss in detail the quality of the data collected and the possibility of alternative interpretations of the findings. An extensive discussion of these matters can be found elsewhere

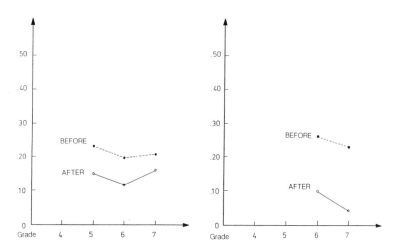

Figure 5.5. Effects of Intervention Program on "Bullying Other Students" for Girls.

NOTE: Left-hand panel shows effects after 8 months of intervention, and right-hand panel displays results after 20 months of intervention. Upper curves (designated Before) show baseline date (Time 1), and the lower curves (designated After) display data collected at Time 2 in the left-hand panel and at Time 3 in the right-hand panel.

(Olweus, 1991). Here I limit myself to summarizing the conclusions in the following point statements:

- Self-reports, which were implicated in most of the analyses conducted so far, are in fact the best data source for the purposes of this study.
- It is very difficult to explain the results obtained as a consequence of (a) underreporting by the students; (b) gradual changes in the students' attitudes to bully/victim problems; (c) repeated measurement; and (d) concomitant changes in other factors. All in all, it is concluded that the reductions in bully/victim and associated problems described above are likely to be mainly a consequence of the intervention program and not of some other "irrelevant" factor.

In addition, a clear "dosage-response" relationship ($r = .51$, $n = 80$) has been established in preliminary analyses at the class level (which is the natural unit of analysis in this case): Those classes that showed larger reductions in bully/victim problems had implemented three presumably essential components of the intervention program (including the use of class meetings and the establishment of class rules against bullying) to a greater extent than those with smaller changes (additional information on these analyses can be found in Olweus & Alsaker, in press). This finding certainly provides corroborating evidence for the effects of the intervention program. It will be followed up with more systematic and comprehensive analyses.

Brief Comments

The reported effects of the intervention program must be considered quite positive, particularly since most previous attempts systematically to reduce aggressive and antisocial behavior in preadolescents/adolescents have been relatively unsuccessful (e.g., Dumas, 1989; Gottfredson, 1987; Kazdin, 1987). The importance of the results is also accentuated by the fact that there has been a highly disturbing increase in the prevalence of violence and other antisocial behavior in most industrialized societies in the past decades. In the Scandinavian countries, for instance, various forms of registered criminality have typically increased by 300%-500% since the 1950s (and these increases cannot, or only to a very small degree, be explained as a consequence of changes in risk of detection).

As mentioned above, we can estimate that approximately 80,000 students in Norwegian comprehensive schools were involved in bully/victim problems in 1983. On the basis of the reported results the following conclusion can be drawn: *If all comprehensive schools in Norway used the intervention program in the way it was used in Bergen, the number of students involved in bully/victim problems would be reduced to 40,000 or less in a relatively short period.* Effective use of the intervention program would also result in lower levels of theft, vandalism, and other antisocial behavior, which would save society large amounts of money. In all probability, it would also improve classroom discipline and other aspects of the social climate of the class and the school.

Basic Principles

Having reported the main goals and components of the intervention program as well as some of its effects, it is now natural to present its underlying principles and major subgoals.

The intervention program is built around a limited set of key principles, derived chiefly from research on the development and modification of the implicated problem behaviors, in particular aggressive behavior. It is considered important to try to create a school (and ideally, also a home) environment characterized by *warmth, positive interest, and involvement from adults* on one hand and *firm limits to unacceptable behavior* on the other. Third, in cases of violations of limits and rules, *nonhostile, nonphysical sanctions* should be consistently applied. Implied in the latter two principles is also a certain degree of *monitoring and surveillance* of the students' activities in and out of school (Patterson, 1986). Finally, *adults* are supposed to *act as authorities in at least some respects.*

The first three of these principles largely represent the opposite of the child-rearing dimensions that have been found in our research to be important in the development of an aggressive personality pattern (Olweus, 1980): negativism on the part of the primary caretaker, permissiveness and lack of clear limits, and use of power-assertive methods. In a sense, the present intervention program is based on an authoritative adult-child interaction, or child-rearing, model (cf. e.g., Baumrind, 1967) applied to the school setting.

The principles listed above can be translated into a number of specific measures to be used at school and class—as well as individual—levels. It is considered important to work on all of these levels, if possible. Figure 5.6 lists a number of such measures that were recommended in the intervention program (a few of the measures in Figure 5.6, including cooperative learning, were not proposed in the original program). Space limitations prevent a detailed description of the various measures suggested but such an account can be found in a small book designed for teachers and parents (Olweus, 1986; an English version is now available, Olweus, 1992; this book also describes a reduced program of "core components" that are considered to be particularly important in any implementation of the program).

With regard to implementation and execution, the program is mainly based on a utilization of the existing social environment: teachers and other school personnel, students, and parents. Non-mental health professionals thus play a major role in the desired restructuring of the social environment. Experts such as school psychologists and social workers may also serve important functions, such as planning and coordinating, counseling teacher and parent groups, and handling more serious cases.

COMPONENTS TO PROGRAM PACKAGE AGAINST BULLYING

GENERAL PREREQUISITES: AWARENESS + INVOLVEMENT

SCHOOL LEVEL	CLASS LEVEL	INDIVIDUAL LEVEL
• Better supervision of recess • More attractive school playground • Contact telephone • Meeting staff--parents • Teacher groups for the development of the "school climate" • Parent circles (study and discussion groups)	• Class rules against bullying: clarification, praise, and sanctions • Regular class meetings • Cooperative learning • Meeting teacher--parents/children • Common positive activities • Role playing • Literature	• Serious talks with bullies and victims • Serious talks with parents of involved children • Teacher use of imagination • Help from "neutral" students • Advice to parents (parent brochure) • "Discussion" groups with parents of bullies and victims • Change of class or school

Figure 5.6. Overview of Measures at the School, Class, and Individual Levels.

Additional Characteristics

Further understanding of the program and its ways of working can be gained from a brief description of four major subgoals:

(1) *To increase awareness of the bully/victim problem and advance knowledge about it,* including dispelling some of the myths about the problem and its causes. Use of the questionnaire is an important step in obtaining more specific knowledge about the frequency and nature of the problems in a particular school.

(2) *To achieve active involvement on the part of teachers and parents.* This implies, among other things, that adults must recognize that it is their responsibility to control to a certain degree what goes on among the children at school. One way of doing this is to provide adequate supervision during recess time. Further, the teachers are encouraged to intervene in possible bullying situations and give a clear message to the students: Bullying is not accepted in our school. Teachers are also strongly advised to initiate serious talks with victims and bullies, and their parents, if a bully/victim problem has been identified in the class. Again, the basic message should be: We don't tolerate bullying in our school and will see

to it that it comes to an end. Such an intervention on the part of the school must be regularly followed up and closely supervised—otherwise the situation may easily become worse for the victim than before the intervention.

(3) *To develop clear rules against bullying behavior,* such as: (a) We shall not bully others; (b) We shall try to help students who are being bullied; (c) We shall make a point to include students who become easily left out. Such a set of rules may serve as a basis for class discussions about what is meant by *bullying behavior* in concrete situations and what kind of sanctions should be used for students who break the rules. The behavior of the students in the class should be regularly related to these rules in class meetings ("social hour"), and it is important that the teacher make consistent use of sanctions (some form of nonhostile, nonphysical punishment) in cases of rule violations and also give generous praise when the rules have been followed.

(4) *To provide support and protection for the victims.* If followed, class rules against bullying certainly support children who tend to be victimized. In addition, the teacher may enlist the help of "neutral" or well-adjusted students to alleviate the situation of the victims in various ways. Also, teachers are encouraged to use their imagination to help victimized students to assert themselves in the class, to make them valuable in the eyes of their classmates. Parents of victims are exhorted to help their children develop new peer contacts and to teach them in detail how to make new acquaintances and to maintain friendships.

It may be added that the intervention program has been evaluated by more than 1,000 Norwegian and Swedish teachers. In short, their reactions have generally been quite favorable, indicating among other things that the teachers see the proposed principles and measures as useful and realistic.

Some Possible Reasons for Program Effectiveness

In this concluding section, I will discuss briefly some of my personal views about why the intervention program has been effective. I will present my comments in six main points:

(1) First, I think it is important to emphasize generally that the intervention program rests on a *decent knowledge base* (cf. Cowen, 1984). Over the years, we have devoted a considerable amount of time to testing in empirical research a number of more or less popular conceptions or hypotheses about the causes and mechanisms behind

bully/victim problems. As shown elsewhere (e.g., Olweus, 1978, 1991), several of these conceptions have proven to be "myths" with no or little empirical support. In this way, it has been possible to avoid at least some false leads about how to reduce or prevent bully/victim problems in school (by avoiding the focusing of intervention efforts on, for example, external deviations in the victims, anxiety and poor self-esteem in the bullies, or on reducing class or school size).

At the same time, research-based knowledge has been accumulating about the causes and mechanisms involved in bully/victim problems, as well as in the two broader categories of "adjustment reactions," of which these problems form a part:aggressive, conduct-disordered, externalizing and anxious, withdrawn, and internalizing reaction patterns, respectively. We have tried to build a good deal of this knowledge into the program. As stated above, several of the principles underlying the program are directly derived from research on the development and modification of the implicated problem behaviors.

(2) An additional reason for the relative efficacy of the program probably lies in its *direct focus on the relevant behaviors and associated norms* (e.g., "we don't accept bullying in our school and will see to it that it comes to an end") rather than on some assumed underlying or mediating mechanism.

Implied in the above is also a view of aggressive behavior that differs in important respects from several contemporary approaches. Many present-day researchers and clinicians seem to have the understanding that aggressive children usually share society's and the school's values and norms about appropriate behavior and are basically interested in conforming to them. However, due to such personal characteristics as lack of conflict-management capacities, cognitive or behavior (social) deficits, or a poor self-image, they are believed to be unable to do so.

Although I recognize that a certain proportion of aggressive children may have skills deficits or poor self-esteem (which may or may not show up as statistically significant differences in group comparisons), I do not think there is much evidence to support the hypothesis that these factors actually cause aggressive behavior (or at least are major causal factors; cf. Dumas, 1989). In my own approach, I stress the view that a good deal of *aggressive behavior,* and in particular bullying, can be seen as *"self-initiated behavior"* with the deliberate aim of inflicting pain and discomfort, of dominating and oppressing others, and of obtaining tangible and prestigious rewards through coercion. In this view, bullying behavior is not primarily seen as a consequence of lack of skills or abilities but rather as *a function of "deviant" motivations and habits.* It is more a question of what the aggressors want to do and are used to doing than what they are able to do. In line with this view, major foci of the present intervention program are the bullying behavior itself and its "opportunity structure" (opportunities to bully others with associated expected positive or negative consequences), to borrow a term from criminology.

(3) Related to the above formulations is the fact that program participants are encouraged via the program to *take a clear stance against bullying behavior:* "Bullying is not tolerated in our class/school." The program also makes clear the power relationships in that regard: The adults are in charge and have the authority (and responsibility) to stop such behavior.

It is also important, however, to make the students take a clear stance. This can be done, for example, in the context of the development of class rules (norms) against bullying as well as in follow-up discussions at class meetings.

While the program stresses the importance of repudiating bullying behavior, it also makes it clear that such repudiation should not be made in a harsh, hostile, or punitive way. Consistent use of nonhostile, noncorporal sanctions in cases of rule violations is an important part of the intervention program. At the same time, it is considered essential to develop a class/school climate characterized by warmth and involvement.

(4) Another presumably important aspect of the program is that it is *directed toward the school as "system" and works simultaneously at several levels*: the school, the class, and the individual levels. In addition, it is highly desirable to get the students' parents involved, although less control over this is possible. In this way, measures used at different levels and in different settings can support each other and will result, under favorable conditions, in *consistent messages* from most of the students' social environment. This approach also makes it possible to achieve a certain degree of *collective commitment* to the program, in particular on the part of the adults at school. If these possibilities are adequately realized, the program is likely to have powerful effects that may also generalize from one setting to another.

From a somewhat different perspective it may be said that the program is *both environment- or systems-oriented and person-oriented.* Although its main focus is on the environment or the system (a restructuring of the social environment), it also contains person-oriented components (e.g., serious talks with the students involved in an identified bully/victim problem and with their parents). It is likely that the combination of these two approaches is better than either alone.

(5) The positive effects of the intervention, and in particular their maintenance, are likely to be related to the fact that the program is designed to *achieve not only relatively immediate, more or less short-lived effects on already existing bully/victim problems, but also to prevent the development of new problems and the reemergence of earlier problems.* It is reasonable to assume that bully/victim problems may occur whenever several children are together without adequate adult supervision. Accordingly, it is important for the school always to be ready to detect such problems and to counteract them effectively. For example, by use of class rules against bullying in combination with regular class meetings, problems can be discovered at an early stage before they have become ingrained or have taken a dramatic turn. In this way, these and similar mechanisms built into the program are likely to prevent the emergence of new problems or the reemergence of problems from earlier periods. They may also have preventive effects; for example, through change of the class or school norms and the nature of the interactions among students.

(6) Finally, there are several *advantages to formulating the problems* to be targeted in the intervention *as bully/victim problems* and not in some other way, such as problems with aggressive and antisocial behavior or conduct disorder problems.

In the first place, by conceptualizing it as a bully/victim problem, the aggressive behavior is placed or anchored in a social context: The recipient of the aggression, the victim, comes into focus in addition to the aggressor. In this way, the repeated humiliation and suffering of the victim are brought into the foreground. This serves an important function in justifying use of the program.

To a considerable degree, installment of the program is in fact legitimized by the suffering of the victims, that is, by reference to the immediate, current situation and not to possible long-term effects on the aggressive, antisocial students. Future beneficial effects for the bullies will hopefully occur, but in trying to use such effects as an argument for an intervention program, one is usually met (at least in more sophisticated quarters) with the problem of false positives—individuals who are predicted to have a "deviant" outcome but who in fact become "non-deviant" over time. As is well known from research, a sizeable proportion of aggressive antisocial children and youths will "normalize" when they grow older and will not turn delinquent or criminal (or whatever outcome is expected) in the absence of any systematic intervention. Since there is usually no way of knowing with suitable accuracy which students will become "false positives" (or "true positives"), this may make it difficult to argue for the necessity of installing an intervention program, at least if it is person-oriented.

These problems are nicely avoided when the main justification of the program lies in the current suffering of the victims as in the present antibullying program. Here the possible long-term changes of the bullies, though highly desirable, are not the key argument for use of the program; they only serve as accessory justification.

By focusing on bully/victim problems, it is usually also relatively *easy to reach consensual agreement* among teachers, parents, and (the majority of) students that such problems should not be tolerated in the class or the school: Psychologically and physically stronger students must not be allowed to harass and humiliate weaker and more anxious students. For several reasons, it may be much more difficult to come to consensus about the desirability of counteracting aggressive or antisocial behavior in general.

Though it is certainly important to address bully/victim problems for their own sake, it should be noted that the program had beneficial effects with regard to other forms of antisocial or conduct-disordered behavior, such as vandalism and truancy, as well. In addition, it increased the students' satisfaction with school life and was probably conducive to improved classroom discipline. In this way, bully/victim problems can be regarded as a nice entry point for dealing with several other major problems that plague present-day schools.

Related to the last point is the fact that many components and activities of the program (e.g., class rules against bullying, regular class meetings, role playing, better recess supervision, PTA meetings) are aimed at the total population of students, not only at particularly targeted, "deviant" or at-risk children. Due to this "universal" orientation, the necessity of deciding which students will and will not be involved or focused on in the program—and possible stigmatization problems—is (partly) avoided. The program may not only reduce and prevent undesirable behaviors and attitudes; it is also likely to improve social relationships generally (as evidenced, e.g., in a better social climate in the class) and to enhance prosocial behavior. In this way, the present program shares some of the features of what have been called "mental health promoting" programs (Peters, 1990).

All in all, the above characteristics of the program may make it not only acceptable but often even attractive to the school staff (and to many parents). Formulating the problems in this way is likely *to make schools more willing to "take ownership of the problems"* and to recognize that it is primarily their responsibility to do something about them. Again, if the problems were conceptualized in a different way, for instance, in terms of the level of conduct-disordered behavior, the schools would be more inclined to disengage themselves from responsibility for the problems and to regard their solution as a task for the child psychiatrist or school psychologist. In sum, the way in which a problem is conceptualized, formulated, and presented to the school has important implications for the school's readiness to do something about it.

Concluding Words

Although what has been presented in this chapter about the effects of the intervention program represents only the first stages of analysis, the basic message of our findings is clear: *It is definitely possible substantially to reduce bully/victim problems and related problem behaviors in school with a suitable intervention program.* Nor need such a program entail large costs in terms of money or time. Whether these problems will be tackled or not no longer depends on whether we have the knowledge necessary to achieve desirable changes. It is much more a matter of our willingness to involve ourselves and to use the existing knowledge to counteract the problems.

Notes

1. There is now an (expanded) English version of this questionnaire (one version for Grades 1-4, and another for Grades 5-9 and higher grades). This questionnaire as well as other materials related to the intervention program (see Note 2) are copyrighted, which implies certain restrictions on their use. For more details, please write to Dan Olweus, University of Bergen, Øysteinsgate 3, N-5007 Bergen, Norway.

2. The updated "package" related to the intervention program against bully/victim problems consists of the questionnaire for the measurement of bully/victim problems (above and Note 1), a copy of a small book titled *Bullying at School—What We Know and What We Can Do* (Olweus, 1986, 1992) aimed at teachers and parents, and the 20-minute video cassette (with English subtitles; for European or North American electrical current). These materials are copyrighted, which implies certain restrictions on their use. For more information, please write to the author at the address given in Note 1.

References

Baumrind, D. (1967). Child care practices anteceding three patterns of preschool behavior. *Genetic Psychology Monographs, 75,* 43-88.

Cook, T. D., & Campbell, D. T. (1979). *Quasi-experimentation.* Chicago: Rand McNally.

Cowen, E. L. (1984). A general structural model for primary program development in mental health. *Personnel and Guidance Journal, 62,* 485-490.

Dumas, J. E. (1989). Treating antisocial behavior in children: Child and family approaches. *Clinical Psychology Review, 9,* 197-222.

Gottfredson, G. D. (1987). Peer group interventions to reduce the risk of delinquent behavior: A selective review and a new evaluation. *Criminology, 25,* 187-203.

Kazdin, A. E. (1987). Treatment of antisocial behavior in children: Current status and future directions. *Psychological Bulletin, 102,* 187-203.

Lagerspetz, K. M., Björkqvist, K., Berts, M., & King, E. (1982). Group aggression among school children in three schools. *Scandinavian Journal of Psychology, 23,* 45-52.

Loeber, R., & Dishion, T. (1983). Early predictors of male delinquency: A review. *Psychological Bulletin, 94,* 69-99.

Magnusson, D., Stattin, H., & Dunér, A. (1983). Aggression and criminality in a longitudinal perspective. In K. T. Van Dusen & S. A. Mednick (Eds.), *Prospective studies of crime and delinquency.* Boston: Kluwer-Nijhoff.

Manger, T., & Olweus, D. (1985). Tilbakemelding til skulane. *Norsk Skoleblad [Oslo, Norway], 35,* 20-22.

Olweus, D. (1973a). *Hackkycklingar och översittare: Forskning om skol-mobbning.* Stockholm: Almqvist & Wiksell.

Olweus, D. (1973b). Personality and aggression. In J. K. Cole & D. D. Jensen (Eds.), *Nebraska symposium on motivation, 1972* (Vol. 20, pp. 261-321). Lincoln: University of Nebraska Press.

Olweus, D. (1977). Aggression and peer acceptance in adolescent boys: Two short-term longitudinal studies of ratings. *Child Development, 48,* 1301-1313.

Olweus, D. (1978). *Aggression in the schools: Bullies and whipping boys.* Washington, DC: Hemisphere.

Olweus, D. (1979). Stability of aggressive reaction patterns in males: A review. *Psychological Bulletin, 86,* 852-875.

Olweus, D. (1980). Familial and temperamental determinants of aggressive behavior in adolescent boys: A causal analysis. *Developmental Psychology, 16,* 644-660.

Olweus, D. (1981). Bullying among school boys. In N. Cantwell (Ed.), *Children and violence* (pp. 97-131). Stockholm: Akademilitteratur.

Olweus, D. (1983). Low school achievement and aggressive behavior in adolescent boys. In D. Magnusson & V. Allen (Eds.), *Human development. An interactional perspective* (pp. 353-365). New York: Academic Press.

Olweus, D. (1984). Aggressors and their victims: Bullying at school. In N. Frude & H. Gault (Eds.), *Disruptive behavior in schools* (pp. 57-76). New York: John Wiley.

Olweus, D. (1985). 80 000 barn er innblandet i mobbing. *Norsk Skoleblad [Oslo, Norway], 35,* 18-23.

Olweus, D. (1986). *Mobbning—vad vi vet och vad vi kan göra.* Stockholm: Liber.

Olweus, D. (1987). Bully/victim problems among schoolchildren. In J. P. Myklebust & R. Ommundsen (Eds.), *Psykologprofesjonen mot år 2000* (pp. 395-413). Oslo: Universitetsforlaget.

Olweus, D. (1989). Prevalence and incidence in the study of anti social behavior: Definitions and measurement. In M. Klein (Ed.), *Cross-national research in self-reported crime and delinquency* (pp. 187-201). Dordrecht, The Netherlands: Kluwer.

Olweus, D. (1991). Bully/victim problems among school children: Basic facts and effects of a school based intervention program. In D. Pepler & K. H. Rubin (Eds.), *The development and treatment of childhood aggression* (pp. 411-448). Hillsdale, NJ: Lawrence Erlbaum.

Olweus, D. (1992). *Bullying at school—What we know and what we can do.* Stockholm: Liber.

Olweus, D. & Alsaker, F.D. (in press). Assessing change in a cohort longitudinal study with hierarchical data. In D. Magnusson, L. Bergman, G. Rudinger, & B. Törestad (Eds.), *Matching problems and methods in longitudinal research.* New York: Cambridge University Press.

Olweus, D., & Roland, E. (1983). *Mobbing—Bakgrunn og tiltak.* Oslo, Norway: Kirke-og Undervisningsdepartementet.

Patterson, G. R. (1986). Performance models for antisocial boys. *American Psychologist, 41,* 432-444.

Perry, D. G., Kusel, S. J., & Perry, L. C. (1988). Victims of peer aggression. *Developmental Psychology, 24,* 807-814.

Peters, R. DeV. (1990). Adolescent mental health promotion: Policy and practice. In R. J. McMahon, & R. DeV. Peters (Eds.), *Behavior disorders of adolescence.* New York: Plenum.

Smith, P. (1989). *The silent nightmare: Bullying and victimization in school peer groups.* Paper presented at the meeting of the British Psychological Society, London, England.

6

Helping Families With Aggressive Children and
Adolescents Change

JEAN E. DUMAS

ELAINE A. BLECHMAN

RONALD J. PRINZ

Aggressive children and adolescents present a formidable challenge
for society as a whole, and for the professionals who come in
contact with them on a regular basis. Although multifaceted, aggressive, antisocial conduct in childhood and adolescence is generally
characterized by repeated violations of familial and social rules and of
the basic rights of others, a characteristic that gives such conduct
considerable interpersonal and social significance. This significance is
highlighted in comprehensive reviews (Dumas, 1989a; Kazdin, 1987)
that show that aggressive and antisocial conduct: (a) has a prevalence
rate as high as 10% in the general population if one considers official
statistics, and even higher if one relies on youth self-reports (Rutter,

AUTHORS' NOTE: Preparation of this manuscript was supported in part by grants from
the Social Sciences and Humanities Research Council of Canada, the Medical Research
Council of Canada, and the William T. Grant Foundation to Jean E. Dumas, and by grants
from the National Institute of Mental Health (MH38667) and the William T. Grant
Foundation to Ronald J. Prinz.

Cox, Tupling, Berger, & Yule, 1975); (b) represents as many as half of all child and adolescent referrals for professional services of a clinical nature (Robins, 1981); (c) tends to be chronic and stable over time (Loeber, 1982; Olweus, 1979) and to be associated with serious problems in adolescence and adulthood, including peer rejection (Cantrell & Prinz, 1985), delinquency and academic failure (Eron, 1988), adult psychopathy and criminality (Olweus, 1979; Robins, 1966), and other psychopathology (Weintraub, Prinz, & Neale, 1978); (d) often runs across generations (e.g., Huesmann, Eron, Lefkowitz, & Walder, 1984); and (e) involves truly exorbitant costs to society in terms of clinical (e.g., psychiatric, psychological, counseling care), educational (e.g., remedial education, special school placements), legal (e.g., law enforcement, juvenile adjudication, incarceration), and social (e.g, harm to others, property destruction) repercussions (e.g., Robins, 1981; U.S. Senate Judiciary Committee, Subcommittee to Investigate Juvenile Delinquency, 1976).

Research Implementation and Evaluation Issues

Dumas's (1989a) and Kazdin's (1987) reviews of empirically based interventions for aggressive, antisocial children and adolescents demonstrate that no single data-driven approach has yet emerged as a treatment of choice in this area. Rather, evidence suggests that a variety of approaches appear promising, with the strongest support available today for interventions aimed at training parents in effective child-rearing skills. A major stumbling block in the interpretation of empirical findings stems from the fact that most therapeutic interventions have been found to be differentially effective: Treatments that have been reported to work with some children and their families have been found to be unsuccessful with others. Although this situation must reflect, in part, the complexity of antisocial behavior and the multiplicity of its correlates, we believe that it is also a reflection of major methodological limitations that have been characteristic of most interventions in this field and that the development and evaluation of viable treatments will require a concerted effort to overcome these limitations (Loeber & Lahey, 1989; Sechrest & Rosenblatt, 1987). These limitations reflect related diagnostic, developmental, and contextual issues.

Diagnostic Issues

Two major diagnostic issues presently limit research implementation and evaluation. The first one stems from the fact that there is no agreed upon definition of aggressive, antisocial behavior to guide the selection and description of treated samples. The second, related issue arises from growing evidence showing that aggressive, antisocial behavior, however defined, is often associated with other forms of psychological disturbances.

Definition

Despite considerable heterogeneity in the characteristics of children and adolescents with disruptive behavior disorders, most interventions describe their samples as aggressive or antisocial children, or even less clearly as deviant or problematic youths, without defining what is meant by such broad labels or on what basis the dysfunction was established. This implies that experimental samples may often contain children with considerable behavioral heterogeneity. As the effectiveness of any intervention can be expected to depend in part on the nature and extent of a child's problems, borderline results may reflect differential treatment effects in samples that contained children with a variety of antisocial behavior patterns (Dumas, 1989a; Loeber & Lahey, 1989).

The situation is further complicated by the fact that the most commonly used diagnostic manual in North America, the Diagnostic and Statistical Manual of Mental Disorders (American Psychiatric Association, 1980, 1987), underwent considerable changes in the past decade in its definitions of the aggressive, antisocial disorders of childhood. These changes make comparisons among studies conducted at different times difficult and require that the reliability and validity of the diagnostic criteria be studied with each new version of the manual. The third edition of the manual (DSM-III; American Psychiatric Association, 1980) provides two broad categories to classify aggressive, antisocial behavior of childhood and adolescence. Oppositional Disorder (OD) refers to a behavior pattern characterized by disobedience, negativism, provocation, and opposition to authority, while Conduct Disorder (CD), which may include important features of OD, is usually a more severe condition characterized by repeated violations of the basic rights of others and/or of major social rules. DSM-III distinguishes further among four subtypes of CD: undersocialized aggressive, socialized aggressive, undersocialized nonaggressive, and socialized nonaggressive. The revised version of the DSM-III (DSM-III-R; American Psychiatric Association, 1987) maintains the distinction between OD (now relabeled Oppositional Defiant Disorder-ODD) and CD, but describes three rather than four subtypes of CD: solitary aggressive, group, and undifferentiated. This last subtype is described as a remainder category, although DSM-III-R notes that it may comprise more children than the other two subtypes. Another important change stems from the fact that ODD and CD could be diagnosed as occurring concurrently according to DSM-III, but that a diagnosis of CD hierarchically preempts a diagnosis of ODD according to DSM-III-R. This imposed mutual exclusivity may be misleading, as children who qualify for a CD diagnosis may or may not have pronounced ODD features. Although ODD is often a precursor of CD (Loeber, 1990), the distinction is not only developmental as the behaviors in CD generally are not only more severe than in ODD, but they have also legal ramifications.

Comorbidity

To add to this definitional complexity, children with an ODD or CD diagnosis may qualify for additional diagnoses, such as Attention-deficit Hyperactivity Disorder (ADHD) and childhood depression. Considerable overlap between childhood aggression and hyperactivity has been reported (Prinz, Connor, & Wilson, 1981). Relying on careful diagnostic procedures, Shapiro and Garfinkel (1986) found in a sample of 7- to 13-year-olds that 45% of those who qualified for a diagnosis of ODD or CD also qualified for a diagnosis of ADHD. In a large Canadian sample of 4- to 11-year-olds, Offord and his colleagues (Szatmari, Offord, & Boyle, 1989) found that 36% of girls and 42% of boys with ADHD also qualified for a CD diagnosis. There is also evidence that some aggressive, antisocial children share a codiagnosis of childhood depression. Based on seven studies relating depressive and disruptive behavior disorders (e.g., Kovacs, Paulauskas, Gatsonis, & Richards, 1988; Marriage, Fine, Moretti, & Haley, 1986; Puig-Antich, 1982), estimates of depressive comorbidity in children and adolescents range from 15% to 33% depending upon the reference population and the level of depressive symptoms required to diagnose the disorder. Because treatment research has not yet compared outcomes for subgroups of aggressive children based on presence or absence of ADHD or depressive comorbidity, it is not known whether and in what ways their treatment needs may differ.

A related issue concerns the presence of cofeatures of covert-antisocial problems (e.g., theft). Although not a diagnostic category in its own right, covert-antisocial symptomatology can be present to varying degrees in the profile of ODD or CD children. (Note, however, that DSM-III-R lists covert-antisocial problems under CD only, assuming presumably that these problems tend to appear later in the developmental progression of children with disruptive behavior disorders.) Loeber and Schmaling (1985) demonstrated the utility of considering covert-antisocial problems as an additional subgrouping variable for children with disruptive behavior disorder, while Stouthamer-Loeber, Loeber, and Green (1989) found that parental report of covert-antisocial symptoms in adolescents was strongly associated with delinquent conduct, police contact, self-reported theft, and verbal aggression. The rate of comorbidity between the disruptive disorders and covert-antisocial symptomatology has not yet been established, because the covert dimension is a relatively new construct and because there is a very wide range of covert problems, which makes it difficult to set absolute cutoffs. Similarly, the treatment literature is only beginning to take into account the potential significance of covert-antisocial problems with respect to treatment planning and outcome (Miller & Prinz, 1990).

Developmental Issues

Most researchers and clinicians have paid little attention to developmental considerations in the assessment and treatment of aggressive, antisocial youths. That such considerations are essential is suggested by a growing body of evidence that can be reviewed under the two broad markers of age and gender.

Age

Symptoms of opposition and aggression are very common in young children and may play an important role in normal development (Maccoby & Martin, 1983). These generally subside with age, so that children who still present a constellation of these symptoms by age 8 represent a truly deviant group (Loeber, personal communication). Work by Patterson and colleagues is particularly relevant here (e.g., Patterson & Bank, 1986; Patterson, Dishion, & Bank, 1984), as they have found empirical support for a developmental progression in oppositional-aggressive conduct in childhood. According to Patterson's model, CD in boys may have its roots in dysfunctional parent-child interactions at home that are characterized by direct training in coercion and lead over time to the appearance of dysfunctional peer relationships, academic failure, and a poor self-concept. This model is "contextualized" in that this developmental trajectory can be influenced by psychosocial factors, such as parental psychopathology. Related evidence that stresses the importance of developmental issues in this area has been summarized by McMahon (1987).

Gender

Treatment studies of aggressive, antisocial children have devoted little attention to girls. A review of 15 studies published in refereed journals in the past five years revealed that 7 of them excluded girls from their samples, while none of the other 8 studies examined treatment effects separately for boys and girls. Evidence that girls may present different symptom patterns and higher desistance rates than boys (Loeber & Lahey, 1989) suggests that data should be analyzed separately for each gender and aggregated only if no differences are found. The primary obstacle to studying treatment effects for girls has been lack of sufficient numbers at any one site to generate an adequately large sample. However, the rate of disruptive behavior disorders in girls is not so low as to prohibit the study of this population. The ratio of boys to girls with ODD or CD has been estimated to be between 2:1 and 3:1 (Quay, 1986).

Contextual Issues

Differential treatment effects may be due not only to differences among children, but also to differences among their families. Although clinical experience shows that treatment outcome may be influenced by contextual variables not taken into account in treatment specification or design, such variables have commonly been ignored in the development of interventions for aggressive, antisocial youths (Dumas, 1989b). At least three types of variables may be important: maternal depression, marital adjustment, and social isolation.

Maternal Depression

A large body of evidence supports the existence of an association between child aggressive, antisocial conduct, and maternal self-reports of depressive symptomatology or general emotional distress (Forehand, Wells, McMahon, Griest, & Rogers, 1982). Besides discriminating between referred and nonreferred families, studies show that depression predicts maternal perception of their children (Griest, Forehand, Wells, & McMahon, 1980), and child behavior toward their mothers and other family members (Dumas, Gibson, & Albin, 1989; Forehand, Lautenschlager, Faust, & Graziano, 1986; Hops et al., 1987). Emotional distress may play as important a role as actual child behavior in predicting maternal perception. For example, Brody and Forehand (1986) compared four groups of mother-child dyads (high maternal distress/high child noncompliance, low distress/high noncompliance, high distress/low noncompliance, and low distress/low noncompliance) and found a significant interaction effect, as children in the first group were perceived to be more maladjusted than their counterparts in the other groups, who did not differ from each other. Similarly, maternal depressive symptomatology may be associated with differences in child behavior toward all family members. Although the nature of this association remains unclear, Dumas and Gibson (1990) found that aggressive, antisocial children whose mothers were distressed were more compliant and less aversive toward them than toward their fathers and siblings, while the opposite applied to children whose mothers were not distressed. Not surprisingly, maternal depressive symptomatology has also been found to be associated with the effectiveness of interventions for aggressive, antisocial child behavior. Griest et al. (1982) reported that to supplement a parent skills training with treatment for maternal depression led to a reduction in the latter and an improvement in treatment outcome. Similarly, Forehand, Wells, and Griest (1980) and Patterson (1980) found that the elevated depression scores of mothers of conduct disordered children decreased after parent training.

Marital Adjustment

It has often been reported that separation and divorce are more common in referred than in nonreferred families (e.g., Love & Kaswan, 1974), and that intact families who seek help for child behavior problems commonly present high levels of marital discord, whether this is assessed by self-report measures of marital satisfaction (Johnson & Lobitz, 1974) or open marital conflict (Rutter et al., 1974). In general, parents who experience marital stress see their children as presenting more behavior problems than do parents who do not experience such stress, a perception that is often confirmed by third parties, such as teachers. Similarly, marital discord plays a significant role in a child's adjustment to divorce, and children of divorced parents may be better adjusted if they are no longer exposed to parental conflict than children who remain in intact but conflicted families (Emery, 1982). For example, Rutter et al. (1974) found that ratings of marital adjustment in families of clinically disturbed children were significantly worse than in comparison families, and that child deviance was particularly associated with open discord, tension, and hostility, rather than with parental apathy and indifference toward each other. In keeping with this evidence, some studies suggest that marital discord may undermine behavior therapy with children and families (e.g., Kent & O'Leary, 1976).

Social Isolation

Aggressive, antisocial child behavior may also reflect the adverse nature of the social context in which the child's family functions (Dumas & Wahler, 1985; Wahler, 1980). For example, Dumas (1986) studied 14 mothers who experienced severe management problems with their children and reported high levels of aversive interactions with adults in their environment. The study compared mother and child behaviors between baseline home observations preceded by maternal self-reports of positive community contacts and observations preceded by aversive community contacts. Child behavior did not differ under the two contact conditions, but mothers were found to be more likely to act in an aversive and indiscriminate manner toward their children when they had experienced a large proportion of aversive contacts with adults prior to an observation than when they had not. This suggests that daily changes in mother-child interactions in the families of aggressive, antisocial children may reflect changes in the socioemotional context in which mothers function when they are not with their children. This conclusion is supported by findings that treatment effectiveness may be related to the socioemotional and socioeconomic conditions in which families function (e.g., Dumas, 1984; Dumas & Wahler, 1983; Wahler, 1980; Wahler & Dumas, 1987). Dumas and Wahler (1983) found that the long-term effectiveness of a standardized parent training program was related to pretreatment measures of socioeconomic disadvantage and social isolation, as the probability of treatment failure increased steadily in the presence of disadvantage, isolation, or both.

Treatment Implementation and Evaluation Issues

Assuming that the issues just described can be taken into account, researchers and clinicians still face major challenges when implementing and evaluating a treatment program. Two types of treatment issues will be considered here: the demonstration of treatment effectiveness (in particular, through the establishment of treatment fidelity and follow-up evaluations), and the effective engagement of families in treatment.

Demonstration of Treatment Effectiveness

Treatment Fidelity

To evaluate any treatment strategy requires that one demonstrates that the intervention was conducted as specified; that is, that all participants actually received the particular treatment they were meant to receive. With notable exceptions (Kazdin, Bass, Siegel, & Thomas, 1989; Kazdin, Esveldt-Dawson, French, & Unis, 1987), fidelity has not been demonstrated in intervention studies with aggressive, antisocial youths. Without such demonstration, however, it is almost impossible to interpret positive or negative findings unambiguously; the former may reflect a host of unspecified treatment characteristics, or the fact that treatment was not delivered to all participants in the same manner, while the latter might not justify the modification or abandonment of a treatment approach.

Follow-Up

To establish treatment effectiveness requires not only a demonstration of reliable change following intervention but the maintenance of such change over time. To call a treatment successful, a significant drop in referral problems, without a concomitant increase in other behavior difficulties, should be observed one or two years after intervention. Although this may be an obvious minimum, very few treatment studies of childhood aggressive, antisocial disorders have followed their subjects for even a year. However, the chronic and stable nature of these disorders suggests that a one-year follow-up should be a minimum. Typically, aggressive, antisocial children come to the attention of professionals only after months, if not years, of problematic conduct, and often continue to exhibit such conduct even though an intervention program may temporarily bring a change in their behavior (Wahler, 1980; Wahler & Dumas, 1987). If maintenance of treatment gains can be established after a year, a progressively longer follow-up should be set up in order to monitor positive and negative effects that may only be detected years after termination. For example, McCord (1978) followed up more than 500 men who had participated in the Cambridge-Somerville Youth Study (an early delinquency prevention program) in the 1930s and 1940s. Although participants reported that they had generally benefited from the program, detailed comparisons between treated and control subjects showed that the program had adverse long-term effects on measures such as criminality, death, disease, occupational status, and job satisfaction.

Parental Engagement

Attrition

The integrity of any treatment evaluation is likely to be undermined by subject attrition during the study. This is a particularly serious threat when one considers that families who enter treatment programs for childhood aggression are often more difficult to engage than other clinical populations, especially when samples are carefully selected to include only children with unquestionably chronic and serious problems. Forehand, Middlebrook, Rogers, and Steffe (1983) reviewed 45 studies of family-based interventions for children with oppositional, disruptive behavior problems, 22 of which reported attrition data that averaged 28%. (This rate may actually be an underestimate, as families who make initial contact but decline to begin treatment—e.g., because of extensive research requirements, home observations, etc.—are typically not counted.) Although this rate may compare favorably with other forms of intervention for children and adolescents, it is not so much the magnitude of attrition that should be of concern as the fact that attrition may have a differential impact on a treated sample. For example, McMahon, Forehand, Griest, and Wells (1981) reported that families who dropped out from treatment differed in socioeconomic status and maternal depression from families who did not drop out.

Resistance

Potentially related to the same construct underlying attrition is the problem of resistance in parents who remain in therapy but show limited treatment benefits (Chamberlain & Baldwin, 1988; Chamberlain, Patterson, Reid, Kavanagh, & Forgatch, 1984; Fleischman, Horne, & Arthur, 1983). Resistance is a difficult construct to operationalize as it could take several forms, such as refusal to cooperate with an assignment, debating a topic in therapy, or missing an appointment. Few studies have systematically evaluated resistance in family intervention in general (Pinsoff, 1986) or in family-based treatment of childhood aggression in particular (Chamberlain & Ray, 1988), probably because the construct (a) lacks a widely agreed upon definition, and (b) requires the assessment of micro- rather than macrosocial interactions between therapist and clients to capture the process accurately. One observation system that addresses these two problems is the Therapy Process Code (TPC), which was developed specifically to study family treatment for child antisocial behavior (Chamberlain & Baldwin, 1988; Chamberlain & Ray, 1988). This system, in which resistance generally refers to client statements that block or impede therapist efforts toward change, assesses three clusters of client resistance behaviors: self-deprecation, family conflict, and refusal. Results from recent research with the TPC suggest that high levels of resistance affect engagement in therapy and are associated with limited child behavior change. Higher resistance was observed in dropout families compared with nondropouts (Chamberlain et al., 1984), while lower resistance, especially in the last phase of treatment, was related to higher therapist ratings of success after treatment termination. More importantly, Chamberlain and Ray (1988) reported preliminary findings that mid-therapy parental resistance was significantly related to lower child treatment gains for a sample of aggressive children. Two other potentially important findings point to areas for future inquiry. First, parental resistance is influenced by specific therapist behaviors. Patterson and Forgatch (1985) found that therapist teaching or confronting (in contrast to supporting) was more likely to be followed by resistant behaviors, and that manipulating these therapist behaviors in ABAB reversal designs produced systematic changes in the occurrence of resistance. Second, personal or familial factors may covary with resistance. For example, Chamberlain et al. (1984) found greater resistance in agency-referred than self-referred families.

Client Expectations

Client expectations are commonly conceived as ideas, attitudes, or perceptions pertaining to the client's role or that of the therapist in treatment. The adult psychotherapy literature shows that clients who drop out often report that the therapist or treatment did not conform to their expectations (Garfield, Affleck, & Muffly, 1963; Overall & Aronson, 1963). When these expectations are addressed in initial sessions, clients are more likely to continue treatment (Hoen-Saric et al., 1964; Kissen, Platz, & Su, 1971). In contrast to the extensive work on individual client expectancy factors, there is a dearth of such work within the family intervention literature (Sager, Masters, Ronall, & Normand, 1967; R. Shapiro & Budman, 1970). Several sources of misalignment between parental expectations and child/family therapy have been identified, including the expected level of parental involvement, the assignment of tasks outside of therapy, and the lack of discussion about problems not directly connected to the child's behavior problems (Gaines & Stedman, 1981; R. Shapiro & Budman, 1970). Similarly, Dumas (1984), Griest and Forehand (1982), and Dumas and Wahler (1983) identified strong links between parental perceptions of problems within the family system (i.e., personal adjustment, marital status, and extrafamilial interaction difficulties) and improvements in child problem behavior. More specifically, improved engagement and more persistent child gains occur when child treatment is augmented by addressing parental perceptions, concerns, and attitudes regarding personal difficulties (Griest et al., 1982; Patterson & Fleischman, 1979), marital adjustment, and extrafamilial interactions (Wahler & Afton, 1980; Wahler & Dumas, 1984). Enhancing treatment by addressing parental concerns that go beyond child conduct appears to be of particular significance when treating multiproblem families who are struggling with considerable difficulties in addition to their children's aggressive, antisocial behavior.

Treatment Enhancement Approaches

Enhancement of Parental Engagement

In an investigation of parental engagement in a parent training program for childhood aggression, R. J. Prinz and Miller (1988) demonstrated the

importance of attending to concerns that parents have in addition to the
clinical problems of the child. The study contrasted two treatment
approaches (that both lasted approximately 20 sessions): (1) Standard
Parent Training (SPT) used a social-learning model in a mastery-oriented
therapy format to focus exclusively on parent-child interactions and
improvement of child behavior; (2) Enhanced Parent Training (EPT)
combined the SPT skill-based modules and procedures with an additional, adult-focused component designed to make the social-learning
intervention more effective. EPT therapists systematically elicited from
parents concerns and topics that were not directly related to child
behavior change, such as job stress, health problems, personal worries,
disputes with relatives, and other feelings and external demands.

The sample consisted of 147 preadolescent boys with severe cross-
situational oppositional-aggressive problems selected from a referred
sample of 609 children. Mean T-scale aggression scores on the Child
Behavior Checklist (Achenbach & Edelbrock, 1983) at pretreatment
were 79.9, 73.6, and 74.8 as rated by mothers, fathers, and teachers
respectively. The 147 families were assigned to EPT or SPT using
stratified random assignment to control for one- versus two-parent
families and SES level. EPT and SPT families did not differ significantly at pretreatment with respect to severity of child aggression at
home or school, child IQ, marital discord, parental depression and
overall psychopathology, parental social support, family income, overall SES level, and family history of alcohol or drug abuse and criminality. Nine therapists with at least a master's degree or equivalent plus
additional therapy experience conducted both treatments (counterbalanced within each therapist). Fidelity of both treatments was verified
by independent observers. Results showed that, despite random assignment and comparable initial profiles for the two groups, 29% of EPT
families dropped out of treatment prematurely in comparison with 45%
of SPT families ($\chi^2 = 4.1, p < .05$). EPT parents were also more diligent
than SPT parents in completing homework assignments (92.4% vs.
85.4%, $p < .05$) and reported greater satisfaction with treatment ($p <$
.05). These results support the conclusion that by exploring parental
concerns in addition to child behavior problems, EPT gave parents an
opportunity to discuss problems that might have interfered with their
ability to benefit from the child-oriented aspects of treatment. This
study underscores the need to build an adult-oriented component into
family treatment for childhood aggression.

Other Enhancements

Although family-based social learning interventions are promising treatments for children exhibiting severe aggressive, antisocial behavior, investigators readily acknowledge that high levels of resistance, poor engagement, and inadequate maintenance of improvements are observed in many treated families (McMahon & Forehand, 1984; Sanders & James, 1983). These obstacles have inspired enhancement efforts to improve basic social-learning programs. Miller and Prinz (1990) reviewed the literature for family treatments of childhood conduct disorder and identified some promising approaches. Studies fell into three groups: enhancements and expansions (a) within a dyadic (parent-child) interaction model, (b) within a broad-based model that acknowledges a wider range of family influences, and (c) through a multisystems model. Enhancements within a dyadic model have centered on either the strengthening of parental skills already included in the core intervention or the adding of new interactional strategies (e.g., child self-control training, conflict resolution training, marital therapy). Only partial success has been achieved with this model. Expansions from a broader based model have focused on parental adjustment, parental expectations, and social-environmental stressors, while multisystems adjuncts have included cognitive-behavioral interventions to affect peer relations and ecological approaches to intervene across domains. These generally more complex expansions have produced promising but, for the most part, untested treatment regimens. Related areas of investigation included therapy process research, medication combined with family treatment, and the involvement of fathers in treatment. Miller and Prinz concluded that: (a) most of the enhancement strategies have been underevaluated and not subjected to replication by independent investigators, (b) some of the enhancement approaches were only tested with less severe populations, and (c) the current social learning models of childhood aggression and its treatment need to be expanded to make further progress. In line with this last conclusion, we turn to an overview of Family Skills Training (Blechman, 1985), a relatively new approach that was specifically developed to address the multifaceted difficulties of multiproblem families and their aggressive, antisocial children and thus enhance not only parental engagement but the overall effectiveness of intervention.

Family Skills Training

Family Skills Training (FST) builds on the pioneering work of the developers of Parent Management Training (PMT), Gerald Patterson, Robert Wahler, and Rex Forehand, but is specifically designed to engage families faced with multiple stressors, such as poverty, social isolation, illiteracy, and a disorganized life-style (Blechman, 1985, in press a; Hargis & Blechman, 1979). Like PMT, FST appears to be a promising approach to the treatment of youth with DSM-III-R disruptive behavior disorders, especially if they do not evidence the most severe symptoms of CD (such as cruelty to persons or animals, coerced sexual activity, theft, initiation of physical fights, and use of weapons in fights).

Like PMT, FST strives to reduce the referred child's symptoms, promote successful parent-child behavior management, increase the child's social competence (especially in relationships with peers), and reduce the family's common reliance on a generally coercive style of interaction. These changes in child and family functioning are taught via modules and role plays that help the family institute concrete solutions to circumvent behavior problems and maximize effective communication (Table 6.1 lists these modules and illustrates their relevance to the symptoms of aggressive, antisocial children who would qualify for a diagnosis of ODD). FST therapists use Blechman's (1985) *Solving Child Behavior Problems at Home and at School* as a therapy manual. They rely on the BLOSSOM (Blechman On-Site Skill Observation Measure) (Blechman, Bass, & Newman, 1987; Blechman, Tryon, McEnroe, & Ruff, 1989) for continuing role play assessment of skills targeted by the modules and use the outcome of each role play as a stage for practicing these skills until the family demonstrates proficiency.

Distinctive Features of FST

In contrast with traditional PMT approaches, FST seeks not only to eliminate the behavior problems of the referred child, but also to promote family-wide competence and effective communication (Blechman, 1984a; Blechman & McEnroe, 1985; Blechman & Tryon, in press). By definition, the symptoms of the aggressive, antisocial child are not the sole challenge to the multiproblem family. Other family members often evidence psychiatric and physical health impairments together with low competence in the domains of affect regulation, social

TABLE 6.1   Relevance of FST Modules to the Symptoms of Aggressive, Antisocial Children Who Qualify for a Diagnosis of ODD

FST Modules

a. Good-Day System
b. Communication
c. Putting away clothes and toys
d. Hygiene/bedtime/curfew
e. Toileting (optional)
f. Temper tantrums
g. Fighting
h. Following instructions and arguing
i. Good behavior away from home
j. Morning routine and school attendance
k. Chores and allowance

Diagnostic Features of ODD	*Relevant FST Modules*
1. Loses temper	b, f, g
2. Argues with adults	b, c, h
3. Defies, refuses adult requests, rules	a, b, c, d, f, g, h, i, j, k
4. Deliberately annoys other people	b, f, g, h
5. Blames others for mistakes	b, f, g, h, i, k
6. Touchy, easily annoyed	b, f, g
7. Angry, resentful	b, f, g, k
8. Spiteful, vindictive	b, f, g, k
9. Swears, uses obscene language	a, b, f, g

interaction, and achievement at school or work. At the same time, communication within the family and between the family and outsiders tends to be limited, characterized by ineffective information exchange, behavior management, and problem solving.

Table 6.2 presents an overview of differences between PMT and FST. Note that some of these differences are obscured whenever PMT includes innovative developments emerging from social-learning clinical laboratories, such as Wahler's combination of PMT with synthesis teaching (Wahler & Dumas, 1989).

The Entire Family Participates in FST

In traditional PMT, parents or mothers only (with or without the target child) are the usual participants and the focus is on long-term

TABLE 6.2   Comparison of the Major Features of Parent Management Training (PMT) and Family Skills Training (FST)

Features	PMT	FST
Participants:		
Parents +/– child	yes	no
Entire family	no	yes
Processes of Family/Therapist Communication:		
Information exchange	no	yes
Behavior management	yes	yes
Problem solving	no	yes
Data Driving Treatment:		
Parent skill acquisition	no	yes
Child behavior change	yes	no
Teaching Strategy:		
Abstract principles	yes	no
Concrete routines	no	yes
Long-Term Goals for Participants:		
Child symptoms –	yes	yes
Coercive communication –	yes	yes
Effective communication +	no	yes
Affective competence +	no	yes
Social competence +	yes	yes
Achievement competence +	no	yes

benefits for the target child as perceived by parents, teachers, and other
adults. If siblings and parents benefit from treatment, their improvement is unplanned and not explicitly accounted for by the intervention
process. In contrast, FST views the maintenance of treatment gains in
the referred child as highly dependent upon comparable benefits to
other family members. In particular, mothers must benefit in their
relationships with other adults (e.g., spouses, relatives, authority figures) in order for them to sustain solution strategies instituted during
FST (Blechman, 1980, 1981, 1984b). Consequently, all nuclear family
members and household residents take part in FST (including if possible
parents who live elsewhere and parents' long-term sexual partners),
which from the outset is focused on the implementation of long-term
changes that will benefit all participants.

In FST, Information Exchange Is Presumed Necessary
For Parent-Child Behavior Management and Problem Solving

In traditional PMT, family interaction is equated with behavior management. Parents are presumed to control important concrete and social consequences that they can use to weaken children's antisocial behavior and strengthen their prosocial behavior. Most importantly, communication is presumed effective when parental behavior management is successful. In contrast, FST presumes that effective family communication consists of processes of information exchange, behavior management, and problem solving (Blechman, 1990a, 1990b) that must be actively taught for therapy to be successful.

Information Exchange. In information exchange, family members use words and actions to disclose their feelings, thoughts, and experiences to each other. They also watch and listen attentively and nonjudgmentally to these disclosures in order to understand each other's perspectives and needs. Information exchange is thus seen as the foundation of family social support. During information exchange, family members exposed to stress at school, at work, or in the neighborhood, express their feelings, share their experiences, and formulate their thoughts. Other family members listen attentively and in so doing convey acceptance of negative feelings, frustrating experiences, and verbal experimentation with potential coping strategies. Through information exchange, problems can dissipate without overt behavior management or problem solving.

From the standpoint of social-learning theory, information exchange enables family members to reinforce each other's effective molecular communication behaviors (e.g., statements of self-disclosure, facilitative listening). When a family lacks the capacity for information exchange, premature attempts at behavior management and problem solving often magnify the speaker's negative feelings and experiences. Thus a family capable of information exchange will allow a boy who has been chastised by a teacher to talk about his anger and to experiment aloud with various plans of action, some quite inappropriate ("I'll kill him" or "I'll poison him. You wait and see."). Given the opportunity to express his feelings, the child may at least calm down and at best choose a future strategy likely to yield maximally favorable consequences and minimally punishing ones ("Next time that teacher gets on my case, I'm going to ask him to talk to me alone. And if he doesn't I'll just pretend

I'm listening but I'll really ignore him."). When a family is both unskilled at information exchange and overvalues behavior management, the latter, paradoxically, rarely succeeds (Father: "That's no way to talk about your teacher. If you try to do anything like that, I'll wring your neck." Son: "Yeah, well f . . . you.").

Behavior Management. Behavior management is a successful control process during which A influences B through a combination of clear requests for action, positive consequences for compliance, and extinction of noncompliance. Behavior management is present-oriented when family members make requests of each other for immediate action ("Please turn the TV down, I can't hear you.") and comply with such requests ("O.K. Is that better?"). Behavior management becomes future-oriented when members formulate plans or contingency contracts supplying extrinsic incentives for compliance ("If you help me prepare dinner, I'll let you watch TV after dinner"). Thus we believe that much of what is called problem solving and negotiation in PMT would be more accurately labeled as behavior management.

Families in which members are unaware of or uninterested in each other's points of view (evident in minimal and ineffective information exchange) are necessarily inept at behavior management. Without concrete information, family members cannot even identify behaviors likely to prove effective reinforcers and punishers. Note in this regard how often parents of aggressive, antisocial children claim (in advance of trying the procedure) that time out will not work because the child will enjoy isolation from family activities, that positive reinforcement will not work because nothing the child does deserves praise, or that punishment does work (even though it has obviously failed to reduce the child's symptoms).

Problem Solving. Problem solving is a bilateral (or multilateral) verbal communication process in which each participant recognizes a common problem and expresses an interest in solving it in the future by changing his or her own behavior. The incentive for problem solving lies in its impact on the quality of the relationship rather than in any extrinsic reward.

Problem solving depends on information exchange (allowing understanding of the same problem from multiple vantage points) and behavior management (providing evidence of willingness to accommodate). Problems can and often are satisfactorily resolved through repetitive information exchange and behavior management. However, problem solving as such requires that family members act proactively, taking time to consider future dilemmas and invent mutually satisfying methods of resolving future conflicts. Given such challenging requirements, even for functional families, FST strives to promote information exchange and behavior management and anticipates that a minority of families may spontaneously acquire problem-solving skills.

In FST, Information Exchange Is Presumed Necessary For Therapist-Client Behavior Management and Problem Solving

FST therapists are expected to use effective communication with clients as operationalized in INTERACT/BLISS (Dumas & Blechman, 1990). This coding system, when applied to videotapes of therapist-family interaction, can be used to assess treatment fidelity.

FST presumes that information exchange and behavior management are both necessary for parental engagement. Information exchange is particularly crucial in the engagement of parents from multiproblem families. To this end, therapists use questions to elicit self-disclosure, thereby stimulating information exchange, and build on family members' answers to promote behavior management. This enhancement of traditional PMT thus bridges the gap between a parent's adult concerns (e.g., about her boyfriend) and her child-rearing difficulties. In other words, FST assumes that parents in a multiproblem family will not follow instructions as they are typically provided during early PMT sessions until the therapist has used extensive information exchange to explore the parents' points of view and given them a clear sense that their concerns are understood and taken seriously. Although their theoretical rationales may differ, the process of information exchange has much in common with Wahler's synthesis teaching (Wahler & Dumas, 1989). Consider this hypothetical dialogue between a therapist and the mother of a 16-year-old aggressive boy. Note how the therapist uses questions to engage the mother in information exchange and move her toward behavior management.

> *Therapist:* Let me see if I've got it right. You've tried everything but you feel angry and frustrated that nothing has worked. You feel that you have as little control over your son as you do over your boyfriend. You want things to be better with your son and you want your boyfriend to quit drinking so much, but you don't know how to make that happen. Is that right?

Mother: That's it. That's just how I feel. I want my boy to get better. But I don't know what to do that will work.

Therapist: You are looking for something you can do that will help your son and your boyfriend?

Mother: Yeah, that's what I want. But what can I do?

Therapist: When a woman wants to lose weight, what's more important, exercising every day and eating the right foods or getting on the scale every day and worrying about her weight?

Mother: Exercising, eating right. That's smarter than worrying about your weight. (Laughs.) But what's that got to do with me and my son?

Therapist: What do you think it's got to do with you and your son?

Mother: Oh, you mean if I want him to get better, instead of worrying about him I should just do whatever is right and keep on doing it until it works?

Therapist: Does that make sense to you, doing the right thing until your son and maybe your boyfriend gets better?

Mother: I think so. Sounds OK.

Therapist: If you did that, just kept doing the right thing no matter what your son does, would you feel in control of yourself?

Mother: Yes, I would. Even if I can't control my son, I can at least control myself.

In FST, Treatment Is Driven by Direct Observations of Parents' Behavior Change

In traditional PMT, parental reports (principally about rates of child behavior) are used to gauge how effectively parents are applying social-learning principles to manage child behavior (except in criterion-based programs, such as Forehand & McMahon, 1981). Clearly, these reports can be biased and lacking in information about the manner in which parents apply abstract principles to particular problem situations. In FST, all family members work through a series of modules, tailoring and instituting solutions to the home problems of all members and the school and community behavior problems of all children. Progress through these modules is driven by data collected during the family's role-played enactment of a solution to a particular problem, which takes place before and repeatedly after each module to measure skill acquisition and maintenance. Instructions for enactment and scoring of the role plays that are keyed to each module are found in the BLOSSOM; for charting parental adherence to solutions developed during each module, in the Home Problem Chart; for family-wide ratings of problems targeted by each module, in the Problem-Severity Ratings.

The FST Teaching Strategy Centers on Parental Enactment of Concrete Solutions for Child Behavior Problems

In PMT, parents commonly learn abstract social-learning principles and are guided in the application of these principles to troublesome child behavior. For example, parents may be required to master a self-instructional text (such as Patterson's, 1976, *Living with Children*). During treatment they are then asked to observe and chart child behavior and to deliver their observations in writing or by daily telephone interview. This teaching strategy is most suitable for parents who are fairly skilled at abstract reasoning, literate, organized, and knowledgeable about optimum child development.

The FST teaching strategy was designed for multiproblem families in which parents reason concretely, are semiliterate, disorganized, and lack child development knowledge. Rather than teach abstract principles, therapists rely on modules to help families enact, rehearse, and adopt concrete solutions to specific problems. Steps involved in each module include: (a) administration of the BLOSSOM pretest, (b) scoring and discussion of pretest results, (c) tailoring of a solution strategy to the family's specific circumstances and preferences, (d) rehearsal of the strategy in the clinic, (e) rehearsal of the strategy at home, (f) collection of data about the strategy's implementation, (g) administration of the BLOSSOM posttest, (h) scoring and discussion of the BLOSSOM posttest, (i) administration of the next module's pretest if the family reached criterion on the previous posttest.

In each module, solution strategies are developed so that they apply to all children in the family. For example, when treatment begins, a "Good-Day" system may be set up to reinforce behavior incompatible with the excesses of the aggressive, antisocial child and all other siblings. As a result, each child is rewarded at the end of a "good day" when no behavioral excesses (e.g., stealing at school) by that child have been reported to parents. If several siblings share the same problem (e.g., stealing), then a Good-Day system is set up to reinforce each one for the absence of any stealing.

Families of dysfunctional children can readily sabotage any solution strategy. Parents might undermine the Good-Day system by inventing evidence of wrongdoing (e.g., taking food from the refrigerator without permission is now equated with stealing). Children might sabotage the Good-Day system by covering up evidence of wrongdoing until after they have been rewarded. Therefore, experienced FST therapists continually troubleshoot solution strategies by asking questions about what could go or has gone wrong in practical situations. As a result, parents may agree to change an agreed-upon definition of stealing only during an FST session. Children may agree that whenever evidence of wrong-doing surfaces (even if it occurred 3 days ago), the current day will not qualify as a "good day." Parents and children may agree to reward honesty about wrongdoing. An act of stealing not reported by the stealer to the parent may (when it surfaces) disqualify the next three days from being "good days." In contrast, an act of stealing reported by the child may disqualify only that day from being a "good day."

Looking Ahead

This chapter began with a review of research and treatment issues that limit the interpretation of available findings on aggressive, antiso-cial youths and that, we believe, should be considered in the implemen-tation of any new treatment program. Looked at optimistically, these issues present a formidable challenge to researchers and clinicians. Seen in a more pessimistic light, the same issues may only offer a recipe for despair. We hope that the second half of this chapter will encourage cautious optimism, as enhancements to traditional programs or new therapeutic approaches like FST become more widely used, although we are aware that these new developments may not withstand empirical scrutiny. As we continue to gather data, however, we may want to consider a theoretical question: to make significant progress in the modification of childhood and adolescent aggression, will it be suffi-cient to rely on enhancements or other improvements of the social-learning model that has underlined most empirical investigations to date, or will it be necessary to question the ultimate usefulness of this model and offer alternatives? Blechman (1990a) is pointing to the latter in her emphasis on the importance of communication in healthy human relationships, as are Dumas (1989b) in his critique of the operant model and Wahler and Dumas (1989) in their presentation of an interbehavio-ral model of dysfunctional mother-child interactions. Will it suffice to do what we have always been doing better, or will we need to think about what we should be doing differently? Time will tell.

References

Achenbach, T. M., & Edelbrock, C. (1983). *Manual for the Child Behavior Checklist and Revised Child Behavior Profile.* Burlington: University of Vermont, Department of Psychiatry.

American Psychiatric Association. (1980). *Diagnostic and statistical manual of mental disorders* (3rd ed.). Washington, DC: Author.

American Psychiatric Association. (1987). *Diagnostic and statistical manual of mental disorders* (3rd ed., rev.). Washington, DC: Author.

Blechman, E. A. (1980). Ecological sources of dysfunction in women: Issues and implications for clinical behavior therapy. *Clinical Behavior Therapy Review, 2,* 1-16.

Blechman, E. A. (1981). Competence, depression and behavior modification with women. In M. Hersen, R. M. Eisler, & P. M. Miller (Eds.), *Progress in behavior modification* (Vol. 12, pp. 227-263). New York: Academic Press.

Blechman, E. A. (1984a). Competent parents, competent children: Behavioral objectives of parent training. In R. F. Dangel & R. A. Polster (Eds.), *Behavioral parent training: Foundations of research and practice* (pp. 34-63). New York: Guilford.

Blechman, E. A. (1984b). Women's behavior in a man's world: Sex differences in competence. In E. A. Blechman (Ed.), *Behavior modification with women* (pp. 3-33). New York: Guilford.

Blechman, E. A. (1985). *Solving child behavior problems at home and at school.* Champaign, IL: Research Press.

Blechman, E. A. (1990a). Effective communication: Enabling the multi-problem family to change. In P. Cowan & M. Hetherington (Eds.), *Advances in family research* (Vol. 2). Hillsdale, NJ: Lawrence Erlbaum.

Blechman, E. A. (1990b). A new look at emotions and the family: A model of effective family communication. In E. A. Blechman (Ed.), *Emotions and the family: For better or for worse* (pp. 201-224). Hillsdale, NJ: Lawrence Erlbaum.

Blechman, E. A., Bass, C., & Newman, D. (1987). *BLOSSOM: Blechman On-Site Skill Observation Measure. Technical Manual.* Albert Einstein College of Medicine/Montefiore Medical Center, Department of Psychiatry, Behavior Therapy Program, The Bronx, NY.

Blechman, E. A., & McEnroe, M. J. (1985). Effective family problem solving. *Child Development, 56,* 429-437.

Blechman, E. A., & Tryon, A. S. (in press). Familial origins of affective competence and depression. In K. Schlesinger & B. Bloom (Eds.), *Boulder Symposium on Clinical Psychology: Depression.* Hillsdale, NJ: Lawrence Erlbaum.

Blechman, E. A., Tryon, A. S., McEnroe, M. J., &, Ruff, M. H. (1989). Behavioral approaches to psychological assessment: A comprehensive strategy for the measurement of family interaction. In M. M. Katz & S. Wetzler (Eds.), *Contemporary approaches to psychological assessment* (pp. 43-65). New York: Brunner/Mazel.

Brody, G. H., & Forehand, R. (1986). Maternal perceptions of child maladjustment as a function of the combined influence of child behavior and maternal depression. *Journal of Consulting and Clinical Psychology, 54,* 237-240.

Cantrell, V. L., & Prinz, R. J. (1985). Multiple perspectives of rejected, neglected, and accepted children: Relationship between sociometric status and behavioral characteristics. *Journal of Consulting and Clinical Psychology, 53,* 884-889.

Chamberlain, P., & Baldwin, D. V. (1988). Client resistance to parent training: Its therapeutic management. In T. R. Kratochwill (Ed.), *Advances in school psychology* (Vol. 6, pp. 131-171). Hillsdale, NJ: Lawrence Erlbaum.

Chamberlain, P., Patterson, G. R., Reid, J., Kavanagh, K., & Forgatch, M. (1984). Observation of client resistance. *Behavior Therapy, 15,* 144-155.

Chamberlain, P., & Ray, J. (1988). The therapy process code: A multidimensional system for observing therapist and client interactions in family treatment. In R. J. Prinz (Ed.), *Advances in behavioral assessment of children and families* (Vol. 4, pp. 189-217). Greenwich, CT: JAI Press.

Dumas, J. E. (1984). Child, adult-interactional, and socioeconomic setting events as predictors of parent training outcome. *Education and Treatment of Children, 7,* 351-364.

Dumas, J. E. (1986). Indirect influence of maternal social contacts on mother-child interactions: A setting event analysis. *Journal of Abnormal Child Psychology, 14,* 205-216.

Dumas, J. E. (1989a). Treating antisocial behavior in children: Child and family approaches. *Clinical Psychology Review, 9,* 197-222.

Dumas, J. E. (1989b). Let's not forget the context in behavioral assessment. *Behavioral Assessment, 11,* 231-247.

Dumas, J. E., & Gibson, J. A. (1990a). Behavioral correlates of maternal depressive symptomatology in conduct-disorder children. II: Systemic effects involving fathers and siblings. *Journal of Consulting and Clinical Psychology, 58,* 877-881.

Dumas, J. E., & Blechman, E. A. (1990b). *INTERACT/BLISS—A coding system to assess small group interaction.* Unpublished coding manual, University of Montreal, Department of Psycho-Education.

Dumas, J. E., Gibson, J. A., & Albin, J. B. (1989). Behavioral correlates of maternal depressive symptomatology in conduct-disorder children. *Journal of Consulting and Clinical Psychology, 57,* 516-521.

Dumas, J. E., & Wahler, R. G. (1983). Predictors of treatment outcome in parent training: Mother insularity and socioeconomic disadvantage. *Behavioral Assessment, 5,* 301-313.

Dumas, J. E., & Wahler, R. G. (1985). Indiscriminate mothering as a contextual factor in aggressive-oppositional child behavior: "Damned if you do, damned if you don't." *Journal of Abnormal Child Psychology, 13,* 1-17.

Emery, R. E. (1982). Interparental conflict and the children of discord and divorce. *Psychological Bulletin, 92,* 310-330.

Eron, L. D. (1988). Aggression in middle childhood—A harbinger of future problems. *Canadian Journal of Public Health Supplement, 79,* 17-21.

Fleischman, M. J., Horne, A. M., & Arthur, J. L. (1983). *Troubled families, a treatment approach.* Champaign, IL: Research Press.

Forehand, R., Lautenschlager, G. J., Faust, J., & Graziano, W. G. (1986). Parent perceptions and parent-child interactions in clinic-referred children: A preliminary investigation of the effects of maternal depressive moods. *Behaviour Research and Therapy, 24,* 73-75.

Forehand, R., & McMahon, R. J. (1981). *Helping the noncompliant child: A clinician's guide to parent training.* New York: Guilford.

Forehand, R., Middlebrook, J., Rogers, T., & Steffe, M. (1983). Dropping out of parent training. *Behaviour Research and Therapy, 21,* 663-668.

Forehand, R., Wells, K. C., & Griest, D. L. (1980). An examination of the social validity of a parent training program. *Behavior Therapy, 11,* 488-502.

Forehand, R., Wells, K. C., McMahon, R. J., Griest, D., & Rogers, T. (1982). Maternal perception of maladjustment in clinic-referred children: An extension of earlier research. *Journal of Behavioral Assessment, 4,* 145-151.

Gaines, T., & Stedman, J. M. (1981). Factors associated with dropping out of child and family treatment. *American Journal of Family Therapy, 9,* 45-51.

Garfield, S. L., Affleck, D. C., & Muffly, R. A. (1963). Psychotherapy interaction and continuation of psychotherapy. *Journal of Clinical Psychology, 19,* 473-478.

Griest, D. L, & Forehand, R. (1982). "How can I get any parent training done with all these other problems going on?": The role of family variables in child behavior therapy. *Child and Family Behavior Therapy, 4,* 73-80.

Griest, D. L., Forehand, R., Rogers, T., Breiner, J., Furey, W., & Williams, C. A. (1982). Effects of parent enhancement therapy on the treatment outcome and generalization of a parent training program. *Behaviour Research and Therapy, 20,* 429-436.

Griest, D. L., Forehand, R., Wells, K. C., & McMahon, R. J. (1980). An examination of differences between nonclinic and behavior-problem clinic-referred children and their mothers. *Journal of Abnormal Psychology, 89,* 497-500.

Hargis, K. R., & Blechman, E. A. (1979). Social class and training of parents as behavior change agents. *Child Behavior Therapy, 1,* 69-74.

Hoen-Saric, R., Frank, J. D., Imber, S. D., et al. (1964). Systematic preparation of patients for psychotherapy: Effects on behavior and outcome. *Journal of Psychiatric Research, 2,* 267-281.

Hops, M., Biglan, A., Sherman, L., Arthur, J., Friedman, L., & Osteen, V. (1987). Home observations of family interactions of depressed women. *Journal of Consulting and Clinical Psychology, 55,* 341-346.

Huesmann, L. R., Eron, L. D., Lefkowitz, M. M., & Walder, L. O. (1984). Stability of aggression over time and generations. *Developmental Psychology, 20,* 1120-1134.

Johnson, S. M., & Lobitz, G. K. (1974). The personal and marital adjustment of parents as related to observed child deviance and parenting behaviors. *Journal of Abnormal Child Psychology, 2,* 193-207.

Kazdin, A. E. (1987). Treatment of antisocial behavior in children: Current status and future directions. *Psychological Bulletin, 102,* 187-203.

Kazdin, A. E., Bass, D., Siegel, T., & Thomas, C. (1989). Cognitive-behavioral therapy and relationship therapy in the treatment of children referred for antisocial behavior. *Journal of Consulting and Clinical Psychology, 57,* 522-536.

Kazdin, A. E., Esveldt-Dawson, K., French, N. H., & Unis, A. S. (1987). Problem-solving skills training and relationship therapy in the treatment of antisocial child behavior. *Journal of Consulting and Clinical Psychology, 55,* 76-85.

Kent, R. N., & O'Leary, K. D. (1976). A controlled evaluation of behavior modification with conduct problem children. *Journal of Consulting and Clinical Psychology, 44,* 586-596.

Kissen, B., Platz, A., & Su, W. H. (1971). Selective factors in treatment choice and outcome in alcoholics. In N. K. Mello & J. H. Mendelson (Eds.), *Recent advances in studies of alcoholism* (pp. 781-802). Washington, DC: Government Printing Office.

Kovacs, M., Paulauskas, S., Gatsonis, C., & Richards, C. (1988). Depressive disorders in childhood: III. A longitudinal study of comorbidity with and risk for conduct disorders. *Journal of Affective Disorders, 15,* 205-217.

Loeber, R. (1982). The stability of antisocial and delinquent child behavior: A review. *Child Development, 53,* 1431-1446.

Loeber, R. (1990). Development and risk factors of juvenile antisocial behavior and delinquency, *Clinical Psychology Review, 10,* 1-41.

Loeber, R., & Lahey, B. B. (1989). Recommendations for research on disruptive behavior disorders of childhood and adolescence. In B. B. Lahey & A. E. Kazdin (Eds.), *Advances in clinical child psychology* (Vol. 12, pp. 221-251). New York: Plenum.

Loeber, R., & Schmaling, K. B. (1985). Empirical evidence for overt and covert patterns of antisocial conduct problems: A meta-analysis. *Journal of Abnormal Child Psychology, 13,* 337-352.

Love, L. R., & Kaswan, J. W. (1974). *Troubled children: Their families, schools, and treatments.* New York: John Wiley.

Maccoby, E. E., & Martin, J. A. (1983). Socialization in the context of the family: Parent-child interaction. In E. M. Hetherington (Ed.), *Handbook of child psychology: Vol. 4. Socialization, personality, and social development* (pp. 1-101). New York: John Wiley.

Marriage, K., Fine, S., Moretti, M., & Haley, G. (1986). Relationship between depression and conduct disorder in children and adolescents. *Journal of the American Academy of Child Psychiatry, 25,* 687-691.

McCord, J. (1978). A thirty-year follow-up of treatment effects. *American Psychologist, 33,* 284-289.

McMahon, R. J. (1987). Some current issues in the behavioral assessment of conduct-disordered children and their families. *Behavioral Assessment, 9,* 235-252.

McMahon, R. J., & Forehand, R. (1984). Parent training for the noncompliant child: Treatment outcome, generalization, and adjunctive therapy procedures. In R. F. Dangel & R. A. Polster (Eds.), *Parent training: Foundations of research and practice* (pp. 298-328). New York: Guilford.

McMahon, R. J., Forehand, R., Griest, D. L., & Wells, K. C. (1981). Who drops out of therapy during parent behavioral training? *Behavioral Counseling Quarterly, 1,* 79-85.

Miller, G. E., & Prinz, G. E. (1990). Enhancement of social learning family interventions for childhood conduct disorder. *Psychological Bulletin, 108,* 291-307.

Olweus, D. (1979). Stability of aggressive reaction patterns in males: A review. *Psychological Bulletin, 86,* 852-875.

Overall, B., & Aronson, H. (1963). Expectations of psychotherapy in patients of lower socioeconomic class. *American Journal of Orthopsychiatry, 33,* 421-430.

Patterson, G. R. (1976). *Living with children: New methods for parents and teachers* (rev. ed.). Champaign, IL: Research Press.

Patterson, G. R. (1980). Mothers: The unacknowledged victims. *Monographs of the Society for Research in Child Development, 45*(5, Serial No. 186).

Patterson, G. R., & Bank, L. (1986). Bootstrapping your way in the nomological thicket. *Behavioral Assessment, 8,* 49-73.

Patterson, G. R., Dishion, T. J., & Bank, L. (1984). Family interaction: A process model of deviancy training. *Aggressive Behavior, 10,* 253-267.

Patterson, G. R., & Fleischman, M. J. (1979). Maintenance of treatment effects: Some considerations concerning family systems and follow-up data. *Behavior Therapy, 10,* 168-185.

Patterson, G. R., & Forgatch, M. S. (1985). Therapist behavior as a determinant for client noncompliance: A paradox for the behavior modifier. *Journal of Consulting and Clinical Psychology, 53*, 846-851.

Pinsoff, W. M. (1986). The process of family therapy: The development of the Family Therapist Coding System. In L. S. Greenberg & W. M. Pinsoff (Eds.), *The psychotherapeutic process: A research handbook* (pp. 201-284). New York: Guilford.

Prinz, R. J., Connor, P., & Wilson, C. (1981). Hyperactive and aggressive behaviors in childhood: Intertwined dimensions. *Journal of Abnormal Child Psychology, 9*, 191-202.

Prinz, R. J., & Miller, G. E. (1988, November). Behavioral family treatment of conduct disorder: Learning from the dropouts. In R. J. Prinz (Chair), *Advances in behavioral family therapy.* Symposium conducted at the meeting of the Association for Advancement of Behavior Therapy, New York.

Puig-Antich, J. (1982). Major depression and conduct disorder in prepuberty. *Journal of the American Academy of Child Psychiatry, 21*, 118-128.

Quay, H. C. (1986). Conduct disorders. In H. C. Quay & J. S. Werry (Eds.), *Psychopathological disorders of childhood* (3rd ed.) (pp. 35-72). New York: John Wiley.

Robins, L. N. (1966). *Deviant children grown up.* Baltimore, MD: Williams & Wilkins.

Robins, L. N. (1981). Epidemiological approaches to natural history research: Antisocial disorders in children. *Journal of the American Academy of Child Psychiatry, 20*, 566-580.

Rutter, M., Cox, A., Tupling, C., Berger, M., & Yule, W. (1975). Attainment and adjustment in two geographical areas: I. The prevalence of psychiatric disorder. *British Journal of Psychiatry, 126*, 493-509.

Rutter, M., Yule, B., Quinton, D., Rowlands, O., Yule, W., & Berger, M. (1974). Attainment and adjustment in two geographical areas: III. Some factors accounting for area differences. *British Journal of Psychiatry, 125*, 520-533.

Sager, C. J., Masters, Y. J., Ronall, R. E., & Normand, W. C. (1967). Selection and engagement of patients in family therapy. *American Journal of Orthopsychiatry, 37*, 715-723.

Sanders, M. R., & James, J. E. (1983). The modification of parent behavior: A review of generalization and maintenance. *Behavior Modification, 7*, 3-27.

Sechrest, L., & Rosenblatt, A. (1987). Research methods. In H. C. Quay (Ed.), *Handbook of juvenile delinquency* (pp. 417-450). New York: John Wiley.

Shapiro, R. J., & Budman, S. H. (1970). Defection, termination, and continuation in family and individual therapy. In N. W. Ackerman (Ed.), *Family process* (pp. 55-67). New York: Basic Books.

Shapiro, S. K., & Garfinkel, B. D. (1986). The occurrence of behavior disorders in children: The interdependence of attention deficit disorder and conduct disorder. *Journal of the American Academy of Child Psychiatry, 25*, 809-819.

Stouthamer-Loeber, M., Loeber, R., & Green, S. M. (1989, February). *Dishonesty and covert problem behavior in adolescence and early adulthood.* Paper presented at the meeting of the Society for Research in Child and Adolescent Psychopathology, Miami, FL.

Szatmari, P., Offord, D. R., & Boyle, M. H. (1989). Ontario Child Health Study: Prevalence of attention deficit disorder with hyperactivity. *Journal of Child Psychology and Psychiatry, 30*, 219-230.

U.S. Senate Judiciary Committee, Subcommittee to Investigate Juvenile Delinquency. (1976). *School violence and vandalism: The nature, extent and cost of violence and vandalism in the nation's schools.* Washington, DC: Government Printing Office.

Wahler, R. G. (1980). The insular mother: Her problems in parent-child treatment. *Journal of Applied Behavior Analysis, 13,* 207-219.

Wahler, R. G., & Afton, A. D. (1980). Attentional processes in insular and noninsular mothers: Some differences in their summary reports about child problem behavior. *Child Behavior Therapy, 2,* 25-42.

Wahler, R. G., & Dumas, J. E. (1984). Changing the observational coding styles of insular and noninsular mothers: A step toward maintenance of parent training effects. In R. F. Dangel & R. A. Polster (Eds.), *Parent training: Foundations of research and practice* (pp. 379-416). New York: Guilford.

Wahler, R. G., & Dumas, J. E. (1987). Family factors in childhood psychopathology: A coercion-neglect model. In T. Jacob (Ed.), *Family interaction and psychopathology: Theories, methods, and findings* (pp. 581-627). New York: Plenum.

Wahler, R. G., & Dumas, J. E. (1989). Attentional problems in dysfunctional mother-child interactions: An interbehavioral model. *Psychological Bulletin, 105,* 116-130.

Weintraub, S., Prinz, R. J., & Neale, J. M. (1978). Peer evaluations of the competence of children vulnerable to psychopathology. *Journal of Abnormal Child Psychology, 6,* 461-473.

7

Post-Traumatic Stress Disorder:
Clinical Features and Treatment

EDNA B. FOA

BARBARA O. ROTHBAUM

The purpose of this chapter is to examine the various clinical aspects of post-traumatic stress disorder and to evaluate existing studies of treatment methods and their effectiveness. Post-traumatic stress disorder (PTSD), before being labeled as such, was recognized in soldiers for more than 100 years and was commonly referred to as battle fatigue, combat neurosis, shell shock, and hysteria. These suffering soldiers typically reported strong feelings of being overwhelmed and confused, and endured excessive fear responses such as sweating, trembling, and shaking. Many veterans experienced psychological dysfunctioning associated with these reactions long after the battle had ended and their physical encounter with war had ceased.

Other trauma survivors also experience severe stress reactions that sometimes render them psychologically disabled. Victims of aggravated assault (Kilpatrick, Saunders, Veronen, Best, & Von, 1987; Rothbaum & Foa, 1988), rape (Rothbaum & Foa, 1992), accidents (Burstein et al., 1988; Muse, 1986), and natural disasters (Lindy, Green, Grace, &

AUTHORS' NOTE: Preparation of this manuscript was supported by NIMH Grant No. MH42178-02 awarded to the author.

Titchener, 1983) can also experience painful and enduring symptoms similar to those encountered by war veterans.

An example of the devastating effects of PTSD is found in a 23-year-old rape victim (Sarah) who sought treatment from the Crime Victims Program at the Medical College of Pennsylvania/Eastern Pennsylvania Psychiatric Institute three years after her assault. She was experiencing symptoms associated with PTSD: nervousness, depression, sleep difficulties, intrusive thoughts, and nightmares. She avoided being home alone, going out after dark, or talking about the incident. All of these problems developed after a man had held her at gunpoint, stolen her jewelry and money, beat her repeatedly in the chest and face, and raped her. Although the incident occurred three years prior to her presentation for treatment, Sarah's life was still governed by the suffering resulting from her assault. It thus becomes apparent that post-traumatic reactions can be pervasive, chronic, emotionally painful, and life-altering.

Diagnostic Features

Post-traumatic stress syndrome was first included as an anxiety disorder in the DSM-III Diagnostic Manual (American Psychiatric Association, 1980). The revised diagnostic manual (DSM-III-R; American Psychiatric Association, 1987) classified the characteristic symptoms into three main categories: reexperiencing, avoidance, and increased arousal.

The primary distinguishing characteristic of PTSD is the reexperiencing of the traumatic event through nightmares and flashbacks (Keane, Zimering, & Caddell, 1985). Indeed, although agoraphobics generally recall their first panic attack with dread, they do not tend to report recurrent dreams or flashbacks of it. Obsessive-compulsives who are often preoccupied with thoughts about contamination throughout the day also rarely report contamination nightmares. However, "intense psychological distress [caused by] exposure to events that symbolize or resemble an aspect of the traumatic material" (American Psychiatric Association, 1987, p. 250) is also listed as a reexperiencing symptom but does resemble a phobic reaction.

The second category of PTSD symptoms includes cognitive and behavioral avoidance manifestations. These symptoms also define simple phobia. Thus both disorders involve the persistent fear and avoidance of threat-related situations (American Psychiatric Association, 1987, p. 244).

The third PTSD symptom category includes arousal symptoms that are quite similar to those that characterize generalized anxiety disorder (GAD). As illustrated by the DSM-III-R (American Psychiatric Association, 1987), symptoms such as excessive anxiety and worry, motor tension, autonomic hyperactivity, vigilance, and scanning are shared by the syndromes of GAD and PTSD.

Not only do diagnostic criteria demonstrate symptom similarities among PTSD, phobias, and GAD, experimental data suggest such relations as well. These will be summarized below.

Psychological Reactions to Stressors

Several studies (Blanchard, Kolb, Gerardi, Ryan, & Pallmeyer, 1986; Kozak, Foa, & Olasov, 1987; Malloy, Fairbank, & Keane, 1983; Pitman, Orr, Forgue, deJong, & Claiborn, 1987) demonstrated that people suffering from PTSD, just like phobics, experience fear when confronted with trauma-related information. Pitman et al. (1987) explored psychophysiological responses to relevant stressors in Vietnam combat veterans diagnosed with PTSD. Based on a paradigm developed by Lang, Levin, Miller, and Kozak (1983), the authors presented subjects with tape-recorded scripts (neutral and individualized combat descriptions). Each one lasted for 30 seconds. For each script presentation, a baseline measure was first recorded. Subjects then listened to each script (read period), imagined the scene as vividly as possible after the story ended (imagery period), and then stopped imagining the scene and relaxed (recovery period). Recordings of heart rate, skin conductance, muscle tension, and self-report measures indicated that skin conductance and muscle tension increased as a result of combat script presentation. Neutral passages, however, did not yield increased results.

Kozak, McCarthy, Foa, Rothbaum, and Murdock (1989), also using the paradigm developed by Lang et al. (1983), examined psychophysiological responses in rape victims and non-rape victims (controls). In this study, however, rape-related scripts were not individualized. Results demonstrated a tendency for rape presentations to increase heart rate in PTSD rape victims, particularly when they listened to the rape-related scripts. No increase was found for the controls.

It is interesting to note that when the rape victim's response is compared to those of snake phobics (Lang et al., 1983), their heart rate elevation is identical when they listened to threat-related passages. Differences between the two groups, however, became apparent during the imagery periods. Phobics' heart rates further increased at this time, while PTSD rape victims' decreased. Differences between imagery reactions in phobics and PTSD sufferers may be due to the dissociative aspects of PTSD. Someone with PTSD may cognitively avoid thoughts about upsetting or threatening occurrences, whereas phobics may be more successful in imagining fear presentations.

With regard to the overlap between GAD and PTSD, psychopathological studies have shown that baseline physiologic arousal is higher among individuals diagnosed as having anxiety states (Lader, 1967). Blanchard et al. (1986) demonstrated heightened general arousal in PTSD sufferers. They compared Vietnam veterans with PTSD to combat veterans without PTSD and to simple phobics. They found that PTSD sufferers had higher baseline heart rates than did the other two groups. Phobics' arousals were similar to that of normals.

In summary, both DSM-III-R criteria and psychophysiological experiments demonstrate similarity of PTSD to simple phobia on some aspects and to GAD on other aspects.

Prevalence of the Disorder

Epidemiological studies suggest that PTSD is a serious mental health problem. In the United States, lifetime prevalence of this disorder in the general population is estimated at 8%, but the prevalence in risk groups is much higher. In a national study of Vietnam veterans, Kulka et al. (1988) found 31% lifetime prevalence among males and 27% among females. At the time of the interviews, the prevalence was 15% and 8.5% for males and females respectively. Eighteen percent of fire fighters had PTSD eight months postfire (McFarlane, 1989). Twenty-five percent of Buffalo Creek Dam Collapse survivors reported current PTSD 14 years post-trauma (Green, 1989). Sixteen percent of rape victims report current PTSD after an average of 17 years postassault (Kilpatrick et al., 1987).

It seems that the chronicity of PTSD among rape victims is similar to that found in other traumatized populations. However, wars are not currently being fought by the United States, and natural disasters are relatively rare. On the other hand, recent studies estimate that one out of four women is likely to become a victim of rape (Koss, Gidycz, & Wisniewski, 1987). Rape victims may therefore constitute the largest group of PTSD sufferers in this country.

Rothbaum, Foa, Murdock, Riggs, and Walsh (in press) conducted a study that examined the incidence of PTSD following rape. Female sexual assault victims were interviewed soon after the rape and then once a week for a total of 12 weeks. PTSD symptoms were evaluated through the use of a semistructured interview. Rape-related symptoms were assessed with standardized self-report measures. Results demonstrated that almost all rape victims reported sufficient PTSD symptoms to meet a diagnosis of PTSD one week after the assault. At a three-month postassault evaluation, the incidence of PTSD had gradually been decreased but almost half of the victims still suffered from PTSD. It then becomes apparent that many rape victims manifest long-term PTSD that may remain unchanged without treatment.

Cognitive-Behavioral Treatment

Knowledge pertaining to the treatment of PTSD is limited, perhaps due to its relatively recent inclusion as a diagnostic category. A great deal of knowledge does, however, exist about the treatment of anxiety disorders. Because of symptom similarities, treatments of anxiety disorders may be applicable to the attempted amelioration of PTSD. Two commonly used behavioral treatment procedures for these disorders are exposure-based methods and anxiety management techniques (AMT).

Exposure treatment requires patients to confront their feared situations. It is designed to activate fear and promote habituation to the feared material. Such techniques are used to treat disorders involving excessive fear and avoidance of circumscribed anxiety-provoking situations. In fact, exposure treatment is the most effective form of therapy for simple phobias (Barlow, Leitenberg, Agras, & Wincze, 1969; Gelder & Marks, 1968; Williams, Dooseman, & Kleinfield, 1984).

Often used in conjunction with exposure, the purpose of AMT is to manage anxiety that hinders daily functioning. Such management is achieved by teaching patients how to control their fear through methods such as relaxation training (e.g., Bernstein & Borkovec, 1973; Jacobson,

1938), stress inoculation training (Meichenbaum, 1974), breathing re-training (Clark, Salkovskis, & Chalkley, 1985), distraction techniques (e.g., thought stopping; Wolpe, 1973), and cognitive restructuring (Beck, 1972; Ellis, 1977). AMT is, in fact, the most effective form of treatment for generalized anxiety disorders (Borkovec & Mathews, 1987; Butler, Covington, Hibbut, Klimes, & Gelder, 1987; Jannoun, Oppenheimer, & Gelder, 1982; for comprehensive review of cognitive-behavioral treatment for anxiety disorders, see Foa, Rothbaum, & Kozak, 1989).

Exposure Techniques

Exposure treatment for PTSD was first used with war veterans. Several case studies (Fairbank, Gross, & Keane, 1983; Fairbank & Keane, 1982; Johnson, Gilmore, & Shenoy, 1982; Keane & Kaloupek, 1982; Schindler, 1980) demonstrated the treatment effectiveness of exposure to trauma-related stimuli. Both imaginal flooding (e.g., Fairbank & Keane, 1982; Keane, Fairbank, Caddell, & Zimering, 1989) and in vivo flooding (e.g., Johnson et al., 1982) were found equally therapeutic. These treatment studies, however, included the use of other therapeutic methods such as anger control or relaxation training. Although proven effective, the contribution of exposure to patients' overall improvement is thus unclear.

Peniston (1986) conducted a study of Vietnam veterans with PTSD. The effect of EMG biofeedback-assisted desensitization was compared with a no-treatment condition. Treatment was administered three times per week for a total of 48 30-minute sessions. In the first 3 sessions, patients were trained in visualization/imagery and progressive relaxation. A 10-item hierarchy of stressors was then conducted. Three to five desensitization sessions were spent on each item. Presentations were continually repeated until they no longer elicited an anxiety response. Results showed that EMG desensitization was better at reducing muscle tension, nightmares, and flashbacks than was no treatment. Assessment taken two years after study completion emphasized the effectiveness of EMG desensitization; none of the treatment patients had been rehospitalized, whereas five out of eight controls had been hospitalized.

Keane et al. (1989) studied the use of exposure as a primary treatment method. They randomly assigned 24 PTSD Vietnam veterans to either relaxation and imaginal flooding treatments (14 to 16 sessions of 90 minutes each) or to a waiting list control group. In each session, patients were first instructed to relax. They then received 45 minutes of imaginal flooding, followed again by relaxation. Results of this study showed that the treatment group reported significantly less depression, general anxiety, fear, hypochondriasis, and hysteria at post-treatment and follow-up assessments than did the controls. Therapists also rated patients' experiencing of trauma, startle reactions, memory/concentration problems, impulsivity, irritability, and legal problems to be significantly lower than those of the control group. Differences pertaining to other PTSD symptoms were not, however, discussed. Keane et al.'s (1989) utilization of relaxation before and after exposure is a unique procedure not often used. It would thus be interesting to examine the potentially separate effects of exposure and relaxation training on their results.

Frank and Stewart (1983, 1984) found that systematic desensitization (Wolpe, 1958) was effective in the treatment of PTSD. Rape victims received 14 sessions of systematic desensitization. After treatment completion, the victims' rape-related anxiety and depression were reduced and their social adjustment increased. Most subjects also voluntarily exposed themselves in vivo to situations that had been desensitized only in imagination during treatment. Whether or not this apparent treatment effectiveness is the result of natural symptom reduction with passage of time is unclear because patients received treatment immediately after the rape. This study also did not include a control group, again making it difficult to interpret the results (see Kilpatrick & Calhoun, 1988, for critique).

Exposure techniques have also been successfully applied to the treatment of accident-related PTSD. McCaffrey and Fairbank (1985) studied a person who had been in a helicopter crash and another who had experienced a series of automobile accidents. Treatment consisted of relaxation training, imaginal exposure, and self-exposure in vivo. With treatment, PTSD symptoms improved a great deal. Only minor changes, however, were noted in patients' self-reported anxiety.

Fairbank, DeGood, and Jenkins (1981) treated a 32-year-old woman who had experienced a head-on collision in which she and her children were injured. As a result, this woman was enduring a persistent post-traumatic motoric startle response (jerking the steering wheel when a car approached). Treatment consisted of three weekly sessions of relaxation training and daily exposure to highway driving. Self-reported anxiety decreased during the relaxation training phase, remained at a reduced level during the driving exposure phase, and decreased further at a six-month follow-up assessment. Self-monitored motoric startle responses varied throughout the relaxation phase, dissipated during the driving exposure phase, and remained extinct at follow-up.

Muse (1986) applied systematic desensitization to the treatment of three automobile accident victims suffering from chronic pain syndromes and PTSD. Patients received two to four months of pain clinic treatments (exercise therapy, biofeedback training, supportive group counseling, and medication) beginning one month to two years following the accident. After pain treatment completion, all patients were still suffering from PTSD. They then received systematic desensitization (13 to 18 sessions) with the final two sessions devoted to in vivo exposure. Results showed a reduction in therapist-observed and patient-reported fear and anxiety, PTSD symptoms, depression, and pain. Patients also resumed activities in which they had previously lost interest. Although limited by a case study approach, this report demonstrated that exposure techniques are especially effective in relieving PTSD symptoms.

Anxiety Management Techniques

Hickling, Sison, and Vanderploeg (1986) investigated the efficacy of EMG biofeedback and progressive muscle relaxation training in the treatment of PTSD. Six veterans received treatment (7 to 14 sessions; 8- to 16-week period) that included the use of autogenic phrases (e.g., suggesting increased warmth or calm; Schultz & Luthe, 1969) and cue-controlled relaxation techniques. Most PTSD symptoms improved upon treatment completion. Although this type of therapy seemed beneficial, full interpretation of results was limited because only patients who believed they would profit from this behavioral treatment were included. However, Blanchard and Abel (1976) also found the use of biofeedback helpful in alleviating disturbances associated with PTSD. They treated a rape victim with cardiovascular problems (episodic sinus tachycardia and syncope) with systematic biofeedback training and helped her control tachycardia. These results lend further support to the previously discussed findings of Hickling et al. (1986).

Frank and Stewart (1984) studied the effects of anxiety and depression targeted cognitive therapy on 25 rape victims. Treatment began an average of two weeks after the assault. Based on Beck's (1972) theories and therapy methods, treatment included self-monitoring of activities with mastery and pleasure responses, grading task assignments (e.g., going out alone), and identifying and modifying maladaptive cognitions. All patients showed significant improvement upon treatment completion.

The premise of this procedure is the hypothesis that individual cognitions are filtered through preexisting assumptions about the world. For example, a rape victim may focus on distorted perceptions of inadequacy, incompetence, helplessness, and worthlessness. Such a person may also feel in some way responsible for the rape occurrence. Cognitive therapy techniques are intended to help the patients identify such distorted perceptions and to test their reality. As demonstrated by Frank and Stewart (1984), this form of therapy seems quite effective. Again, the interpretation of the results is limited by the fact that patients entered treatment two weeks after the rape.

Stress inoculation training (SIT) is a treatment program developed especially for rape victims who remained highly fearful several months after their assault (Kilpatrick, Veronen, & Resick, 1982). This treatment technique originally consisted of 20 therapy hours and homework assignments conducted in two phases. The first phase was educational and it included an explanation of the rationale and theoretical basis for the treatment. Therapy was described to patients as a cognitive-behavioral approach to the management of rape-related fear (explained as a classical conditioning phenomenon) and anxiety. The patient was also told that coping strategies would be used to help alleviate rape-associated fear and avoidance. The concept of anxiety was described as a multichannel system incorporating various behavioral/motoric, cognitive, and physiological responses that occur in stages. Such detailed explanation was presented because of the belief that "if one can identify the early indicators of the fear response, one can better control [the] reaction to it" (Veronen & Kilpatrick, 1983, p. 359).

The second SIT phase consisted of the coping skills training. It started with deep muscle relaxation and breathing control training. Patients were instructed to tense and relax various muscles systematically (Jacobson, 1938). This was also practiced at home, with the use of taped relaxation sessions, until patients were able to relax on their own in a variety of situations within a short period of time. Breathing control exercises emphasized slow, rhythmic breathing from the diaphragm and were similar to those taught in yoga or Lamaze natural childbirth classes. Through the use of covert modeling (imagery) and role playing (in vivo), patients were taught communication skills. Thought stopping (Wolpe, 1958) was also taught to control for the intrusive effects of obsessive thinking.

D. G. Kilpatrick (personal communication, 1986) considered guided self-dialogue to be the most important technique used in SIT. Using Meichenbaum's (1974) approach, patients were taught to focus on internal dialogue and to identify irrational, faulty, or negative self-statements. Rational and positive statements were generated and substituted for the negative ones. Veronen and Kilpatrick (1982) investigated the efficacy of this program. They examined and treated 15 female rape victims who showed elevated fear and avoidance to specific phobic stimuli three months postrape. Results showed a treatment effect for rape-related fear, anxiety, phobic anxiety, tension, and depression. A control group, however, was not included in this study. Interpretations of the data are thus limited.

Stress inoculation training has since been revised. Treatment duration was shortened to eight therapy hours. In addition to fear and avoidance, various other rape-related problems were also addressed in the coping skills training phase. Kilpatrick and Amick (1985) conducted a case study using the revised SIT. A 21-year-old woman was assessed for psychophysiological reactions to stressors. A polygraph and self-monitor of anxiety-related physical symptoms (e.g., headaches, itchy scalp, nausea, sleep disturbances, chest tightness) measured reactions. Self-report measures (SCL-90-R, Veronen-Kilpatrick MFS, Profile of Mood States Scale, IES) and therapist interviews that addressed dreams and irrational beliefs about the assault (e.g., self-blame) assessed patients' cognitive responses. Self-monitoring of social withdrawal, fear of driving, interpersonal difficulty, and substance abuse of meprobamate and alcohol provided measures of behavioral responses. Information gathered from the above assessments was used in the development of treatment goals and was monitored throughout the study. Results demonstrated treatment success. The thoroughness of the assessment procedures in this report was exemplary.

Resick, Jordan, Girelli, Hutter, and Marhoefer-Dvorak (1988) compared three types of therapy: stress inoculation training, assertion training, and supportive psychotherapy with information distribution. Thirty-seven rape victims were divided into these three treatment groups and a wait-list control group. The SIT used was similar to the program outlined in Kilpatrick et al. (1982). However, exposure in vivo was added to this study; cognitive restructuring, assertiveness training, and role playing were omitted. Assertion training began with an explanation of how assertion can be used to counter fear and avoidance. Training included

behavioral rehearsal via role playing with feedback regarding performance. Such specific techniques used in assertion training were based
on the writings of Lange and Jakubowski (1976) and Ellis (1977;
Rational Emotive Therapy). Supportive psychotherapy with information provision began with an educational period. Participants then
selected discussion topics that included their sense of anxiety that
resulted from the assault, others' reactions to what happened, and their
amount of felt support. All three treatments proved to be equally
effective in alleviating rape-related symptoms. Measures of general
psychopathology, general fear, and specific fear, as well as intrusion
and avoidance symptoms, demonstrated improvement. Measures of
depression, self-esteem, and social fears did not. The wait list control
group did not show change.

SIT, Exposure, and Supportive Counseling

Foa, Rothbaum, Riggs, and Murdock (1991) compared the use of SIT,
exposure treatment, supportive counseling, and a no-treatment control.
They studied sexual assault victims (randomly assigned to one of the
treatment groups) who met PTSD diagnostic criteria at least three
months following their attack. Conducted twice a week for a total of
nine 90-minute sessions, SIT treatment included: educating, information
gathering, treatment planning, breathing retraining and deep muscle relax-
ing, thought stopping, cognitive restructuring (Beck, 1972; Ellis, 1977),
self-dialogue guiding (Meichenbaum, 1974), covert modeling, and role
playing. In vivo exposure to feared situations was not included.

Each coping skills session began with a review of the previous
session's activity, an update on the use of coping skills in the victim's
natural environment, and a review of the patient's homework assignments. Therapists then introduced a new skill to the patient. This was
first practiced with a non-assault-related situation and then with an
assault-related event. After all sessions were completed, the therapist
and patient reviewed progress accomplished in treatment. At this time,
the patient informed the therapist about which skills she had acquired
and successfully applied in real-life situations. The future use of these
skills was also discussed.

Exposure treatment was also administered in nine 90-minute bi-
weekly sessions. Therapists gathered information from patients assigned to this group, provided an explanation of treatment rationale, and

planned treatment in the first two sessions. A hierarchy of avoided situations was also constructed at this time for in vivo exposure homework. Such homework began with exposure to situations that elicited low levels of anxiety (Subjective Units of Discomfort [SUDs] = 50) and progressed to events that elicited higher levels of anxiety (e.g., SUDs = 100). Other sessions involved reliving the rape scene in imagination. Patients were instructed to imagine the assault as vividly as possible and to describe it aloud, in detail, as if it were happening at that moment. They repeatedly imagined and described the scene several times within a 60-minute period in order to promote habituation. Narratives were audiotaped for patients to listen to at home once a day. In the last session, the therapists reminded the patients that avoidance of safe situations and/or rape-associated thoughts could exacerbate PTSD symptoms. In order to prevent this, the patients were asked to practice exposure in their everyday lives.

Patients assigned to receive supportive counseling (nine 90-minute sessions, twice a week) were assisted, by therapists, in discussing and solving current daily problems. Discussion of the assault itself was prevented and topics varied from rape-related to non-rape-related issues. This method of communicating and problem-solving was aimed at promoting patients' perceptions of self-control.

Results from the above comparison study showed that SIT was better in reducing PTSD symptoms immediately after treatment than wait list control. At this point, however, SIT effectiveness did not differ from exposure and supportive counseling. At a follow-up assessment averaging 3½ months post-treatment, patients who received exposure treatment showed greater PTSD symptom improvement than did those who received the other treatments. Patients treated with exposure continued to improve whereas those who received SIT lost some of their gains.

Summary

Over the past 10 years, knowledge pertaining to the psychological impact of crime on its victims has increased and advanced. Methods of treating chronic post-traumatic stress disorder have also been studied. The controlled studies and case reports discussed in this chapter were consistent in reporting that exposure and anxiety management techniques are somewhat effective in reducing PTSD symptoms. A greater understanding of the underlying mechanisms and theoretical basis for these treatments, however, is needed. Future research will also need to focus on trauma and personality variables that are likely to produce chronic PTSD. Once such issues are understood, the development of prevention programs and improvement of treatment methods will be facilitated.

References

American Psychiatric Association. (1980). *Diagnostic and statistical manual of mental disorders* (3rd ed.). Washington, DC: Author.

American Psychiatric Association. (1987). *Diagnostic and statistical manual of mental disorders* (3rd ed., rev.). Washington, DC: Author.

Barlow, D. H., Leitenberg, H., Agras, W. S., & Wincze, J. P. (1969). The transfer gap in systematic desensitization: An analogue study. *Behaviour Research and Therapy, 7,* 191-196.

Beck, A. T. (1972). *Depression: Causes and treatment.* Philadelphia: University of Pennsylvania Press.

Bernstein, D. A., & Borkovec, T. D. (1973). *Progressive relaxation training.* Champaign, IL: Research Press.

Blanchard, E. B., & Abel, G. G. (1976). An experimental case study of the biofeedback treatment of a rape induced psychophysiological cardiovascular disorder. *Behavior Therapy, 7,* 113-119.

Blanchard, E. B., Kolb, L. C., Gerardi, R. J., Ryan, D., & Pallmeyer, T. P. (1986). Cardiac response to relevant stimuli as an adjunctive tool for diagnosing post-traumatic stress disorder in Vietnam veterans. *Behavior Therapy, 17,* 592-606.

Borkovec, T. D., & Mathews, A. M. (1987). Treatment of non-phobic anxiety disorders. *Journal of Consulting and Clinical Psychology, 55,* 883-888.

Burstein, A., Ciccone, P. E., Greenstein, R. A., Daniels, N., Olsen, K., Mazarek, A., Decatur, R., & Johnson, N. (1988). Chronic Vietnam PTSD and acute civilian PTSD: A comparison of treatment experiences. *General Hospital Psychiatry, 10,* 245-249.

Butler, G., Covington, A., Hibbut, G., Klimes, I., & Gelder, M. (1987). Anxiety management for persistent generalized anxiety. *British Journal of Psychiatry, 151,* 535-542.

Clark, D. M., Salkovskis, P. M., & Chalkley, A. J. (1985). Respiratory control as a treatment for panic attacks. *Journal of Behavior Therapy and Experimental Psychiatry, 16,* 23-30.

Ellis, A. (1977). The basic clinical theory and rational-emotive therapy. In A. Ellis & R. Grieger (Eds.), *Handbook of rational-emotive therapy* (pp. 3-34). New York: Springer.

Fairbank, J. A., DeGood, D. E., & Jenkins, C. W. (1981). Behavioral treatment of a persistent post-traumatic startle response. *Journal of Behavior Therapy and Experimental Psychiatry, 12,* 321-324.

Fairbank, J. A., Gross, R. T., & Keane, T. M. (1983). Treatment of posttraumatic stress disorder: Evaluation of outcome with a behavioral code. *Behavior Modification, 7,* 557-568.

Fairbank, J. A., & Keane, T. M. (1982). Flooding for combat-related stress disorders: Assessment of anxiety reduction across traumatic memories. *Behavior Therapy, 13,* 499-510.

Foa, E. B., Rothbaum, B., & Kozak, M. J. (1989). Behavioral treatments of anxiety and depression. In P. Kendall & D. Watson (Eds.), *Anxiety and depression: Distinctive and overlapping features.* New York: Academic Press.

Foa, E. B., Rothbaum, B. O., Riggs, D., & Murdock, T. (1991). Treatment of post-traumatic stress disorder in rape victims: A comparison between cognitive behavioral procedures and counseling. *Journal of Consulting and Clinical Psychology, 59,* 715-723.

Frank, E., & Stewart, B. D. (1983). Treating depression in victims of rape. *The Clinical Psychologist, 8,* 65-74.

Frank, E., & Stewart, B. D. (1984). Depressive symptoms in rape victims. *Journal of Affective Disorders, 1,* 269-277.

Gelder, M. G., & Marks, I. M. (1968). Desensitization and phobias: A cross-over study. *British Journal of Psychiatry, 114,* 323-328.

Green, B. (1989). *Disasters and PTSD.* Position Paper prepared for DSM-IV.

Hickling, E. J., Sison, G. F. P., & Vanderploeg, R. D. (1986). Treatment of posttraumatic stress disorder with relaxation and biofeedback training. *Biofeedback and Self-Regulation, 11,* 125-134.

Jacobson, E. (1938). *Progressive relaxation.* Chicago: University of Chicago Press.

Jannoun, L., Oppenheimer, C., & Gelder, M. (1982). A self-help treatment program for anxiety state patients. *Behavior Therapy, 13,* 103-111.

Johnson, C. H., Gilmore, J. D., & Shenoy, R. Z. (1982). Use of a feeding procedure in the treatment of a stress-related anxiety disorder. *Journal of Behavior Therapy and Experimental Psychiatry, 13,* 235-237.

Keane, T. M., Fairbank, J. A., Caddell, J. M., & Zimering, R. T. (1989). Implosive (flooding) therapy reduces symptoms of PTSD in Vietnam combat veterans. *Behavior Therapy, 20,* 245-260.

Keane, T. M., & Kaloupek, D. G. (1982). Imaginal flooding in the treatment of post-traumatic stress disorder. *Journal of Consulting and Clinical Psychology, 50,* 138-140.

Keane, T. M., Zimering, R. T., & Caddell, J. M. (1985). A behavioral formulation of post-traumatic stress disorder in Vietnam veterans. *The Behavior Therapist, 8,* 9-12.

Kilpatrick, D. G., & Amick, A. E. (1985). Rape trauma. In M. Hersen & C. G. Last (Eds.), *Behavior therapy casebook* (pp. 86-103). New York: Springer.

Kilpatrick, D. G., & Calhoun, K. S. (1988). Early behavioral treatment for rape trauma: Efficacy or artifact? *Behavior Therapy, 19,* 421-427.

Kilpatrick, D. G., Saunders, B. E., Veronen, L. J., Best, C. L., & Von, J. M. (1987). Criminal victimization: Lifetime prevalence, reporting to police, and psychological impact. *Crime and Delinquency, 33,* 479-489.

Kilpatrick, D. G., Veronen, L. J., & Resick, P. A. (1982). Psychological sequelae to rape: Assessment and treatment strategies. In D. M. Dolays & R. L. Meredith (Eds.), *Behavioral medicine: Assessment and treatment strategies* (pp. 473-497). New York: Plenum.

Koss, M. P., Gidycz, C. A., & Wisniewski, N. (1987). The scope of rape: Incidence and prevalence of sexual aggression and victimization in a national sample of higher education students. *Journal of Consulting and Clinical Psychology, 55,* 162-170.

Kozak, M. J., Foa, E. B., & Olasov, B. (1987, October). *Psychophysiological response of rape victims during imagery of rape and neutral scenes.* Paper presented at the annual meeting of the Society for Psychophysiological Research, Amsterdam, the Netherlands.

Kozak, M. J., McCarthy, P. R., Foa, E. B., Rothbaum, B. O., & Murdock, T. B. (1988, November). *Rape survivors with post-traumatic stress disorder: Autonomic responding to single auditory tones.* Presented at the Association for the Advancement of Behavior Therapy, Phobia SIG, New York.

Kulka, R. A., Schlenger, W. E., Fairbank, J. A., Hough, R. L., Jordan, B. K., Marmar, C. R., & Weiss, D. S. (1988). *Contractual report of findings from the national Vietnam veterans readjustment study.* Research Triangle Park, NC: Research Triangle Institute.

Lader, M. H. (1967). Palmer skin conductance measure in anxiety and phobic states. *Journal of Psychosomatic Research, 11,* 271-281.

Lang, P. J., Levin, D. N., Miller, G. A., & Kozak, M. J. (1983). Fear behavior, fear imagery, and the psychophysiology of emotion: The problem of affective response integration. *Journal of Abnormal Psychology, 92,* 276-306.

Lange, A. J., & Jakubowski, P. (1976). *Responsible assertive behavior.* Champaign, IL: Research Press.

Lindy, J. D., Green, B. L., Grace, M., & Titchener, J. (1983). Psychotherapy with survivors of the Beverly Hills Supper Club fire. *American Journal of Psychotherapy, 4,* 593-610.

Malloy, P. E., Fairbank, J. A., & Keane, T. M. (1983). Validation of a multimethod assessment of post-traumatic stress disorder in Vietnam veterans. *Journal of Consulting and Clinical Psychology, 51,* 488-494.

McCaffrey, R. J., & Fairbank, J. A. (1985). Post-traumatic stress disorder associated with transportation accidents: Two case studies. *Behavior Therapy, 16,* 406-416.

McFarlane, A. C. (1989). The aetiology of post-traumatic morbidity: Predisposing, precipitating and perpetuating factors. *Psychiatry, 154,* 221-228.

Meichenbaum, D. (1974). *Cognitive behavior modification.* Morristown, NJ: General Learning Press.

Muse, M. (1986). Stress-related, posttraumatic chronic pain syndrome: Behavioral treatment approach. *Pain, 25,* 389-394.

Peniston, E. G. (1986). EMG biofeedback-assisted desensitization treatment for Vietnam combat veterans post-traumatic stress disorder. *Clinical Biofeedback and Health, 9,* 35-41.

Pitman, R. K., Orr, S. P., Forgue, D. F., deJong, J. B., & Claiborn, J. M. (1987). Psychophysiologic assessment of post-traumatic stress disorder imagery in Vietnam combat veterans. *Archives of General Psychiatry, 44,* 970-975.

Resick, P. A., Jordan, C. G., Girelli, S. A., Hutter, C. K., & Marhoefer-Dvorak, S. (1988). A comparative outcome study of behavioral group therapy for sexual assault victims. *Behavior Therapy, 19,* 385-401.

Rothbaum, B. O., & Foa, E. B. (1988, September). *Treatments of post-traumatic stress disorder in rape victims.* Presented at the World Congress of Behaviour Therapy Conference, Edinburgh, Scotland.

Rothbaum, B. O., & Foa, E. B. (1992). Cognitive-behavioral treatment of post-traumatic stress disorder. In P. A. Saigh (Ed.), *Posttraumatic stress disorder: A behavioral approach to assessment and treatment.* Elmsford, NY: Pergamon.

Rothbaum, B. O., Foa, E. B., Murdock, T., Riggs, D., & Walsh, W. (in press). Post-traumatic stress disorder following rape. *Journal of Traumatic Stress.*

Schindler, F. E. (1980) Treatment by systematic desensitization of a recurring nightmare of a real life trauma. *Journal of Behavior Therapy and Experimental Psychiatry, 11,* 53-54.

Schultz, F. H., & Luthe, W. (1969). *Autogenic therapy.* New York: Grune & Stratton.

Veronen, L. J., & Kilpatrick, D. G. (1982, November). *Stress inoculation training for victims of rape: Efficacy and differential findings.* Presented in a symposium entitled "Sexual Violence and Harassment" at the 16th Annual Convention of the Association for Advancement of Behavior Therapy, Los Angeles, CA.

Veronen, L. J., & Kilpatrick, D. G. (1983). Stress management for rape victims. In D. Meichenbaum & M. E. Jaremko (Eds.), *Stress reduction and prevention* (pp. 341-374). New York: Plenum.

Williams, S. L., Dooseman, G., & Kleinfield, E. (1984). Comparative effectiveness of guided mastery and exposure treatments for intractable phobias. *Journal of Consulting and Clinical Psychology, 52,* 505-518.

Wolpe, J. (1958). *Psychotherapy by reciprocal inhibition.* Stanford, CA: Stanford University Press.

Wolpe, J. (1973). *The practice of behavior therapy.* Elmsford, NY: Pergamon. Press.

8

Cognitive Treatment of a Crime-Related Post-Traumatic Stress Disorder

PATRICIA A. RESICK

Although crime is depicted daily in the news and in the entertainment media, it has only been in the past decade that mental health professionals have developed an awareness of the impact of crime on victims. If one were to depend on the media as a source of information regarding the effects of crime (with the possible exception of recent talk shows), the overwhelming impression would be that crime has a minimal psychological impact on victims and that they recover quickly from any kind of victimization, including rape or the homicide of a loved one. At the end of the hour, in a typical drama, the case has been solved and the victim, if "she" (victims are usually presented as young, beautiful women) ever exhibited any distress, is now walking arm in arm with the detective or attorney into the sunset.

Faced with these constant changes, it is not surprising that many victims of crime are stunned by the extent of their trauma reaction and feel that they have failed to cope as well as they assume others do, if they are still symptomatic a few weeks after the event. Crime-trauma victims often arrive in therapy, after delaying treatment for years, with the secret fear that the therapist will pronounce them crazy or particularly bad at coping.

There are several purposes of this chapter. One purpose will be to review the prevalence of post-traumatic stress disorder (PTSD) in crime victims and to describe recovery patterns typically seen. A second purpose is to discuss recent theories of PTSD. Third, a new therapy for crime-related PTSD, cognitive processing therapy (CPT), will be described and the results of CPT used with four clients will be presented. Finally, there will be a brief discussion of special considerations for treatment of various types of crime victims with CPT.

Prevalence of Crime-Related Post-Traumatic Stress Disorder and Recovery Patterns

Post-traumatic stress disorder (PTSD) has been identified as the most common psychological disorder that may occur in the aftermath of criminal victimization (Foa, Chapter 7 this volume; Kilpatrick, Veronen et al., 1987; Steketee & Foa, 1987). In the only randomly drawn survey of PTSD in female crime victims, Kilpatrick, Saunders, Veronen, Best, & Von (1987) found that more than 75% of a sample of 391 Charleston, SC, respondents had been a victim of crime. Fifty-three percent of the women reported having been sexually assaulted, 9.7% reported having been the victim of aggravated assault, 5.6% of robbery, and 45.3% of burglary. Of these victims, 27.8% were found to have developed post-traumatic stress disorder following the crime.

Sexual assault victims were much more likely to develop PTSD than victims of other types of crime. Fifty-seven percent of rape victims developed PTSD after the crime and 16.5% still reported meeting criteria for PTSD an average of 17 years postcrime. Thirty-seven percent of aggravated assault, 18% of robbery, and 28% of burglary victims reported meeting the criteria for PTSD for some (unspecified) period after their victimization.

In a separate report on the same study, Kilpatrick, Saunders et al. (1989) reported on variables affecting the development of PTSD in their sample of female crime victims. They found that life threat, physical injury, and completed rape each made significant contributions to explaining the development of PTSD. Those women whose crimes included all three variables were 8.5 times more likely to develop PTSD than those with none of the three variables.

In another random community survey, Kilpatrick, Amick, and Resnick (1988; also, Amick-McMullan, Kilpatrick, & Resnick, 1988; Amick-McMullan, Kilpatrick, Saunders, & Resnick, 1988), determined the prevalence of surviving family members of criminal homicide or alcohol-related vehicular homicides. In the first stage of the project, 12,500 subjects were screened through a random telephone survey. In stage two, 500 subjects were interviewed by telephone. In this stage, 214 subjects interviewed had a close family member who had been killed. Based on the total number surveyed in stage one, the researchers estimated the prevalence of family homicide. They found that 1.55% were family members of criminal homicide victims while 1.22% were family survivors of alcohol-related vehicular homicide victims. They estimated that 4.5 million adults in the United States have experienced this type of secondary victimization.

The researchers found that of those in the second stage of the research, 28.7% of the criminal homicide survivors and 34.1% of the alcohol-related vehicular homicide survivors developed PTSD after the crime. At the time of the interviews, 7% of the criminal homicide survivor group and 2.2% of the alcohol-related vehicular homicide survivors still met criteria for a diagnosis of PTSD. The researchers did not report the average length of time since the crime nor the duration of PTSD symptoms afterward.

In a prospective longitudinal study of rape victims, Foa (1990, Chapter 7 this volume) found that 94% of the sampled women met the criteria for PTSD in the first week after the event. At three months postcrime, 47% still met criteria for PTSD. Although earlier longitudinal studies on reactions to rape or robbery did not examine PTSD as a diagnostic entity, their results were compatible with those of Foa (Calhoun, Atkeson, & Resick, 1982; Kilpatrick, Resick, & Veronen, 1981; Resick, 1986). The greatest amount of recovery occurs in the first three months postcrime with relatively little more recovery thereafter.

While there has been very little research on reactions of male victims of crime, Resick (1988) compared reactions of male and female robbery victims in a longitudinal prospective study for 18 months postcrime. Female robbery victims reported more anxiety, depression, and PTSD symptoms in the first month after the crime. Thereafter, however, there were no sex differences in reactions.

Theories of PTSD

Two-Factor Theory

Until the past few years, the prevailing theory of victim reactions was two-factor theory (Holmes & St. Lawrence, 1983; Kilpatrick, Veronen, & Resick, 1982). Classical conditioning was assumed to account for the fear reactions that were observed while escape and avoidance learning were hypothesized to account for the maintenance of these fear reactions. Through higher order conditioning and stimulus generalization, many stimuli, including cognitive stimuli such as images and thoughts, acquire the ability to elicit anxiety reactions.

Information Processing Theory

With the acceptance of post-traumatic stress disorder as the most likely reaction to follow victimization, two-factor theory became a less viable theory. Two-factor theory does not explain satisfactorily the reexperiencing phenomena, the flashbacks, nightmares, or intrusive recollections in the absence of environmental stimuli. These intrusive recollections are present in no other anxiety disorder (Foa, Steketee, & Rothbaum, 1989). Because of the prevalence of these cognitive symptoms, cognitive theories have been proposed recently (Chemtob, Roitblat, Hamada, Carlson, & Twentyman, 1988; Foa, Steketee, & Olasov-Rothbaum, 1989; Litz & Keane, 1989; McCann, Sakheim, & Abrahamson, 1988).

Information processing theories propose that people develop PTSD symptoms because they have not adequately processed the crime. As a result of traumatic victimization, the victim develops a fear schema, which is essentially a program for escape and avoidance behavior (Chemtob et al., 1988; Foa et al., 1989). This "threat" schema, according to Chemtob et al. (1988) is always at least weakly potentiated in PTSD. This would account for the greater physiological reactivity observed in PTSD sufferers (Blanchard, Kolb, Pallmeyer, & Gerardi, 1982; McNally et al., 1987; Pitman et al., 1990; Pitman, Orr, Forgue, de Jong, & Claiborn, 1987). When someone with PTSD detects even ambiguous evidence of a possible threat, he or she is biased to perceive that threat and activate the schema. Memories of the event would then be activated in the form of flashbacks, intrusive recollections, strong physiological reactions, emotions, and behavior.

Similar to Foa et al. (1989), Jones and Barlow (1990) have conceptualized PTSD as an anxiety disorder much like panic disorder. They propose that PTSD symptoms are accounted for by a state of anxious apprehension that develops as a result of a trauma-induced learned alarm. This state of anxious apprehension is moderated by the individual's coping skills and social support.

While the theories proposed by Foa et al. (1989), Chemtob et al. (1988), and Jones and Barlow (1990) fit the information currently available on PTSD, it appears that PTSD consists of more than fearful memories and apprehension. Intrusive recollections and avoidance might be activated by other strong affects and beliefs as well. For instance, crime victims often report experiencing anger, disgust, humiliation, and guilt. They also report conflicts between prior schema and the current event ("Rape doesn't happen to nice women," "My son was minding his own business. He never hurt anyone. Why was he killed?"). In fact, Veronen, Kilpatrick, and Resick (1979) found that rape victims reported experiencing a range of reactions besides fear during, immediately after, and hours following the crime.

Furthermore, in the case of homicide-victim family members, fear may not play a role in their PTSD at all. They may not have been present at the crime and do not feel personally threatened by the event. Yet, they suffer from PTSD. They have intrusive memories of their imagined images of the crime, of their loved one's suffering and death, of waiting at the hospital, or of being informed of the death by the police either in person or on the phone. They cannot reconcile the sudden, unexpected, and violent death with their beliefs about justice or their memories of their loved one.

Pitman et al. (1990) found the same range of emotions among Vietnam veterans. Combat veterans with PTSD reported experiencing a variety of feelings such as anger, surprise, and sadness, as well as fear, significantly more than non-PTSD anxious veterans when listening to individualized traumatic scripts. In fact, PTSD veterans were no more likely to report feeling fear than other emotions.

Hollon and Garber (1988) have suggested that when people are exposed to events that are incompatible with their existing schemata, one of two things usually happens. Assimilation occurs when the new information is altered or distorted to be consistent with preexisting schemata (e.g., "It wasn't rape" or "It must have been my fault"). Accommodation is the process whereby schemata are altered to integrate the new information. ("The event did happen. I was helpless to stop it."). Perhaps the symptoms of PTSD occur when someone is unable to accomplish either of these tasks successfully. Assimilation may be inadequate because distorted excuses or explanations create conflict with the reality of the event, yet accommodation may threaten a person's sense of safety and security in the world.

Both Chemtob et al. (1988) and Foa et al. (1989) have proposed that flooding or anxiety management techniques are the most logical form of therapy because they allow accommodation of the event by activating the fear network in a safe environment. However, Resick and Schnicke (1990) have suggested that while activation of schemata in a safe environment may sufficiently alter perceptions of danger (and therefore fear), there may be no change in emotional reactions other than fear unless direct confrontation of misattributions or distortions occurs. Victims may still blame themselves, feel that they have not recovered or handled the event quickly enough, or feel shame, disgust, or anger, all of which could be sufficiently intense to facilitate intrusive recollections and avoidance reactions.

Cognitive Processing Therapy

Because PTSD is largely a cognitive disorder (intrusive recollections, nightmares, flashbacks, concentration problems, cognitive avoidance, and numbing), it is possible that a cognitive approach may be beneficial in helping crime victims more adaptively process the event. Cognitive processing therapy (CPT) was developed to elicit and identify emotional reactions and to recognize and modify distorted/maladaptive thoughts and beliefs about the event. While there is an exposure component in CPT, much of the emphasis in therapy is focused on identifying and resolving conflicts between prior beliefs regarding oneself and the world and the schema-discrepant experience of victimization.

While CPT borrows some components from Beck's cognitive therapy for depression and anxiety (Beck, Rush, Shaw, & Emery, 1979; Beck & Emery, 1985), there are also some distinct differences. Beck's cognitive therapy is based on the assumption that anxiety and depression result from faulty cognitions and distorted thinking patterns. The therapy de-emphasizes the expression of emotion. However, following traumatic events, victims experience overwhelming emotions that they attempt to suppress and avoid. Perceptions and beliefs about the traumatic event could be reasonably accurate but so horrifying that the victims cannot reconcile the event with their prior beliefs about the world and human behavior.

In addition, Beck's therapy for depression focuses a great deal on the modification of behavior (scheduling behavior and graded assignments) and the use of experiments to confront maladaptive cognitions. Unlike the typical depressed person, it is this author's experience that women who have been raped do not need to increase their activity level. In fact, they are often overscheduled, holding down two jobs, taking classes, or working overtime, as a strategy to avoid thinking and as an excuse for not having a social life. CPT is strictly a cognitive therapy, and while there are daily homework assignments and worksheets, there are no experiments set up to test assumptions. Most of their conflicting cognitions have to do with events surrounding the crime or the meaning of the event. Appropriate experiments to test those beliefs are not feasible.

CPT attempts to assist the client process accurate emotion-laden memories and to resolve conflicts between memories of the event that cannot be avoided entirely but that cannot be integrated into existing schemata. Because avoidance is part of PTSD, emotions should not be minimized or avoided in therapy. CPT includes an exposure component, in which clients are encouraged to activate their schemata of the event and to experience their emotions fully. They are then taught to differentiate accurate interpretations from faulty cognitions. Both the exposure technique and the focus on possible faulty or conflicting beliefs are attempts to locate areas of incomplete processing, which, in CPT, are called "stuck points."

CPT also includes a component that addresses specific areas of functioning that are likely to be affected by the crime. While clients may have specific stuck points about the crime itself ("Why did he choose *me*?", "It must have been my fault," "I thought I was going to die"), it is also likely that beliefs about other areas of functioning are affected by the crime. McCann et al. (1988) identified five areas of functioning that are frequently affected by victimization: safety, trust, power/control, esteem, and intimacy. Each of these areas can be divided into beliefs regarding oneself and beliefs regarding others. McCann et al. (1988) propose that if victims had positive beliefs in these areas prior to the event, these beliefs may become disrupted because of the crime.

However, if one had negative beliefs due to prior traumas or poor parenting, then victimization may confirm and entrench these negative beliefs. Such disruptions or faulty confirmations would result in inadequate and incomplete processing of the event. Therefore, CPT includes specific modules to help the client analyze and modify problematic beliefs in these areas.

Treatment Program

CPT consists of 12 sessions. During the first 3 sessions, clients are given a description of the symptoms of PTSD and are presented with an explanation of information processing. (See Resick & Schnicke, in press, for wording that is used with clients.) The therapist describes how the client may assimilate (alter) schema-discrepant events rather than accommodate prior schemata to incorporate this new information. Clients are also told that while assimilation is more likely, it is also possible that they may have over-accommodated some schemata as a result of the incident ("I am never safe," "No man can be trusted"). The therapist also describes how prior beliefs (e.g., belief in a just world) may interfere with the processing of this schema-discrepant event. Because of conflicting beliefs or overwhelming emotions, memories that need to be integrated are avoided and interpretations about the event and oneself can become automatic and outside of awareness. Clients are taught to label four basic feelings (mad, sad, glad, and scared) and are asked to become aware of the connection between thoughts and feelings using A-B-C sheets (to monitor Activating events, Beliefs, and Consequences).

The goals of the next three sessions are to help the client accept the reality of the victimization and to begin to look for stuck points. After the therapist provides the rationale, the client is asked to write about the incident, including sensory details, thoughts, and feelings. The client is to move beyond the sterilized version usually recounted, which sounds more like an emotionless police report. At the next session, the client reads the account to the therapist and they discuss the client's feelings, then and now, as well as the client's thoughts. If the client fails to complete the assignment, she is asked to tell the therapist what she would have said if she had written it (no avoidance allowed). If the client stopped or skipped over part of the incident (e.g., ". . . and then he raped me. Afterwards . . ."), this is assumed to be a stuck point and the cognitions and accompanying emotions are elicited and discussed in great detail. The client is then asked to repeat the assignment in even greater detail. The client is given a list of questions to ask herself in order to begin confronting stuck points. Beck's faulty thinking patterns (e.g., jumping to conclusions, either/or thinking) are also introduced. These patterns are introduced in order to help the client to begin to recognize how she may have established patterns of responding that preclude accurate assessment of situations in which she finds herself.

At the seventh session, the client discusses relevant thinking patterns and continues to identify and question stuck points relevant to the crime. In order to facilitate cognitive restructuring, the client is given a set of more elaborate tracking sheets to help her confront and alter those cognitions that are maladaptive and to resolve conflicting beliefs and information. The worksheet used is adapted from Beck and Emery's (1985) book on cognitive treatment of anxiety. The first of the five themes, safety, is introduced and discussed with the client. The client is then asked to complete worksheets on the theme of safety as well as the stuck points already identified.

During the next four sessions, the other four themes are introduced: trust, power, esteem, and intimacy. The therapist helps the client to identify stuck points and negative beliefs pertaining to these themes and the worksheets are used to restructure beliefs. Beliefs that existed before the crime are examined, and if necessary, challenged, as well as those resulting from the crime. During the final session, all of the material is reviewed, progress in therapy is discussed, any remaining stuck points for the client to work on are identified, and future goals are established. A therapist manual is available for specific information on the exact implementation of CPT and results of treatment for 45 subjects (Resick & Schnicke, in press).

Case Studies

CPT was implemented with four female rape victims whose incidents occurred at least three months prior to beginning treatment. Prior to receiving therapy, the clients were interviewed about the assault and given the Structured Clinical Interview for DSM-III-R (SCID) in order to diagnose anxiety disorders, including PTSD, and mood disorders (Spitzer, Williams, & Gibbon, 1987). They were also asked to complete the SCL-90-R (Derogotis, 1977), the Impact of Event Scale (Horowitz,

Wilner, & Alvarez, 1979), the Beck Depression Inventory (Beck, Ward, Mendelson, Mock, & Erbaugh, 1961), and a self-report version of the PTSD Symptom Scale (Foa, Riggs, Dancu, & Rothbaum, in press). The SCL-90-R was scored to include the recently constructed PTSD scale by Saunders, Arata, and Kilpatrick (1990). All of the scales are used frequently in research on crime-related PTSD or depression.

Table 8.1 presents demographic information, some information about the crime, social support, prior criminal victimizations, and treatment sought following the rape, prior to seeking treatment with us. Two of the women had been raped less than one year prior to receiving treatment, one woman had been raped two years earlier, and one woman had been raped 13 years ago. Two of them had been raped twice before seeking treatment from us, while the other two had been raped once. They ranged in age from 20 to 31. Two of the women had histories of family abuse or domestic violence (client B reported a very extensive history of childhood abuse, including repeated sexual victimization by her father and severe physical abuse by both parents). The other two clients reported no childhood violence or adult domestic abuse.

Three of the clients were treated by a clinical psychology doctoral student under the author's supervision and one client was treated by the author. The therapy was conducted as described above in 12 sessions, which were spaced, as much as possible, 2 sessions per week for six weeks.

At the pretreatment assessment, all four of the women met DSM-III-R criteria for PTSD and three of them also met criteria for major depressive disorder. The scores on the self-report measures were comparable and elevated. As can be seen in Table 8.2, three of the women scored five standard deviations above the normative mean on overall distress (GSI) on the SCL-90-R, while one woman's scores were elevated two standard deviations above the normative mean.

At the post-treatment assessment none of the women met criteria for PTSD or major depression on the SCID interview, and their scores on the self-report scales had dropped considerably. On the SCL-90-R subscales, most of their scores were now within one standard deviation of the normative means. At the three-month follow-up, three of the women continued to maintain their improvement on the self-report scales and none of the four met criteria for PTSD or depression on the SCID interview. One woman, client B, exhibited some decrement in her improvement, but the scores had not returned to pretherapy levels. During CPT for the rape, it was clear that client B also had major trauma reactions regarding her abusive childhood. While dealing with the rape, memories and issues regarding her father kept emerging. After completion of CPT, she decided to receive therapy to deal with these issues. It is likely that some of the symptoms that were reported at the three-month follow-up were the result of emerging memories and reactions to childhood abuse.

At the six-month follow-up, the four women were functioning well. Client A was experiencing a slight increase in anxiety symptoms because she was about to be married the week after the six-month follow-up. Client B had shown some improvement over the three-month follow-up but had experienced some losses three weeks earlier. The therapist she had been seeing about her childhood issues moved away, and the same week her uncle died. The other two clients continued to do very well. Client C had to complete her assessment long-distance but wrote that she was in a dating relationship that had developed since she completed treatment.

Special Clinical Considerations for Various Types of Crime

Thus far, CPT has only been tested with rape victims (although we have been using it clinically with other crime victims). There is every reason to believe that CPT will be successful with other types of crime victims. Robbery victims suffering from PTSD have very similar reactions to those of rape victims (Resick, 1988). Kilpatrick, Resnick, and Amick (1989) found that homicide-victim families who continue to search for meaning are most likely to suffer from PTSD. This finding appears to indicate that a cognitive approach that helps the person reconcile the event and his or her beliefs should be beneficial with homicide survivors as well as rape victims.

Clinicians should be aware that particular types of crime are likely to produce specific issues or problems for victims. For example, rape victims are probably more likely to be subjected to blaming attitudes by others and, because of the sexual nature of the crime, they may be less able or willing to discuss some of the most important aspects of the trauma with their significant others. It is important for the therapist to correct or refute the negative statements made by others and to encourage the victims to remember and discuss the most sensitive parts of their experience. Women who have been raped are most likely to avoid recalling the details of the sexual part of the assault, particularly if it was bizarre or especially disgusting. It is important that the therapist not engage in complicity and inadvertently encourage this avoidance.

TABLE 8.1 Client Information on Four Rape Victims Receiving Cognitive Processing Therapy

Subject:	A	B	C	D
Demographics				
Age	31	31	23	20
Race	Caucasian	Hispanic	Caucasian	Caucasian
Marital status	Divorced	Divorced	Single	Single
Years school	14	11	14	14
Crime Information				
Number of rapes	2	1	1	2
Months since most recent	8	162	7	33
Number assailants	1	1	1	1
Relationship	Employer	Stranger	Friend	Date
Threatened?	Yes	Yes	Yes	No
Length of incident	2 hours	17 hours	1 hour	3 hours
Reported to police?	No	Yes	Yes	No
How long before told someone?	6 months	Within 1st hour	Within 1st hour	Within 24 hours
Social Support				
People talked to in first month	0	7	4	2
Reactions of important people	Positive	Positive/neutral	Positive	Positive
Reactions of others	Negative	Neutral	Positive	Positive
Overall quality	Very good	Mixed	Excellent	Mixed
Number people talked to regularly	16	2	25	6

Other Victimizations	Child abuse Sexual molestation Domestic violence Burglary	Child abuse Sexual molestation Domestic violence	No	No
Other Treatment Since Rape	Medication	Medication Therapy (25 sessions)	Therapy (2 sessions)	Therapy (5 sessions)

TABLE 8.2 Pretherapy, Posttherapy, and Three-Month Follow-Up Scores of Four Rape Victims Receiving Cognitive Processing Therapy

Subject:	A			B			C			D		
	Pre	Post	3-Month	Pre	Post	3-Month	Pre	Post	3-Month	Pre	Post	3-Month
SCL-90	t-score											
Somatization	95	46	51	97	51	69	55	51	41	75	59	51
Ob-Comp	106	46	55	104	52	77	77	52	50	97	59	57
Int-Sen	91	45	43	114	54	68	77	45	48	97	60	54
Depression	103	44	51	94	57	72	61	47	47	121	54	52
Anxiety	104	55	58	128	58	91	80	42	47	96	64	53
Hostility	76	43	47	72	47	43	93	55	55	55	47	47
Phobic	120	55	46	129	69	106	69	46	46	64	64	55
Paranoid	80	58	46	95	61	58	76	54	50	73	54	46
Psychoticism	104	44	44	92	60	56	56	44	44	108	56	44
PTSD	88	46	47	93	48	69	64	49	45	82	53	47
Global Severity Index	111	47	49	117	56	79	76	49	47	101	58	52
PTSD Scale Raw Scores												
Total	38	5	11	43	13	20	26	6	9	31	7	5
Reexperience	11	3	1	10	2	4	8	1	4	8	3	2
Avoidance	15	0	3	17	5	7	5	1	1	13	2	1
Arousal	12	2	7	16	6	9	13	4	4	10	2	2

IES												
Intrusion	33	3	5	37	13	25	21	13	7	19	5	5
Avoidance	28	5	0	23	12	15	22	12	7	21	8	5
BDI	19	1	5	33	14	17	15	8	10	33	0	3
SCID												
PTSD	Yes	No	No	Yes	No	No	Yes	No	No	Yes	No	No
Major Depression	Yes	No	No	Yes	No	No	No	No	No	Yes	No	No

While robbery, assault, and burglary victims may find it easier to discuss the incident with other people than rape victims, they may still be subjected to some prejudicial attitudes or insensitivity on the part of others. The label "victim" has a negative connotation that may elicit negative comments. Also, because people want to believe they are immune from such events, they typically look for reasons to blame the victim for having been the occasion for a crime. Furthermore, while the general public is becoming more aware of the trauma of rape, they are still rather uninformed that other types of crime may be traumatic to the victim. They are more likely to focus on what the assailant stole or whether he or she is being prosecuted than how the victim is reacting and recovering.

Homicide surviving family members have a double trauma reaction. They may have PTSD symptoms compounding their grief reactions. Because homicide is sudden and unexpected, as well as violent, the loved ones of victims often have additional difficulty in three areas. First, there is no time for them to repair the relationship with the loved one or to say good-bye. If family members had fought or had been estranged in some fashion, the survivors may experience great guilt that their family member died not knowing how much they were loved. Second, the family may also be haunted by images of the pain, suffering, or terror experienced by the victim as he or she died. Third, the event does not end with the death of their relative. It may be the beginning of a strange relationship with the assailant.

If someone is apprehended for the homicide, there is typically a lengthy period of time during which the family is involved with the media and the legal system. In states in which there is the death penalty, there may be numerous hearings and appeals. In other cases, the family may wish to appear at parole hearings. Their lives become inexorably bound to the life of the assailant in their pursuit for justice. Unfortunately, because the family has no official role in the criminal justice system, they are often thwarted in their efforts to find out about and participate in the process.

Finally, in the case of alcohol-related vehicular homicide, the chief frustration for family members is often the apparent lack of seriousness with which the criminal justice system seems to handle these cases. Family members are often furious because drunk drivers are frequently given little more than a "slap on the hand" while they are left to grieve the loss of a loved one.

These are all issues with which therapists should be prepared to deal, in working with family members of homicide victims. They are difficult issues with no easy answers. The profoundly distressing emotions of the survivors may not be based on distortions, which therapists are more accustomed to dealing with, but on uncomfortable realities that the survivors (and therapist) must learn to accept.

Child victims also suffer from PTSD following trauma (Goodwin, 1988; Kiser et al., 1988; McLeer, Deblinger, Atkins, Foa, & Ralphe, 1988; Wolfe, Gentile, & Wolfe, 1989). However, because of their limited cognitive development and verbal skills, it is frequently difficult for children to express their beliefs or symptoms in a direct manner. The reexperiencing symptoms of PTSD in children are often revealed through nightmares, play, or behavioral reenactments rather than through the intrusive cognitive symptoms that are typically reported by adults. The clinician must be sensitive to this possibility and listen and watch for any indications of behavioral reenactments.

It should be recognized that the children are often put in a no-win situation when they have been abused by parents. If they tell the non-offending parent (if there is one) and that parent believes them, these children may believe they have broken up the family and may, in fact, be told so by angry siblings, the assailant, or the other parent. If the parents do not believe them or minimize the impact, they have essentially lost a second parent.

Finally, it should be noted that children typically engage in either-or thinking because of their level of cognitive development. It is, thus, very difficult for children to integrate two opposing sets of memories, those of the perpetrator being loving and kind, and those of the perpetrator being abusive. They need a great deal of help in processing this seemingly discrepant information and in feeling their emotions about it. The children's ambivalence regarding their abusive parent may be difficult for others to understand and respond to appropriately. For further information please refer to Browne and Finkelhor (1986), Finkelhor and Browne (1985), and Lyons (1987).

Conclusion

While the literature on the treatment of crime victims is still in its infancy, the results thus far appear optimistic for successful recovery from these traumatic events. There have been reports of the success of stress inoculation and direct therapeutic exposure (Foa, Chapter 7 this volume; Foa, Rothbaum, Riggs, & Murdock, in press; Kilpatrick, Veronen,

& Resick, 1982; Resick, Jordan, Girelli, Hutter, & Marhoefer-Dvorak, 1988; Veronen & Kilpatrick, 1983), cognitive therapy (Frank et al., 1988), and now a combined exposure and cognitive therapy (CPT) for the treatment of crime victims. These initial efforts appear promising, but considerable work remains to be done in determining which treatment or combination of treatments will be most effective for various types of clients with different victimization histories. Therapy research thus far has only included rape victims. Integration of some of the special issues of crime victims that were discussed above will need to be addressed as these different types of crime victims become the focus of therapy outcome research.

References

Amick-McMullan, A., Kilpatrick, D. G., & Resnick, H. S. (1988, September). *Survivors of homicide victims: National prevalence and psychological adjustment.* Paper presented at the Fourth Annual Meeting of the Society for Traumatic Stress Studies, Dallas, TX.

Amick-McMullan, A., Kilpatrick, D. G., Saunders, B. E., & Resnick, H. S. (1988, April). *Indirect victims of homicide: An epidemiological study.* Paper presented at the 9th Annual Meeting of the Society of Behavioral Medicine, Boston.

Beck, A. T., & Emery, G. (1985). *Anxiety disorders and phobias: A cognitive perspective.* New York: Basic Books.

Beck, A. T., Rush, A. J., Shaw, B. F., & Emery, G. (1979). *Cognitive therapy of depression.* New York: Guilford.

Beck, A. T., Ward, C. H., Mendelson, M., Mock, J., & Erbaugh, J. (1961). An inventory for measuring depression. *Archives of General Psychiatry, 4,* 561-571.

Blanchard, E. B., Kolb, L. C., Pallmeyer, T. P., & Gerardi, R. J. (1982). A psychophysiological study of post traumatic stress disorder in Vietnam veterans. *Psychiatric Quarterly, 54,* 220-229.

Browne, A., & Finkelhor, D. (1986). Impact of child sexual abuse: A review of the research. *Psychological Bulletin, 99,* 66-77.

Calhoun, K. S., Atkeson, B. N., & Resick, P. A. (1982). A longitudinal examination of fear reactions in victims of rape. *Journal of Counseling Psychology, 29,* 655-661.

Chemtob, C., Roitblat, H. L., Hamada, R. S., Carlson, J. G., & Twentyman, C. T. (1988). A cognitive action theory of post-traumatic stress disorder. *Journal of Anxiety Disorders, 2,* 253-275.

Derogotis, L. R. (1977). *SCL-90-R: Administration, scoring, & procedures manual-II.* Towson, MD: Clinical Psychometric Research.

Finkelhor, D., & Browne, A. (1985). The traumatic impact of child sexual abuse: A conceptualization. *American Journal of Orthopsychiatry, 55,* 530-541.

Foa, E. (1990, March). *The development of post traumatic stress disorder and its treatment in rape victims.* Presented at XXII Banff International Conference, Banff, Alberta.

Foa, E. B., Riggs, D. S., Dancu, C. V., & Rothbaum, B. O. (in press). Reliability and validity of a brief instrument for assessing post-traumatic stress disorder. *Journal of Traumatic Stress.*

Foa, E. B., Rothbaum, B. O., Riggs, D. S., & Murdock, T. B. (in press). Treatment of PTSD in rape victims: A comparison between cognitive-behavioral procedures and counseling. *Journal of Consulting and Clinical Psychology.*

Foa, E. B., Steketee, G., & Olasov-Rothbaum, B. (1989). Behavioral/cognitive conceptualizations of post-traumatic stress disorder. *Behavior Therapy, 20,* 155-176.

Frank, E., Anderson, B., Stewart, B. D., Dancu, C., Hughes, C., & West, D. (1988). Efficacy of cognitive behavior therapy and systematic desensitization in the treatment of rape trauma. *Behavior Therapy, 19,* 403-420.

Goodwin, J. (1988). Post-traumatic symptoms in abused children. *Journal of Traumatic Stress, 1,* 475-488.

Hollon, S. D., & Garber, J. (1988). Cognitive therapy. In L. Y. Abramson (Ed.), *Social cognition and clinical psychology: A synthesis* (pp. 204-253). New York: Guilford.

Holmes, M. R., & St. Lawrence, J. (1983). Treatment of rape-induced trauma: Proposed behavioral conceptualization and review of the literature. *Clinical Psychology Review, 3,* 417-433.

Horowitz, M. D., Wilner, N., & Alvarez, W. (1979). Impact of event scale: A measure of subjective stress. *Psychosomatic Medicine, 41,* 209-218.

Jones, J. C., & Barlow, D. H. (1990). The etiology of posttraumatic stress disorder. *Clinical Psychology Review, 10,* 299-328.

Kilpatrick, D. G., Amick, A., & Resnick, H. S. (1988, September). *Preliminary research data on post traumatic stress disorder following murders and drunk driving crashes.* Paper presented at the 14th Annual Meeting of the National Organization for Victim Assistance, Tucson, AZ.

Kilpatrick, D. G., Resick, P. A., & Veronen, L. J. (1981). Effects of a rape experience: A longitudinal study. *Journal of Social Issues, 37,* 105-121.

Kilpatrick, D. G., Resnick, H. S., & Amick, A. (1989, August). *Family members of homicide victims: Search for meaning and post-traumatic stress disorder.* Presented at the 97th Annual Meeting of the American Psychological Association, New Orleans.

Kilpatrick, D. G., Saunders, B. E., Amick-McMullan, A., Best, C. L., Veronen, L. J., & Resnick, H. S. (1989). Victim and crime factors associated with the development of crime-related post-traumatic stress disorder. *Behavior Therapy, 20,* 199-214.

Kilpatrick, D. G., Saunders, B. E., Veronen, L. J., Best, C. L., & Von, J. M. (1987). Criminal victimization: Lifetime prevalence, reporting to police, and psychological impact. *Crime and Delinquency, 33,* 479-489.

Kilpatrick, D. G., Veronen, L. J., & Resick, P. A. (1982). Psychological sequelae to rape. In D. M. Doleys, R. L. Meredith, & A. R. Ciminero (Eds.), *Behavioral medicine: Assessment and treatment strategies* (pp. 473-497). New York: Plenum.

Kilpatrick, D. G., Veronen, L. J., Saunders, B. E., Best, C. L., Amick-McMullan, A., & Paduhovich, J. (1987, March). *The psychological impact of crime: A study of randomly surveyed crime victims (Final Report, Grant No. 84-IJ-CX-0039).* Washington, DC: National Institute of Justice.

Kiser, L. J., Ackerman, B. J., Brown, E., Edwards, N. B., McColgan, E., Pugh, R., & Pruitt, D. B. (1988). Post-traumatic stress disorder in young children: A reaction to purported sexual abuse. *Journal of the American Academy of Child and Adolescent Psychiatry, 27,* 645-649.

Litz, B. T., & Keane, T. M. (1989). Information processing in anxiety disorders: Application to the understanding of posttraumatic stress disorder. *Clinical Psychology Review, 9,* 243-257.

Lyons, J. A. (1987). Posttraumatic stress disorder in children and adolescents: A review of the literature. *Journal of Developmental and Behavioral Pediatrics, 8,* 349-356.

McCann, I. L., Sakheim, D. K., & Abrahamson, D. J. (1988). Trauma and victimization: A model of psychological adaptation. *The Counseling Psychologist, 16,* 531-594.

McLeer, S. V., Deblinger, E., Atkins, M. S., Foa, E. B., & Ralphe, D. L. (1988). Post-traumatic stress disorder in sexually abused children. *Journal of the American Academy of Child and Adolescent Psychiatry, 27,* 650-654.

McNally, R., Luedke, D. L., Besyner, J. K., Peterson, R. A., Bohm, K., Lips, O. J. (1987). Sensitivity to stress-relevant stimuli in posttraumatic stress disorder. *Journal of Anxiety Disorders, 1,* 105-116.

Pitman, R. K., Orr, S. P., Forgue, D. F., de Jong, J. B., & Claiborn, J. M. (1987). Psychophysiologic assessment of posttraumatic stress disorder imagery in Vietnam combat veterans. *Archives of General Psychiatry, 44,* 970-975.

Pitman, R. K., Orr, S. P., Forgue, D. F., Altman, B., de Jong, J. B., & Herz, L. R. (1990). Psychophysiologic responses to combat imagery of Vietnam veterans with posttraumatic stress disorder versus other anxiety disorders. *Journal of Abnormal Psychology, 99,* 49-54.

Resick, P. A. (1986). *Reactions of female and male victims of rape or robbery* (Final Report, Grant No. 85-IJ-CX-0042). Washington, DC: National Institute of Justice.

Resick, P. A., Jordan, C. G., Girelli, S. A., Hutter, C. H., Marhoefer-Dvorak, S. (1988). A comparative outcome study of behavioral group therapy for sexual assault victims. *Behavior Therapy, 19,* 385-401.

Resick, P. A., & Schnicke, M. K. (1990). Treating symptoms in adult victims of sexual assault. *Journal of Interpersonal Violence, 5,* 488-506.

Resick, P. A., & Schnicke, M. K. (in press). *Cognitive processing therapy for rape victims: A treatment manual.* Newbury Park, CA: Sage.

Saunders, B. E., Arata, C. M., & Kilpatrick, D. G. (1990). Development of a crime-related post-traumatic stress disorder scale for women within the Symptom Checklist-90-Revised. *Journal of Traumatic Stress, 3,* 439-448.

Spitzer, R. L., Williams, J. B. W., & Gibbon, M. (1987). *Structured clinical interview for DSM-III-R: Nonpatient version.* New York State Psychiatric Institute, Biometrics Research Department.

Steketee, G., & Foa, E. B. (1987). Rape victims: Post-traumatic stress responses and their treatment: A review of the literature. *Journal of Anxiety Disorders, 1,* 69-86.

Veronen, L. J., & Kilpatrick, D. G. (1983). Stress management for rape victims. In D. Meichenbaum & M. E. Jaremko (Eds.), *Stress reduction and prevention* (pp. 341-374). New York: Plenum.

Veronen, L. J., Kilpatrick, D. G., & Resick, P. A. (1979). Treating fear and anxiety in rape victims: Implications for the criminal justice system. In W. H. Parsonage (Ed.), *Perspectives on victimology* (pp. 148-159). Beverly Hills, CA: Sage.

Wolfe, V. V., Gentile, C., & Wolfe, D. A. (1989). The impact of sexual abuse on children: A PTSD formulation. *Behavior Therapy, 20,* 215-228.

9

Theoretical and Empirical Perspectives on the Etiology and Prevention of Wife Assault

DONALD G. DUTTON

One of the most serious forms of aggression between intimates is wife assault, which we define as any physical act of aggression by a man against a woman with whom he is in an intimate (i.e., sexual-emotional) relationship, regardless of whether they are actually married. While husband assault does exist, the effects of male violence are far more serious than those of female violence. Berk, Berk, Loseke, and Rauma (1981) analyzed 262 domestic disturbance incidents reported to police, using a scale of effects that ranked the severity of injuries sustained by the victim. When assaultive incidents are classified by injurious effects rather than by use of violence, women are the victims 94% of the time, compared to 14% for men. Berk et al. also report that data from the U.S. National Crime Survey, collected from a nationally representative sample of households, indicated that when victimization occurs between spouses, 95% of the time it is the woman who suffers.

Incidence of Wife Assault: The Magnitude of the Problem

Surveys of Incidence

Two U.S. national surveys (Straus, Gelles, & Steinmetz, 1980; Straus & Gelles, 1985), a study of the U.S. state of Kentucky (Schulman, 1979), and a survey of the Canadian province of Alberta (Kennedy & Dutton, 1989), used the Straus Conflict Tactics Scale (CTS; Straus, 1979) as a measure of the type of actions used to resolve family conflicts. The CTS asks respondents to list the frequency of discrete actions they have used in a dispute during the last year. This common measure enables some direct comparison between the surveys. Both the Straus et al. (1980; $n = 2,143$) and the Schulman (1979; $n = 1,793$) surveys use Straus's definition of *severe assault* as anything from item O on the CTS (kicked, bit, or hit you with a fist) to item S (used a knife or fired a gun), as shown in Table 9.1.

Using this definition, the victimization rates for husband-to-wife violence on the two surveys were 8.7% (Schulman) and 12.6% (Straus et al.). Using the more inclusive measure of any violent husband-to-wife acts (including slapping, pushing, and shoving), the rates were 21% (Schulman) and 27.8% (Straus et al.). These figures refer to the use of violence at any time in the marriage.

In 1985 Straus and Gelles conducted a second U.S. National Survey of family violence using the CTS. A national probability sample of 6,002 households was obtained through telephone interviews conducted by Louis Harris and Associates (Straus & Gelles, 1985). A subsample of 3,520 married/cohabiting couples was compared with Straus et al.'s 1975 sample. Husband-to-wife violence had declined between 1975 to 1985. Rates for assaultive behavior in the year preceding the survey on the Physical Violence Scale dropped from 12.1 to 11.3 (a 7% decrease) and rates on the Severe Violence Scale dropped from 3.8 to 3.0 (a decline of 21%). There was a slight (nonsignificant) increase in wife-to-husband violence. Kennedy and Dutton (1989) conducted a survey using the Conflict Tactics Scale in Alberta ($n = 1,045$). Respondents self-reported the use of conflict tactics by and against them during the year prior to the survey (1987). Wife assault

TABLE 9.1 Straus *Conflict Tactics Scale*

1. No matter how well a couple gets along, there are times when they disagree on major decisions, get annoyed about something the other person does, or just have spats or fights because they're in a bad mood or tired or for some other reasons. They also use different ways of trying to settle their differences. I'm going to read a list of some things that you and your (spouse/partner) might have done when you had a dispute, and would first like you to tell me for each one how often you did it in the past year.

| | You | | | | | | | Partner | | | | | |
Frequency of:	1	2	5	10	20	+20	Ever?	1	2	5	10	20	+20	Ever?
a. Discuss the issue calmly.	1	2	3	4	5	6	X	1	2	3	4	5	6	X
b. Got information to back up (your/his) side of things.	1	2	3	4	5	6	X	1	2	3	4	5	6	X
c. Brought in or tried to bring in someone to help settle things.	1	2	3	4	5	6	X	1	2	3	4	5	6	X
d. Argued heatedly but short of yelling.	1	2	3	4	5	6	X	1	2	3	4	5	6	X
e. Insulted, yelled, or swore at other one.	1	2	3	4	5	6	X	1	2	3	4	5	6	X
f. Sulked and/or refused to talk about it.	1	2	3	4	5	6	X	1	2	3	4	5	6	X
g. Stomped out of the room or house (or yard).	1	2	3	4	5	6	X	1	2	3	4	5	6	X
h. Cried.	1	2	3	4	5	6	X	1	2	3	4	5	6	X

	1	2	3	4	5	6	X		1	2	3	4	5	6	X
i. Did or said something to spite the other one.	1	2	3	4	5	6	X		1	2	3	4	5	6	X
j. Threatened to hit or throw something at the other one.	1	2	3	4	5	6	X		1	2	3	4	5	6	X
k. Threw or smashed or hit or kicked something.	1	2	3	4	5	6	X		1	2	3	4	5	6	X
l. Threw something at the other one.	1	2	3	4	5	6	X		1	2	3	4	5	6	X
m. Pushed, grabbed, or shoved the other one.	1	2	3	4	5	6	X		1	2	3	4	5	6	X
n. Slapped the other one.	1	2	3	4	5	6	X		1	2	3	4	5	6	X
o. Kicked, bit, or hit with a fist.	1	2	3	4	5	6	X		1	2	3	4	5	6	X
p. Hit or tried to hit with something.	1	2	3	4	5	6	X		1	2	3	4	5	6	X
q. Beat up the other one.	1	2	3	4	5	6	X		1	2	3	4	5	6	X
r. Threatened with a knife or gun.	1	2	3	4	5	6	X		1	2	3	4	5	6	X
s. Used knife or gun.	1	2	3	4	5	6	X		1	2	3	4	5	6	X
t. Other _____	1	2	3	4	5	6	X		1	2	3	4	5	6	X

rates were higher in urban settings (12.8%) than in rural settings (8.3%). Overall violence rates (of all self-reported aggressive acts) were virtually identical to those found in the Straus and Gelles 1985 U.S. survey. In the U.S. sample, 11.3% reported use of violence against wives, compared to 11.2% of the Canadian sample. However, use of severe violence was less in Canada (assuming Alberta to be representative of Canadian rates), with only 77% of the U.S. incidence rate reported.

When interpreting the findings of all these surveys it is important to view them in their social context. In North American culture, the assault of women by men, with its potentially serious consequences to the victim (see Kennedy & Dutton, 1989), is becoming increasingly negatively sanctioned by society. Male perpetrators and female victims may both underreport the incidence and negative effects of such violence (Frieze & Browne, 1989). In the case of male perpetrators this underreporting is probably due to guilt about the violence, while for the female victim it is more to avoid the stigma attached to being a "battered woman."

Explanations for Wife Assault

Sociological Explanations for Wife Assault

Sociological explanations for wife assault view it as a common event, generated by social rules that support male domination of women (Dobash & Dobash, 1978; Goode, 1971), and tacit approval by society (Straus, 1976, 1977a, 1977b, 1977c). Straus (1976) and Gelles (1972) suggest that wife assault is mainly normal violence committed by men who believe that patriarchy (any system in which the majority of upper positions in hierarchies are occupied by males) is their right, yet lack the resources to fulfill that role. As Dobash and Dobash (1979) put it, "Men who assault their wives are actually living up to cultural prescriptions that are cherished in Western society—aggressiveness, male dominance and female subordination—and they are using physical force as a means to enforce that dominance" (p. 24).

Little societal approval for wife assault still exists. A survey by Stark and McEvoy (1970) found that 24% of men and 17% of women approved of a man slapping his wife "under appropriate circumstances." This finding hardly seems to prove a cultural norm for the use of violence against wives. First of all, only a minority of men or women approved a man slapping his wife under any circumstances. Viewed from another perspective, the survey result tells us that the majority believe slapping is never appropriate. When we add the Stark and McEvoy survey of acceptance of wife assault to the incidence surveys reviewed above (which indicate that a small minority of men assault their wives), the case for wife assault being normative is weakened. Many men convicted of wife assault do not feel that what they did was acceptable. Instead they feel guilty, minimize the violence and try to exculpate themselves in the manner of one whose actions are unacceptable to oneself. The sociological view of violence as normal would lead us to expect the opposite: that no guilt would follow from "normal" behavior. Furthermore, an examination by Coleman and Straus (1986) of the relationship between family power dynamics and use of violence presents a much more complex picture than that implied by a simple patriarchal model.

Based on the U.S. national sample of 2,143 couples, Coleman and Straus found that 53% of couples had a form of power sharing, 29% described themselves as "equalitarian," 7% as female dominant, and 9% as male dominant. Levels of marital conflict were highest in these male dominant families when disagreement existed as to who should be in power. However, levels of marital violence were highest in female dominant/high conflict families. These results present a more complex picture than that suggested by a defense of patriarchy view.

Psychological Explanations for Wife Assault: Wife Assault in Non-Pathological Populations

Social learning theory views biological factors, observational learning, and reinforced performance as the main origins of aggressive behavior. Biological factors such as activity level, physical stature, and musculature "set limits on the type of aggressive responses that can be developed, influence the rate at which learning progresses" and "predispose individuals to perceive and learn critical features of their immediate environment" (Bandura, 1979, p. 201). Hence, from a social learning point of view, males may be biologically predisposed to act aggressively, since they inherit greater musculature than females. This musculature increases the probability that physically aggressive responses will produce their intended effect, thereby generating reward for the performer of the response.

Observational learning constitutes a major determinant of the acquisition of behaviors, allowing the individual to develop a conception of how an action is performed through attending to the modeled behavior, coding it into permanent symbolic modes, and integrating it through motor reproduction. Studies that indicate a higher likelihood of wife assault among males who had witnessed their mother being assaulted by their father provide data consistent with an observational acquisition of this behavior. Straus et al. (1980), for example, found that males who had observed parents attack each other were three times more likely to have assaulted their wives (35% of men who had seen this had hit their own wives in the year of the study, compared to 10.7% of men who had not witnessed such an event). Straus et al. conclude that the likelihood of violence toward spouses seems to rise fairly steadily with the amount of violence these people, as children, observed between their own parents.

Straus et al. argue that the family of origin is the place where people first experience violence and learn its emotional and moral meaning. For most, this experience occurs by being a victim of violence, for others it is the observation of parental violence. Being hit as a teenager clearly makes people more prone to spouse-assault: People who experienced the most punishment as teenagers had spouse-beating rates four times greater than those whose parents did not hit them.

Kalmuss (1984) analyzed data from the 1975 U.S. National Survey and concluded that both observation of, and victimization by, assault in the family of origin were related to use of aggression as an adult (by both males and females). Kalmuss established that 15.8% of respondents had witnessed parental hitting, and 62.4% had themselves been hit by parents while in their teens. By correlating these responses with CTS scores for their adult relationships, Kalmuss found that witnessing fathers hitting mothers increased the likelihood of both husband-to-wife and wife-to-husband aggression in the next generation. Both sons and daughters were more likely to be victims and/or perpetrators of violence when they had witnessed parental hitting, regardless of which parent was the aggressor. While witnessing parental hitting and being hit as a teenager are both related to severe husband-to-wife and wife-to-husband aggression, the stronger effect comes from observing parental hitting (which doubles the odds of husband-wife violence).

Kalmuss concluded that two types of modeling occur for parental aggression. Generalized modeling communicates the acceptability of aggression between family members and increases the likelihood of any form of family aggression in the next generation. Specific modeling occurs when individuals reproduce the particular types of family aggression to which they were exposed. Although specific modeling occurred in Kalmuss's study, sex-specific modeling did not.

Social learning theory emphasizes symbolic modeling as an important source of response acquisition. Hence, any new behaviors introduced by salient examples of a response (e.g., television portrayals of the "macho" use of violence, use of stereotyped responses to conflict situations) would also contribute to a generalized, adopted role that integrated such responses.

Reinforced Performance

Although the likelihood of wife assault increases with witnessing parental violence, the majority of wife assaulters never witnessed such violence, suggesting that learning may have occurred from another source, from their own experience, or from some blend of the two. Kalmuss and Seltzer (1986) examined continuity in the use of violence across relationships and concluded that a repertoire of aggressive behaviors was not necessarily related to family of origin learning, but frequently developed in a first marriage and was maintained across subsequent relationships.

For an acquired response pattern to be enacted by an individual it must have functional value for them and be either rewarded or, at least, not punished. The enactment of an acquired behavior such as wife assault depends then on: (1) appropriate inducements, (2) functional value, and (3) reward or absence of punishment for performance (Bandura, 1979). An appropriate inducement for wife assault, from the perspective of the assaulter, might be a statement or action by his wife that challenges his authority. The functional value would be the utility and meaning that an individual ascribes to using violence to restore that authority. Reward might include termination of an aversive stimulus (his wife's insubordinate statements or actions). Punishments could include anything from police intervention, to his wife leaving him, to feelings of guilt for his violence. If these punishments are absent, reenactment becomes more likely.

In other words, wife assaulters could learn to use physical aggression in an auto-didactic fashion. The behaviors involved (e.g., punching, shoving) are not complex and, as Bandura points out, have been universally modeled. If a male uses these behaviors against his wife and is rewarded through: (1) regaining control or dominance; (2) feeling expressive or agentic (i.e., acting out and taking charge in a male sex-role consonant fashion [Novaco, 1976]); and/or (3) terminating an aversive state of arousal or upset, and if he is not punished for using violence, the likelihood increases that he will use these actions again in a similar future conflict situation.

Instigators of Wife Assault

Social learning theory holds that acquired behaviors will not be demonstrated unless an appropriate stimulus or "instigator" exists in the contemporary environment. Aversive instigators include the perceptions that the male is "losing" an argument (or symbolic power struggle) to his wife. The arousal generated by aversive stimulation has both a physiological and an experiential component to it. The emotional consequence of such arousal depends, however, on a cognitive appraisal of the instigator and the situation (Hunt, Cole, & Reis, 1958; Schachter & Singer, 1962; Mandler, 1975).

Social learning theory has not placed great emphasis on the role of affect or emotion. It views anger arousal as facilitative rather than necessary for aggression. The arousal itself has a cognitive basis (the appraisal of the situation) and its relationship to aggression also has a cognitive component (based in part on the anticipated consequences of aggressive behavior).

Novaco (1976) describes how the expression of anger has several built-in reward functions: it can be energizing, expressive, lead to feelings of potency, determination, short-cut feelings of vulnerability, generate a sense of personal control, and so on. Many of these functions are shaped by male sex role expectations of agency (taking action). In primary relationships, sex role expectations may also define limits of acceptable male-female behavior by determining expectations of power, dominance, and the mode of conflict expression. Female behavior that exceeds those limits may be viewed as aversive. Hence, both perceived aversiveness and consequent anger expression may be shaped by sex role expectations.

Social learning theory has examined physical assaults, verbal threats and insults, and adverse reductions in the conditions of life, as three types of stimuli that produce aversive arousal. Clinical reports of wife assaulters rarely cite physical attack by a woman as an instigator for assault, although verbal threat, challenge to authority, and feelings of humiliation are frequent. As with the population of assault-prone individuals studied by Toch (1969), high sensitivity to perceived devaluation and deficient verbal skills for dispute resolution (and to restore self-esteem) may characterize wife assaulters. Below we will consider a special case of aversive stimulus that seems especially powerful in the etiology of wife assault: the perception by the male that he is losing control over the degree of intimacy or social-emotional distance in the relationship.

Regulators of Assaultive Behavior

About two thirds of males who commit wife assault once, repeat within a year (Schulman, 1979; Straus et al., 1980). It is these repeatedly assaultive males who constitute the most serious risk for injury to their wives. Bandura (1979) describes a variety of regulators that sustain or inhibit aggression. These include intermittent reinforcement (Walters & Brown, 1963) that functions to make aggression especially persistent, and the presence or absence of internal and external punishment.

Intermittent Reinforcement

In the case of wife assault, when aggression serves to regain control for the male in a male-female conflict, thereby reducing aversive arousal, reinforcement occurs.

Vivian and O'Leary (1987) established that couple communication patterns used early in the marriage predicted later use of violence, with reciprocity of negative affect characterizing the aggressive group. Murphy and O'Leary (1987) studied a subset of this longitudinal sample who were nonviolent during the year prior to marriage. They found that elevated verbal aggression characterized spouses who later reported physical aggression. Marital discord did not predict later physical aggression. The authors speculate that the escalation from verbal to physical aggression may occur because verbal aggression initially succeeds at signaling an end to the conflict, but later loses this functional value as one partner habituates to the outbursts of the other. At this point in the relationship, physical aggression appropriates the function of reducing aversive conflict-based arousal for the conflicted couple (presumably by ending the conflict).

In cases where the preassault conflict tactics used were essentially verbal and the male escalated to physical tactics because he perceived himself to be losing the verbal battle, the physical tactics put a stop to the dispute (in the male's favor) and thus his actions were reinforced. Social learning theory argues that when this outcome (favorable to the male) occurs intermittently, violent behavior will be strongly reinforced. However, even if this outcome does not occur, the feelings of agency associated with anger expression would still have reinforcement value. Hence, from a social learning perspective, wife assault would tend to be a repeated action because of the variety of sources of reward associated with it. Only expectations of punishment would serve to stop the behavior once initiated.

Punishing Consequences

External Punishment

Bandura (1979) concludes that for external punishment to be effective, a variety of factors must be considered. When alternative means of obtaining the goal are available and the risk of punishment is high, aggression decreases rapidly. However, when aggression is rewarded or alternative means of obtaining these rewards are not available, punishment must be forceful and consistent to suppress aggression. Even when this is so, control is only temporary, and functional aggression (i.e., aggression that obtains rewards) recurs when threats are removed and when the probability of punishment is low.

These results have implications for the regulation of wife assault where external punishment for assault could, in theory, be applied by the wife-victim (by leaving or threatening to leave the relationship), by a friendship or kinship group, or by the criminal justice system. In practice, however, the wife-victim may not have sufficient power or resources to punish the aggressor, informal kin groups may not have knowledge of the assault or may be unwilling to interfere, and criminal justice punishment for wife assault is rare (Dutton, 1987). In any event, Bandura's conclusions suggest that for future assault frequency to diminish, alternative means of obtaining a goal (obtained via assault) must be developed. These "means" are typically one objective of treatment groups for wife assaulters that seek to: (1) alter unrealistic male expectations about their wives, (2) improve assertive communications as a means of nonviolent conflict resolution, and (3) improve the male's empathy for his victim and build in processes of self-punishment for aggression.

Internal Punishment

Self-regulatory mechanisms such as self-punishment imply that people respond not only to external consequences of their behavior but to internal reactions as well. With regard to wife assault, there is tremendous variation in self-regulation among males. Walker (1979) describes a cycle of violence in which assaultive males go through a phase of guilt and contrition about their violence, indicated by exaggerated positive responding to their wives. Within a Canadian sample of wife assaulters, Dutton (1986a) found great variation in the men's cognitive processing of their assaultive behavior. Therapy with wife assaulters reflects this variation: some men are court-mandated to treatment and believe their conviction was unjust and their violence justified, others enter treatment filled with self-recrimination.

While there are differing opinions about the propriety of assaultive behavior among wife assaulters (Dutton, 1986a), Bandura's theory suggests that wife assault could have two generally different etiologies. It could occur because some men simply view it as acceptable behavior, obtaining rewards from its use by dominating their partner and feeling personal pride in their use of violence. Sociological theories suggesting wife assault had normative support would favor this etiology (e.g., Dobash & Dobash, 1979). Alternatively, it could occur because some men who have socialized constraints against the use of violence toward their wife choose to violate their own self-constraints because of high arousal, anxiety about relinquishing control to their wife, and the perceived seriousness of the conflict issue. As Bandura (1979) puts it, moral (i.e., normally socialized) people perform culpable acts through processes that disengage evaluative self-reactions from such conduct, rather than through defects in the development or the structure of their conscience.

Neutralization of Self-Punishment

When people violate their own self-standards, a variety of cognitive processes may result to keep negative self-evaluation (and consequent guilt) from becoming too salient. Self-deterring consequences are activated most strongly when the causal connection between conduct and the detrimental effects it produces are unambiguous (Bandura, 1979). To dissociate consequences from behavior, one can cognitively restructure: (1) the behavior through moral justification, palliative comparison or euphemistic labeling; (2) the behavior-effect relationship by displacing responsibility; (3) the detrimental effects by minimizing or ignoring the consequences for the victim; or (4) the victim through blaming her for the violence.

In the case of wife assault, some form of all these cognitive restructurings appears to occur for assaultive males. Treatment manuals (Ganley,

1981; Sonkin & Durphy, 1982) provide explicit directions for therapists to confront clients' use of each of the forms of neutralization of self-punishment described above. Men in treatment for wife assault will frequently cognitively restructure their behavior so that it is described as being less violent than it actually was. Browning and Dutton (1986) obtained Straus CTS ratings from husbands and wives in 30 couples where the man had been convicted of wife assault. Men reported less than half the frequency or severity of violence as their wives reported them committing. Men's recall and reporting of their own violence was frequently at odds with reports of police and hospital emergency room reports of women's injuries. Euphemistic labeling typically occurs through describing a serious assault in nonserious terms (i.e., "the night we had our little problem . . . you know, when I pushed her."). Palliative comparison in treatment groups is also frequent. Some convicted wife assaulters will volunteer the observation that all men beat their wives and only they themselves had the misfortune to get caught. Others will "downward compare" with a more violent member of their treatment group. Moral justification takes the form that their wife's nagging, suspected infidelity, or other unacceptable behavior needed to be brought into line.

The causal connection between their own actions and the injurious consequences to their victim is obscured by displacing responsibility. Some therapists feel that assaultive men sometimes get drunk in order to get violent. Alcohol is involved in 30%-56% of domestic dispute calls attended by police, but in only 10% of cases did the complainant allege that their spouse was drunk (Bard & Zacker, 1974).

The seriousness of injuries and psychological trauma to the victim are frequently overlooked as well, so that the consequences of the assault are restructured by the assaulter. His action is rendered less reprehensible by denying to himself that it caused pain and distress for his victim.

Finally, the victim is frequently blamed as being the cause of the man's violence through her own actions. Ganley and Harris (1978), Walker (1979), and Dutton and Painter (1980) all report the excessive minimizing of personal responsibility for the wife assault that goes on during the first month of therapy with assaultive males. Often this is accompanied by fixating on some aspect of the wife's behavior, real or imagined, that is described by the batterer as having "caused" his violence. A major objective of treatment is to confront and alter these forms of neutralization of self-punishment.

Pathways From Social Structure to Aggression

We will now consider specific factors related to the etiology of wife assault and to social learning theory and review associated empirical research.

Attitudes

Sex-role expectations may shape both the male's perceptions of aversive circumstances (especially around issues of female independence and household responsibilities) and his acceptable mode of affective response. Although a number of empirical studies have found that men who assault their wives do not have more negative attitudes toward women, nor more traditional sex role attitudes, than do non-assaultive controls (Browning, 1983; Neidig, Friedman, & Collins, 1986; Saunders, Lynch, Grayson, & Linz, 1987), strong demand characteristics that cue wife assaulters to socially acceptable responses may be present in research where subjects know they are being studied because of their violent behavior (Dutton & Strachan, 1987). Dutton and Strachan recommend examining less reactive factors, such as motives, rather than attitudes that might be transparently connected to assault.

Power and Intimacy in Male-Female Conflict

Of potentially greater importance than attitudes in shaping both anger and violence toward women are deeper emotional responses to control over emotional distance in intimate relationships. A special category of "aversive instigator" seems to exist for wife assaulters whose violence is relationship specific; these men appear to react with exaggerated arousal and anger to perceptions that the degree of socioemotional distance (or intimacy) between them and their wife is changing uncontrollably. These men also appear to have strong motives to generate control in intimate relationships (Dutton & Strachan, 1987), and poor verbal skills to do so. Consistent with this view is the finding by Coleman and Straus (1986) that wife assault is highest in female-dominant couples (as measured by the Blood & Wolfe [1960] Decision Power Index, which assesses who has the "final say" in major decisions made by the couple). One theoretical explanation for this finding is that this aggression is initiated by males who feel frustrated by their inability to command dyadic power (and feel that they should command such power).

Intimacy anxiety may have both trait and state properties. The latter involves increases in anxiety in response to sudden uncontrollable changes in the socioemotional distance between spouses. This distance is assumed to be negotiated by both parties to a point that represents an optimal zone. An optimal zone for each person is that degree of emotional closeness or distance between themselves and their partner with which they feel comfortable at any given time. This comfort zone may be similar to optimal zones for interpersonal spacing (cf. Patterson, 1976) in that, as with interpersonal spacing zones, invasions (too much intimacy) or evasions (too little) may produce physiological arousal. Clinical reports (e.g., Ganley, 1981; Gondolf, 1985) suggest that assaultive males tend to label such arousal as anger.

Socioemotional distance can serve as a unifying concept to link reports of wife assault occurring in response to ostensibly opposite instigators such as increases and decreases in intimacy. Intimacy issues can relate to engulfment (e.g., the female moving emotionally toward the male through increased demands for closeness, attention, and affection; the female remaining static and the male developing an increased need for greater distance than currently provided; or shifts in formal role demands such as marriage or fatherhood) or to abandonment (e.g., sexual threat or any other instance of the female moving emotionally further away or reinvesting her energy outside the primary relationship; or the male developing an increased need for intimacy but not successfully expressing it so that a "stationary" female stays at a previously optimal distance that is now too far away. Gelles (1975) and Rounsaville (1978) report that for 40% of repeatedly assaulted wives, the onset of assault coincided with a sudden transition in intimacy such as marriage or pregnancy. The consensus clinical report (Ganley & Harris, 1978; Walker, 1979) is that for assaultive males, the psychological and behavioral result of perceived loss of the female produces arousal, which in turn produces panic, anger, and hysterical aggression.

Arousal, Anger, and Aggression

While arousal may be viewed clinically as a component of state anxiety, a variety of mechanisms operate to induce males to experience the arousal as anger (Novaco, 1976; Dutton, Fehr, & McEwan, 1982). Male sex role socialization is more compatible with expressions of anger than fear (Fasteau, 1974; Pleck, 1981; Gondolf, 1985). Feelings of agency, potency, expressiveness, and determination accompany the expression of anger (but not fear) (Novaco, 1976). Dutton and Aron (1989) found that males viewing interpersonal conflict scenarios demonstrated significant positive correlations between self-reports of arousal and anger. Females demonstrated significant positive correlations between arousal and anxiety. This finding is consistent with clinical reports that assaultive males tend to label many forms of emotional arousal as anger (Ganley, 1980; Gondolf, 1985).

Hence, one way that social role expectations may influence violence toward women is through shaping the interpretation of arousal states in males produced by loss of control over intimacy with their wives. If a man perceives his wife to be increasing or decreasing socioemotional distance beyond an optimal zone, and does not have the verbal skills to restore equilibrium, aversive arousal would ensue. Male sex role socialization would increase the probability of that arousal being "felt" as anger (Pleck, 1981; Gondolf, 1985). With men who have developed verbal modes of expression for anger, that expression would serve to reduce anxiety, enhance feelings of power, and so on. However, with men in whom this repertoire was not developed, or where violent aggression had been rewarded in the past, violence would be a more likely response to this aversive arousal.

Therapists working with wife assaulters describe the men as engaging in cognitive processes that are consistent with this aggression model. Ganley (1981), for example, describes wife assaulters as personalizing disagreements with their wife so the conflict is viewed as intentional (i.e., as an intentional personal attack on them). Ganley also describes the tendency wife assaulters have to express a wide range of emotions as anger. As a result, emotional states other than anger can also lead to assault. Gondolf (1985) describes the "male emotional funnel system" whereby a wide range of arousal producing emotions are experienced as anger.

Empirical Studies

Browning (1983) and Dutton and Browning (1988) systematized the material revealed by assaultive males during group therapy sessions into testable hypotheses and then developed tests of these hypotheses. They created videotapes of male-female conflict varying in power (either the male or the female was depicted as more verbal, winning the argument, having the last word, etc.) and intimacy (where the woman was depicted as wanting greater or less intimacy than the male). In one scenario the conflict was not an intimacy issue. Men with a history of wife assault reported the highest amounts of anger while watching these scenarios (compared to men who were maritally conflicted but not assaultive and satisfactorily married men); the anger ratings were highest in the scenario where the woman was attempting to increase her independence and was depicted as verbally superior to the male. As Rosenbaum and O'Leary (1981), Maiuro, Cahn, Vitaliano, and Zegree (1986), and Dutton and Strachan (1987) all found wife assaulters to have deficits in verbal assertiveness with their spouses, it is hypothesized that higher anger would be associated with a higher likelihood of the use of violence to resolve conflict.

A subsequent study using the same technique (Dutton, 1988a) demonstrates that wife assaulters also differ on anger scores from men who are generally assaultive. Obviously, not all wife assaulters are angered by the same issues (or instigators) with their wives, but this line of research indicates that a theme underlying disparate issues is the male's perceived loss of control that results in a sense of emotional vulnerability. The ensuing anger serves a defensive function that overrides the unacceptable feelings of vulnerability, allowing him to act in a sex-role consonant fashion, and may intermittently succeed in restoring control of the situation (cf. Novaco, 1976; Tavris, 1984). These powerful reinforcers serve to establish habits of violence that in most normally socialized men create feelings of guilt or uneasiness.

Dutton (1986a) found that these feelings were mitigated by cognitive distortions of the causes for the assaultive behavior and its consequences. In coding wife assaulters' free descriptions of their assault, Dutton found that they fell into three patterns of justification. Group 1 (33% of the sample) attributed their actions to provocations by the victim, essentially avoiding responsibility for the assault. Group 2 (27%) accepted responsibility but minimized the frequency and severity of their actions and the severity of consequences for the victim. A third group (40%) attributed the assault to some aspect of themselves (a drinking problem, a bad temper, etc.) and did not minimize the actions or their consequences.

Since this approach is limited to post hoc comparison of known wife assaulters with control subjects, it is not known whether heightened anger responses to perceived uncontrollable female independence is a causative factor of wife assault or a reaction to the recent stress (both relationship and from the criminal justice system) in these men's lives.

Situational Determinants of Severe Wife Assault: Deindividuated Violence

Dutton et al. (1982) and Dutton (1988a) have argued that severe forms of wife assault (often termed *battering*) constitute examples of what Zimbardo (1969) has called "deindividuated violence" where normal constraints do not operate and the aggressor launches into a self-reinforced series of progressively more destructive actions that are extremely difficult to terminate. Furthermore, the batterer demonstrates an inability to recall the actual assaultive incident, even after shame and embarrassment about reporting it have subsided. Reconstruction of the assaultive incident from interviews with the wife, and from police and medical testimony, depict the male as being in a highly aroused state of rage, unresponsive to begging or pleading from the victim and, in some cases, beating her until he is too exhausted to continue. The men usually remember the events leading up to the actual battering and the aftermath (some were shocked and sickened by what they had done), but not the intervening battering.

The descriptions of acute battering incidents provided by interviews with victims appear to fit Zimbardo's (1969) analysis of deindividuated aggression. Furthermore, several of the antecedent conditions that Zimbardo postulates as increasing the likelihood of deindividuated violence are present in severe wife battering: anonymity, diminished personal responsibility, generalized arousal, and altered states of consciousness.

Anonymity is a central input variable discussed by Zimbardo, the effect of which is to reduce social control simply because an anonymous individual cannot be identified for reprisal or sanction. While wife battering usually occurs in the home where, in one sense, the batterer should feel most connected to symbols of his identity, it is in this place that the batterer is most freed from public scrutiny and surveillance. In many jurisdictions, policy, attitudes, and beliefs make police less than eager to respond to family dispute calls (Levens & Dutton, 1977; Dutton, 1977; Loving & Farmer, 1980). Furthermore, public attitudes about the privacy of the family (see, for example, Steiner, 1981), and the victim's own shame that often precludes her reporting the assault (Dutton & Painter, 1980, 1981), may contribute to a wife assaulter's feeling of anonymity with respect to this particular offense. Furthermore, Belsky (1980) reports that isolation of a family (absence of informal support networks) is associated with the incidence of assault, and isolation also contributes to anonymity since, by definition, it connotes an absence of others who might make norms salient, judge, and "individuate" the batterer. Diminished personal responsibility is created by the tendency of batterers to blame their wife or other external circumstances for their behavior through the process described above as neutralization of self-punishment. High arousal seems to be frequently generated in intimate conflict. As we shall see below, a combination of high anxiety, anger, and arousal was the prominent reaction of assaultive males viewing intimate conflict scenes (Dutton & Browning, 1988). Finally, altered consciousness, described as "red outs" by assaultive males, seems to occur frequently during extreme rage states.

In other words, all the central features of deindividuated aggression exist during battering incidents. Deindividuation might explain another feature of extreme aggression: the perpetrator's inability to recall the violence might be explicable by the shift in control over his behavior from external, environmental stimuli to internal, proprioceptive (physical) stimuli. With the exception of being able to locate and direct violence toward the victim, an individual in a deindividuated state is attuned to stimuli from within. What has not been stored in memory cannot be retrieved, hence the persistent inability to remember external details of the battering incident.

Personality Contributors to Assaultiveness: Post-Traumatic Stress, Borderline Personality, and Wife Assault

Some recent reviews of the long-term effects of childhood trauma in the family of origin suggest that clinical descriptions of the borderline personality disorder are remarkably similar to descriptions of patients who have been traumatized over periods of time (van der Kolk, 1987). One of the major contributions of studies of assaultive males based on wives' reports has been the attention they have paid to assessing reported trauma in the family backgrounds of the men. The descriptions of their partners given by women in shelters suggest a composite profile of men who were traumatized by abuse in their family of origin, are generally violent, and have substance abuse problems and a high incidence of personality disorders (cf. Saunders, 1987). This composite is consistent with current studies of long-term sequelae of early abuse in male populations (van der Kolk, 1987).

These individuals' affective problems appear as numbing and constriction occasionally described as alexithymia (or the inability to recognize and make use of emotional reactions), followed by hyperarousal and aggressive outbursts. The form of the aggression seems to be influenced by sex-roles: abused boys tend to identify with the aggressor and subsequently act out; females turn more to self-destructive acts (Carmen, Reiker, & Mills, 1984).

As do persons diagnosed as having borderline personalities, trauma victims have exaggerated separation anxiety, problems with regulation of affect and impulse control, an intense dependency on primary interpersonal relationships, and an inability to tolerate being alone. van der Kolk (1987) hypothesizes that childhood trauma may play a significant role in the development of borderline personality disorder.

Clinical and research descriptions of wife assaulters clearly share many of the characteristics attributed to trauma victims. Wife assaulters have been described as poor monitors of affect (Ganley, 1981; Gondolf, 1985) and as suffering from problems with impulse control, exaggerated dependency, and extreme jealousy or "conjugal paranoia" (Dutton & Browning, 1988; Ganley, 1981). As discussed above, it is clear from survey studies (e.g., Kalmuss, 1984) and from the profile of men described by battered women (Hilberman & Munson, 1978; Walker, 1984) that a substantial subgroup of wife assaulters have themselves been victimized by physical abuse in their family of origin. At present, it is not known whether modeling factors per se or a delayed trauma response might mediate the transformation from victim to perpetrator.

The Criminal Justice Response to Wife Assault

Dutton (1987) calculated that only 6.5% of wife assaults are reported to police and only 0.38% of assaultive males are punished with jail or a fine for a first offence. The main impediment to a more comprehensive handling of wife assault by the criminal justice system is the tendency of victims to view the assault in noncriminal terms. When we examine surveys on family conflict (e.g., Schulman, 1979; Straus, Gelles, & Steinmetz, 1980; Straus & Gelles, 1985), we see that the tendency to report potentially arrestible assaults is low: Schulman found a 17% report rate for Severe Aggression items on the CTS and Straus found a 10% report rate in his 1985 national survey (Straus, personal communication, 1986). When assaults are reported and the police arrest, assaultive behavior is reduced temporarily (Dutton, 1988a; Dutton, Hart, Kennedy, & Williams, 1992).

Jaffe, Wolfe, Telford, and Austin (1986) examined police records and conducted interviews with partners of men arrested for wife assault. Their interviews included CTS assessments of the men's use of violence for a one-year period prior to and following arrest. When police charged a man for wife assault, significant decreases in postcharge violence occurred, whether measured by the number of new contacts he had with police in the ensuing year, or by his wife's report of his use of violence using the CTS. Specific violent acts against wives were reduced by two thirds for the year following arrest compared to the year preceding arrest.

Sherman and Berk (1984) randomly assigned 314 cases of misdemeanor wife assault attended by the Minneapolis police to treatments of arrest, separation, or mediation. The recidivism of arrested men was significantly lower during the next six-month period (13% repeated assault on police reports, 19% repeated assault based on interviews with wives) than men who received other resolution treatments for a six-month period following the event. Corresponding recidivism rates for separation and mediation were 26% (28%) and 18% (37%) for police and wives' reports, respectively.

Dutton et al. (1992) argued that the reduction in recidivism for the arrested group in the Sherman and Berk study was not necessarily due to criminal justice system deterrence but may also have been due to informal sanctions that spin off from arrest. They traced 60 men who had entered a treatment group for wife assaulters three months after arrest and found that these men reported decreased power relative to their wife after arrest (their wives corroborated this finding). Power equalization can also decrease assaultiveness in a relationship (Fagan, 1987).[1] In addition, both the perpetrators and their wives disclosed the assault to more people when an arrest was made (compared to a prior equally serious assault). Disclosure can serve to diminish the isolation that keeps battered women in the relationship and can serve a corrective feedback function for the man (Dutton, 1988a). Hence, factors other than criminal justice system deterrence also are contributors to deterrence. Arrest per se may have only short-term "deterrence" value. Sherman and Berk's follow-up period showed a recidivism rate of 13% for six months after arrest. A treatment evaluation study by Dutton (1986b) found a 16% recidivism rate for arrested men after six months; in the absence of treatment, the rate increased to 40% after 2.5 years (see below for a discussion of recidivism rates with treatment).

Treatment for Wife Assault

At present a variety of court-mandated treatment groups have been developed based on social learning notions of development and maintenance of aggressive behavior patterns (Bandura, 1979). While arrest may challenge some of the regulating mechanisms of self-justification, they are further confronted through court-mandated treatment. To the extent that a wife assaulter believes that: (1) his wife's injuries were minimal; or (2) she was to blame for the conflict; or (3) his use of violence was justified, his ability to neutralize self-punishment is reduced and his habit of violence is sustained.

Another objective of treatment is to enable wife assaulters to improve their ability to detect the warning signs of their own violence (e.g., increased arousal, anger) and to develop a more elaborate set of behaviors for managing previously violence-evoking situations. The empirical question for such treatment is whether these improved cognitive and behavioral abilities, when linked with the belief that future assault will lead to punishment, can decrease recidivism for a treatment population.

Descriptions of therapy with assaultive males (e.g., Ganley, 1981; Gondolf, 1985; Sonkin, Martin, & Walker, 1985; Dutton & McGregor, 1991) outline the variety of techniques that are used in treatment groups to generate the learning of new perceptions and behaviors. These include having the men keep "anger diaries" in which they log the instigators (i.e., events that made them angry), an analysis of the violent event in the group, a discussion of emotional reactions to specific behaviors of others (empathy building), and relaxation exercises while imagining anger-provoking situations. While the emphasis and form of these practices may vary from group to group, the objective they serve remains constant: they demonstrate to the clients how their use of violence is a learned behavior sustained by their own perceptions. This presents the possibility of learning alternative behaviors with less destructive consequences. Many men come to treatment for assaultive behavior with the belief that their violence is "hard wired" or immutable. Having a therapist confront their interpretation of their wife's motives, their denial of emotions other than anger, and their refusal to use other behaviors to express anger, gradually develops their perception that alternatives to violence are possible.

Clinical descriptions of men who are directed by the courts for such treatment (Ganley, 1981; Sonkin et al., 1985) underscore the need for highly structured, confrontative techniques. These men are described as cognitively rigid and unassertive, with strong tendencies to external-ize blame for their behavior. They rarely have experience in psycholog-ical treatment groups (unless involved in alcohol treatment programs) and typically have had little interest in considering the possibility of self-change. Hence, highly directive treatment and the provision of motivation-builders are required. Since many court-directed treatment programs are short term in nature (i.e., 3-6 months), therapeutic prior-ities must be selected carefully.

Treatment Groups for Wife Assaulters

The development of treatment groups to work specifically with wife assaulters was pioneered by Anne Ganley (Ganley & Harris, 1978; Ganley, 1981). Ganley developed her treatment program from a social learning orientation, focusing on poor conflict resolution skills learned by wife assaulters in their family of origin. With these individuals, violence was often the only means of dealing with conflict-generated anger, listening skills were poor, verbal problem-solving skills were poor, and emotional self-disclosure was equated with loss of control. As a step toward rectifying these deficits, Ganley included assertive-ness training as part of her treatment model.

Ganley viewed battering as a learned tension-reducing response that occurred in the family setting because that was the safest place to aggress without punishment and because batterers had stereotyped views of the man as being the absolute ruler at home. Ganley described the tendency of batterers to deny or minimize their violence and to externalize it by holding others responsible and culpable for their own moods and outbursts. She recommended confrontation as a therapeutic strategy for dealing with these forms of neutralization of self-punish-ment. She also developed a highly structured treatment format that stressed personal accountability to each participant. Exercises such as maintaining an anger diary emphasized the need for personal responsi-bility in the constant monitoring of anger.

Batterers also tend to express emotions such as hurt, anxiety, excite-ment, sadness, guilt, humiliation, and helplessness as anger. Ganley's treatment program develops batterer's motivation to change by helping the batterer to identify the negative feelings about his violence. Anger diaries help the man to recognize the instigators of his anger, and his physical and cognitive responses to anger. For a complete description and examples of anger diaries, the reader is referred to Sonkin and Durphy (1982), or to Sonkin, Martin, and Walker (1985). When men are successfully in treatment groups and consistently completing anger diaries, the diaries are used as a step to assertiveness training.

While anger recognition and improved communication skills provide the essence of treatment for assaultive males, other issues also constitute an important adjunct to this treatment. Since the treatment is for male-female violence, the role of sex-role socialization in setting the stage for aggression is important. Male socialization both narrows the range of acceptable emotions (Fasteau, 1974; Pleck, 1981) and creates occasionally unrealistic expectations about family roles that provide a source of chronic conflict (Coleman & Straus, 1986). Treatment should address these issues and attempt to develop empathy for the victim. One way of developing empathy is to have assaultive males describe their own experiences as victims of parental abuse. Exploring the feelings connected to these experiences in a group context and explicitly relating the feelings to their wife's experience as a victim can serve to strengthen empathy by making salient the negative consequences of violence for the victim.

Treatment should also include an attempt to get males to think about power in a different way. Men typically enter treatment thinking about power vis-à-vis their wives in an adversarial fashion. Their gain is their wife's loss and vice versa. We attempt to encourage them to view power in interdependent terms: by diminishing their wife they lose a vital partner and by accepting her empowerment they also gain.

Finally, since treatment for assaultive males usually occurs in a group setting, group process issues (Yalom, 1975) are also important. Assaultive males are described in most clinical texts as isolated (Ganley, 1981; Sonkin et al., 1985). They frequently feel anxious about describing personal problems and feelings in front of other men. Therapists have to do considerable "bridge building" by explicitly connecting the experiences of men in the groups in order to establish some camaraderie and a sense of safety for self-disclosure. On the other hand, the therapist must not allow group cohesiveness to generate mutual protection in the service of denial and minimizing. Confrontation must be presented as necessary for learning new conflict management skills in order to avoid the feeling these men frequently have of being attacked or judged negatively.

Are Treatment Groups Effective?

The past decade has seen a proliferation in North America of court-mandated treatment groups for men convicted of wife assault. Browning (1984) and Eddy and Meyers (1984) provide descriptors of 24 Canadian and 54 U.S. treatment programs for assaultive males. Treatment groups for wife assaulters originated from public pressure on the criminal justice system to respond more effectively to the problem of wife assault (Dutton, 1981; Standing Committee of Health, Welfare and Social Affairs, 1982; U.S. Commission on Civil Rights, 1978). In order to estimate the recidivism rate for men arrested and convicted of wife assault but not treated, Dutton (1986b) scrutinized police records of a group of 50 men for up to 3.0 years post conviction. During the same period, records for a matched group of 50 men arrested, convicted, and treated for wife assault were examined. The treatment program consisted of four months of court-mandated group therapy that included cognitive behavior modification, anger management, and assertiveness as described above. According to police records, the untreated group repeated assaults in 20/50 cases; the treated group in 2/50 cases. Treatment improved the nonrecidivist success rate from 60% to 96%.

An examination of pretreatment and post-treatment CTS reports by a subsample of 37 couples (64%) who remained together throughout the treatment program reveals that both husbands' and wives' reports of husbands' violence show significant pre-post drops. Treated husbands still used acts of severe violence an average of 1.7 times a year (wives' report), down from an average of 10.6 times a year. Thirty-one of the 37 wives (84%) reported no acts of severe violence since termination of treatment. Reports of use of verbal aggression were similar to use of severe violence. Overall rates of use of verbal aggression dropped after treatment based on both husband's reports and wives' reports.

Since Dutton's initial outcome study above, several other attempts have been made to evaluate treatment groups for wife assaulters. Shepard (1987) found that 70% of the women reported no physical abuse at follow-up (n = 77), and 40% reported no psychological abuse at that time. The major reduction in physical abuse came during the first three months of the program, suggesting that brief therapy of this sort is as effective as more protracted intervention.

Edleson, Syers, and Brygger (1987) and Edleson and Grusznski (1988) reported data evaluating the Domestic Abuse Project in Minneapolis, which constitutes the largest (in terms of sample size) evaluation project performed to date. Follow-up data were obtained using the

Conflict Tactics Scale at six months after treatment completion. Edleson and Grusznski assessed three cohorts of men who completed treatment and compared them to dropouts for repeat violence. Based on reports of female partners of men in cohort 1, 67% ($n = 18$) of the men who completed counseling were completely nonviolent; in cohort 2, 67% were both nonviolent and nonthreatening at follow-up. Cohort 3 data indicated less treatment success, with only 59% of men completely nonviolent. Treated men also used significantly less violence (as reported by their partners) than did a group of men who had dropped out of the program.

The results of the majority of studies reviewed here tend to support the case for arrest/treatment combinations to diminish recidivist wife assaults. Through this model, arrest serves both a didactic and deterrent function: It shows the man that wife assault is unacceptable and will be punished by the state. The treatment group then provides the opportunity for the man to learn new responses to the interchanges with his wife that formerly generated violent behavior. In this sense, treatment and law-and-order approaches operate symbiotically to reduce future violence.

Note

1. At present, much remains to be clarified about the role of power in wife assault. Coleman and Straus (1986) and Fagan (1987) suggest that less assault occurs in egalitarian relationships, yet other studies cited above (e.g., Dutton & Browning, 1988) suggest that frustrated power needs predispose men to violence. Part of the problem is that many definitions and ways of measuring power have been used in published studies.

References

Bandura, A. (1979). The social learning perspective: Mechanisms of aggression. In H. Toch (Ed.), *Psychology of crime and criminal justice.* New York: Holt, Rinehart & Winston.

Bard, M., & Zacker, J. (1974). Assaultiveness and alcohol use in family disputes: Police perceptions. *Criminology, 12*(3), 281-292.

Belsky, J. (1980). Child maltreatment: An ecological integration. *American Psychologist, 35*(4), 320-335.

Berk, R. A., Berk, S. F., Loseke, D. R., & Rauma, D. (1981). Mutual combat and other family violence myths. In D. Finkelhor, R. J. Gelles, G. T. Hotaling, & M. A. Straus (Eds.), *The dark side of families: Current family violence and research.* Beverly Hills, CA: Sage.

Blood, R., Jr., & Wolfe, D. (1960). *Husbands and wives: The dynamics of married living.* Glencoe, IL: Free Press.

Browning, J. J. (1983). *Violence against intimates: Toward a profile of the wife assaulter.* Unpublished doctoral dissertation, University of British Columbia, Vancouver.

Browning, J. J. (1984). *Stopping the violence: Canadian programmes for assaultive men.* Ottawa: Health and Welfare Canada.

Browning, J. J., & Dutton, D. G. (1986). Assessment of wife assault with the conflict tactics scale: Using couple data to quantify the differential reporting effect. *Journal of Marriage and the Family, 48,* 375-379.

Carmen, E. H., Reiker, P. P., & Mills, T. (1984). Victims of violence and psychiatric illness. *American Journal of Psychiatry, 141*(3), 378-383.

Coleman, D. H., & Straus, M. A. (1986). Marital power, conflict, and violence in a nationally representative sample of American couples. *Violence and Victims, 1*(2), 141-157.

Dobash, R. E., & Dobash, R. P. (1978). Wives: The appropriate victims of marital assault. *Victimology: An International Journal, 2,* 426-442.

Dobash, R. E., & Dobash, R. P. (1979). *Violence against wives: A case against the patriarchy.* New York: Free Press.

Dutton, D. G. (1977). Domestic dispute intervention by police. *Proceedings from Symposium on Family Violence.* Vancouver, British Columbia: United Way.

Dutton, D. G. (1981). *The criminal justice system response to wife assault.* Ottawa: Solicitor General of Canada, Research Division.

Dutton, D. G. (1986a). Wife assaulters' explanations for assault: The neutralization of self-punishment. *Canadian Journal of Behavioural Science, 18*(4), 381-390.

Dutton, D. G. (1986b). The outcome of court-mandated treatment for wife assault: A quasi-experimental evaluation. *Violence and Victims, 1*(3), 163-175.

Dutton, D. G. (1987). The criminal justice response to wife assault. *Law and Human Behavior, 11*(3), 189-206.

Dutton, D. G. (1988a). *The domestic assault of women: Psychological and criminal justice perspectives.* Boston: Allyn & Bacon.

Dutton, D. G. (1988b). Profiling of wife assaulters: Preliminary evidence for a trimodal analysis. *Violence and Victims, 3*(1), 5-30.

Dutton, D. G., & Aron, A. (1989). Romantic attraction and generalized liking for others who are sources of conflict-based arousal. *Canadian Journal of Behavioural Science, 21*(3), 246-257.

Dutton, D. G., & Browning, J. J. (1988). Power struggles and intimacy anxieties as causative factors of violence in intimate relationships. In G. Russell (Ed), *Violence in intimate relationships.* Great Neck, NY: PMA Publishing.

Dutton, D. G., & McGregor, B. M. S. (1991). The symbiosis of arrest and treatment for wife assault: The case for combined intervention. In M. Steinman (Ed.), *Woman battering: Policy responses* (pp. 131-154). Cincinnati, OH: Anderson.

Dutton, D. G., & Painter, S. L. (1980). *Male domestic violence and its effects on the victim.* Ottawa: Health and Welfare Canada.

Dutton, D. G., & Painter, S. L. (1981). Traumatic bonding: The development of emotional attachments in battered women and other relationships of intermittent abuse. *Victimology: An International Journal, 6,* 139-155.

Dutton, D. G., & Strachan, C. E. (1987). Motivational needs for power and dominance as differentiating variables of assaultive and non-assaultive male populations. *Violence and Victims, 2*(3), 145-156.

Dutton, D. G., Fehr, B., & McEwan, H. (1982). Severe wife battering as deindividuated violence. *Victimology: An International Journal, 7,* 13-23.

Dutton, D. G., Hart, S., Kennedy, L., & Williams, K. (1992). Arrest and the reduction of recidivist wife assault: An exploratory study of alternative mechanisms to deterrence. In E. Buzawa (Ed.), *The criminal justice response to wife assault.* Dover, MA: Auburn.

Eddy, M. J., & Meyers, T. (1984). *Helping men who batter: A profile of programs in the U.S.* Arlington: Texas Council on Family Violence.

Edleson, J. L., & Grusznski, R. J. (1988). Treating men who batter: Four years of outcome data from the Domestic Abuse Project. *Journal of Social Science Research, 12*(1/2), 3-22.

Edleson, J. L., Syers, M., & Brygger, M. P. (1987). *Comparative effectiveness of group treatment for men who batter.* Paper presented at the Third National Family Violence Conference, Durham, NH.

Fagan, J. (1987). Cessation of family violence: Deterrence and dissuasion. In M. Tonry & N. Morris (Eds.), *Crime and justice: A review of research* (Vol. 2, pp. 377-426). Chicago: University of Chicago Press.

Fasteau, M. F. (1974). *The male machine.* New York: McGraw-Hill.

Frieze, I. H., & Browne, A. (1989). Violence in marriage. In L. Ohlin & M. Tonry (Eds.), *Crime and justice: An annual review of research: Family violence.* Chicago: University of Chicago Press.

Ganley, A., & Harris, L. (1978). *Domestic violence: Issues in designing and implementing programs for male batterers.* Paper presented at the 86th annual convention of the American Psychological Association, Toronto.

Ganley, A. (1980, March). [Interview: Whatcom County Counseling and Psychiatric Center, Bellingham, WA.]

Ganley, A. (1981). *Participants' manual: Court-mandated therapy for men who batter.* Washington, DC: Center for Women's Policy Studies.

Gelles, R. J. (1972). *The violent home: A study of physical aggression between husbands and wives.* Beverly Hills, CA: Sage.

Gelles, R. J. (1975). Violence and pregnancy: A note on the extent of the problem and needed services. *Family Co-ordinator, 24,* 81-86.

Gondolf, E. W. (1985). *Men who batter: An integrated approach for stopping wife abuse.* Holmes Beach, CA: Learning Publications.

Goode, W. G. J. (1971). Why men resist. *Dissent,* pp. 181-193.

Hilberman, E., & Munson, K. (1977-1978). Sixty battered women. *Victimology: An International Journal, 2,* 460-470.

Hunt, J. M., Cole, M. W., & Reis, E. E. A. (1958). Situational cues distinguishing anger, fear, and sorrow. *American Journal of Psychology, 71,* 136-151.

Jaffe, P., Wolfe, D. A., Telford, A., & Austin, G. (1986). The impact of police charges in incidents of wife abuse. *Journal of Family Violence, 1*(1), 37-49.

Kalmuss, D. S. (1984, February). The intergenerational transmission of marital aggression. *Journal of Marriage and the Family, 46,* 11-19.

Kalmuss, D. S., & Seltzer, J. A. (1986). Continuity of marital behavior in remarriage: The case of spouse abuse. *Journal of Marriage and the Family, 48,* 113-120.

Kennedy, L. W., & Dutton, D. G. (1989). The incidence of wife assault in Alberta. *Canadian Journal of Behavioural Science, 21*(1), 40-54.

Levens, B. R., & Dutton, D. G. (1977). Domestic crisis intervention: Citizens' requests for service and the Vancouver Police Department response. *Canadian Police College Journal, 1,* 29-50.

Loving, N., & Farmer, M. (1980). *Police handling of spouse abuse and wife beating calls: A guide for police managers.* Washington, DC: Police Executive Research Forum.

Maiuro, R. D., Cahn, T. S., Vitaliano, P. P., & Zegree, J. B. (1986). *Anger control treatment for men who engage in domestic violence: A controlled outcome study.* Paper presented at the annual convention of the Western Psychological Association, Seattle, WA.

Mandler, G. (1975). *Mind and emotion.* New York: John Wiley.

Murphy, C. M., & O'Leary, K. D. (1987). *Verbal aggression as a predictor of physical aggression in early marriage.* Paper presented at the Third National Conference for Family Violence Researchers, Durham, NH.

Neidig, P. H., Friedman, D. H., & Collins, B. S. (1986). Attitudinal characteristics of males who have engaged in spouse abuse. *Journal of Family Violence, 1*(3), 223-234.

Novaco, R. (1976, October). The functions and regulation of the arousal of anger. *American Journal of Psychiatry, 133*(1), 1124-1128.

Patterson, G. R. (1976). The aggressive child: Victim and architect of a coercive system. In E. Mash, L. Hamerlynck, & L. Handy (Eds.), *Behavior modification and families: I. Theory and research.* New York: Brunner/Mazel.

Pleck, J. H. (1981). *The myth of masculinity.* Cambridge: MIT Press.

Rosenbaum, A., & O'Leary, K. D. (1981). Marital violence: Characteristics of abusive couples. *Journal of Consulting and Clinical Psychology, 41,* 63.

Rounsaville, B. (1978). Theories in marital violence: Evidence from a study of battered women. *Victimology: An International Journal, 3*(1-2), 11-31.

Saunders, D. G. (1987). *Are there different types of men who batter? An empirical study with possible implications for treatment.* Paper presented at the Third National Conference for Family Violence Researchers, Durham, NH.

Saunders, D. G., Lynch, A. B., Grayson, M., & Linz, D. (1987). The inventory of beliefs about wife beating: The construction and initial validation of a measure of beliefs and attitudes. *Victims and Violence, 2*(1), 39-55.

Schachter, S., & Singer, J. (1962). Cognitive, social and physiological determinants of emotional state. *Psychological Review, 69,* 379-399.

Schulman, M. (1979). *A survey of spousal violence against women in Kentucky.* Washington, DC: U.S. Department of Justice, Law Enforcement.

Shepard, M. (1987). *Interventions with men who batter: An evaluation of a domestic abuse program.* Paper presented at the Third National Family Violence Research Conference, Durham, NH.

Sherman, L. W, & Berk, R. A. (1984). *The Minneapolis domestic violence experiment* (Police Foundation Reports, 1). Washington, DC: The Police Foundation.

Sonkin, D. J., & Durphy, M. (1982). *Learning to live without violence: A handbook for men.* San Francisco: Volcano Press.

Sonkin, D. J., Martin, D., & Walker, I. E. (1985). *The male batterer: A treatment approach.* New York: Springer.

Standing Committee on Health, Welfare, and Social Affairs. (1982). *Report on violence in the family: Wife battering.* House of Commons, Ottawa.

Stark, R., & McEvoy, J. (1970). Middle class violence. *Psychology Today, 4*(6), 107-112.

Steiner, G. (1981). *The futility of family police.* Washington, DC: Brookings Institution.

Straus, M. A., & Gelles, R. J. (1985, November). *Is family violence increasing? A comparison of 1975 and 1985 national survey rates.* Paper presented at the American Society of Criminology, San Diego, CA.

Straus, M. A. (1976). Sexual inequality, cultural norm and wife beating. *Victimology: An International Journal, 1,* 54-76.

Straus, M. A. (1977a). Societal morphogenesis and intrafamily violence in cross cultural perspective. *Annals of the New York Academy of Sciences, 285,* 718-730.

Straus, M. A. (1977b, March). Violence in the family: How widespread, why it occurs and some thoughts on prevention. In *Proceedings from Symposium on Family Violence.* Vancouver, British Columbia: United Way.

Straus, M. A. (1977c). Wife beating: How common and why? *Victimology: An International Journal, 2*(3-4), 443-459.

Straus, M. A. (1979). Measuring family conflict and violence: The conflict tactics scale. *Journal of Marriage and the Family, 41,* 75-88.

Straus, M. A., Gelles, R. J., & Steinmetz, S. (1980). *Behind closed doors: Violence in the American family.* Garden City, NY: Doubleday.

Tavris, C. (1984). *Anger: The misunderstood emotion.* New York: Simon & Schuster.

Toch, H. (1969). *Violent men: An inquiry into the psychology of violence.* Chicago: Aldine.

U.S. Commission on Civil Rights. (1978). *Battered women: Issues of public policy.* Washington, DC: Government Printing Office.

van der Kolk, B. (1987). *Psychological trauma.* Washington, DC: American Psychiatric Press.

Vivian, D., & O'Leary, K. D. (1987). *Communication patterns in physically assaultive engaged couples.* Paper presented at the Third National Conference for Family Violence Researchers, Durham, NH.

Walker, L. E. (1979). *The battered woman.* New York: Harper & Row.

Walker, L. E. (1984). *The battered woman syndrome.* New York: Springer.

Walters, R. H., & Brown, M. (1963). Studies of reinforcement of aggression. III. Transfer of responses to an interpersonal situation. *Child Development, 34,* 563-571.

Yalom, T. D. (1975). *The theory and practice of group psychotherapy.* New York: Basic Books.

Zimbardo, P. G. (1969). The human choice: Individuation, reason and order vs. deindividuation, impulse and chaos. In *Nebraska Symposium on Motivation.* Lincoln: University of Nebraska Press.

10

The Relapse Prevention Model:
Can It Work With Sex Offenders?

JANICE K. MARQUES
CRAIG NELSON

In recent years, our society has become increasingly aware of the very significant personal and societal consequences of rape and child molestation. This heightened awareness of the extent and impact of sexual aggression has resulted in new attempts to keep sex offenders from repeating their crimes. Although the past decade has seen an unprecedented number of special commissions, conferences, and legislation pertaining to sexual aggression, ambiguity and controversy continue to surround efforts to find the appropriate societal response to the problem. Indeed, at the same time some states in the United States were rescinding statutes providing for treatment (vs. incarceration) of sex offenders, others were establishing new rehabilitative programs (Knopp, 1984). As Furby, Weinrott, and Blackshaw (1989) recently observed, "With respect to the relative appropriateness of simple incarceration versus inpatient treatment, states appear to be passing one another like ships in the night" (p. 3).

AUTHORS' NOTE: The authors gratefully acknowledge the contributions of project staff members Michael H. Miner, Ph.D., Mary Ann West, Ph.D., and Tom Wilson, who performed the data analyses required for this chapter.

Although the controversy about how society should respond to sexual aggression has a number of determinants, the lack of convincing empirical data on the impact of sex offender treatment on recidivism has certainly been an important factor. According to Furby et al. (1989), past outcome studies of the psychological treatment of sex offenders have generally not supported its effectiveness. Eight of the nine studies of untreated offenders they reviewed, with follow-up periods ranging from 6 months to 10 years, had recidivism rates below 12%. In contrast, the rates reported in two thirds of the treated offender studies were higher than 12%. The authors attribute these discouraging results to a variety of factors, ranging from the lack of adequate research designs to the possibility that follow-up supervision was tighter for the treated samples. More encouraging results have recently been reported with newer programs using a combination of cognitive and behavioral interventions (Marshall & Barbaree, 1990). The effectiveness of such approaches, however, still requires validation with scientifically sound comparisons between randomly selected groups of treated and control subjects before the sex offender treatment controversy can be resolved.

As was noted at the 1988 New York Academy of Sciences meeting on sexual aggression, there is a developing consensus regarding at least a rudimentary treatment model for sex offenders (Laws, 1988). At the core of this model are treatments addressing deviant sexual interests, social incompetencies, and cognitive distortions about sexual offending. Most recently, a number of programs have added a relapse prevention (RP) focus to this model, an approach that emphasizes teaching offenders self-management skills to apply in various high-risk situations (Laws, 1989).

In this chapter, we will present a relapse prevention program for sex offenders. First, we will describe how the RP model can be used to understand and interrupt the chain of events leading to relapse in rapists and child molesters. Second, we will describe California's Sex Offender Treatment and Evaluation Project (SOTEP), an experimental test of the effectiveness of one RP program in reducing recidivism. Finally, we will present some preliminary SOTEP findings, highlighting those related to the basic assumptions of the RP model, and to the program's effect on recidivism.

Relapse Prevention With Sex Offenders

Although it has been our experience that most convicted sex offenders report that they will never reoffend, they are often either vague or
evasive regarding how they will prevent committing similar offenses in
the future. They may project blame onto the victim by claiming they
were seduced or wrongly accused, but seem oblivious to ways of
escaping future "seductions" or false allegations. Others justify and
rationalize their actions as due to being under the effects of illicit drugs
or alcohol, yet they are unable to explain how other substance abusers
have not committed sexual crimes. Some offenders claim that they now
understand that their actions were wrong and will, therefore, never
commit such mistakes again. Although this may suggest that the criminal justice system serves to educate offenders, it is difficult to believe
that these men did not comprehend that molesting children or raping
women was legally and morally wrong until they were arrested. In short,
offenders often appear to believe sincerely that they will not rape or
molest again, but rarely have specific plans regarding how they will
maintain their abstinence from the sexual abuse of others.

According to Bandura (1977), "expectation alone will not produce
desired performance if the component capabilities are lacking" (p. 194).
From this perspective, it is necessary not only to have a sense of
self-efficacy regarding one's ability to avoid raping or molesting, but
also to insure that the requisite skills and abilities are present to do so.
Thus, for sex offenders, relapse prevention (RP) attempts to enhance
the client's sense of self-control by developing specific skills for avoiding
relapse into sexually illicit behavior (George & Marlatt, 1989; Marques,
1984, 1988; Marques & Nelson, 1989b; Nelson, Miner, Marques, Russell,
& Achterkirchen, 1988).

Although RP was originally developed for the addictive behaviors of
drinking, smoking, gambling, and so on (Marlatt & Gordon, 1980,
1985), the adaptation of this model to sexual offending does not necessarily imply that child molestation and rape are addictive. Rather, it
implies that there are certain similarities in the way smokers or alcoholics may relapse after having committed themselves to abstinence and
the manner in which offenders may reoffend after having made a sincere
commitment not to do so. Both types of behaviors are characterized by
a problem of immediate gratification in which there are immediate
positive consequences to returning to the forbidden behavior while the
negative consequences are delayed. Other commonalities include: (a)

both addicts and sex offenders tend to deny the severity of their destructive patterns, and minimize their risk of relapse; (b) there are similar precursors, such as the experience of negative emotional states, in the relapses of both types of behaviors (Marques & Nelson, 1989b; Marques, Pithers, & Marlatt, 1984); and (c) the treatment of both addicts and sex offenders presents serious maintenance problems—that is, many successfully start a period of abstinence but fail to maintain control over time and across situations. RP, specifically designed for the maintenance phase of behavior change programs, appears to have promise for helping sex offenders learn to understand and cope with the relapse process itself.

In the following sections, we will describe how RP conceptualizes the relapse process and how clients are taught to intervene to avoid relapse. Although the basic tenets of RP are taken from Marlatt and Gordon's (1985) model, they have been modified for our use with sex offenders.

The Relapse Process

RP describes a general progression of steps that lead from the point at which individuals commit themselves to abstain from a prohibited behavior to the point at which they are again engaging in the behavior. Teaching offenders these steps provides a "cognitive map" they can use to gauge their risk of reoffending and the necessity for intervening with coping responses to reduce that risk. The first step in this process is abstinence, the state in which one has made the commitment not to reoffend. Obviously, however, not all offenders have made such a commitment. For some, their interest is only in not getting caught again, or in finding ways to express their deviance without getting arrested. We should point out that the following account of the relapse process does not apply to these individuals, due to their lack of motivation to modify the targeted behavior. If a commitment is made and abstinence is achieved, however, RP proposes that the individual experiences a sense of self-control and an expectation of continued success. At this point, many incarcerated offenders are able to proclaim sincerely that they are no longer at risk to molest or rape again, even though they may be unaware as to how to achieve this goal.

The next step for the offender heading toward relapse is a decision or behavior that unwittingly places him in a situation that challenges his abstinence commitment. These decisions have been labeled as Apparently Irrelevant Decisions (AIDs) because they "appear" to the offender to be unrelated to his maintaining abstinence. On the surface the offender is able to rationalize or justify these behaviors, but the decisions are actually quite relevant because they place him at risk for relapse. An AID for a rapist, for example, may be picking up a hitch-hiker. This act may be rationalized as a kindly gesture, a rationale that may be legitimate for many men who are not at risk to rape. For the rape-prone offender, however, such a decision may represent the covert engineering of his own relapse. An AID for a child molester, on the other hand, may be the decision to supervise an activity for children even when other adults are present. Although such an action can be justified as supporting one's community and innocuous because of the supervision of others, it may well provide cues that arouse deviant sexual interests. Therefore, it too would be clearly an AID.

When an AID is committed, the offender finds himself in a high-risk situation, which the RP model defines as a predicament that threatens his sense of self-control. In our view of the relapse process, such a situation is seen as a constellation of risk factors or elements. Some risk elements may be environmental (e.g., access to a potential victim, interpersonal stressors, etc.), while others may be intrapersonal (e.g., deviant sexual arousal patterns, negative emotional states, intoxication, cognitive distortions and misinterpretations, etc.). These elements or factors interact to jeopardize the commitment to abstinence and create a danger of relapse (Marques & Nelson, 1989a).

The next step in the progression is a lapse, a slip, or a mistake that precedes the full return of the prohibited behavior. For example a lapse might be a first cigarette for an ex-smoker, or a single drink for the abstinent alcoholic. In dealing with sex offenses, however, we consider a single violation of the abstinence rule to be a full-scale return to the problem. Therefore, a lapse is defined as the behavior that immediately precedes an offense. It may be cruising for a potential victim, "grooming" a child for future sexual relations, or fantasizing about deviant sexual behavior (Marques et al., 1984).

Committing a lapse is frequently associated with a reaction that propels an offender on to a full-blown relapse, or reoffense. This reaction, the Abstinence Violation Effect (AVE), is characterized by thoughts and feelings that are mirror opposites of those associated with abstinence. While abstinence involves feelings of self-control and confidence in one's ability not to reoffend, the AVE is characterized by a decreased sense of control. The offender, at this point, believes he is unable to keep himself from acting upon his deviant sexual urges. In a state of abstinence, the offender expects to be successful; when experiencing the AVE, he comes to expect failure. Although the abstinent offender experiences a sense of self-worth, the offender who has lapsed is likely to feel worthless and engage in self-recriminations.

The final stage in this progression is relapse. This is the point at which there is a return to the offending pattern by the commission of a new sex crime. At this point, it is too late for the offender to intervene to divert the process because a new victim has been created.

Intervening in the Relapse Process

From an RP perspective, if an offender is to maintain his commitment to abstinence and avoid reoffending, he must develop realistic, concrete ways to intervene in the relapse process. This task involves learning to:

(a) identify the steps leading to relapse, and
(b) develop, plan, and practice coping responses to the unique factors that place him at risk for reoffense.

The first step in intervening in the relapse process is for the offender to have an overview of the progression from abstinence to relapse described above. Once this has occurred, he must then individualize his particular relapse pattern into concrete, specific terms. If an offender is to be able to implement specific responses to divert himself from reoffending, he must first be able to identify and recognize those situations in which such coping responses are necessary. The preparation of cognitive-behavioral offense chains is a technique that has been developed to identify these risks and to individualize the relapse process for a particular offender (Nelson & Jackson, 1989). In this technique, the offender is first asked to identify a limited number of environmental events that preceded his offense(s). Such factors as interpersonal stressors, "provocative" victim behaviors, or drug and alcohol abuse may be identified. The offender is then asked to describe particular thoughts and feelings that were associated with each of these events and that served as antecedents to their crimes. This second step allows him to begin to recognize some of the intrapersonal factors that place him at risk for relapse. A properly constructed cognitive-behavioral chain will funnel directly toward the offense and offer a road map of the relapse process. Specific events, thoughts, and feelings are highlighted as concrete and individualized examples of the types of AIDs, high-risk situations, lapses, and AVEs that can lead to relapse for a given offender. The completed cognitive-behavioral chain is like a

recipe of how this particular offender, with his various high-risk ingre-
dients, engineered his particular rape or molestation. Similar, although
not necessarily identical, steps are postulated for the offender as risks
for a future relapse.

When the offender has identified the particular factors that place him
at risk, he is ready to begin the process of developing, planning, and
practicing coping responses to minimize these dangers. In developing
coping responses, an offender is instructed that there are three places
that he can intervene to divert himself from reoffending: (a) he can
avoid making the decisions (AIDs) that place him in high-risk situations; (b) if an AID is committed, he can escape the high-risk situation
or cope with it through any other behavior that would reduce its threat
to his sense of control, and (c) if he fails to cope adequately with the
high-risk situation, and lapses as a result, he can still cope through
appropriate self-statements that counteract his sense of failure (the
AVE) and reestablish his sense of self-control.

Once the unique set of high-risk factors to which the offender must
respond has been delineated, the next step is to plan effective coping
responses that could be used in the future to prevent relapse. In a
concrete fashion, offenders are trained in the following four steps to an
adequate coping response.

Identify the Risk

If an offender fails to determine that he is in a high-risk situation,
there will be no incentive to formulate a coping response even if he is
highly motivated to avoid reoffending. The potential risks involved in
the AIDs, high-risk situations, and AVEs that are encountered must be
highlighted by the offender to insure that he attends to them. This
identification may be a simple self-statement such as, "Being alone with
this child is risky for me because I might get turned on to her."

Reinterpret the Situation

AIDs, high-risk situations, and AVEs always involve some form of
distorted cognition. Therefore, the interpretation that poses a risk must
be reevaluated and corrected by the offender. In the case of an AID this
reinterpretation must center around the surface justification that allowed the offender to place himself in a high-risk situation in the first
place. In the previous rapist example, the reinterpretation may go along
the lines of, "It's no favor for me to pick up a hitchhiker because she's

at more risk with me than with other people driving around." In the instance of the child molester, the reinterpretation may be, "It's no community service for someone with a history of molestation to supervise children, even if another adult is present." At the level of the high-risk situation, the reinterpretation must be made to the thoughts that increase the likelihood of a lapse or relapse. For example, a child molester who is confronted with a girl he believes is being seductive might reinterpret the situation as, "The attention she is paying to me is not a sign of sexual interest; that's coming from me." A rapist at risk when he becomes angry with women may need to be prepared to reinterpret the situation by saying, "It's crazy for me to think my masculinity is being challenged whenever a woman disagrees with me."

When encountering an AVE, the coping reinterpretations are directed toward reestablishing the offender's sense of self-control by reminding himself that: (a) he has only committed a lapse and not a relapse; (b) he can still remove himself from the relapse process without reoffending; (c) to lapse from time to time in learning new behaviors is to be expected and is not a sign of his worthlessness, weakness, or failure in treatment; and (d) he can go back and attempt to understand how he placed himself in a situation that led him to lapse so that he will be better prepared in the future.

Self-Instruct

The offender must then tell himself how to behave in a way that will reduce the risk. That is, he must instruct himself in an appropriate coping response. "I need to turn down this offer to supervise children," "I'm angry at this woman right now and need to get out of here to cool down before I blow it," or "I need to sit down and write a description of the chain of events that led me to this lapse," might all be examples of coping self-instructions.

Follow Through

The final step in the coping process is to follow through with the self-instruction by emitting the appropriate behavioral response. It is not enough for the child molester just to tell himself that he should turn down an offer to supervise children. He must actually do it.

Using these steps, specific coping responses can be developed by the offender for each of the major events and interpretations in his cognitive-behavioral offense chain. It should be clear how each coping response would have decreased the probability of a sexual assault. An examination of the coping responses for the entire chain provides a blueprint with specific behaviors and self-statements designed to avoid a molestation or rape. Thus the offender begins to plan coping strategies that could be used in similar situations in the future.

After specific coping responses have been planned, as much practice in implementing them as possible is given in order to enhance the offender's confidence in his ability actually to produce the desired response. Obviously, practicing in real-life situations with potential victims is unrealistic when working in the area of sexual abuse, given the catastrophic consequences of coping failures. Several techniques, however, have been devised to provide an opportunity for such practice. Relapse rehearsal (Hall, 1989), for example, is a technique in which an offender imagines situations that would be difficult for him to handle without relapsing. The offender is then instructed to imagine (in detail) how he could successfully cope with the situation, and to experience the positive feelings he is likely to feel after conquering the risks. In this way, he gets to practice coping skills and to experience the reinforcement of appropriate responses.

The coping skills game is another form of practice that has been used to help offenders learn and practice appropriate coping responses (Steenman, Nelson, & Viesti, 1989). In this procedure, an offender is asked either to describe or role play his reaction to scenarios that are presented by therapists or other offenders familiar with his high-risk factors. Initially, the situations are rather simple or only slightly risky. If an adequate coping response is given, the circumstances are made more complex or difficult in an attempt to trap the offender in a situation in which he cannot readily produce a coping response that would decrease his chances of committing a rape or molestation. Offenders are pressured to respond quickly with their coping solutions in order to make these responses as automatic as possible. The game continues until either the offender is unable to produce a coping response or no new risk factors can be manufactured that would foil his strategy to handle the situation. Only credible, realistic coping responses are permitted, and unrealistic or fantastic responses lead to disqualification. Following each game, the effectiveness of the responses, the likelihood that the offender would actually emit such responses, and the potential for alternative coping behaviors is analyzed. Successful coping strategies are reinforced, and unsuccessful approaches are modified to make them more effective. This therapeutic technique can be likened to the drills and scrimmages that many athletes undertake as part of their training to prepare them for athletic contests.

In summary, RP rejects the notion that sex offenders will be "cured" and never need worry about molesting or raping again. Instead, the approach emphasizes that success in one's commitment to not reoffend is based upon constant vigilance and control. Successful control relies upon the offender's abilities to recognize the factors that place him at risk for relapse and to be prepared to meet these risks with effective coping responses that minimize the chances of reoffense.

Testing the RP Model

As was noted earlier, the RP model is currently very popular in the field of sex offender treatment. The notion that sex offenders can learn to anticipate and cope with the problem of relapse has great appeal, and many programs now use RP as either a primary treatment framework or as a supplemental treatment component. One program, California's Sex Offender Treatment and Evaluation Project (SOTEP), is an experimental test of the effectiveness of a comprehensive RP program for rapists and child molesters. In the remainder of this chapter, we will describe SOTEP's organization, design, treatment structure, and some preliminary findings.

Project Description

In 1981, the California State Legislature repealed the state's Mentally Disordered Sex Offender statute and required convicted sex offenders to be delivered to the Department of Corrections after sentencing. Thus, after 42 years of providing state hospital treatment for certain sex offenders, California required convicted rapists and child molesters to be delivered to the Department of Corrections after sentencing. Although this legislation eliminated the direct commitment of these offenders to state hospitals, it did allow for the voluntary transfer of sex offenders to a Department of Mental Health treatment facility during the last two years of their prison terms. The state hospital program for these offenders was to be "established according to a valid experimental design in order that the most effective, newest and promising methods of treatment of sex offenders may be rigorously tested" (*California*

Penal Code, Sec. 1365). Subsequent legislation limited the experimental program to 50 beds and required formal evaluation reports to be submitted biennially to the Legislature (*California Penal Code,* Sec. 1364, 1365).

In 1985, the California Department of Mental Health initiated the Sex Offender Treatment and Evaluation Project (SOTEP) (Marques, 1984, 1988; Marques, Day, Nelson, & Miner, 1989a, 1989b), a clinical research program designed to meet the two goals specified in the legislative mandate: (a) the development and operation of a small, innovative treatment unit for sex offenders; and (b) the evaluation of the effectiveness of the treatments provided in the new program. In order to achieve these goals, SOTEP's project director oversees two separate but interrelated projects: (a) the treatment project, which is housed on a 46-bed treatment unit at Atascadero State Hospital, and is staffed by a clinical director, a psychiatrist, 3 clinical psychologists, 4 clinical social workers, 5 social work associates, 2 rehabilitation therapists, and 28 nursing personnel (mostly psychiatric technicians); and (b) the evaluation project, which is directed from the Department's central office in Sacramento, and is staffed by three research professionals and two assistants.

Method

Subjects

Study participants are male inmates from the California Department of Corrections who have been convicted of one or more violations of Penal Code sections pertaining to rape and child molestation. Inmates who have offended only in concert (e.g., gang rape) or only against their biological children (incest) are not included. The study is also limited to inmates who are between 18 and 30 months of their release from prison, have no more than two prior felony convictions, admit they committed the offense(s) for which they are incarcerated, have IQs greater than 80, are between 18 and 60 years of age, can speak English, do not have severe medical conditions, do not have psychotic or organic mental conditions, and have not presented severe management problems in prison.

Procedure

Participants are involved in four phases of the project: selection, treatment, aftercare, and follow-up.

Selection Phase. In this phase, project staff screen and recruit inmates at California's prisons. Qualified inmates who volunteer are matched on the characteristics of type of offense, age, and criminal history, and are assigned at random to either the Treatment Group or to the Volunteer Control group. A third matched group, the Nonvolunteer Control Group, consists of qualified inmates who did not elect to volunteer.

The primary data collected by evaluation project staff in the selection phase are those used to determine eligibility and matching categories, and to describe the subjects in terms of their demographic characteristics, crime patterns, and history.

Treatment Phase. During this phase, the Treatment Group participates in a comprehensive RP program at Atascadero State Hospital for approximately two years, while both Volunteer and Nonvolunteer Control Groups remain in prison. As applied in SOTEP, RP provides a framework within which a variety of behavioral, cognitive, educational, and skill-training approaches are prescribed to teach offenders how to recognize and interrupt the chain of events leading to reoffense (Marques et al., 1989a, 1989b; Marques & Nelson, 1989b; Nelson et al., 1988).

The focus of both assessment and treatment procedures is on the specification and modification of the steps in this chain, from broad life-style factors to specific risk factors such as cognitive distortions, deviant sexual arousal patterns, and interpersonal skill deficits.

The primary treatment structure is the core RP group, which meets five hours each week throughout the program. This highly structured group is the setting in which subjects learn the RP model, construct their cognitive behavioral offense chains, and practice the RP skills described above. This activity also serves to integrate other treatment components into an individualized RP program for each offender. In addition to the core group, subjects attend specialty groups that focus on the knowledge, attitudes, and skills that are needed to identify and cope with high-risk situations. These include groups specializing in: sex education, human sexuality, relaxation training, stress and anger management, social skills, substance abuse, and prerelease (preparation for return to the community). In order to maintain treatment consistency and fidelity, all SOTEP groups follow treatment manuals that describe the major goals, procedures, and behavioral assignments for the group sessions.

All Treatment Group subjects also participate in individual therapy and structured rehabilitation activities, and work 30 hours a week in the hospital. In addition, individual behavior therapy sessions in SOTEP's sexual behavior laboratory are offered to those with deviant sexual arousal patterns. The most frequently used intervention is olfactory aversion, although masturbatory satiation and orgasmic reconditioning approaches are also used.

During the treatment phase, evaluation project staff focus on measures of in-treatment change. First, the impact of individual treatment components is measured by relevant pre-post measures. For the core group, tests on RP are used. Other treatment components are evaluated by analyzing the pre-post changes in variables relevant to the focus of intervention (e.g., social skills, stress management skills, patterns of sexual arousal). Second, the overall effects of the program are addressed by a battery of measures administered at admission and at discharge. These include standardized personality tests (e.g., MMPI, MCMI, etc.), locus of control scales (Nowicki & Strickland, 1973; Rotter, 1966), measures of cognitive distortions related to sex offending (Nichols & Molinder, 1984), a standardized laboratory assessment of deviant sexual arousal patterns (Laws & Osborne, 1983), and a behavioral measure of coping skills (Miner, Day, & Nafpaktitis, 1989).

Just prior to their release from the hospital, Treatment Group members also participate in a prerelease assessment session, which includes an interview about the program and the subject's postrelease situation, two self-report measures (addressing cognitive distortions and perceptions about high-risk situations), and an introduction to the randomized response technique (RRT) (Warner, 1965). RRT, a statistically based technique designed to ascertain group differences without identifying individual responses, is used to supplement official criminal records in determining offense rates. For the subject, RRT involves using a randomizing device, such as dice, to determine whether he gives a set answer (e.g., "no") to a reoffense question, or whether he answers truthfully. For the experimenter, since the overall probability that a given answer is truthful is known, RRT allows estimates of group reoffense rates to be calculated.

Volunteer Control Group members receive no treatment services from SOTEP during the treatment phase, but those who consent are paid for participating in a prerelease assessment session that includes the same measures as does the session conducted with Treatment Group members. As a result of a recent project enhancement grant from NIMH, consenting members of the Nonvolunteer Control Group will also be assessed prior to release, in order for us to learn more about this group of offenders.

Aftercare Phase. In this phase, which lasts one year, Treatment Group members are required to attend two sessions a week in the Sex Offender Aftercare Program (SOAP) as a condition of parole. SOAP services are provided on a contractual basis by clinicians who are individually trained by project staff to provide an extended version of the RP program in the subject's community.

Treatment progress is monitored during the aftercare phase by monthly reports from SOAP providers. In addition, providers must report any parole violations to the Department of Corrections. Members of the two control groups are also on parole during this period, and may be returned to custody if they violate conditions of parole.

At the end of the one-year aftercare period, evaluation project staff conduct a parole assessment session with members of the Treatment and Volunteer Control Groups and collect information on their work, housing, social conditions, and perceived high-risk situations. Also in this session, specific questions about whether the subject has reoffended during the aftercare period are asked using the randomized response technique. As a result of our NIMH enhancement funds, we will also be reassessing consenting Nonvolunteer Controls one year after release.

Follow-Up Phase. This phase overlaps the aftercare phase, and will continue for five years following the release of all study participants. At this time, we expect that our last subjects will be discharged in 1995, and that our follow-up will end in 2000. Since the first participants were released in 1986, we plan to have follow-up data on subjects for a range of 5 to 14 years.

During this final project phase, information on all three groups is gathered on a routine basis from the California Departments of Justice and Corrections, and arrangements are being made to secure similar data from the U.S. Department of Justice. These data concern contacts between participants and the criminal justice system. When documented contacts occur, local criminal justice agencies are asked to provide data on the nature and context of the offense, victim characteristics, and other pertinent variables.

Our recently acquired NIMH grant will also allow us to supplement these official record data on reoffense, by adding: (a) yearly parole assessment sessions with all consenting participants for five years postrelease; (b) confidential self-reports regarding reoffense; (c) interviews with collateral informants regarding high-risk situations, lapses, and relapses; and (d) in-depth interviews with subjects regarding the relapse process.

Preliminary Findings

As the above description indicates, SOTEP is collecting an enormous amount of data on participant characteristics, in-treatment changes, and reoffense rates. As a result, a full report of our preliminary findings is beyond the scope of this chapter. A more complete presentation of our findings, along with more detailed descriptions of our treatment and evaluation methods, is presented in Marques et al. (1989a, 1989b). In the following sections, we will provide a brief overview of the results of SOTEP's first 4½ years of operation, highlighting some of the measures that are most directly related to the RP model, as well as our current data on reoffense rates for the three study groups.

Selection Phase Results

Our selection phase data thus far have indicated that only 20% of the eligible offenders in prison have volunteered for the project. Comparing the volunteers with the nonvolunteers revealed only these significant differences: (a) homosexual and bisexual child molesters were more likely to volunteer than were rapists and heterosexual child molesters, (b) the volunteers were younger, and (c) the volunteers had been less violent in their offending.

In-Treatment Changes

As of the end of 1989, 116 Treatment Group participants (88 child molesters and 28 rapists) were admitted to the hospital program. Twelve withdrew from SOTEP, and 7 were returned to Corrections because they presented severe management problems. For analysis, we are retaining in the Treatment Group individuals who return to prison after at least one year of treatment, and their data are included in the treatment component evaluations and in the follow-up (recidivism) analyses. Our current Treatment Group (those who were in the program as of December 31, 1989 and those who were in the program at least 12 months before they left) includes 107 individuals. By offense type, the group is comprised of 49 heterosexual child molesters, 23 homosexual child molesters, 9 bisexual child molesters, and 26 rapists. A description of the demographic and clinical characteristics of this group is presented in Marques et al. (1989b).

Thus far, analyses of the test scores of the Treatment Group members who took both the pre- and postassessment batteries indicate that completion of the hospital program is associated with the following significant ($p < .05$) changes: (a) an increase in personal responsibility and decrease in the use of justifications for sexual crimes, as measured by the Justifications Scale and the Cognitive Distortions and Immaturity Scale of the Multiphasic Sex Inventory (Nichols & Molinder, 1984); (b) improved self-esteem as measured by the Tennessee Self-Concept Scale (Roid & Fitts, 1988); and (c) fewer symptoms of depression, thought disturbance, and social introversion as measured by subscales of the MMPI and the Carlson Psychological Survey (Carlson, 1982). The penile plethysmographic assessment data indicate that subjects with deviant arousal patterns at admission show significant reductions in this arousal, and that the patterns of subjects at discharge are generally nondeviant.

The treatment component evaluations have indicated that the core RP group members are learning the tenets of the RP model, and that completion of the sex education, human sexuality, stress management, social skills, and substance abuse groups has been associated with changes in the predicted directions on relevant measures. Finally, subjects completing the behavior therapy component (most often olfactory aversion) showed significant reductions in arousal to deviant stimuli, but no significant changes in arousal to nondeviant (consenting adult) stimuli.

Prerelease comparisons of our Treatment and Volunteer Control subjects have revealed: (a) different patterns of evaluating potential high-risk situations that the two groups might encounter (described in the following section); (b) fewer cognitive distortions in treated child molesters compared with controls (not so among rapists); and (c) for the Treatment Group, a high correlation ($r = .99$) between RRT estimates and actual arrests for prior sex crimes (while the correlation was not significantly different from 0.0 for controls). Again, a more complete presentation of these findings is available in Marques et al. (1989b).

Measures of RP Constructs

Most of SOTEP's assessment instruments are related to or derived from our RP treatment framework (e.g., measures of locus of control, empathy, cognitive distortions, sexual deviance, social and stress management skills), and several measures directly address the subjects' knowledge of the RP model. What we have chosen to highlight, however, are two measures that are closely related to our basic assumptions regarding RP treatment effects. The findings in the following section address the questions of whether treatment: (a) increases subjects' awareness of high-risk situations, and (b) improves their abilities to cope in these situations.

In order to address these issues, two assessment procedures have been developed. The first is the High-Risk Situations Test, created to assess an offender's ability to acknowledge and identify factors that affect his chances of reoffending. This instrument consists of 58 items that are rated from −3 ("Greatly decrease your chances of reoffending") to +3 ("Greatly increase your chances of reoffending"). A midpoint (0) is anchored as "No effect on your chances of reoffending." The items have been rationally grouped into six themes or types of risks:

(1) Negative Emotional States (e.g., "If I were angry or frustrated");
(2) Temptations and Testing Personal Control (e.g., "If I found an old collection of pornographic pictures depicting illegal sex acts");
(3) Interpersonal Conflict (e.g., "If there were fights at home");
(4) Negative Physical States (e.g., "If my stomach felt like it was tied in knots");
(5) Enhancing Positive Emotional States (e.g., "If good friends dropped by, and I became full of good feelings"); and
(6) Social Pressure (e.g., "If someone pressured me to 'be a good sport' and see some deviant pornography with them").

Currently, 63 Treatment subjects and 52 Volunteer Control subjects have completed the instrument immediately prior to their release on parole. The Treatment Group rated the following factors as presenting significantly greater risks than did the Volunteer Control Group: Negative Emotional States, $t(113) = 2.38$, $p < .05$; Temptations and Testing Personal Control, $t(113) = 2.76$, $p < .01$; and Interpersonal Conflict, $t(113) = 2.23$, $p < .05$. In contrast, the Volunteer Controls did not rate any of the factor areas as presenting significantly greater risks than did the Treatment Group. These results suggested that those offenders who completed the intensive inpatient phase of treatment were more able, or at least more willing, to acknowledge and identify factors that place them at risk for reoffense. Thus the program appears to be achieving one of its primary in-treatment goals.

A second instrument has been developed to assess offenders' coping skills in high-risk situations (Miner, Day, & Nafpaktitis, 1989). Patterned after an instrument developed by Chaney, O'Leary, & Marlatt (1978), the Sex Offender Situational Competency Test (SOSCT) consists of audiotaped descriptions of situations that could lead to a reoffense. Fourteen such situations are individually presented and the subject is asked to report what he would do, think, and say in order to cope with the situation. The responses are videotaped and rated on a number of factors by independent observers. To date, 15 Treatment Group subjects have completed this procedure both at their admission to and their discharge from the hospital program. The results indicated that the coping responses at discharge, compared with those at admission, were rated as significantly more effective, $F(1, 14) = 15.41$, $p <$ .005; more assertive, $F(1, 14) = 10.89$, $p < .005$; more complex, $F(1, 14) = 12.17$, $p < .005$; and presented a greater number of coping alternatives, $F(1, 14) = 8.2$, $p < .05$. Thus, it appeared the subjects were able to articulate more effective coping responses to high-risk situations after completion of their inpatient phase of treatment, achieving this primary treatment objective as well.

Another RP assumption we examined is the proposal of an association between an offender's recognition of his risks for reoffense and the development of coping responses to reduce those risks. In our view, offenders who recognize and acknowledge they are in danger of committing another rape or molestation are more motivated to prepare for those dangers than are offenders who deny reoffense risks. In order to test this assumption, we analyzed the ratings of the 42 Treatment Group Subjects who completed both the High-Risk Situations Test and the SOSCT immediately prior to their discharge on parole. The expectation that high-risk identification and coping response abilities would be related was partially supported by modest, but significant, correlations between effectiveness ratings on the Sex Offender Situational Competency Test and ratings of risk on the Negative Emotional States ($r = .31$, $p < .05$), Temptations and Testing Personal Control ($r = .38$, $p < .05$), and Social Pressure ($r = .46$, $p < .01$) factors on the High-Risk Situations Test. Thus it appeared that there was indeed some association between identifying risks and describing effective coping responses in at least three high-risk areas.

Aftercare and Follow-Up Data

Our numbers for the parole assessment (one year postrelease) results are still too small to examine changes within groups on the questionnaires used. We also have too few data to draw conclusions from the randomized response (RRT) data; at this time only one question, concerning deviant fantasies rather than actual reoffenses, has yielded an estimate significantly above 0. We do have some preliminary indications that prerelease measures of cognitive distortions and high-risk recognition may be useful in predicting parole revocations among our subjects, but these are based on a very small sample at this time.

While it is also too soon to analyze our follow-up phase data (reoffense rates), we will present a summary of our preliminary findings here because of the importance of this information. Reoffense is, after all, the most important variable in the study of sex offender treatment, as well as the final indication of whether an RP program has succeeded or failed.

By the end of 1989, 72 subjects originally selected for the Treatment Group had been released. Of these, 57 were discharged from the treatment program, and 15 were released from prison after having been returned (either voluntarily or involuntarily) to the Department of Corrections. As was noted above, for purposes of our follow-up analysis, the 9 individuals who left from prison but had at least a year of SOTEP treatment are included in our Treatment Group. The remaining 6, those who returned to prison with less than one year of treatment, are not considered members of the Treatment Group and will be considered separately, as the Ex-Treatment Group. As of the end of 1989, 66 Volunteer Controls and 56 Nonvolunteer Controls had been released from prison.

Data from official state records (rap sheets from the Department of Justice and inmate data from the Department of Corrections) for the four study groups are presented in Table 10.1. The "arrest-no disposition" offenses are charges that are either still pending or have been dropped. The "return to custody" events are charges that resulted in the subject's return to prison, either with a new conviction or by parole revocation. As can be seen in the table, the Ex-Treatment Group has the most criminal justice involvement thus far, and the Treatment Group the least. It is, however, much too early to draw conclusions from these preliminary indications for several reasons. First, our study groups are still quite small. Also, as Marshall and Barbaree (1990) have most recently emphasized, sex offender treatment outcome studies must have follow-up periods of at least several years, and should not rely on official record data alone in estimating actual reoffense rates. As we described above, SOTEP's evaluation project will collect subject follow-up data for 5-14 years postrelease, and will include multiple data sources (interviews with subjects, parole agent notes, confidential self-reports, and RRT data) in order to supplement official records. At this time, these data are still being collected and analyzed, and are not ready to report.

TABLE 10.1 SOTEP Reoffense Summary (12/31/89)

Status	Treatment	Ex-Treatment	Volunteer Control	Nonvolunteer Control
N	66 (57 completed, 9 > 1 yr. treatment)	6 (< 1 yr. treatment)	66	56
$\overline{X}$ time since release	18 months	27 months	21 months	22 months
Arrest, No Disposition				
Sex offense	1 (2%)	1 (17%)	—	2 (4%)
Other violent offense	—	—	—	2 (4%)
Substance	1 (2%)	—	1 (2%)	—
Property	—	—	—	—
Return to Custody				
Sex offense	1 (2%)	2 (33%)	4 (6%)	2 (4%)
Other violent offense	2 (3%)	—	2 (3%)	2 (4%)
Substance	2 (3%)	—	5 (8%)	4 (7%)
Property	—	—	1 (2%)	2 (4%)
Reason unknown/ Parole violation	6 (9%)	2 (33%)	8 (12%)	14 (25%)
TOTALS	13 (20%)	5 (83%)	21 (32%)	28 (50%)

Conclusions

California's Sex Offender Treatment and Evaluation Project is an experimental test of a relapse prevention program specifically designed for rapists and child molesters. Data from the first 57 subjects leaving the program are encouraging, in that completion of the program is associated with a number of positive changes in variables considered relevant to sexual offending (e.g., decreases in cognitive distortions and deviant sexual arousal), and variables closely tied to the RP model (improved skills in the areas of recognizing and planning coping responses for high-risk situations). We do not, however, have sufficient data to evaluate the effect of the program on the most important RP variable—

whether the subject can indeed follow through with his planned coping response in a high-risk situation. As is the case with all sex offender treatment programs, our RP program will be a success only if the subjects succeed in avoiding reoffense.

Note

1. Treatment manuals for the core RP group and specialty groups are available from Craig Nelson, Ph.D., Sex Offender Treatment Project, Atascadero State Hospital, P.O. Box 7001, Atascadero, CA 93423.

References

Bandura, A. (1977). Self-efficacy: Toward a unifying theory of behavioral change. *Psychological Review, 84,* 191-215.

California Penal Code. (1981). Sections 1364 & 1365.

California Penal Code. (1982). Sections 1364 & 1365.

Carlson, K. A. (1982). *Carlson Psychological Survey.* Port Huron, MI: Research Psychologists Press.

Chaney, E. F., O'Leary, M. R., & Marlatt, G. A. (1978). Skill training with alcoholics. *Journal of Consulting and Clinical Psychology, 46,* 1092-1104.

Furby, L., Weinrott, M. R., & Blackshaw, L. (1989). Sex offender recidivism: A review. *Psychological Bulletin, 105,* 3-30.

George, W. H., & Marlatt, G. A. (1989). Introduction. In D. R. Laws (Ed.), *Relapse prevention with sex offenders.* New York: Guilford.

Hall, R. L. (1989). Relapse rehearsal. In D. R. Laws (Ed.), *Relapse prevention with sex offenders.* New York: Guilford.

Knopp, F. H. (1984). *Retraining adult sex offenders: Methods and models.* Syracuse, NY: Safer Society Press.

Laws, D. R. (1988). Introductory comments. In R. Prentky & V. Quinsey (Eds.), Human sexual aggression: Current perspectives. *Annals of the New York Academy of Sciences, 528,* 203-205.

Laws, D. R. (Ed.). (1989). *Relapse prevention with sex offenders.* New York: Guilford.

Laws, D. R., & Osborne, C. A. (1983). How to build and operate a behavioral laboratory to evaluate and treat sexual deviance. In J. G. Greer & I. R. Stuart (Eds.), *The sexual aggressor: Current perspectives on treatment* (pp. 293-335). New York: Van Nostrand Reinhold.

Marlatt, G. A., & Gordon, J. R. (1980). Determinants of relapse: Implications for the maintenance of behavior change. In P. Davidson & S. Davidson (Eds.), *Behavioral medicine: Changing health lifestyles.* New York: Brunner/Mazel.

Marlatt, G. A., & Gordon, J. R. (Eds.). (1985). *Relapse prevention: Maintenance strategies in the treatment of addictive behaviors.* New York: Guilford.

Marques, J. K. (1984). *An innovative treatment program for sex offenders: Report to the Legislature.* Sacramento: California State Department of Mental Health.

Marques, J. K. (1988). The Sex Offender Treatment and Evaluation Project: California's new outcome study. *Annals of the New York Academy of Sciences, 528,* 235-243.

Marques, J. K., Day, D. M., Nelson, C. S., & Miner, M. H. (1989a). The Sex Offender Treatment and Evaluation Project: California's relapse prevention program. In D. R. Laws (Ed.), *Relapse prevention with sex offenders.* New York: Guilford.

Marques, J. K., Day, D. M., Nelson, C. S., & Miner, M. H. (1989b). *The Sex Offender Treatment and Evaluation Project: Third report to the Legislature in response to PC 1365.* Sacramento: California State Department of Mental Health.

Marques, J. K., & Nelson, C. (1989a). Elements of high-risk situations for sex offenders. In D. R. Laws (Ed.), *Relapse prevention with sex offenders.* New York: Guilford.

Marques, J. K., & Nelson, C. (1989b). Understanding and preventing relapse in sex offenders. In M. Gossop (Ed.), *Relapse and addictive behavior.* London: Routledge & Kegan Paul.

Marques, J. K., Pithers, W. D., & Marlatt, G. A. (1984). Relapse prevention: A self-control program for sex offenders [Appendix]. In J. K. Marques, *An innovative treatment program for sex offenders: Report to the Legislature.* Sacramento: California State Department of Mental Health.

Marshall, W. L., & Barbaree, H. E. (1990). Outcome of comprehensive cognitive-behavioral treatment programs. In W. L. Marshall, D. R. Laws, & H. E. Barbaree (Eds.), *Handbook of sexual assault: Issues, theories and treatment of the offender.* New York: Plenum.

Miner, M. H., Day, D. M., & Nafpaktitis, M. (1989). Assessment of coping skills: Development of a situational competency test. In D. R. Laws (Ed.), *Relapse prevention with sex offenders.* New York: Guilford.

Nelson, C., Miner, M., Marques, J., Russell, K., & Achterkirchen, J. (1988). Relapse prevention: A cognitive-behavioral model for treatment of the rapist and child molester. *Journal of Social Work and Human Sexuality, 7,* 125-143.

Nelson, C., & Jackson, P. (1989). High-risk recognition: The cognitive-behavioral chain. In D. R. Laws (Ed.), *Relapse prevention with sex offenders.* New York: Guilford.

Nichols, H. R., & Molinder, I. (1984). *The multiphasic sex inventory manual.* (Available from Nichols and Molinder, 437 Bowes Drive, Tacoma, WA 98466).

Nowicki, S., & Strickland, B. (1973). A locus of control scale. *Journal of Consulting and Clinical Psychology, 40,* 148-154.

Roid, G. H., & Fitts, W. H. (1988). *Tennessee Self-Concept Scale: Revised manual.* Los Angeles: Western Psychological Services.

Rotter, J. B. (1966). Generalized expectancies for internal versus external control of reinforcement. *Psychological Monographs, 80,*(1, No. 609).

Steenman, H., Nelson, C., & Viesti, C. (1989). Developing coping strategies for high-risk situations. In D. R. Laws (Ed.), *Relapse prevention with sex offenders.* New York: Guilford.

Warner, S. L. (1965). Randomized response: A survey technique for eliminating evasive answer bias. *Journal of the American Statistical Association, 60,* 63-69.

11

Dealing With Dangerousness:
Community Risk Management Strategies
With Violent Offenders

VERNON L. QUINSEY

WILLIAM D. WALKER

This chapter concerns the community supervision and treatment of persons whose histories of violent misbehaviors raise serious societal concerns about their commission of further violent acts. For ease of exposition, these persons will be referred to as "offenders," although some (such as violent psychiatric patients) have not been convicted of any crime, despite their violent histories. In addition, because most of these offenders are male, "offenders" will be referred to as males throughout this chapter.

Typically, problems in offender management surface when an offender is considered for release from an institution in which he was initially placed because of some violent behavior. It is difficult to strike the proper balance between the offender's civil liberties and community

AUTHORS' NOTE: Preparation of this chapter was supported by a contract with the Kingston Psychiatric Hospital. We wish to thank C. Earls, G. Harris, and M. Rice for their comments on an earlier version of this chapter. Address correspondence to V. L. Quinsey, Psychology Department, Queen's University, Kingston, Ontario, K7L 3N6.

safety; that is, to answer the questions of who should be released and when. Such decisions must be made with little help from the literature on the prediction of violence. Basically, this literature asserts that, although certain historical variables statistically predict future violence, a large proportion of offenders, perhaps the majority, who are assessed as dangerous (by whatever method) in fact turn out to have been inaccurately judged to be dangerous (false positives). Regardless of the scientific defensibility of these predictions, however, they are ubiquitous and there is a very real political need for decision makers to appear to have done a proper and careful "scientific" assessment in case the offender commits a further violent act that becomes public knowledge.

Persons who are responsible for the community management of offenders with histories of serious aggressive behaviors, sex offenses, or firesetting often greet their task with a mixture of worry and despair. And no wonder; much of the scientific literature argues that neither treatment nor supervision has demonstrable effects on recidivism, and thus it is often unclear to practitioners what should be done with or for the offender. In any event, the resources and expertise available for specific programming are often slender.

The community serves as the final common path for patients discharged from psychiatric facilities, developmentally handicapped persons discharged from institutions, and inmates released from correctional institutions. Within the psychiatric hospital system, the "revolving door" syndrome of frequent short hospital admissions is well known. Within the system for the developmentally handicapped, policies of normalization and deinstitutionalization have resulted in large numbers of developmentally handicapped individuals living in the community with varying amounts of support. Similarly, because of probation and parole orders, large numbers of convicted offenders live in the community under supervision.

It is striking that the issues involved in managing or reducing the risk of violence posed by offenders in these three traditionally separate human service sectors are almost identical. These similarities are ironic given the great attention paid to making the initial disposition to a particular human service system and the difficulties in dealing with persons who do not fit neatly within any one of the three, such as dually diagnosed persons or mentally disordered offenders. This concern with initial placement, as reflected in such legal dispositions as "not guilty by reason of insanity," is based not so much on the behaviors that initially led to institutionalization or the kind of programs that are actually delivered within a sector, but rather the perceived appropriateness of the confine and medicate, confine and train, or confine and punish paradigms traditionally characterizing the three human service sectors.

This is not, of course, to assert that the same proportions of offenders in each of these sectors pose a risk for violence or that the type of violent behavior of concern is necessarily of the same kind or severity. Although one associates propensities for violence primarily with the criminal justice system, the proportion of persons posing such a risk within any service sector is dependent on a variety of substantively uninteresting bureaucratic and legal arrangements within particular jurisdictions (e.g., Axelson & Wahl, in press). This is summed up for mental health and corrections by Penrose's Law, which asserts that the number of persons in the mental health and correctional systems is a constant (Penrose, 1939). Although in fact only a minority of offenders within any of the three service sectors pose a high risk of exhibiting serious violent behaviors, there are a sufficient number in each that the absolute number living in the community is large.

The purpose of this chapter is to argue that community risk management can be improved by combining what is already known from three areas of inquiry: The prediction of violence, the study of decision making and clinical judgment, and the literature on treatment outcome and program evaluation. It will be argued that, although these literatures certainly can (and have) induced therapeutic and supervisory nihilism among practitioners, more recent developments offer grounds for some optimism, particularly when an integrative approach is taken.

Predicting Violent Recidivism and Community Supervision

The prediction of both general and violent criminal recidivism of persons released from correctional and psychiatric institutions has received extensive study (for reviews see Gabor, 1986; Monahan, 1981; Quinsey, 1984; Waller, 1974; Webster & Menzies, 1987). Enough work has been completed to establish a general consensus within the research community about the classes of variables that are valid predictors of recidivism and the degree to which they are related to the criterion behaviors of interest.

American and Canadian studies of released inmates (for a list contact the senior author) agree that youthfulness and number of previous convictions are positively related to the probability of criminal recidivism. Most studies have found that recidivism rates are inversely related to offense severity. However, because of the relative rarity of serious offenses against the person, most studies of criminal recidivism, even those with large samples, essentially examine predictors of robbery, breaking and entering, and other property crimes. This is an important problem because there is evidence that the variables that predict violent crimes against the person are different than those that predict general (both violent and nonviolent) recidivism (Holland, Holt, & Brewer, 1978; Mandelzys, 1979; Nuffield, 1982).

Other predictors, including age at first arrest, criminal versatility (variety of offending), alcohol abuse, and low educational attainment, are usually found to be positively but more weakly related to recidivism rates. Although there are conflicting findings on the relation between institutional behavior and postrelease recidivism, escape and escape attempts have consistently been found to be related to higher recidivism rates. A number of investigators have combined these and related predictors in various ways to obtain summary scores that are more closely related to recidivism than any predictor taken singly. Those developed in Canada include the general recidivism and violent recidivism scales of Nuffield (1982), the Level of Supervision Inventory (Andrews, Kiessling, Mickus, & Robinson, 1986; Bonta & Motiuk, 1985), and the Psychopathy Checklist (Hare, Chapter 13 this volume).

Studies of offenders released from or assessed in psychiatric institutions (for a list contact the senior author) have reached essentially the same conclusions as those drawn on the basis of inmate follow-up studies. Previous criminal history emerges as the best single variable predictor of subsequent recidivism and violent recidivism. Typically, a diagnosis of personality disorder is associated with higher recidivism than a diagnosis of psychosis. Psychopathy, as defined by the Hare Checklist, emerges as a good predictor of both general and violent recidivism just as it does in correctional samples (Harris, Rice, & Cormier, 1991).

The identification of robust and theoretically interpretable predictors of violent recidivism encourages their exploration as moderators or typological variables. Although many investigators have argued that typologies of offenders should be developed for which different predictive variables would be relevant (e.g., Deitz, 1985; Mandelzys, 1979; Quinsey & Maguire, 1986), this work has not proceeded very far until recently. One particularly good candidate for such a typological scheme is psychopathy because of its close association with instrumental and predatory violent recidivism. As an illustrative thought experiment, one can contrast the types of predictive variables likely to prove useful with overcontrolled-hostile men characterized by extreme acts of aggression directed at family members or close associates, lack of criminal history, and severe assertive deficits (Megargee, Cook, & Mendelsohn, 1967; Quinsey, Maguire, & Varney, 1983) with psychopaths characterized by versatile criminal histories, violence for instrumental purposes committed against strangers, and exploitative life-style.

Further conceptual work, however, is needed before psychopathy can be employed in intervention work. It is not clear whether its categorical nature is relevant (Harris, Rice, & Quinsey, in press a), whether the temperament factor of the Psychopathy Checklist should be considered independently of its criminal history factor, and how Checklist scores should be considered in relation to supervision and treatment. Psychopathy could be interpreted as influencing responsivity to treatment, mediating compliance, or both.

Regrettably, however, there remains a yawning chasm between the bulk of the empirical prediction literature and practical violent offender release policies. Barring recent exceptions, the empirical literature deals almost exclusively with static or "tombstone" predictors such as age, offense history, and length of institutionalization. Because both community and institutional service providers require information about predictors that they can modify in order to plan interventions effectively, the bulk of this empirical follow-up literature is essentially irrelevant to them, particularly inasmuch as so few offenders are institutionalized under indeterminate conditions. For the vast majority of offenders, the question is not whether they will be released but when.

The gap between the needs of program managers and the dominant focus of the empirical literature is most readily apparent in an area where one might least expect it: The prediction of violent reoffending among mentally disordered offenders. Although mentally disordered offenders are typically dealt with by mental health professionals working in a psychiatric hospital system that explicitly espouses a treatment-rehabilitation model, of 28 follow-up studies of released mentally disordered offenders identified in a recent review of this literature, 25 employed only static predictors and only 3 (of which 2 were essentially pilot investigations) attempted to predict recidivism from measures of therapeutic change (Quinsey, 1988).

With respect to violent recidivism, the inability of most of the prediction literature to inform treatment and release policies is even more pronounced. Under many circumstances the probability of violent recidivism is low. This welcome infrequency of postrelease violence means that efforts to predict it inevitably result in unacceptably high rates of false positives. Much of this literature appears to suggest that the optimal prediction for violent offenders is that none of them are dangerous; treatments designed to reduce violent recidivism, therefore, are superfluous and supervision unnecessary.

However, contrary to the impression given by the prediction literature, the base rate of violence is sometimes high enough to make predictions well worth while (e.g., Harris, Rice, & Quinsey, in press b). First, it is certain that the base rate of violent behavior has often been underestimated by recidivism research because investigators have used lists of criminal charges ("rap sheet" data) instead of police descriptions of the behaviors involved, follow-up periods that are too short (because serious violent crimes are often low frequency phenomena), and unlikely populations of offenders (e.g., old persons). For a discussion of these and other interpretive problems see Gordon, 1977; Quinsey, 1980; Quinsey & Maguire, 1986). Offenders likely to exhibit high base rates of violent behaviors include those with lengthy histories of violent crime (e.g., Walker, Hammond, & Steer, 1967), psychopaths (e.g., Hare & McPherson, 1984), and persons repeatedly passed over for release when held under fully indeterminate conditions (Quinsey, 1980; Quinsey, & Maguire, 1986).

Thus the bulk of the follow-up literature provides very little information for choosing appropriate programs for violent offenders or in making decisions based upon offender change. All of the above leads to a reconsideration of what might be done to reduce recidivism; that is, not so much how to predict it (except to identify high-risk groups as opposed to individuals) but how to reduce or prevent it in the community. The key, therefore, lies in the effectiveness of postrelease supervision and treatment.

We are not the first to arrive at this conclusion. In the preface to Waller's (1974) book on prison releasees, Edwards (p. vii) states:

> What is called for is a major realignment of the time and energies of those engaged in the fields of correction and related organizations towards the alleviation of those problems associated with employment, family and community relationships, and alcoholism which are at the root of most failures following release.

It is, of course, difficult to know what sorts of community programs need to be developed in the absence of knowing the antecedents of recidivism. *Antecedents* in this context means specifiable dynamic conditions of the offender or identifiable environmental events that precede recidivism. Antecedent conditions are, therefore, variables that supervisory authorities or offenders themselves could potentially do something about in order to prevent the commission of a criminal act. Static personal characteristics of offenders are useful in this context as variables that define the risk group to which an offender belongs and as moderator variables, that is, variables that determine the manner in which antecedents affect behavior.

Determinants of sexual reoffending among 136 child molesters and 64 rapists have been examined in detail by Pithers, Kashima, Cumming, Beal, and Buell (1988). Nearly 90% of their sample of sex offenders reported experiencing strong emotional states before relapse (the commission of a new sex offense): 94% of the rapists reported feeling anger, usually occasioned by interpersonal conflict; 46% of the child molesters reported experiencing anxiety and 38% reported depression (these emotional states appeared to be related to social disaffiliation). The chain leading to relapse seemed to begin with negative affect leading to paraphiliac sexual fantasies, then cognitive distortions, and, finally, passive planning just prior to the offense. Frisbie (1969), based on 550 interviews of 311 child molesters under supervision, concluded that, in addition to alcohol abuse, factors predicting recidivism were "the desire for and selection of physically immature children as sexual objects, unorthodox ethical values, and grave difficulties in establishing meaningful relationships with adult females on a mature basis" (p. 223). The similarities between Frisbie's observations and those of Pithers et al. (fantasies, disaffiliation, and cognitive distortion) are striking. Planning and behavioral rehearsal as antecedents to serious sexual offenses have also been noted by MacCulloch, Snowden, Wood, and Mills (1983). It is of interest in the present context that Frisbie (1969) was surprised at how much her interviewees would disclose to a project interviewer; because of their home visits, the research team was often aware of impending relapse before the parole authorities.

The use of dynamic theoretically chosen predictors of recidivism among sex offenders has proven useful. For example, follow-up studies of patients released from a maximum security psychiatric institution have shown that phallometric measures of sexual preference predict new sexual convictions among both rapists (Rice, Harris, & Quinsey, 1990) and child molesters (Rice, Quinsey, & Harris, 1991).

With respect to the antecedents of supervisory failure in the form of general recidivism, Waller (1974) found that lack of employment, undesirable associates, fighting, not seeing one's children, and frequent drinking predicted reoffending. Hart, Kropp, and Hare (1988) also observed that instability in both employment and relationships during the follow-up period predicted reoffending. Recently, more direct evidence relating to the usefulness of identifying antecedents of general recidivism has been provided (Andrews, 1982, 1989). Motiuk and Porporino (1989), for example, have shown that parole officers' crude assessment of parolees' needs at the beginning of supervision was more accurate in predicting general recidivism than the well validated Nuffield Scale (Nuffield, 1982) for evaluating risk based on criminal history. The needs that demonstrated predictive validity were: criminal companions, alcohol/drug use, instability in living arrangement, and lack of responsiveness to supervision. The finding that postrelease factors are closely related to recidivism is extremely important because they provide potential targets for both supervision and intervention. The combination of traditional static predictors with dynamic predictors, measured postrelease, appears very promising.

Although it is obvious that a great deal of work remains to be accomplished, a clear picture is emerging of the approach to be taken if prediction research is to inform supervisory and release policies. It involves first, the further identification of factors that determine risk and, therefore, whether an offender requires supervision, and, second, the establishment of links between postrelease dynamic variables and violent crime. It is highly likely that some of these antecedents are specific to certain types of offenders. In short, prediction research should be used to establish theories of recidivism for homogeneous groups of offenders that can be tested by the evaluation of specific interventions.

Clinical Judgment

The past quarter century of research has severely shaken confidence in the accuracy of clinical judgment both in absolute terms and in comparison to actuarial models (Dawes, 1989; Meehl, 1986). This research will not be reviewed here except where it bears upon the prediction of violent behavior or the treatment of offenders (for a recent review of the clinical appraisal of dangerousness see Webster & Menzies, 1987). Early research indirectly evaluated assessments of dangerousness by following offenders who were released from secure psychiatric institutions because of court orders (Steadman & Cocozza, 1974; Thornberry & Jacoby, 1979). Because these offenders were at least implicitly considered to be dangerous, their very low rates of violent recidivism spoke to the conservative bias of clinical judgment. Similarly, a statistical model derived from forensic clinicians' predictions of violence was not significantly related to violent recidivism for a sample of offenders released from a maximum security psychiatric sample (Quinsey & Maguire, 1986).

In a study that controlled the amount and kind of clinical file information available to forensic psychiatrists who were asked to make predictions of future violent behavior and mock release decisions concerning mentally disordered offenders (Quinsey & Ambtman, 1979), it was found that the clinicians showed low rates of agreement with each other on the patients' dangerousness and based their appraisal primarily on the seriousness of the index offense. The average of the psychiatrists' judgments closely corresponded to those of high school teachers who were asked to rate the same clinical material. The lack of difference between clinicians' and lay peoples' appraisals of dangerousness has also been demonstrated in ratings of fictitious case histories (Quinsey & Cyr, 1986) and the low amount of interclinician congruence has been replicated in studies of actual case conferences (Quinsey & Ambtman, 1978; Quinsey & Maguire, 1983, 1986; Menzies, Webster, & Sepejak, 1985).

Of the variety of clinical prediction tasks, it would be expected that violence prediction would be among the most problematic because of the low base rate of violent behavior. Human judges are known to be insensitive to differing base rates under a variety of conditions, such as when they are asked to assess the likelihood of some event given the base rate of the alternatives plus worthless diagnostic information (Kahneman & Tversky, 1973). For example, subjects may be asked to guess whether a person is an engineering or arts student based upon a physical description and a specification of what proportion of students are in engineering or arts. The Kahneman and Tversky task actually requires subjects to postdict rather than predict because they are asked, for example, whether a person is an engineer or arts student instead of whether a person will become an engineer or arts student. Prediction tasks (those that inquire about future events such as violent behavior) appear to lead to even greater departure from base rates under the worthless information condition than the formally identical postdiction tasks of Kahneman and Tversky with both student and forensic clinician subjects (Preston & Quinsey, 1990).

Despite the kind of evidence presented here that documents the unreliability and poor validity of clinical appraisals of dangerousness, these clinical appraisals continue to be the dominant method of making dispositional decisions pertaining to security and supervision within the corrections/criminal justice system, psychiatric hospitals, and the system for the developmentally handicapped.

One might expect forensic clinicians on the basis of their training to do better in assessing the treatability of offenders and in selecting specific treatments for them than in assessing dangerousness. Although there are fewer data on this form of judgment than on the clinical prediction of violence, what data exist are even more discouraging. Quinsey and Maguire (1983) studied 200 consecutive court remands to a maximum security psychiatric facility. The treatability of each offender was independently rated by forensic clinicians after each case conference preceding his return to the court. The clinicians showed poorer agreement on the rating of general treatability than they did on the dangerousness of these offenders. Interclinician agreement on ratings of the efficacy of discrete types of treatment were extremely low, with the exception of neuroleptic medication. Agreement did not improve when the most senior or the most optimistic pair of clinicians was compared. In general, clinicians were extremely pessimistic about the prospects for treatment, especially for offenders diagnosed as personality disordered as opposed to psychotic.

Quinsey and Cyr (1986) constructed fictitious case histories of offenders and had them evaluated by clinicians and laypersons. Half of the offenders' histories were crime free and essentially normal (the index offense was out of character and severely provoked) and half contained descriptions of many acts that were similar to but less serious than the index offense (suggesting a diagnosis of personality disorder and an internal attribution). Clinicians and laypersons made similar judgments. Ratings of dangerousness were negatively correlated with ratings of treatability and the normal offenders were judged to be more treatable than those with lengthy histories of similar behaviors.

Fortunately, it has been shown to be possible for clinicians and decision makers to improve the quality of their decisions through the use of actuarial information. Gottfredson, Wilkins, and Hoffman (1978) have shown how actuarial predictions of risk (a salient factor score) can be used by parole authorities in establishing a range of sentence for each risk category. Using Gottfredson's scheme, parole authorities can simply select the midpoint of the range of sentence lengths appropriate to a given offender's risk category or instead elect to use their judgment to increase or decrease the time served from the midpoint within the range. More rarely, they may choose to go outside the normal range by exercising a clinical override provision, providing they articulate specific reasons for so doing. This scheme for structuring discretion makes the basis for the decisions explicit (and thus open to examination and revision), and anchors or calibrates the decision makers by focusing their attention on specific base rates or risk values. In addition, this strategy preserves the involvement of human decision makers while aiding their judgment. Ongoing computerized feedback could be used with such a system to indicate to decision makers whether they exhibit conservative or liberal bias relative to their peers or the model itself and the degree of rigidity in their implicit decision policy by examining the variance in their recommended sentence lengths. Such a method could, in principle, be elaborated to combine static and dynamic variables into a release, supervision, and treatment plan. Essentially, the idea is to develop an "expert system" to aid, but not dictate to, clinical decision makers.

Treatment

Intervention is usually bound to prediction. Given that a person possesses characteristics that predict a high probability of further violent behavior, societal options are limited to incapacitation or treatment. It is clear that successful treatment, unlike incapacitation, serves both the interests of society and the individual offender. Incapacitation is also an apocalyptic alternative: What of the false positives generated by the most accurate of the present generation of actuarial-clinical prediction models? Given the options, these offenders must be confined until age takes them out of the high-risk category.

One of the few ethical ways in which the base rate problem can be addressed is through the design of interventions that are positive enough (i.e., neither aversive nor intrusive) and inexpensive enough that they can be implemented for an entire high-risk group. The cost of this strategy is that a substantial number of false positives have to receive a given intervention in order to ensure that all of the true positives have received it. A simple example of this strategy involves airport security procedures. Extremely few passengers that pass through airport screening are carrying weapons but everyone is treated as though this is a real possibility; such screening is socially acceptable because it is brief, benign, and reasonably effective. A more closely related example is the program developed in Norway by Olweus (Chapter 5 this volume), who administered a program to reduce bullying to an entire population of children. The nature of the program was such that there was no problem with nonbullying children receiving it.

Treatment is also bound to prediction in another way. The evidence with respect to the efficacy of interventions designed to reduce general recidivism among correctional populations suggests that efficacy is determined in part by whether the interventions are focused on high-risk cases and actually target dynamic risk factors or "criminogenic needs" (Andrews, 1982, 1989). This means that interventions designed to reduce recidivism should be both reserved for high risk cases and individualized so as to target idiosyncratic risk factors.

However, recidivism follow-up studies employing only static risk and/or institutional treatment predictors leave it both empirically and conceptually unclear, as Mandelzys (1979) has pointed out, how much criminal recidivism is a result of unresolved problems within a released offender that could have been addressed during a period of incarceration and what proportion of new offenses are caused by new environmental or offender problems. Of course, the longer the time between release and recidivism, the less likely a within-institution intervention will be relevant. Another way of thinking about this issue is that recidivism studies do not evaluate the effects of institutional interventions directly but rather their generalization and maintenance because the intervention and the measurement of its effects occur in different settings (Gottschalk, Davidson, Mayer, & Gensheimer, 1987). Moreover, the recent literature on psychological and behavioral interventions for delinquents and adult offenders strongly suggests that treatment effects seldom generalize across settings (Braukmann & Wolf, 1987; Milan, 1987a, 1987b; Rice, Quinsey, & Houghton, 1990). The unequivocal conclusion from this literature is that interventions must occur in the settings in which the behaviors of concern occur. In offender programming, therefore, interventions that are designed to reduce postrelease recidivism must continue in the community. This conclusion requires that the purpose of intervention be reconceptualized from attempting to produce a cure from a temporally restricted treatment given in an institutional environment to enhancing long-term adjustment through continuing intervention (e.g., Kazdin, 1987).

It is of interest that this conclusion has been arrived at in several different areas of psychopathology at about the same time. Consider the treatment of schizophrenia. This area is interesting both because the disorder (or, more correctly, the construct) has some genetic and physiological determinants and because schizophrenia is part of the cause of some offenders' violent behaviors or, at least, part of the context in which the violent behaviors must be addressed. Schizophrenic offenders are, of course, most common in secure psychiatric hospitals. It is well known that phenothiazines are the treatment of choice for active schizophrenic symptoms (such as delusions and hallucinations), particularly in the acute phase of the illness. It is less well accepted, although well documented, that social learning programs can be very effective with chronic, severe, and assaultive schizophrenic patients (Paul & Lentz, 1977).

The problem of schizophrenic relapse and readmission following even successful treatment has proven to be an intractable problem until recently (see Paul & Lentz, 1977, for a review). Demographic and symptom-severity data gathered in-hospital typically predict little of the variance in readmission data (e.g., Abramowitz, Tupin, & Berger, 1984). The prevailing view that relapse is usually caused by medication noncompliance now appears to be incorrect (Hogarty et al., 1986). Although a complete theory of relapse is not yet developed, recent evidence obtained prospectively indicates that specific stressful events (outside the subjects' control and independent of their illness) are related to subsequent relapse among schizophrenic patients (Ventura, Nuechterlein, Lukoff, & Hardesty, 1989). In line with this finding, a number of studies have observed much higher relapse rates among schizophrenics released to families high in "expressed emotion"; that is, highly critical of and sometimes hostile toward the identified patient. Further work has shown that educational and behavioral interventions focused on helping high-risk families deal with their schizophrenic relatives and social skill training of the patients can markedly lower relapse rates (Falloon et al., 1985; Hogarty et al., 1986; Liberman, 1988). The relevance of the expressed emotion variable is readily apparent to any clinician who has worked with schizophrenic murderers found not guilty by reason of insanity.

Lukoff, Liberman, and Nuechterlein (1986) have described a system of ongoing symptom monitoring for determining when to alter drug levels, psychosocial programs, and amount of supervision for schizophrenic patients that is similar in spirit to what is required for the community management of high-risk offenders, whether schizophrenic or not. There is also some evidence that uncontrollable adverse events causing significant disruption in a person's life increase the risk of developing depression (e.g., Swindle, Cronkite, & Moos, 1989). The potential relevance of this observation to the supervision and treatment of violent offenders is illustrated by Cote and Hodgins (1992) who found that a representative sample of Canadian homicide offenders suffered significantly more frequently from depression associated with alcohol abuse than other prison inmates and that the depression ante-dated the murder for 83% of these offenders.

Alcohol abuse is a common antecedent of violent crime and an extremely high proportion of correctional inmates have alcohol and drug abuse problems (Ross & Lightfoot, 1985). One of the most prom-ising approaches to substance abuse in recent years is relapse preven-tion, an approach that teaches clients to avoid idiosyncratic high-risk situations and to cope with them if they cannot avoid or escape them (e.g., Brownell, Marlatt, Lichenstein, & Wilson, 1986). The relapse prevention approach is explicitly rehabilitative and does not purport to offer a cure for the problem. This approach has recently been adapted for use in treating sex offenders, teaching coping skills to deal with the antecedents of sexual crime described earlier in the section on predic-tion (Pithers et al., 1988).

Our argument is that if more effective programs for violent offenders are to be developed, the rehabilitative focus found in the treatment of other and related problems should be adopted. The problem of violence is not unique except in that it requires incapacitation in extremely high-risk cases, such as serial murderers (because no conceivable treatment outcome could give a decision maker sufficient confidence to recommend release), and levels of supervision, such as electronic monitoring for high-risk cases, not usually required for other sorts of problems.

The costs of not basing interventions on the scientific literature can be high because programs developed using incorrect theoretical models can not only be ineffective (Gendreau & Andrews, 1989), they can actually increase recidivism. For example, Andrews (1982) points out that evocative or insight-oriented therapeutic models have been associ-ated with increased recidivism rates among criminal offenders. Wormith (1984) found that recidivism rates were positively related to inmate self-esteem under conditions where the inmates maintained procriminal attitudes. Harris et al. (1991) have recently reported that violent recidivism was higher among psychopaths exposed to a rigorous milieu therapy program in a secure psychiatric facility than among psychopaths placed in correctional facilities. The reverse was true for nonpsychopaths.

The treatment literature suggests that outcome is improved when specific problems affecting recidivism or relapse among specific kinds of offenders, patients, or clients are addressed on an ongoing basis as they arise. Careful problem or risk factor identification and monitoring of individuals is one of the keys to successful supervision and intervention. Problem, need, or dynamic risk factors, however, can also be used to facilitate treatment and supervision practices through the development of overall treatment programs and policies.

In a maximum security psychiatric facility, Rice and Harris (1988) used a Problem Survey (Quinsey, Cyr, & Lavallee, 1988) to assess the frequency with which patients exhibited various problem behaviors (e.g., assaultiveness, litigiousness, suspiciousness, depression, poor self-care, alcohol abuse) in the community or in the institution by soliciting clinical staff opinions. Using factor analysis, these problems were combined into problem scales (such as, positive psychotic symptoms and institutional management problems) and then submitted to cluster analyses to identify homogeneous groups of patients that shared similar problem distributions.

Patient groups identified by their unique problem distributions were labeled as: good institutional citizens, social isolates, personality disorders, institutional management problems, institutionalized psychotics, psychotics, and the developmentally handicapped. An organizational structure for the institution was developed by determining first which problems had living unit implications (level of functioning and assaultiveness) and which patient types required similar or compatible programs. The power of this approach lies in the fact that programs are not delivered to problems but to patients. For a fuller discussion of the treatment implications of this approach see Rice, Harris, Quinsey, and Cyr (1990).

The next steps suggested by this approach are to use actual measurement of these problem areas instead of a survey methodology, to examine the interaction of static risk factors with patient type in predicting violent behavior, and to evaluate treatment and supervisory programs designed to reduce violent recidivism for each type of offender.

Conclusions

In conclusion, the literature on the prediction of violence suggests that high-risk groups can be established on the basis of combinations of static variables. Predictive power is considerably enhanced by the inclusion of dynamic variables that are measured in the postrelease community environment. Actuarial models incorporating static and dynamic variables can be used to aid decision makers in establishing the level and type of supervision required for a given offender and a specification of what must be accomplished through treatment to reduce the amount of supervision required. Problems or dynamic risk factors can be used to establish groups of offenders for which particular types of treatment and supervisory programs are likely to be appropriate. A supervision/treatment plan established in such a way is an instantiation of a more general theory pertaining to the proximal causes of violent crime.

Effective policies for the community supervision and treatment of persons with violent histories thus require the integration of findings and concepts from the literatures on the prediction of violent behavior, clinical judgment, and intervention evaluation. Some of the problems dealing with persons assessed as dangerous may be overcome with a reconceptualization based upon an integration of these literatures. In this approach to risk management and rehabilitation: (a) Actuarial data are explicitly used to guide clinical appraisals of dangerousness, (b) postrelease risk assessment is performed on an ongoing basis and linked to supervisory decisions, (c) alterable risk factors are identified postrelease and targeted for intervention, and (d) treatment and supervision strategies are developed for homogeneous groups of offenders identified on the basis of their shared risk factors.

References

Abramowitz, S. L., Tupin, J. P., & Berger, A. (1984). Multivariate prediction of hospital readmission. *Comprehensive Psychiatry, 25,* 71-76.

Andrews, D. A. (1982). *The supervision of offenders: Identifying and gaining control over the factors which make a difference.* Ottawa: Solicitor General Canada.

Andrews. D. A. (1989). Recidivism is predictable and can be influenced: Using risk assessments to reduce recidivism. *Forum on Corrections Research, 1,* 11-18.

Andrews, D. A., Kiessling, J. J., Mickus, S., & Robinson, D. (1986). The construct validity of interview-based risk assessment in corrections. *Canadian Journal of Behavioural Science, 18,* 460-471.

Axelson, G. L., & Wahl, O. F. (in press). Psychotic vs. non-psychotic misdemeanants in a large county jail: An analysis of pre-trial treatment by the legal system. *International Journal of Law and Psychiatry.*

Bonta, J., & Motiuk, L. (1985). Utilization of an interview-based classification instrument: A study of correctional halfway houses. *Criminal Justice and Behavior, 12,* 333-352.

Braukmann, C. J., & Wolf, M. M. (1987). Behaviorally based group homes for juvenile offenders. In E. K. Morris & C. J. Braukmann (Eds.), *Behavioral approaches to crime and delinquency: A handbook of application, research, and concepts* (pp. 109-133). New York: Plenum.

Brownell, D. K., Marlatt, G. A., Lichtenstein, E., & Wilson, G. T. (1986). Understanding and preventing relapse. *American Psychologist, 41,* 765-782.

Cote, G., & Hodgins, S. (1992). The prevalence of major mental disorders among homicide offenders. *International Journal of Law and Psychiatry, 15,* 89-100.

Dawes, R. M. (1989). Experience and validity of clinical judgment: The illusory correlation. *Behavioral Sciences and the Law, 7,* 457-467.

Deitz, P. E. (1985). Hypothetical criteria for the prediction of individual criminality. In C. D. Webster, M. Ben-Aron, & S. J. Hucker (Eds.), *Dangerousness: Probability and prediction, psychiatry and public policy* (pp. 87-102). Cambridge: Cambridge University Press.

Falloon, R. H., et al. (1985). Family management in the prevention of morbidity of schizophrenia. *Archives of General Psychiatry, 42,* 887-896.

Frisbie, L. V. (1969). *Another look at sex offenders in California* (California Mental Health Research Monograph, No. 12). Sacramento: State Department of Mental Hygiene.

Gabor, T. (1986). *The prediction of criminal behaviour: Statistical approaches.* Toronto: University of Toronto Press.

Gendreau, P., & Andrews, D. A. (1989). What the meta-analyses of the offender treatment literature tells us about "what works." *Canadian Journal of Corrections.*

Gordon, R. A. (1977). A critique of the evaluation of Patuxent Institution, with particular attention to the issues of dangerousness and recidivism. *Bulletin of the American Academy of Psychiatry and the Law, 5,* 210-255.

Gottfredson, D. M., Wilkins, L. T., & Hoffman, P. B. (1978). *Guidelines for parole and sentencing.* Toronto: Lexington.

Gottschalk, R., Davidson, W. S., Mayer, J., & Gensheimer, L. K. (1987). Behavioral approaches with juvenile offenders: A meta-analysis of long-term treatment efficacy. In E. K. Morris & C. J. Braukmann (Eds.). *Behavioral approaches to crime and delinquency: A handbook of application, research, and concepts* (pp. 399-422). New York: Plenum.

Hare, R. D., & McPherson, L. M. (1984). Violent and aggressive behavior by criminal psychopaths. *International Journal of Law and Psychiatry, 7,* 35-50.

Harris, G. T., Rice, M. E., & Cormier, C. A. (1991). Psychopathy and violent recidivism. *Law and Human Behavior, 15,* 625-637.

Harris, G. T., Rice, M. E., & Quinsey, V. L. (in press a). *Psychopathy as a taxon: Evidence that psychopaths are a discrete class.*

Harris, G. T., Rice, M. E., & Quinsey, V. L. (in press b.) *Violent recidivism among mentally disordered offenders: The development of a statistical prediction instrument.*

Hart, S. D., Kropp, P. R., & Hare, R. D. (1988). Performance of male psychopaths following conditional release from prison. *Journal of Consulting and Clinical Psychology, 56,* 227-232.

Hogarty, G. E., et al. (1986). Family psychoeducation, social skills training, and maintenance chemotherapy in the aftercare treatment of schizophrenia. I: One year effects of a controlled study on relapse and expressed emotion. *Archives of General Psychiatry, 43,* 633-642.

Holland, T. R., Holt, N., & Brewer, D. L. (1978). Social roles and information utilization in parole decision-making. *Journal of Social Psychology, 106,* 111-120.

Kahneman, D., & Tversky, A. (1973). On the psychology of prediction. *Psychological Review, 80,* 237-251.

Kazdin, A. E. (1987). Treatment of antisocial behavior in children: Current status and future directions. *Psychological Bulletin, 102,* 187-203.

Liberman, R. P. (1988). Behavioral family management. In R. P. Liberman (Ed.), *Psychiatric rehabilitation of chronic mental patients* (pp. 199-244). Washington, DC: American Psychiatric Press.

Lukoff, D., Liberman, R. P., & Nuechterlein, K. H. (1986). Symptom monitoring in the rehabilitation of schizophrenic patients. *Schizophrenia Bulletin, 12,* 578-602.

MacCulloch, M. J., Snowden, P. R., Wood, P. J. W., & Mills, H. E. (1983). Sadistic fantasy, sadistic behaviour and offending. *British Journal of Psychiatry, 143,* 20-29.

Mandelzys, N. (1979). Correlates of offense severity and recidivism probability in a Canadian Sample. *Journal of Clinical Psychology, 35,* 897-907.

Meehl, P. E. (1986). Causes and effects of my disturbing little book. *Journal of Personality Assessment, 50,* 370-375.

Megargee, E. I., Cook, P. E., & Mendelsohn, G. A. (1967). Development and validation of an MMPI scale of assaultiveness in overcontrolled individuals. *Journal of Abnormal Psychology, 72,* 519-528.

Menzies, R. J., Webster, C. D., & Sepejak, D. S. (1985). Hitting the forensic sound barrier: Predictions of dangerousness in a pretrial psychiatric clinic. In C. D. Webster, M. H. Ben-Aron, & S. J. Hucker (Eds.), *Dangerousness: Probability and prediction, psychiatry and public policy.* New York: Cambridge University Press.

Milan, M. A. (1987a). Basic behavioral procedures in closed institutions. In E. K. Morris & C. J. Braukmann (Eds.), *Behavioral approaches to crime and delinquency: A handbook of application, research and concepts* (pp. 161-193). New York: Plenum.

Milan, M. A. (1987b). Token economy programs in closed institutions. In E. K. Morris & C. J. Braukmann (Eds.), *Behavioral approaches to crime and delinquency: A handbook of application, research and concepts* (pp. 195-222). New York: Plenum.

Monahan, J. (1981). *Predicting violent behavior: An assessment of clinical techniques.* Beverly Hills, CA: Sage.

Motiuk, L. L., & Porporino, F. J. (1989). *Offender risk/needs assessment: A study of conditional releases.* Ottawa: Solicitor General Canada.

Nuffield, J. (1982). *Parole decision-making in Canada: Research towards decision guidelines.* Ottawa: Supply and Services Canada.

Paul, G. L., & Lentz, R. J. (1977). *Psychosocial treatment of chronic mental patients: Milieu versus social-learning programs.* Cambridge, MA: Harvard University Press.

Penrose, L. S. (1939). Medical disease and crime: Outline of a comparative study of European statistics. *British Journal of Medical Psychology, 18,* 1-15.

Pithers, W. D., Kashima, K. M., Cumming, G. F., Beal, L. S., & Buell, M. M. (1988). Relapse prevention of sexual aggression. In R. A. Prentky & V. L. Quinsey (Eds.), *Human sexual aggression: Current perspectives, 528,* (pp. 244-260). Annals of the New York Academy of Sciences.

Preston, D. L., & Quinsey, V. L. (1990, June). *The accuracy of clinical judgment: Predictions and postdictions.* Paper presented at the meeting of the Canadian Psychological Association, Ottawa.

Quinsey, V. L. (1980). The baserate problem and the prediction of dangerousness: A reappraisal. *Journal of Psychiatry and Law, 8,* 329-340.

Quinsey, V. L. (1984). Institutional release policy and the identification of dangerous men: A review of the literature. *Criminologie, 17,* 53-78.

Quinsey, V. L., & Ambtman, R. (1978). Psychiatric assessments of the dangerousness of mentally ill offenders. *Crime and Justice, 6,* 249-257.

Quinsey, V. L., & Ambtman, R. (1979). Variables affecting psychiatrists' and teachers' assessments of the dangerousness of mentally ill offenders. *Journal of Consulting and Clinical Psychology, 47,* 353-362.

Quinsey, V. L., & Cyr, M. (1986). The effects of internal versus external attributions of crime causality on the perceived dangerousness and treatability of offenders. *Journal of Interpersonal Violence, 1*, 458-471.

Quinsey, V. L., Cyr, M., & Lavallee, Y. (1988). Treatment opportunities in a maximum security psychiatric hospital: A problem survey. *International Journal of Law and Psychiatry, 11*, 179-194.

Quinsey, V. L., & Maguire, A. (1983). Offenders remanded for a psychiatric examination: Perceived treatability and disposition. *International Journal of Law and Psychiatry, 6*, 193-205.

Quinsey, V. L., & Maguire, A. (1986). Maximum security psychiatric patients: Actuarial and clinical prediction of dangerousness. *Journal of Interpersonal Violence, 1*, 143-171.

Quinsey, V. L., Maguire, A. M., & Varney, G. W. (1983). Assertion and overcontrolled hostility among mentally disordered murderers. *Journal of Consulting and Clinical Psychology, 51*, 550-556.

Rice, M. E., & Harris, G. T. (1988). An empirical approach to the classification and treatment of maximum security psychiatric patients. *Behavioral Sciences and the Law, 6*, 497-514.

Rice, M. E., Harris, G. T., & Quinsey, V. L. (1990). A followup of rapists assessed in a maximum security psychiatric facility. *Journal of Interpersonal Violence, 5*, 435-448.

Rice, M. E., Harris, G. T., Quinsey, V. L., & Cyr, M. (1990). Planning treatment programs in secure psychiatric facilities. In D. Weisstub (Ed.), *Law and mental health: International perspectives, 5*, (pp. 162-230). Elmsford, NY: Pergamon.

Rice, M. E., Quinsey, V. L., & Harris, G. T. (1991). Sexual recidivism among child molesters released from a maximum security psychiatric institution. *Journal of Consulting & Clinical Psychology, 59*, 381-386.

Rice, M. E., Quinsey, V. L., & Houghton, R. (1990). Predicting treatment outcome and recidivism among patients in a maximum security token economy. *Behavior Sciences and the Law, 8*, 313-326.

Ross, R. R., & Lightfoot, L. O. (1985). *Treatment of the alcohol-abusing offender.* Springfield, IL: Charles C Thomas.

Steadman, H. J., & Coccoza, J. J. (1974). *Careers of the criminally insane: Excessive social control of deviance.* Toronto: Lexington.

Swindle, R. W., Cronkite, R. C., & Moos, R. H. (1989). Life stressors, social resources, coping, and the 4-year course of depression. *Journal of Abnormal Psychology, 98*, 468-477.

Thornberry, T. P., & Jacoby, J. E. (1979). *The criminally insane: A community follow-up of mentally ill offenders.* Chicago: University of Chicago Press.

Ventura, J., Nuechterlein, K. H., Lukoff, D., & Hardesty, J. P. (1989). A prospective study of stressful life events and schizophrenic relapse. *Journal of Abnormal Psychology, 98*, 407-411.

Walker, N., Hammond, W., & Steer, D. (1967). Repeated violence. *The Criminal Law Review, 207*, 465-472.

Waller, I. (1974). *Men released from prison.* Toronto: University of Toronto Press.

Webster, C. D., & Menzies, R. J. (1987). The clinical prediction of dangerousness. In D. N. Weisstub (Ed.), *Law and mental health: International perspectives, 3*, 158-208.

Wormith, J. S. (1984). Attitude and behavior change of correctional clientele: A three year follow-up. *Criminology, 22*, 595-618.

12

Reducing Violence in Institutions:
Maintaining Behavior Change

GRANT T. HARRIS

MARNIE E. RICE

With many social problems, there is often a body of scientific research that, without providing a complete explanation of the problem, does lend considerable understanding. This understanding often extends to a technology of intervention demonstrated to be effective in reducing or even eliminating the problem. Yet, strangely, this knowledge frequently does not result in the widespread effective implementation of the technology. Behavior therapy for many human disorders exemplifies this paradox. Known behavioral technology is not employed where it could be or when it *is* used, its potency and integrity are seriously weakened by failure to adhere to established behavioral principles. In this chapter we will illustrate this phenomenon with behavioral interventions to reduce institutional violence. We will present some data from our own clinical work to illustrate ways this phenomenon occurs. We will conclude by pointing to some methods that could be used to ensure that effective behavioral interventions are used and

AUTHORS' NOTE: Thanks are due to V. L. Quinsey for helpful comments on an earlier draft of this chapter. Some of the data reported in this chapter were gathered as part of grant DM421 from the Ontario Ministry of Health.

maintained. Our central thesis with respect to institutional violence is that appropriate contingencies must apply not only to the behavior of assaultive patients but also to the behavior of ward staff, supervisors, program managers, administrators, and even government officials if effective interventions are to persist. We begin, however, with a brief review of what is known about violence in institutions.

What Factors Contribute to Violence in Institutions?

In a recent review of institutional violence, Rice, Harris, Varney, and Quinsey (1989) discussed three sources of variance in assault frequency: those pertaining to assaulters, violence-promoting environments, and victims of assault.

Characteristics of Assaulters

Most studies of institutional assaultiveness have been done in psychiatric or health institutions, where the medical model predominates. Perhaps because of this, most investigators begin with the assumption that the problem lies within the assaulter and examine the pathology of the individuals who commit the assaults.

Within psychiatric facilities, there is widespread agreement that, while very few schizophrenics are assaultive, assaultiveness is disproportionately associated with schizophrenia. Organic brain syndrome and mental retardation are also associated with assaultiveness in psychiatric institutions. In other institutions, assaultiveness is associated with acute distress, low functioning, and high degrees of disturbance. In general hospitals, patients suffering from high levels of pain, and patients in intensive care units and emergency rooms are most assaultive. In prisons, assaultive inmates are those with low coping skills and short sentences. In a variety of institutions, assaultiveness has been associated with attempted suicide, self-injurious behavior, withdrawal, and depression. Both within and outside of institutions, it is much more likely among young persons. While assaultiveness outside of institutions is overwhelmingly a male behavior, the evidence of gender bias within institutions is less clear. Finally, individuals with a history of several relatively minor offenses are more likely to be assaultive than those with smaller numbers of relatively serious antisocial acts.

Characteristics of Assaultive Environments

Crowding and high turnover have been linked with institutional assaultiveness. Assaults tend to occur when patients have relatively free access to one another and to staff, and at times when there is little structured activity. Assaults also tend to occur when there is a clear payoff for violence, when it is excused, or when it is expected. There is also evidence that assaults are more likely in settings where the ambient temperature is high (Anderson, 1989).

There is convincing evidence that exposure to aggressive models leads to increased aggression. Most of this evidence has been with normal children exposed to aggressive models on television (e.g., Eron, 1987; Liebert & Sprafkin, 1988), but there is evidence that exposure to aggressive models can increase the assaultiveness of institutionalized adolescents (Parke, Berkowitz, Leyens, West, & Sebastian, 1977) as well as adult male mentally disordered offenders (Harry, 1983).

Although there has been little research on the topic of ward atmosphere or staff-patient relationships and their associations with institutional assaults, there is evidence from work on children's aggression to suggest that the social environment is an important contributor to aggression. Specifically, Eron (1982) concluded that parents' rejecting and nonnurturant child-rearing practices contributed to aggression in their children. By hypothesizing an analogous process in institutions, it is reasonable to predict that patient or inmate aggression would be highest on wards where staff treated their charges in a rejecting and critical manner.

Characteristics of Assault Victims

Assault victims, whether patients or staff, tend to be older and smaller than assaulters. While there is conflicting evidence about whether staff are overrepresented as assault victims relative to patients, there have been several studies of the characteristics of staff behavior that appear to be related to being the victim of an assault. Staff behaviors frequently associated with assault are demanding activity from patients, refusing requests, or imposing sanctions. Staff who approach patients in an authoritarian manner are more likely to be assaulted than other staff, as are staff wearing uniforms.

Maximally Violence-Enhancing Conditions

From the above review, a maximally violence-prone institution would have the following characteristics:

Population

The institution would have a high turnover of young people with histories of institutional aggression. These people would be schizophrenic, developmentally handicapped, depressed, suffering from organic brain disorder, and/or engage in suicidal attempts or self-injurious behavior. These persons would have histories of poor community adjustment, especially histories of many minor crimes rather than one or two major offenses.

Staff

The staff would be inexperienced, and treat patients in a rejecting, hostile, and authoritarian manner. They would be poor models for their charges, exhibiting emotional instability, immaturity, and irritability.

Environment

The clients would engage in few structured activities and live in crowded conditions. They would spend much of their time watching aggressive models on television, movies, or watching one another behave aggressively. There would be no or very inconsistent penalties for exhibiting assaultive behavior. The ward would be overheated in winter and without cooling in summer.

Unfortunately, many large correctional, psychiatric institutions or institutions for the developmentally handicapped have many of these characteristics.

Reducing Institutional Violence

Changing the Assaulter

Not surprisingly in view of the above review, most work (both behavioral and nonbehavioral) on reducing institutional violence has focused on the assaultive individual. Because the majority of assaults are committed by a small proportion of patients, and because the best predictor of future institutional aggression is past institutional aggression, developing programs for those persons who have exhibited institutional violence makes good sense. The approaches that have been tried include such nonbehavioral strategies as the use of restraint, seclusion, and sedating drugs, and a variety of behavioral strategies to train prosocial behaviors incompatible with assault.

Seclusion, Restraint, and Drugs

The most important observation to make about seclusion, restraint, and drugs is that, although they are ubiquitous, there is almost no evidence that they reduce violence in institutions (Rice et al., 1989; Harris, Rice, & Preston, 1989). The existing evidence does permit some conclusions, however (Rice et al. 1989). The use of such strategies varies greatly over institutions with similar patient populations, and these strategies are used with psychiatric patients more often because of agitation and disruptive behavior than because of physical assault. The use of these strategies is related to such institutional characteristics as the amount of structured activity for patients, management style, ratio of male to female staff, the use of drug-free assessment periods, and staff morale. It is possible to reduce drastically the use of these strategies without altering staff morale by promoting the use of behavioral interventions for assaultive behavior (Davidson, Hemingway, & Wysocki, 1984).

When we studied the use of seclusion, restraint, and sedating drugs in a maximum security hospital (Harris et al., 1989) we found that there was considerable agreement among patients and staff as to their relative restrictiveness and aversiveness. For both staff and patients, perceived intrusiveness depended upon the situation and experience with the procedures.

There was considerable disagreement, however, among staff about the likelihood that such strategies would prevent future violent incidents. In addition, patients preferred the use of least restrictive procedures while ward staff preferred the use of much more restrictive methods in the same situations. However, ward staff reported that they actually used the least restrictive methods, while patients stated that considerably more restrictive procedures were actually used. That is, each group's preference coincided precisely with the other group's reported experience. These data provided strong evidence that staff and patients together are not reliable reporters about what actually occurs because the recall of each group is biased in opposite directions, and that such biased recall is responsible for the common staff perception that, although they deal with patients in the least restrictive ways possible, they are under constant and unreasonable pressure to be even less restrictive. Similarly, such biases are likely responsible for the conflicting beliefs by patients that ward staff are unnecessarily restrictive and heavy handed.

Behavioral Treatments

There is considerable evidence that behavioral therapy techniques are effective in teaching assaultive patients alternative behaviors. For example, role play rehearsal and the gradual introduction of increasingly provocative practice stimuli (Elder, Edelstein, & Narick, 1979; Kolko, Dorsett, & Milan, 1981) can improve ward behavior and decrease assaults. However, we have encountered several problems in obtaining on-ward behavior change using these techniques. As noted by Quinsey (1977), assaultive patients reported that other patients were a major source of provocation, but throughout a behavior therapy program, they could not be enlisted to emit practice provocations; staff lost interest in and would forget to administer the program; and staff and patients delivered "unauthorized" provocations. The failure of the treatment to be as effective as hoped was attributed to the problems in implementation.

A closely related behavior therapy for assaultive patients is the use of social skills training in the form of anger management or assertion training. Usually delivered in a group therapy program, these treatments involve modeling, coaching, role play rehearsal, and feedback (often including the use of videotape) to teach behaviors associated with the skillful use of verbal means to deal effectively with anger-provoking social situations. However, though demonstrably effective in teaching relevant skills (Goldstein & Glick, 1987), anger management and assertion training present some problems in implementation. The most important of these is the tendency of institutional staff to discourage socially skillful behavior. That is, generalization to the ward environment is difficult to achieve because institutional staff actually do not regard assertive behavior as appropriate. Rather, the social norms for patients require them to be quiet and compliant (Buehler, Patterson, & Furniss, 1966; Rice, 1985; Ullmann, 1967).

A particularly good example of this phenomenon comes from our recent work in providing assertion training for institutionalized firesetters. Our earlier work showed that firesetters (though not usually assaultive) are a particularly unassertive group of patients and that assertion training is a theoretically and clinically relevant treatment (Harris & Rice, 1984; Rice & Chaplin, 1979; Rice & Harris, 1991). In treating a group of firesetters, we compared assertion training to a plausible alternative treatment (life-skills training). We also collected a variety of pre-post measures of therapeutic effectiveness: role play measures, self-report questionnaires, and staff ratings of patient behaviors.

The results are summarized in Table 12.1. The role play measure consisted of sets of audiotaped sequences of five social situations; each situation required the subject to emit an assertive response that was recorded. Blind ratings of social skill, assertion, and likelihood of success of the response were then performed. The Rathus Assertion Schedule (RAS) is a paper and pencil self-report measure of assertion and contains such items as, "Sometimes I enjoy a good argument," and "I have hesitated to make dates because of shyness." The Mood and Cooperation (MACC) subscales of The Behavior Adjustment Scale (Ellsworth, 1971) are ward staff ratings of subjects' cheerfulness, cooperation, and compliance. The Withdrawal and Belligerence subscales of the Psychotic Reaction Profile are ward staff ratings of social withdrawal (e.g., "Usually stays by himself") and paranoid belligerence (e.g., "Is likely to hit someone for no apparent reason.").

The results in Table 12.1 show that, compared to life skills training, the assertion training improved patients' ability to perform assertively. Although not shown in the table, the control treatment did produce significant improvements on a paper and pencil assessment of life skills. This improvement associated with the assertion training occurred at some cost to the patients. Compared to the control treatment, assertion training was associated with increases in staff ratings of belligerence and noncompliance.

These results are poignant because the subjects in this study were among the very least assertive in an institution where the population as a whole was rated as less assertive than the norm (Harris & Rice, 1984). We wonder whether providing assertion training for institutionalized patients renders them any service at all. Similar observations have been made with the provision of anger management therapy to incarcerated offenders. Kennedy (1990) found that therapy improved offenders' self-reported and role play measures of inappropriate anger and temporarily

TABLE 12.1 The Results of Assertion Training and a Control Therapy (Life Skills) for Arsonists in Maximum Security.

Measure	Assertion				Life Skills		
	Pre	Post	t(20)	Pre	Post		t(12)
Role play test:							
Assertion	22.1 (8.52)	27.0 (7.77)	2.10*	27.1 (6.94)	27.0 (7.81)		.26
Total skill	63.4 (21.1)	74.6 (19.7)	2.26*	78.2 (18.1)	79.5 (21.4)		.51
Self report:							
Rathus	−7.70 (29.7)	5.32 (25.6)	2.66*	5.46 (25.0)	3.54 (29.2)		.50
Self-esteem	26.4 (9.94)	30.7 (10.3)	2.50*	30.2 (10.0)	31.4 (8.9)		.70
Staff measures:							
Social contact	13.9 (4.2)	14.1 (2.7)	1.82	13.9 (2.8)	15.1 (2.8)		1.67
Withdrawal	15.1 (8.0)	12.3 (6.5)	2.19*	12.9 (7.6)	12.7 (9.4)		.10
Belligerence	3.67 (4.7)	4.63 (4.8)	2.11*	7.12 (7.3)	6.3 (6.2)		.56

NOTE: *$p < .05$

reduced misconducts, but she hypothesized that after treatment ended, institutional staff punished even socially appropriate attempts by prisoners to resolve conflicts verbally. Thus behavioral interventions targeted at the individual client, though clearly effective in teaching new behaviors, may not reduce the rate of institutional violence.

Changing Assaultive Environments

Just as the research on institutional violence suggested a variety of behavioral strategies aimed at assaultive individuals, there are several obvious ways one might attempt to alter the social environment of an institution to reduce violence. We have attempted a few of these over the years and again discovered that the environment was either unexpectedly difficult to change, or—if changes did occur—they were not maintained.

Token Economies

There is abundant and persuasive evidence that the application of social learning theory to the social environment in the form of token economies can have profoundly positive effects on a large number of behaviors in a wide variety of subject populations (Rice, Harris, Quinsey, & Cyr, 1991). Chief among these behaviors, for the present discussion, are assaults (Paul & Lentz, 1977; Bostow & Bailey, 1969). Despite the evidence favoring the use of token economy programs with assaultive patients, they are disappearing (Boudewyns, Fry, & Nightingale, 1986). There are several factors advanced to account for this trend (Rice et al., 1991). Bureaucratic practice is often incompatible with effective behavioral programming. It is very difficult to retrain custodially oriented staff who traditionally reward both appropriate and inappropriate behavior inconsistently (Gelfand, Gelfand, & Dobson, 1967) actually to employ behavioral techniques that require careful application of contingencies. Behavior therapists have largely abandoned the chronically institutionalized because of a false belief that serious mental disorders are too severe for behavior modification and that, because of the mounting evidence for biological bases to most mental disorders, only medical treatments will be effective (Bellack, 1986).

In addition, frontline staff invariably seek to punish assaultiveness but frequently fail to reinforce incompatible appropriate responses. Even in token economy programs, there is a continual tendency for frontline staff to lobby for more and larger fines for misbehaviors and simultaneously to give fewer and fewer rewards for appropriate behaviors

(Bassett & Blanchard, 1977). An example of this powerful trend comes from our own work in a maximum security hospital. For more than a decade, there existed simple token economies on the wards housing the most assaultive patients. Throughout the long history of these programs, the ways patients could earn tokens remained remarkably unaltered (Harris, 1989; Quinsey & Sarbit, 1975). Indeed there was good evidence that all the behavioral ratings performed by staff in the program actually corresponded to a single very global dimension of compliance and passivity (Rice, Quinsey, & Houghton, 1990). That is, the behaviors actually rewarded in the program were not necessarily incompatible with occasional or even frequent assaultiveness.

However, over the years the programs did change by becoming more punitive. Figure 12.1 shows the change of two indices of program punitiveness (number of punishable behaviors and mean size of fine). Several other indices of punitiveness (e.g., duration of confinements and number of confineable behaviors) were examined and all showed the same pattern. These changes occurred despite explicit efforts by psychology staff assigned to the unit to resist this trend. Interestingly, assaultive behavior on the same wards generally increased over the same time period (see Figure 12.1). There is additional good evidence that increasing the punitiveness of the programs was ineffective in reducing assaults (Quinsey & Varney, 1977).

Most recently, the programs in operation on these wards have come to rely more heavily upon response cost. Currently, patients are awarded a majority of all possible tokens noncontingently each day. Fines for a variety of behaviors including assaultiveness can then be deducted. Over the years the program has come closer to a traditional milieu where there exists less contingent reinforcement for prosocial, nonsymptomatic, independent behaviors but considerable (and sometimes variable) contingent cost to antisocial, disruptive, and nuisance behaviors. Thus, although response cost can be effective when combined with positive programs (Sullivan & O'Leary, 1990), we conclude that the behavioral integrity of our token economies gradually eroded and they have lost some of their clinical utility, especially in controlling violence.

Removing Violent Models

There have been a few attempts to reduce the effects of aggressive models in institutions' environments. Ross and McKay (1979) showed that positive reinforcement by staff for desirable behavior was ineffective as long as the institutional peer culture reinforced undesirable

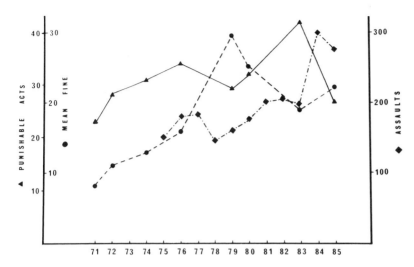

Figure 12.1. Two Indices of Program Punitiveness (Number of Punishable Acts and Mean Magnitude of Program Fines) and Total Assaults as a Function of Calendar Year

behavior. It was necessary to "co-opt" the peer culture through the use of prosocial peer models to effect reductions in problem behaviors.

We attempted to reduce the amount of aggressive modeling in a maximum security hospital by first studying the effects of aggressive television models. However, the attempt encountered an unexpected problem in implementation. The study was conducted on two wards housing the institution's most assaultive patients. Baseline data showed that patients on these wards spent considerable time watching television and especially violent television (including videotaped films). We used published data from the National Coalition on Television Violence (NCTV) to obtain independent estimates of the amount of violence in patients' routine television diet. The baseline was high—a mean rating of 29.30 violent acts per hour. Also, during the baseline period, we surveyed the wards' patients and staff to find out their preferred programs as well as staff opinions about the effect of television violence upon patient assaults. In general, patients and staff liked the same programs except patients were much less fond of televised sports than were staff. Also, on average, both groups reported a preference for shows that obtained high scores for violence on the NCTV lists. The study design called for the manipulation of the amount of television violence on each ward in a counterbalanced fashion such that for one month the staff on duty were to select prescribed violent (mean rating = 34.35) programs (mostly ones patients and staff had reported a preference for) and the next month, were to select prescribed nonviolent (mean rating = 1.27) programs. We were unable to evaluate the effect of this manipulation upon patient-initiated assaults and other antisocial behavior because, despite unqualified administration approval for the project and direct instructions from supervisory personnel, the staff did not comply with the prescribed television regimen.

When the prescribed programming was violent, compliance was approximately 75% but fell to only about 26% during the nonviolent regimen. We were able to obtain a record of what patients and staff actually watched as opposed to what they were supposed to watch. Patients and staff actually saw programs that received mean ratings of 29.58 and 29.17 during the violent and nonviolent periods, respectively. We compared these records to the staff and patient preferences gathered earlier. More often, the substituted program corresponded to reported staff preferences. That is, ward staff simply ignored the prescription and watched what they liked and this was often a violent program.

We assumed that this occurred because the staff cared little for our goal to obtain interesting research data and because they did not believe violent television caused assaults anyway. Curiously, however, an examination of the questionnaire data from the 26 ward staff respondents showed that the majority of staff had earlier strongly endorsed such items as "Viewing aggressive television causes aggressive behavior in viewers" and "Repeated exposure to television violence fosters a more accepting attitude towards aggression." On a 5-point scale where 1 corresponded to "strongly agree" and 5 to "strongly disagree," staff ratings of these two items, for example, were 2.15 and 2.36, respectively. The item "Watching televised aggression relieves tension and reduces aggressive drives" received a mean rating of 4.15. Clearly, effecting a change in staff behavior required more than instructions from their superiors and more even than changing their attitudes and opinions about the causes of assaultiveness. Again, even though everyone agreed about what televised violence would probably do to assaultive behavior, actual changes were difficult to achieve even temporarily.

Changing the Victims of Assaults

Probably the most radical ways we attempted to reduce assaults comes from looking at assaults in an unusual way. After systematically studying more than a thousand assaultive incidents (Harris & Varney, 1986; Quinsey & Varney, 1977), many years' accumulation of staff injuries sustained in altercations with patients (Harris & Rice, 1986), and series of especially serious incidents (Rice et al., 1989, chap. 3), we concluded that some staff and patients unwittingly engage in behavior that increases the likelihood they will be assaulted and injured. This observation has been made in other domains. For example, others (Dutton, 1981; Toch, 1977) have concluded that some police officers were injured or killed in the line of duty partly because of sharply differing perceptions concerning their interactions with citizens. The officers' behavior was regarded as arbitrary, authoritarian, and even aggressive by people with whom they came in contact, some of whom attacked the officer feeling as though they were reacting to extreme provocation. Meanwhile, the officer/victims, because they treated everyone the same way, regarded their own behavior as fair, routine and "just part of the job." Consequently, they regarded attacks by citizens as completely unjustified and even irrational.

It seemed to us that this process characterized many assaults in our institution. A logical consequence of such a view led to the idea that we could decrease assaults by changing the interpersonal behavior of patient and staff victims of assaults. Thus in two separate projects we attempted to improve the social skills of unpopular patients (Rice, 1983; Rice & Josefowitz, 1983), and to equip ward staff with a wide variety of skills to enable them to anticipate, and intervene to prevent patient violence (Rice et al., 1989; Rice, Helzel, Varney, & Quinsey, 1985). There was considerable evidence from both projects that the subjects acquired the skills we attempted to teach them and, in the case of the staff training program, this resulted in a reduction in assaults and injuries. In addition, the staff who took the course gave it very positive ratings for its content, direct usefulness, and enjoyment. Most importantly, our institution's administration adopted the course and it is official policy that all ward staff take the course.

With respect to our training course for staff, we were able to show that participants acquired the target skills and provided evidence that, temporarily at least, these skills were exhibited on the job (Rice et al., 1985). However, the potential of the course has not been realized because on any ward at any time only a small proportion (approximately 45%) of the staff have taken the course or refresher training within the past four years. There are several reasons for this: (1) The course was five days long and therefore, relatively expensive. We resisted pressure to shorten the course for many years but it was finally reduced to three days. (2) Staff turnover is high. Of course, turnover makes it difficult to ensure that all staff are trained. However, given such high turnover, the institution has achieved high rates of training for other courses; for example, legislatively mandated training in Workplace Hazardous Materials Information System (98%), and courses mandatory for the maintenance of nursing registration in Cardiopulmonary Resuscitation (80%). (3) The course is not a requirement for staff. Partly because of the first two points above, the institution sometimes hires persons to work on the wards who have no training and experience in mental health and occasionally even staff who have no clinical or health care experience. Clearly, managers who feel forced to staff the institution in this way will regard a training course in managing aggression as desirable but not essential. Again, we could provide a behavioral strategy that worked, but its impact was weakened or lost over time.

In conclusion, one wonders about the actual contingencies that apply to ward staff behaviors, especially those consistent or compatible with reductions in assaults by patients. For example, we wonder whether the staff experience or perceive much payoff to reductions in assaults. We also wonder about the impact of a labor-management decision to separate our frontline staff from all other provincial psychiatric hospital staff and include them in the category comprised of jail guards. This was done to compensate our staff for working in a dangerous environment. We don't suggest that our staff consciously or unconsciously provoked violence to facilitate or maintain this arrangement—the consequences were too loosely tied to on-ward behaviors to have much impact anyway. However, we do wonder how much incentive the staff actually have to engage in *new* behaviors consistent with reductions in assaults, especially in view of increases in social status associated with "danger pay."

How Can Effective Behavioral Interventions Be Maintained?

The difficulties we describe in ensuring long-term reductions in institutional violence are not limited to assault and not limited to our institution. Rice and Quinsey (1986) discuss several similar examples in other settings. Many powerful psychological interventions do not persist beyond the direct involvement of the program innovator(s). Perhaps the most striking example of this problem is the work of Paul and Lentz (1977) in applying social learning theory to the rehabilitation of chronic mental patients. Although their program yielded impressive data on the cost effectiveness of their technology, amazingly the program has been abandoned at the institution where it began. Another good example is that five years after the pioneering work on token economies done by Ayllon and his colleagues at Weyburn Saskatchewan, many staff at the hospital did not even know the program had ever existed (R. Berry, personal communication, June, 1984), and two of the patients who had provided much of the original data were still institutionalized a decade later (Sherwood & Gray, 1974). It is clear to us that the primary reason for this disturbing phenomenon is that most behavioral interventions in institutions must live in an environment that is itself not behavioral. That is, the contingencies that apply to the behavior of administrators and government bureaucrats often do not promote the long-term maintenance of behavior changes on the part of the institution's inhabitants.

What might be done to increase the likelihood that behavioral strategies discussed above would persist over the long term? There is evidence that psychologists who develop behavioral interventions aimed at individual patients or at the social environment can increase the likelihood of the intervention program being adopted, maintained, and spread to other institutions by applying established behavioral principles to the organization.

We reported above that maintaining behavior change requires institutional staff to provide consistent, appropriate contingencies for patient behaviors. Traditionally, managers have attempted to improve the therapeutic behavior of frontline workers by the simplest means possible. For example, memos describing desired actions and one-shot massed in-service training sessions are often used but are usually ineffective in developing (much less maintaining) appropriate staff behaviors (Willet, 1983). Partly because measuring program performance is difficult, staff promotions often are based on criteria that are completely unrelated to their competence in carrying out programs (such as having a neat ward and having all their paperwork done) but are more visible (Ellsworth, 1968). Staff members infer from promotional practices that following ward treatment programs is unimportant (Ellsworth, 1968). Indeed, managers rarely employ behavioral principles in attempting to alter staff behaviors; they rely almost exclusively on aversive consequences even though they know that such negative contingencies are very unlikely to work (Mayhew, Patience, & Cone, 1979).

Management-level behavioral interventions shown to produce and maintain therapeutic performance among frontline staff include: (a) detailed written descriptions of desired behaviors, (b) frequent supervisor approval of enactments of the behaviors plus a description of precisely what was approved, (c) continuous posted feedback describing progress in staff target behaviors, and (d) provision of rewards to staff for superior performance and (e) monitoring of and feedback to supervisors regarding their performance in giving feedback and rewards to their staff (Andrasik & McNamara, 1977; Burgio, Whitman, & Reid, 1983; Brown, Willis, & Reid, 1981; Ellsworth, 1968).

Another important behavioral factor in implementing new programs is breaking the innovation down into several small steps so that it can be installed one step at a time, with evidence of incremental success (Glaser, Abelson, & Garrison, 1983). Although behavioral psychologists are familiar with developing programs for clients that are broken down into easy steps, thinking about the implementation process in the same way is frequently overlooked.

With respect to management-level interventions specifically aimed at reducing violence, institutional managers must first be in a position to know how much violence is occurring on the wards. Yet institutional records of assaults, seclusions, and other critical incidents are notoriously unreliable (e.g., Lion & Reid, 1983). Specifically developed information systems are required to measure violent incidents, and the quality of the information must be monitored by periodic checks of reliability and validity. Managers could also monitor the quality of staff-patient interactions by the use of instruments such as the Staff-Resident Interaction Chronograph or SRIC (Paul & Lentz, 1977) to ensure that staff are carrying out the programs as specified. The SRIC has been employed to monitor the integrity of milieu therapy and social learning programs. Unfortunately, this instrument is somewhat difficult to learn, and expensive to use, and these factors have been shown to lessen the likelihood of adoption (Backer, Liberman, & Kuehnel, 1986). We have obtained positive preliminary data using a simplified version of this instrument, and others have also used simpler instruments with positive results (Kuehnel, DeRisi, Liberman, & Mosk, 1984). However, future research is required to establish whether simpler instruments are equally effective in monitoring the staff and patient behaviors.

Of course, unless program managers and their supervisors have some knowledge of mental health issues in general and behavior modification in particular, and some knowledge about violence and behaviorally sound ways to reduce violence, they are unlikely to be able to recognize, let alone reward, desirable behaviors in their subordinates. Gendreau (1988) refers to the "MBA Syndrome" in which managers are construed as a generic entity, as persons who need to know about how to manage but need know little, or nothing, about the theory or practice of treatment for the clients over whom they have ultimate authority.

Even when managers and administrators have some understanding of the problems and are aware of the success and cost-effectiveness for behavioral treatments for the populations in the institutions they manage, other factors are necessary to make innovative programs work over the long term. One is the presence of a person who will fight to maintain interest, motivation, enthusiasm, and accountability (Arbuthnot & Gordon, 1988). Gendreau (1989) reviewed the factors related to the implementation and maintenance (for at least 2 years) of 52 innovative programs. Most were in correctional agencies. Some of the factors were behavioral principles mentioned above. Some of the other management-level factors that Gendreau concluded were important were: (1) The initiation for the program comes jointly from the program designer and the host agency, rather than just from one of these or by being imposed strictly from above. That is, program success must be reinforcing to the host agency and staff. (2) The program designer has professional credibility and a history of being associated with successful programs. (3) The funding for the development and implementation of the innovation comes from the host agency or institution. That is, the host agency must bear the financial contingencies for program success or failure, and (4) If the program is in a prison, the program separates the participants from the general population. That is, the counterproductive effects of antisocial models must be eliminated.

Arbuthnot and Gordon (1988) concluded that, while perhaps not so critical as some of the factors mentioned above, careful selection of staff trainees for the necessary intellectual, social, and technical skills, as well as self-confidence and enthusiasm, was also important. Within psychiatric facilities, for example, the optimal staff for programs to reduce the levels of violence and other behavioral programs might be behavior technicians (persons with specific postsecondary training in behavior modification) rather than nurses who are the traditional frontline workers in psychiatric institutions. Changing the qualifications of staff requires intervention at high levels of the system and can take considerable time. Nevertheless, this is another way to increase the likelihood that behavioral interventions will be adopted and maintained.

Most behavioral interventions require a long time, team effort, and systems to ensure program integrity (cf. the Staff Resident Interaction Chronograph mentioned earlier). These factors make behavioral interventions much more difficult to implement than medical interventions such as a new drug, because the response cost of adopting a new drug is relatively low (Backer et al., 1986; Harris, 1989). Another factor that assists in implementation is timing; innovations aimed at solving a problem that happens to be in sharp focus at the time is much more likely to be adopted because there will be a high likelihood of immediate rewards to managers contingent upon successful implementation.

In addition to the problems associated with maintaining a program over the long term at one institution, an additional challenge to researchers, program developers, and clinicians comes as they attempt to promote the spread of new clinical interventions. Traditionally, researchers have attempted to disseminate new clinical interventions through journal articles and conferences. Yet these have many limits. Half of the research articles published in major psychology journals are read by fewer than 17% of psychologists (Garvey & Griffith, 1971), and clinical psychologists working in applied settings read on average only two research articles per month (Cohen, 1979). Most practitioners attend few professional meetings and when they do, there is little evidence to suggest that they utilize the information obtained (Backer et al., 1986). Rather, research on adult education consistently shows that active and direct training procedures are necessary to promote acquisition and utilization of new treatment procedures (Matarazzo, 1971). These procedures are rarely used at professional meetings. Program developers who are interested in having the program adopted elsewhere must attend to established behavioral principles and, for example, be prepared to provide personal consultation. They must also develop detailed step-by-step instructional materials that allow for active practice by participants (Backer et al., 1986). A particularly good example of a well-developed dissemination effort is the comprehensive package of training materials, training sessions, and personal consultation put together by Liberman and his associates (Liberman, 1988). The program is aimed at the adoption of techniques shown to be successful in the rehabilitation of chronic mental patients.

In their review of factors leading to the adoption of three highly successful psychosocial interventions including the Behavior Analysis and Modification Project designed to improve the quality of care in day hospitals (Liberman, Eckman, Kuehnel, Rosenstein, & Kuehnel, 1982), the Teaching Family Model designed for predelinquent and delinquent youths (Phillips, Phillips, Fixsen, & Wolf, 1973), and the Fairweather Lodge Program (Fairweather, Sanders, Maynard, & Cressler, 1969;), Backer et al. (1986) concluded that outside consultation on program adoption and especially on managing the psychological and administrative ramifications of the change was critical in all three cases.

Conclusions

We conclude this chapter with the observation that our own institution appears to be a microcosm. As in the world at large, the noble declarations of politicians, bureaucrats, administrators, and clinicians to the contrary, an examination of the existing contingencies reveals that reductions in institutional violence (or any other improvements in patients' adaptive behavior) are not always the primary concern of the organization. And when such laudable ideals *are* the genuine goals of the organization's leaders, they are often ineffective because their efforts do not embody what is already known about human behavior change. That is, the behavior of assaultive patients, institutional staff, program managers, and bureaucrats does not change (and stay changed) simply because such changes are virtuous, moral, desirable, or commanded. Changes occur when the contingencies applied to the behavior support and continue to support behavior change. A clinician's task is not complete when he or she identifies and demonstrates the effectiveness of a program to reduce the assaultive behavior of an institution's patients. The challenge for behaviorally oriented clinicians is to find ways to aim their behavioral technology at higher and higher levels of the systems in which they work.

References

Anderson, C. A. (1989). Temperature and aggression: Ubiquitous effects of heat on occurrence of human violence. *Psychological Bulletin, 106,* 74-96.

Andrasik, F., & McNamara, J. R. (1977). Optimizing staff performance in an institutional behavior change system. A pilot study. *Behavior Modification, 1,* 235-248.

Arbuthnot, J., & Gordon, D. (1988). Disseminating effective interventions for juvenile delinquents. Cognitively based sociomoral reasoning development programs. *Journal of Correctional Education, 39,* 48-53.

Backer, T. E., Liberman, R. P., & Kuehnel, T. G. (1986). Dissemination and adoption of innovative psychosocial interventions. *Journal of Consulting and Clinical Psychology, 54,* 111-118.

Bassett, J. E., & Blanchard, E. B. (1977). The effect of the absence of close supervision on the use of response cost in a prison token economy. *Journal of Applied Behavior Analysis, 10,* 375-379.

Bellack, A. S. (1986). Schizophrenia: Behavior therapy's forgotten child. *Behavior Therapy, 17,* 199-214.

Bostow, D. E., & Bailey, J. B. (1969). Modification of severe disruptive and aggressive behavior using brief timeout and reinforcement procedures. *Journal of Applied Behavior Analysis, 2,* 31-37.

Boudewyns, P. A., Fry, T. J., & Nightingale, E. J. (1986). Token economy programs in VA medical centers: Where are they today? *The Behavior Therapist, 6,* 126-127.

Brown, K. M., Willis, B. S., & Reid, D. H. (1981). Differential effects of supervisor verbal feedback and feedback plus approval on institutional staff performance. Journal of Organizational Behavior Management, 3, 57-68.

Buehler, R. E., Patterson, F. R., & Furniss, J. M. (1966). The reinforcement of behavior in institutional settings. *Behavior Research and Therapy, 4,* 157-167.

Burgio, L. D., Whitman, T. L., & Reid, D. H. (1983). A participative management approach for improving direct-care staff performance in an institutional setting. *Journal of Applied Behavior Analysis, 16,* 37-53.

Cohen, L. H. (1979). The research readership and information source reliance of clinical psychologists. *Professional Psychology, 10,* 780-785.

Davidson, N. A., Hemingway, M. J., & Wysocki, T. (1984). Reducing the use of restrictive procedures in a residential facility. *Hospital and Community Psychiatry, 35,* 164-167.

Dutton, D. G. (1981). Training police officers to intervene in domestic violence. In R. B. Stuart (Ed.), *Violent behavior: Social learning approaches to prediction, management and treatment.* New York: Brunner/Mazel.

Elder, J. P., Edelstein, B. A., & Narick, M. M. (1979). Adolescent psychiatric patients: Modifying aggressive behavior with social skills training. *Behavior Modification, 3,* 161-178.

Ellsworth, R. B. (1968). *Nonprofessionals in psychiatric rehabilitation: The psychiatric aide and the schizophrenic patient.* New York: Appleton-Century-Crofts.

Ellsworth, R. B. (1971). *The MACC Behavioral Adjustment Scale.* Los Angeles: Western Psychological Services.

Eron, L. D. (1982). Parent-child interaction, television violence, and aggression of children. *American Psychologist, 37,* 197-211.

Eron, L. D. (1987). The development of aggressive behavior from the perspective of a developing behaviorism. *American Psychologist, 42,* 435-442.

Fairweather, G. W., Sanders, D. H., Maynard, H., & Cressler, D. H. (1969). *Community life for the mentally ill.* Chicago: Aldine.

Garvey, W. D., & Griffith, B. C. (1971). Scientific communication: Its role in the conduct of research and creation of knowledge. *American Psychologist, 26,* 349-362.

Gelfand, D. M., Gelfand, S., & Dobson, W. R. (1967). Unprogrammed reinforcement of patients' behavior in a mental hospital. *Behavior Research and Therapy, 5,* 201-207.

Gendreau, P. (1988, August). *Principles of effective treatments for offenders.* Paper presented at a conference on the Antisocial Personality: Research, Assessment and Treatment Programs, Midland, Ontario.

Gendreau, P. (1989, November). *Principles of effective intervention.* Paper presented to Centracare staff, St. John, New Brunswick.

Glaser, E. M., Abelson, H. H., & Garrison, K. N. (1983). *Putting knowledge to use.* San Francisco: Jossey-Bass.

Goldstein, A. P., & Glick, B. (1987). *Aggression replacement training.* Champaign, IL: Research Press.

Harris, G. T. (1989). The relationship between neuroleptic drug dose and the performance of psychiatric patients in a maximum security token economy program. *Journal of Behavior Therapy and Experimental Psychiatry, 20,* 57-67.

Harris, G. T., & Rice, M. E. (1984). Mentally disordered firesetters: Psychodynamic versus empirical approaches. *International Journal of Law and Psychiatry, 7,* 19-34.

Harris, G. T., & Rice, M. E. (1986). Staff injuries sustained during altercations with psychiatric patients. *Journal of Interpersonal Violence, 1,* 193-211.

Harris, G. T., Rice, M. E., & Preston, D. L. (1989). Staff and patient perceptions of the least restrictive alternatives for the short term control of disturbed behavior. *Journal of Psychiatry and Law, 17,* 239-263.

Harris, G. T., & Varney, G. W. (1986). A ten year study of assaults and assaulters on a maximum security psychiatric unit. *Journal of Interpersonal Violence, 1,* 173-191.

Harry, B. (1983). Movies and behavior among hospitalized mentally disordered offenders. *Bulletin of the American Academy of Psychiatry and Law, 11,* 359-364.

Kennedy, S. (1990). *Anger management and training with adult prisoners.* Unpublished doctoral dissertation, University of Ottawa, Ottawa.

Kolko, D. J., Dorsett, P. G., & Milan, M. A. (1981). A total assessment approach to the evaluation of social skills training. The effectiveness of an anger control program for adolescent psychiatric patients. *Behavioral Assessment, 3,* 383-402.

Kuehnel, T. G., DeRisi, W. J., Liberman, R. P., & Mosk, M. D. (1984). Treatment strategies that promote deinstitutionalization of chronic mental patients. In W. P. Christian, G. T. Hannah, & T. J. Glahn (Eds.), *Programming effective human services* (pp. 245-265). New York: Plenum.

Liberman, R. P. (Ed.). (1988). *Psychiatric rehabilitation of chronic mental patients.* Washington, DC: American Psychiatric Press.

Liberman, R. P., Eckman, T., Kuehnel, T., Rosenstein, J., & Kuehnel, J. (1982). Dissemination of new behavior therapy programs to community mental health centers. *American Journal of Psychiatry, 139,* 224-226.

Liebert, R. M., & Sprafkin, J. (1988). *The early window: Effects of television on children and youth* (3rd ed.). Oxford, England: Pergamon.

Lion, J. R., & Reid, W. H. (1983). (Eds.) *Assaults within psychiatric facilities.* Toronto: Grune & Stratton.

Matarazzo, R. G. (1971). Research on the teaching and learning of psychotherapeutic skills. In S. L. Garfield & A. E. Bergin (Eds.), *Handbook of psychotherapy and behavior change: An empirical analysis* (2nd ed.) (pp. 941-966). New York: John Wiley.

Mayhew, G. L., Patience, E., & Cone, J. D. (1979). Approaches to employee management: Policies and preferences. *Journal of Organizational Behavior Management, 2,* 103-112.

Parke, R. D., Berkowitz, L., Leyens, J. P., West, S. G., & Sebastian, R. J. (1977). Some effects of violent and nonviolent movies on the behavior of juvenile delinquents. In L. Berkowitz (Ed.), *Advances in experimental social psychology* (Vol. 10, pp. 135-172). New York: Academic Press.

Paul, G. L., & Lentz, R. J. (1977). *Psychosocial treatment of chronic mental patients: Milieu versus social learning programs.* Cambridge, MA: Harvard University Press.

Phillips, E. L., Phillips, E. A., Fixsen, D. L., & Wolf, M. M. (1973). Achievement place: Behavior shaping works for delinquents. *Psychology Today, 6,* 75-79.

Quinsey, V. L. (1977). Studies in the reduction of assaults in a maximum security psychiatric institution. *Canada's Mental Health, 25,* 21-23.

Quinsey, V. L., & Sarbit, B. (1975). Behavioral changes associated with the introduction of a token economy in a maximum security psychiatric institution. *Canadian Journal of Criminology and Corrections, 17,* 177-182.

Quinsey, V. L., & Varney, G. W. (1977). Characteristics of assaults and assaulters in a maximum security psychiatric unit. *Crime and Justice, 5,* 212-220.

Rice, M. E. (1983). Improving the social skills of males in a maximum security psychiatric setting. *Canadian Journal of Behavioural Science, 15,* 1-13.

Rice, M. E. (1985). Violence in the maximum security hospital: A researcher-clinician's perspective. In M. H. Ben-Aron, S. J. Hucker, & C. D. Webster (Eds.), *Clinical criminology: The assessment and treatment of criminal behaviour.* Toronto: M. M. Graphics.

Rice, M. E., & Chaplin, T. C. (1979). Social skills training for hospitalized male arsonists. *Journal of Behavior Therapy and Experimental Psychiatry, 10,* 105-108.

Rice, M. E., & Harris, G. T. (1991). Firesetters admitted to a maximum security psychiatric institution: Characteristics of offenders and offenses. *Journal of Interpersonal Violence, 6,* 461-475.

Rice, M. E., Harris, G. T., Quinsey, V. L., & Cyr, M. (1991). Planning treatment programs in secure psychiatric facilities. In D. Weisstub (Ed.), *Law and mental health: International perspectives* (pp. 162-230). Elmsford, NY: Pergamon.

Rice, M. E., Harris, G. T., Varney, G. W., & Quinsey, V. L. (1989). *Violence in institutions: Understanding, prevention, and control.* Toronto: Hans Huber.

Rice, M. E., Helzel, M. F., Varney, G. W., & Quinsey, V. L. (1985). Crisis prevention and intervention training for psychiatric hospital staff. *American Journal of Community Psychology, 13,* 289-304.

Rice, M. E., & Josefowitz, N. (1983). Assertion, popularity, and social behavior in maximum security psychiatric patients. *Corrective and Social Psychiatry and Journal of Behavior Technology Methods and Therapy, 29,* 97-104.

Rice, M. E., & Quinsey, V. L. (1986). Contributions of Canadian applied psychological research to correctional and psychiatric institutions. *Canadian Psychology, 27,* 1-21.

Rice, M. E., Quinsey, V. L., & Houghton, R. (1990). Predicting treatment outcome and recidivism among patients in a maximum security token economy. *Behavioral Sciences and the Law, 8,* 313-326.

Ross, R. R., & McKay, H. B. (1979). *Self-mutilation.* Toronto: D. C. Heath.

Sherwood, G. C., & Gray, J. E. (1974). Two "classic" behaviour modification patients: A decade later. *Canadian Journal of Behavioural Science, 6,* 420-427.

Sullivan, M. A., & O'Leary, S. G. (1990). Maintenance following reward and cost token programs. *Behavior Therapy, 21,* 139-149.

Toch, H. (1977). *Police, prisons and the problem of violence.* Rockville, MD: U.S. Department of Health, Education, and Welfare.

Ullmann, L. F. (1967). *Institution and outcome: A comparative study of psychiatric hospitals.* Elmsford, NY: Pergamon.

Willet, T. C. (1983). Prison guards in private. *Canadian Journal of Criminology, 25,* 1-17.

13

Psychopathy and Crime Across the Life Span

ROBERT D. HARE
ADELLE E. FORTH
KATY E. STRACHAN

Psychopathy is a personality disorder defined by a constellation of affective, interpersonal, and behavioral characteristics, central to which are a profound lack of empathy, guilt, or remorse, and a callous disregard for the feelings, rights, and welfare of others (see Cleckley, 1976; Hare & Cox, 1978; McCord & McCord, 1964; Tennent, Tennent, Prins, & Bedford, 1990). Individuals with this disorder—psychopaths—typically are glib, egocentric, selfish, callous, deceitful, manipulative, impulsive, sensation-seeking, irresponsible, and without "conscience." Psychopaths readily flout social conventions and ignore social and interpersonal obligations. Not surprisingly, they frequently come into contact with the criminal justice system.

In this chapter we provide an overview of recent research on the association between psychopathy and criminal behavior across much of

AUTHORS' NOTES: Preparation of this chapter was supported by grant MT-4511 from the Medical Research Council of Canada, and by the Program of Research on Mental Health and Law of the John D. and Catherine T. MacArthur Foundation.

Adelle Forth is now at the Department of Psychology, Carleton University, Ottawa, Ontario.

the life span. First, however, we clarify what we mean by *psychopathy,*
a term that has been the source of some confusion over the years.

The Definition and Assessment of Psychopathy

A variety of terms (e.g., *psychopathy, sociopathy,* and *antisocial
personality)* have been used to describe what is ostensibly much the
same disorder. However, the use of these terms is often idiosyncratic,
and the lack of common diagnostic criteria makes it difficult to determine the extent to which different terms actually refer to the same
construct. For example, the diagnostic criteria for antisocial personality
disorder (APD) contained in the revised third edition of the *Diagnostic
and Statistical Manual of Mental Disorders* (DSM-III-R; American
Psychiatric Association, 1987) consist primarily of easily measured
antisocial and criminal behaviors. The result is a personality disorder
that has good reliability but that bears an uncertain resemblance to the
more traditional clinical concept of psychopathy (Frances & Widiger,
1986; Hare, Hart, & Harpur, 1991; Morey, 1988; Widiger, Frances,
Pincus, Davis, & First, 1991; World Health Organization, 1990). The
problem is that the criteria for APD fail to capture the affective and
interpersonal characteristics of psychopathy long considered fundamental to the disorder. As a consequence of its focus on antisocial
behaviors, APD is more closely allied with persistent criminality than
with psychopathy. Indeed, as many as 80% of incarcerated male offenders in Canadian federal prisons meet the criteria for APD (Correctional
Service of Canada, 1990). Individuals with such a diagnosis, though
antisocial, are heterogeneous with respect to interpersonal and affective
characteristics. Issues of this sort have led the American Psychiatric
Association to undertake field trials to evaluate alternative diagnostic
criteria for possible inclusion in DSM-IV (see below).

The use of self-report scales as a primary method to assess psychopathy is popular. However, their use for this purpose is problematic.
Many of these inventories lack demonstrated reliability and validity. In
addition, self-report scales are susceptible to malingering and impression management, a particular concern with individuals who may be
skilled at deception and manipulation (Hare, Forth, & Hart, 1989).
Moreover, self-report scales designed to measure psychopathy, such as
the Psychopathic Deviate *(Pd)* from the Minnesota Multiphasic Personality Inventory (MMPI), the Socialization *(So)* scale from the California

Psychological Inventory (CPI), or the antisocial scale from the Millon Clinical Multiaxial Inventory (MCMI-II), seem to measure only the social deviance components of psychopathy (Hare, 1985, 1991; Harpur, Hare, & Hakstian, 1989; Hart, Forth, & Hare, 1991). Like the DSM-III-R category, APD, these scales do not do a very good job of measuring the affective and interpersonal features of psychopathy.

The Revised Psychopathy Checklist (PCL-R)

A measure of psychopathy that is closely tied to traditional clinical conceptions of the disorder is the 22-item Psychopathy Checklist (PCL; Hare, 1980) and its 20-item revision (PCL-R; Hare, 1991). The PCL and PCL-R are highly correlated ($r = .88$) and measure the same construct (Hare et al., 1990). Each version consists of a set of clinical rating scales designed to assess behaviors and personality traits considered fundamental to psychopathy. Their immediate predecessor was a 7-point global rating scale for the assessment of psychopathy (Hare, 1985; Hare & Cox, 1978).

The items in the PCL-R are presented in Table 13.1. Each item is scored on a 3-point scale on the basis of extensive institutional files and a semistructured interview. PCL-R scores range from 0 to 40, and represent the degree to which an individual resembles the prototypical psychopath. For research purposes, a cutoff score of 30 (34 for the PCL) has proven useful for the diagnosis of psychopathy. There is a substantial body of evidence attesting to the reliability and validity of the PCL-R (Hare, 1991; Hare et al., 1990; Harpur, Hare, & Hakstian, 1989; Hart, Hare, & Harpur, in press). With respect to the former, Hart et al. (in press) reported that the alpha coefficient for the PCL-R, aggregated over seven samples of male prison inmates from Canada, the United States, and England ($N = 1,192$), was .87; the intraclass correlation was .83 for a single rating and .91 for the mean of two ratings.

Although they meet statistical criteria for a homogeneous measure of a unidimensional construct, both the PCL and the PCL-R consist of the same two stable factors (Hare et al., 1990; Harpur, Hakstian, & Hare, 1988; see Table 13.1 for the items that define these factors in the PCL-R). Although correlated about .5 on average, the factors have differential patterns of intercorrelations with external variables. Factor 1 reflects interpersonal and affective characteristics, such as egocentricity, manipulativeness, callousness, and lack of remorse, considered

TABLE 13.1 Items in the Revised Psychopathy Checklist (PCL-R)

1. Glibness/superficial charm[1]
2. Grandiose sense of self-worth[1]
3. Need for stimulation/proneness to boredom[2]
4. Pathological lying[1]
5. Conning/manipulative[1]
6. Lack of remorse or guilt[1]
7. Shallow affect[1]
8. Callous/lack of empathy[1]
9. Parasitic life-style[2]
10. Poor behavioral controls[2]
11. Promiscuous sexual behavior
12. Early behavior problems[2]
13. Lack of realistic, long-term goals[2]
14. Impulsivity[2]
15. Irresponsibility[2]
16. Failure to accept responsibility for actions[1]
17. Many short-term marital relationships
18. Juvenile delinquency[2]
19. Revocation of conditional release[2]
20. Criminal versatility

NOTES: 1. Item loads on Factor 1.
2. Item loads on Factor 2.
Items 11, 17, and 20 do not load on either factor.

by many clinicians to be the essence of psychopathy. This factor is correlated with classic, clinical descriptions of psychopathy, prototypicality ratings of narcissistic personality disorder, and self-report measures of narcissism; it is negatively correlated with self-report measures of empathy and anxiety. Factor 2 reflects those characteristics of psychopathy associated with an impulsive, antisocial, and unstable life-style. This factor is most strongly correlated with diagnoses of APD, criminal behaviors, substance abuse, and self-report measures of psychopathy. Each of the factors can be measured reliably. Thus, in the seven samples of prison inmates described above, the alpha coefficient was .84 for Factor 1 and .77 for Factor 2. The intraclass correlation for a single rating and for the mean of two ratings was, respectively, .72 and .86 for Factor 1, and .83 and .91 for Factor 2 (Hart et al., in press).

The PCL-R factors form the basis for a 10-item criterion set (5 items from Factor 1 and 5 from Factor 2) currently being tested in the American Psychiatric Association's field trials for APD (see Hare et al. 1991; Widiger et al., 1991).

In contrast to the large percentage of offenders receiving a diagnosis of APD, only about 15% to 25% of offenders meet the PCL-R criteria for psychopathy. An asymmetric association between the two procedures exists: The majority of criminal psychopaths defined by the PCL-R meet the APD criteria, but most offenders with an APD diagnosis do not meet the PCL-R criteria for psychopathy.

In the review that follows we will focus on research in which the assessments of psychopathy were based on the PCL, the PCL-R, or their predecessor, the 7-point rating scale described by Hare & Cox (1978). There are two main reasons for doing so. First, there is an extensive literature attesting to their reliability and validity. Second, they provide a common metric for operationalizing the construct of psychopathy, with the result that method variance is considerably reduced. Because several of the PCL and PCL-R items are directly or indirectly related to criminal behaviors, most investigators delete these items or take them into account statistically when computing psychopathy-crime associations.

Psychopathy and Crime

Characteristics that ordinarily help to inhibit antisocial and aggressive behavior, such as empathy, close emotional bonds, and fear of punishment, are lacking or relatively ineffective in psychopaths. It is not surprising, therefore, that psychopaths are responsible for a disproportionate amount of the serious repetitive crime and violence in our society (see reviews by Hare, 1991; Hare, Strachan, & Forth, in press). For example, studies by Wong (1984), Hare and Jutai (1983), and Kosson, Smith, and Newman (1990), to name but a few, found that psychopathic offenders were more heavily involved in crime than were other offenders.

The psychopathy-violence association has been the subject of considerable interest among researchers. Hare and McPherson (1984) found that between the ages of 16 and 30 psychopaths were generally more violent than were other offenders. Serin (1991) found that compared to other offenders, psychopaths were more likely to have received a conviction for a violent offence, to have used weapons, and to have made threats of violence. Kosson et al. (1990) examined the association between psychopathy and crime in samples of White and Black inmates. Psychopaths of both races had higher rates of convictions for both nonviolent and violent offenses than did nonpsychopaths. In addition, the psychopaths committed a greater variety of different types of offenses than did the nonpsychopaths.

The propensity of psychopaths for violent and aggressive behavior apparently is not inhibited during incarceration. Hare and McPherson (1984) reported that psychopaths engaged in considerably more institutional violence and aggression than did other offenders. Wong (1984) found that psychopaths committed almost four times as many institutional offenses, were given higher ratings for violence, and engaged in significantly more threatening behavior and acts of violence than did other inmates. Similarly, Serin (1991) found that, while in prison, psychopaths were more aggressive, abusive, and threatening, had higher scores on anger inventories, and were more likely to use instrumental aggression, than were other offenders.

The association between psychopathy and crime is not confined to male prison inmates. Hart and Hare (1989) found that psychopathy was significantly related to criminal activity and violence in a sample of consecutive male admissions to a forensic psychiatric hospital. Forth, Hart, and Hare (1990) reported that psychopathic young offenders were more criminally active and violent than were other young offenders. Strachan (1991) found that about one third of a sample of female offenders met the criteria for psychopathy, but that these women were responsible for about half of the nonviolent and violent offenses committed by the entire sample.

Recidivism and the Prediction of Violent Behavior

Most clinical descriptions of psychopathy make reference to a persistent disregard for social norms and conventions. Moreover, it is often assumed that the personality structure of psychopaths is relatively stable over time, and that the characteristics that resulted in criminal and violent behavior in the past will have a similar effect in the future. Until recently, most clinicians and researchers have been pessimistic about the value of diagnoses of psychopathy in predicting recidivism and violence. However, an increasing body of research indicates that this pessimism is unwarranted, provided that reliable and valid measures of psychopathy are used.

For example, Hart, Kropp, and Hare (1988) found that the PCL-R predicted violations of conditional release in a sample of 231 federal offenders. A series of regression analyses demonstrated that the PCL made a significant contribution to the prediction of outcome over and beyond that made by relevant criminal-history and demographic variables. The recidivism rate of the psychopaths was almost three times that of the nonpsychopaths. Similar results were obtained by Serin, Peters, and Barbaree (1990), who compared empirically derived predictors of recidivism with PCL scores in a sample of 93 federal offenders released on temporary absences and parole. The PCL predicted outcome better than did a combination of criminal-history and demographic variables and several standard actuarial risk instruments.

Hemphill (1991) investigated the recidivism rates for 106 inmates released from a forensic psychiatric center; the average follow-up period was 879 days. Each inmate had been assessed with the PCL-R and had taken part in an intensive therapeutic community treatment program (described by Ogloff, Wong, & Greenwood, 1990). The recidivism rate was 73% for the psychopaths and 43% for the nonpsychopaths.

Psychopathy appears to be predictive not only of recidivism in general, but also of violent recidivism. In a five-year follow-up of the subjects in the Serin et al. (1990) study, Serin (1991) reported that PCL scores, but not standard actuarial scales, were significantly correlated with violent reoffending. In a long-term follow-up of release behavior of forensic psychiatric patients, Harris, Rice, and Cormier (1991) reported that the violent recidivism rate of psychopaths (as measured by the PCL-R) was almost four times that of nonpsychopaths.

Rice, Harris, and Quinsey (1990) studied 54 rapists released from a maximum security psychiatric hospital. A combination of PCL-R scores and a phallometric measure of sexual arousal (as measured by penile plethysmography) correctly identified 77% of the violent recidivists.

Criminal History of Psychopaths

The "official" criminal activities of psychopaths begin at a very early age (Hare, 1991; Wong, 1984). Among federal offenders, most psychopaths have had formal contacts with the criminal justice system by age 15 or 16, several years earlier than the nonpsychopath offenders.

Early Criminality

Many clinicians and investigators have argued that the unusually early criminality of psychopaths is related to poor social and environmental factors. However, the results of two studies on the association between family background and early criminality in criminal psychopaths do not support this argument (DeVita, Forth, Hare, & McPherson, 1991). In these studies of male offenders (n = 315 and 107, respectively), diagnoses of psychopathy were unrelated to family background variables typically considered conducive to the development of early criminality. A "poor" family life was associated with the emergence of early criminality in nonpsychopaths, but not in psychopaths. For example, the mean age of formal contact with the criminal justice system was about 15 years for nonpsychopaths from a poor background, and about 22 years for nonpsychopaths from a "good" background. For psychopaths, the mean age of first contact was about 12 years for those from a poor background and about 13 years for those from a good background. Additional analyses on the degree of criminal behavior prior to age 20 lead to the same conclusion, namely, that family background was strongly related to criminal behavior only in nonpsychopathic offenders.

Although there may be some reluctance to describe an adolescent as a psychopath, there is no doubt that the traits and behaviors associated with the disorder are first manifested at an early age. Given the temporal stability of personality and behavioral characteristics, one would expect that the strong psychopathy-crime association found in adult offenders would also be found in adolescent psychopaths.

Forth et al. (1990) investigated the association between psychopathy and crime in a sample of 75 male adolescents held in a maximum-security detention center. Psychopaths, defined by the PCL-R, had a more extensive criminal history, particularly for violent offending, than did other young offenders. The overall pattern of correlations between the PCL-R and criminal behavior variables, including institutional behavior and postrelease recidivism, was consistent with the results reviewed above for adult male offenders.

Age-Related Changes in Middle Age

There is good evidence that the criminality of some habitual criminals decreases in middle age (e.g., Blumstein, Cohen, Roth, & Visher, 1986; Conrad, 1985; Hoffman & Beck, 1984). In some cases this decrease in criminality is quite dramatic, leading some observers to refer to it as "burnout." Clinical folklore and some recent empirical evidence (see Robins, 1966; Hare, McPherson, & Forth, 1988; Suedfeld & Landon, 1978) suggests that the concept of burnout, at least in a descriptive sense, may also apply to criminal psychopaths.

Hare et al. (1988) examined the age-related changes in criminal activities of 317 nonpsychopaths and 204 psychopaths from a medium-security institution. Official criminal records were used to code charges and convictions for criminal offenses and time spent in prison; these were broken down into five-year periods from age 16 to age 45. We have recently extended the study period by another five years, to age 50; the results presented here include these new data.

Analyses were both retrospective (offenses committed prior to the assessment of psychopathy) and prospective (offenses committed after the assessment of psychopathy). Because of group differences in time spent in prison, we converted the conviction data into a rate measure, number of convictions per year free. The data were positively skewed, and for this reason they were subjected to a logarithmic transformation [$\log(x + 1)$] prior to statistical analysis. Due to the differences in age at the time of assessment, the number of subjects decreased across the age periods (see Table 13.2). The data were analyzed in two ways: cross-sectionally, with different sample sizes in each age period; and longitudinally, with the same subjects followed from age 16 to age 50.

Table 13.2 presents the results from the cross-sectional analyses for several criminological variables for each age period: months spent in prison (maximum = 60); percentage of inmates in each group who spent all or part of an age period in prison; percentage of inmates who received at least one conviction; percentage of total convictions that were for a violent offense; and conviction rates for nonviolent and violent offenses.

Inspection of Table 13.2 reveals that until about the age of 40 psychopaths generally were more criminally active than were nonpsychopaths. After age 40 the known criminal activities of psychopaths decreased dramatically, reaching a level that was as low as that of other criminals. An exception involved the percentage of convictions for violent offenses. Although the total number of convictions for both violent and nonviolent crimes decreased with age, the percentage of convictions for violent offenses committed by psychopaths increased after age 45. Thus, in the 46-50 age period, 30% of the convictions received by psychopaths, and only 8.8% of those received by nonpsychopaths, were for violent offenses.

Table 13.2 also indicates that almost half of the psychopaths continued to be convicted of crimes after age 46.

The preceding analyses were performed on data from different numbers of subjects in each age period. Although the data provide a useful cross-sectional picture of criminal history, they do not readily lend

TABLE 13.2 Cross-Sectional Criminal History Data for Psychopaths and Nonpsychopaths

Age period (years)	n^a		Months in Prison	Subjects in Prison (%)[b]	Subjects Convicted (%)[c]	Crimes Violence (%)[d]	Conviction Rate[e]	
							NV	V
Psychopaths								
1. 16-20	204	(1)	19.0	80.4	86.5	14/0	.90	.25
2. 21-25	203	(9)	28.2	90.1	91.6	16.7	.93	.37
3. 26-30	184	(14)	27.5	84.8	79.3	13.1	.75	.28
4. 31-35	126	(16)	29.1	84.1	76.2	22.0	.75	.22
5. 36-40	87	(14)	27.7	75.9	63.2	25.0	.63	.21
6. 41-45	61	(5)	19.6	60.7	60.7	19.0	.50	.12
7. 46-50	35	(5)	16.2	48.4	42.9	30.0	.27	.12
Nonpsychopaths								
1. 16-20	317	(1)	10.7	57.7	70.2	19.0	.59	.14
2. 21-25	313	(2)	17.2	72.8	75.4	23.0	.67	.21
3. 26-30	281	(10)	19.4	68.3	71.5	24.0	.58	.18
4. 31-35	208	(15)	20.5	67.8	66.8	21.0	.57	.16
5. 36-40	137	(11)	19.0	61.3	58.4	16.9	.44	.09
6. 41-45	86	(9)	17.7	59.31	57.0	15.2	.39	.07
7. 46-50	47	(3)	14.2	51.1	40.4	8.8	.31	.03

NOTES: NV = nonviolent offenses; V = violent offenses.
a. Values in parentheses indicate the number of inmates deleted from conviction rate analyses because they spent the entire period in prison.
b. All or part of a period in prison.
c. At least one conviction.
d. Percentage of total crimes that are violent.
e. Per year free (logarithmic transformation).

themselves to analysis of group changes in criminal activity with age (see Farrington, 1986). An alternative depiction of age-related changes is to describe the same subjects over time, that is, longitudinally.

Figure 13.1 presents the mean number of months spent in prison by 35 psychopaths and 47 nonpsychopaths from ages 16 to 50. Psychopaths spent an increasing amount of time in prison until about age 40, after which their prison time decreased sharply.

Conviction rates for violent and nonviolent offenses in each age period are presented in Figure 13.2. For psychopaths, the conviction rate for nonviolent offenses—but not for violent ones—increased until about age 40, and then dropped dramatically. These data suggest that

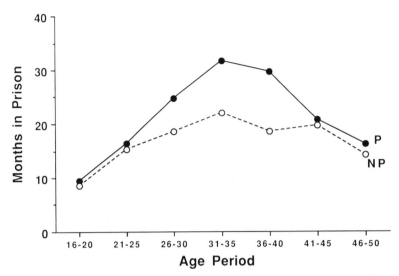

Figure 13.1. Mean Number of Months Spent in Prison by Psychopaths (P; $n = 35$) and Nonpsychopaths (NP; $n = 47$) from Age 16 to 50

the decrease in criminality shown by psychopaths after age 40 is more dramatic for nonviolent crimes than for violent ones. In effect, it appears that the psychopath's propensity for violence and aggression may be relatively persistent across much of the life span.

The reasons for the age-related decline in the criminal activities of some psychopaths remains unknown. Similar decreases in the criminality of habitual offenders have been interpreted in terms of burnout, maturation, the development of new strategies to remain out of prison, or a realization of the negative consequences of a criminal life-style (Shover, 1985). The extent to which these factors are applicable to psychopaths needs to be investigated. It is unlikely, however, that the traditional meaning of *burnout*—with its implications of emotional and physical wear and tear—applies to the psychopath.

Age-related changes in the criminality of psychopaths may reflect changes in core personality traits. Many clinicians and researchers believe, however, that the personality structure of psychopaths is too stable to account for the behavioral changes that sometimes occur in middle age. Robins (1966) has noted, for example, that although some psychopaths become less grossly criminal and antisocial with age, they

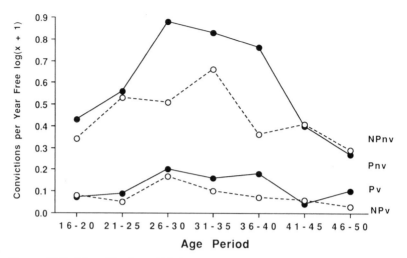

Figure 13.2. Mean Number of Violent (v) and Nonviolent (nv) Convictions per Year Free by Psychopaths (P; n = 35) and Nonpsychopaths (NP; n = 47) from Age 16 to 50

often remain rather disagreeable individuals. In many cases, their social deviance is expressed in ways that, although not criminal, are socially and emotionally distressing to others.

Assessment of Psychopathy as a Function of Age

The two-factor structure of the PCL/PCL-R may prove useful in determining the extent to which age-related changes in the criminality/social deviance of psychopaths is related to parallel changes in personality. We can ask, for example, whether decreases in criminality are associated with a corresponding decrease in both the social deviance (Factor 1) and the personality (Factor 2) components of psychopathy, or with only the social deviance components.

As a first step, Harpur and Hare (1991) obtained PCL/PCL-R scores for 889 male inmates, ranging in age from 16 to 70 at the time of assessment. The sample for this cross-sectional study was divided into six groups according to the age at which the assessments were made: 16-20, 21-25,

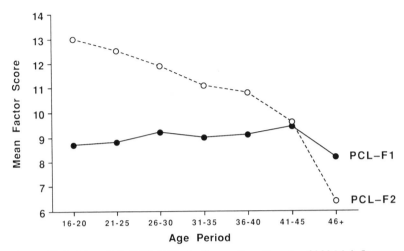

Figure 13.3. Mean PCL/PCL-R Factor Scores for a Sample of 889 Male Inmates as a Function of Age of Assessment. The Number of Inmates in Each Age Period was 86, 244, 240, 147, 82, 48, and 42, respectively.

26-30, 31-35, 36-40, 41-45, and 46-70 (n = 86, 244, 240, 147, 82, 48, and 42, respectively).

Mean Factor scores for each group are presented in Figure 13.3. It is clear that mean scores on Factor 1 remained constant across all the ages, whereas mean Factor 2 scores declined with age.

These results are consistent with a conceptualization of psychopathy as encompassing two correlated but distinct constructs, one defined by affective and interpersonal traits and the other by socially deviant behaviors. They also suggest that age-related changes in social deviance and antisocial behavior are not necessarily paralleled by changes in the egocentric, manipulative, and callous traits fundamental to psychopathy.

Conclusions

The antisocial behavior of psychopaths begins at an early age and persists throughout much of the life span. Although the criminality of a significant proportion of criminal psychopaths decreases in middle age, many others remain criminally active well beyond age 40. In addition, estimates of illegal behavior are typically based on official records detailing time spent in prison and convictions for criminal offenses. Even if many psychopaths receive fewer convictions as they age, this does not necessarily mean that they have become model citizens or that their behavior is no longer antisocial. The available evidence suggests that the reduction in criminality and social deviance shown by some psychopaths in middle age may not be the result of fundamental changes in personality or in the way they view other people. From society's perspective, this may not be as important as the fact that some reduction in criminality has occurred. However, a more detailed picture of the social behaviors of "reformed" psychopaths may reveal that these individuals remain capable of generating considerable social and interpersonal distress.

References

American Psychiatric Association. (1987). *Diagnostic and statistical manual of mental disorders* (3rd ed., rev.). Washington, DC: Author.

Blumstein, A., Cohen, J., Roth, J. A., & Visher, C. A. (1986). *Criminal careers and "career criminals"* (Vol 1.). Washington, DC: National Academy Press.

Cleckley, H. (1976). *The mask of sanity* (5th ed.). St. Louis, MO: C. V. Mosby.

Conrad, J. P. (1985). *The dangerous and the endangered.* Lexington, MA: Lexington.

Correctional Service of Canada. (1990). *Forum on corrections research, 2,* No. 1. Ottawa: Author.

DeVita, E., Forth, A. E., Hare, R. D., & McPherson, L. M. (1991). *Early criminal behavior of psychopaths.* Manuscript under review.

Farrington, D. P. (1986). Age and crime. In M. Tonry & N. Morris (Eds.), *Crime and justice: An annual review of research* (Vol. 7, pp. 189-250). Chicago: University of Chicago Press.

Forth, A. E., Hart, S. D., & Hare, R. D. (1990). Assessment of psychopathy in male young offenders. *Psychological Assessment: A Journal of Consulting and Clinical Psychology, 2,* 342-344.

Frances, A. J., & Widiger, T. (1986). The classification of personality disorders: An overview of problems and situations. In A. J. Frances & R. E. Hales (Eds.), *American Psychiatric Association annual review* (Vol. 5, Psychiatry update, pp. 24-257). Washington, DC: American Psychiatric Press.

Hare, R. D. (1980). A research scale for the assessment of psychopathy in criminal populations. *Personality and Individual Differences, 1,* 111-119.

Hare, R. D. (1985). Comparison of procedures for the assessment of psychopathy. *Journal of Consulting and Clinical Psychology, 53,* 7-16.

Hare, R. D. (1991). *The Hare Psychopathy Checklist-Revised. Toronto: Multi-Health Systems.*

Hare, R. D., & Cox, D. N. (1978). Clinical and empirical conceptions of psychopathy, and the selection of subjects for research. In R. D. Hare & D. Schalling (Eds.), *Psychopathic behaviour: Approaches to research.* Chichester, England: John Wiley.

Hare, R. D., Forth, A. E., & Hart, S. D. (1989). The psychopath as prototype for pathological lying and deception. In J. C. Yuille (Ed.), *Credibility assessment* (pp. 25-49). Dordrecht, The Netherlands: Kluwer.

Hare, R. D., Harpur, T. J., Hakstian, A. R., Forth, A. E., Hart, S. D., & Newman, J. P. (1990). The revised Psychopathy Checklist: Reliability and factor structure. *Psychological Assessment: A Journal of Consulting and Clinical Psychology, 2,* 338-341.

Hare, R. D., Hart, S. D., & Harpur, T. J. (1991). Psychopathy and the DSM-IV criteria for antisocial personality disorder. *Journal of Abnormal Psychology, 100,* 391-398.

Hare, R. D., & Jutai, J. W. (1983). Criminal history of the male psychopath: Some preliminary data. In K. T. Van Dusen & S. A. Mednick (Eds.), *Prospective studies of crime and delinquency* (pp. 225-236). Boston: Kluwer-Nijhoff.

Hare, R. D., & McPherson, L. M. (1984). Violent and aggressive behavior by criminal psychopaths. *International Journal of Law and Psychiatry, 7,* 35-50.

Hare, R. D., McPherson, L. M., & Forth, A. E. (1988). Male psychopaths and their criminal careers. *Journal of Consulting and Clinical Psychology, 56,* 710-714.

Hare, R. D., Strachan, K. E., & Forth, A. E. (in press). Psychopathy and crime: A review. In K. Howells & C. Hollin (Eds.), *Clinical approaches to mentally disordered offenders.* New York: John Wiley.

Harpur, T. J., & Hare, R. D. (1991). *The assessment of psychopathy as a function of age.* Manuscript under review.

Harpur, T. J., Hakstian, A. R., & Hare, R. D. (1988). Factor structure of the Psychopathy Checklist. *Journal of Consulting and Clinical Psychology, 56,* 741-747.

Harpur, T. J., Hare, R. D., & Hakstian, A. R. (1989). Two-factor conceptualization of psychopathy: Construct validation and assessment implications. *Psychological Assessment: A Journal of Consulting and Clinical Psychology, 1,* 6-17.

Harris, G. T., Rice, M. E., & Cormier, C. A. (1991). Psychopathy and violent recidivism. *Law and Human Behavior, 15,* 625-637.

Hart, S. D., Forth, A. E., & Hare, R. D. (1991). Assessing psychopathy in male criminals using the MCMI-II. *Journal of Personality Disorders, 5,* 318-327.

Hart, S. D., & Hare, R. D. (1989). Discriminant validity of the Psychopathy Checklist in a forensic psychiatric population. *Psychological Assessment: A Journal of Consulting and Clinical Psychology, 1,* 211-218.

Hart, S. D., Hare, R. D., & Harpur, T. J. (in press). The Psychopathy Checklist: An overview for researchers and clinicians. In P. McReynolds & J. Rosen (Eds.), *Advances in psychological assessment* (Vol. 8). New York: Plenum.

Hart, S. D., Kropp, P. R., & Hare, R. D. (1988). Performance of male psychopaths following conditional release from prison. *Journal of Consulting and Clinical Psychology, 56,* 227-232.

Hemphill, J. (1991). *Efficacy of the therapeutic community for treating criminal psychopaths.* Unpublished master's thesis, Department of Psychology, University of Saskatchewan, Saskatoon.

Hoffman, P. B., & Beck, J. L. (1984). Burnout—Age at release from prison and recidivism. *Journal of Criminal Justice, 12,* 617-623.

Kosson, D. S., Smith, S. S., & Newman, J. P. (1990). Evaluating the construct validity of psychopathy on Black and White male inmates: Three preliminary studies. *Journal of Abnormal Psychology, 99,* 250-259.

McCord, W., & McCord, J. (1964). *The psychopath: An essay on the criminal mind.* Princeton, NJ: Van Nostrand.

Morey, L. C. (1988). The categorical representation of personality disorder: A cluster analysis of DSM-III personality features. *Journal of Abnormal Psychology, 97,* 314-321.

Ogloff, J. R., Wong, S., & Greenwood, A. (1990). Treating criminal psychopaths in a therapeutic community program. *Behavioral Sciences and the Law, 8,* 81-90.

Rice, M. E., Harris, G. T., & Quinsey, V. L. (1990). A follow-up of rapists assessed in a maximum security psychiatric facility. *Journal of Interpersonal Violence, 4,* 435-448.

Robins, L. N. (1966). *Deviant children grown up.* Baltimore, MD: Williams & Wilkins.

Serin, R. C. (1991). Psychopathy and violence in criminals. *Journal of Interpersonal Violence, 6,* 423-431.

Serin, R. C., Peters, R. D., & Barbaree, H. E. (1990). Predictors of psychopathy and release outcome in a criminal population. *Psychological Assessment: A Journal of Consulting and Clinical Psychology, 2,* 419-422.

Serin, R. C. (1991). *Violence and recidivism in criminal psychopaths.* Manuscript under review.

Shover, N. (1985). *Aging criminals.* Beverly Hills, CA: Sage.

Strachan, K. E., (1991). [Psychopathy and female offenders]. Unpublished data. Department of Psychology, University of British Columbia, Vancouver.

Suedfeld, P., & Landon, P. B. (1978). Approaches to treatment. In R. D. Hare & D. Schalling (Eds.), *Psychopathic behavior: Approaches to research* (pp. 347-376). Chichester, England: John Wiley.

Tennent, G., Tennent, D., Prins, H., & Bedford, A. (1990). Psychopathic disorder—A useful clinical concept? *Medicine, Science, and Law, 30,* 39-44.

Widiger, T. A., Frances, A. K., Pincus, H. A., Davis, W. W., & First, M. (1991). Toward an empirical classification for DSM-IV. *Journal of Abnormal Psychology, 100,* 280-288.

Wong, S. (1984). *Criminal and institutional behaviours of psychopaths.* Programs Branch Users Report. Ottawa: Ministry of the Solicitor-General of Canada.

World Health Organization. (1990). *International classification of diseases and related health problems* (10th ed.). Geneva: Author.

14

Elder Abuse in Canada and the United States:
Prevalence, Legal, and Service Issues

JOSEPH P. HORNICK

LYNN McDONALD

GERALD B. ROBERTSON

W ithout doubt, the majority of older Canadians enjoy positive
relationships with their families, friends, and relatives and, if
institutionalized, with their professional caregivers. Nevertheless, there
is a growing awareness that some elderly Canadians suffer abuse at the
hands of these groups. Sensitization to this "new" form of violence has
generated public, professional and political concern and pressure to
respond to the problem. The demand for legal and social remedies has,

AUTHORS' NOTES: Early drafts of this chapter were presented at the XXII Banff
International Conference on Behavioural Sciences, March 1990, Banff, Alberta, and at
the Canadian Institute for the Administration of Justice Conference: Health Care Ethics
and Law, October 1990, Toronto, Ontario.
   Table 14.1 used by permission: *Elder Abuse and Neglect in Canada,* (Markham:
Butterworths, 1991). Some sections of this chapter have also been summarized from the
same work.
   The authors' names are in alphabetical order; their contribution to this chapter is equal.
The views expressed in this chapter are those of the authors and do not necessarily reflect
the views of the Canadian Research Institute for Law and the Family.

however, outpaced the research knowledge necessary for the creation of cohesive approaches to combat the problem. In fact, elder abuse as a topic of research has had a very abbreviated history—a decade at most.

The problem of the lack of research knowledge in this area is exacerbated by the lack of consensus among researchers and Canadians in general as to what constitutes elder abuse and neglect and, as a result, estimates of the incidence and prevalence of the problem are imprecise at best. However, common sense seems to tell us that with the reality of longer life spans and the changing configuration of the family structure, elder abuse and neglect may simply increase because of the growing number and proportion of persons 65 years and older.

The dangers of developing both legal and social responses to elder abuse in the absence of knowledge of the relevant issues are substantial. In the name of protection, older persons could be forced to accept services they do not want. Family relations could be severely strained, and in some instances, the older adult could be institutionalized. The potential for "revictimizing the victim" is readily apparent. Thus, in order to contribute to the development of a knowledge base in the area of elder abuse, this chapter reviews and summarizes the relevant literature to date. Specifically, the purpose of this chapter is to identify relevant issues and information concerning the following: (1) the incidence and prevalence of elder abuse, (2) the legal response to elder abuse, and (3) the social service response to elder abuse.

The Incidence and Prevalence of Elder Abuse

Research Definitions

The first task in researching and responding to any social problem is to identify the problem accurately, in a manner that can be understood by all who may have to deal with it. Unfortunately, concepts such as "elder abuse" and "elder mistreatment" developed as folk categories; that is, labels were applied by those directly involved with the manifestation of the phenomena. Such labels, of course, are rarely parsimoniously conceptualized or designed for research. Thus definitions of "elder abuse" in the research literature tend to be vague and vary from author to author (Crystal, 1987; Giordano & Giordano, 1984; Hudson & Johnson, 1986; Pedrick-Cornell & Gelles, 1982; Podnieks, 1985; Valentine & Cash, 1986).

First, it is important to note that attention has been placed almost exclusively on defining and identifying abuse and neglect of the elderly that takes place in domestic settings and perpetrated by caregivers. Little research has been undertaken to examine abuse and neglect of the elderly in institutional settings such as hospitals and nursing homes and offenses committed by noncaregivers would simply be considered criminal acts.

In terms of the type of abuse, most social researchers differentiate between physical abuse, and psychological or verbal/emotional abuse, (Chen, Bell, Dolinsky, Doyle, & Dunn, 1981; Crouse, Cobb, Harris, Kopecky, & Poertner, 1981; Douglass, Hickey, & Noel, 1980; Giordano & Giordano, 1984; Lau & Kosberg, 1979; H. O'Malley, Segars, Perez, Mitchell, & Knuepfel, 1979; L. Phillips & Rempusheski, 1985; Podnieks, Pillemer, Nicholson, Shillington, & Frizzell, 1989; Wolf, Strugnell, & Godkin, 1982). Neglect is also included by many authors (Gioglio & Blakemore, 1983; Hageboeck & Brandt, 1981; Hall & Andrew, 1984; Levenberg, Milan, Dolan, & Carpenter, 1983; McLaughlin, Nickell, & Gill, 1980; O'Brien, Hudson, & Johnson, 1984; H. O'Malley et al., 1979). Other authors differentiate between active and passive neglect (Crouse et al., 1981; Douglass et al., 1980; Wolf et al., 1982). Still others have added self-abuse and self-neglect to these categories of elder abuse (Chen et al., 1981; Hall & Andrew, 1984; O'Brien et al., 1984).

The literature reveals that many authors apply different terms to similar concepts. Thus, although categories have different names, they are in fact referring to the same phenomena. For example, exploitation (Hall & Andrew, 1984; Lau & Kosberg, 1979; O'Brien et al., 1984; H. O'Malley et al., 1979), financial abuse (Gioglio & Blakemore, 1983; Giordano & Giordano, 1984; Hageboeck & Brandt, 1981), and material abuse (Hall & Andrew, 1984; L. Phillips & Rempusheski, 1985; Wolf et al., 1982) often refer to the same type of elder abuse.

The lack of precise definitions of the different types of elder abuse and neglect and the subsequent lack of accurate predictive criteria have made it difficult for both practitioners and the general public to identify cases of elder abuse and neglect (L. Phillips & Rempusheski, 1986). It has been suggested that "research on the causes of abuse and neglect rather than on the symptoms can assist in the identification of at-risk persons and in the development of preventive programs" (Hudson, 1986, p. 161).

A number of methods have been proposed for detecting elder abuse, ranging from formal protocols to general guidelines (Fulmer, 1982;

T. O'Malley, Everett, O'Malley, & Campion, 1983). However, in order
for these tools to be useful, some consensus on the definitions of elder
abuse and neglect is necessary to establish standardized identification
and detection procedures (Hudson & Johnson, 1986).

A Taxonomy of Elder Abuse

The first step in developing a comprehensive and useful definition is
to develop a taxonomy of the various subcomponents or specific types
included in the concept. The work of Wolf et al. (1982) provides the
basis for the description of the different types of abuse and neglect
contained in Table 14.1.

These researchers divided elder abuse into three types: (1) physical
abuse, (2) psychological abuse, and (3) material abuse. Elder neglect is
divided into two major categories: (1) active neglect, and (2) passive
neglect. For the most part, this framework is adopted in Table 14.1;
however, active and passive neglect are categorized as intentional and
unintentional neglect since intention is an important dimension and
neglect, by definition, tends to be passive.

Physical abuse of the elderly receives the most attention in the
literature and is the most easily identified category. Physical elder abuse
refers to acts of commission that involve the intentional infliction of
physical discomfort, pain, or injury (e.g., slapping, cutting, burning, physical coercion, or restraint) and lead to bodily harm to the aged individual
(Chen et al., 1981; Douglass & Hickey, 1983; Lau & Kosberg, 1979; T.
O'Malley et al., 1983; L. Phillips & Rempusheski, 1985; Valentine &
Cash, 1986; Wolf, 1986). Physical abuse could also consist of medical
maltreatment or sexual assault.

Psychological abuse of the elderly is sometimes referred to as verbal
or emotional abuse (Crouse et al., 1981; Douglass et al., 1980). This
may include verbal assaults upon the elderly (e.g., name calling), being
humiliated or intimidated, threats of placement in a nursing home or
isolation, or being treated as a child (Chen et al., 1981; Giordano &
Giordano, 1984; Lau & Kosberg, 1979; T. O'Malley et al., 1983; L.
Phillips & Rempusheski, 1985; Valentine & Cash, 1986; Wolf, 1986).
Since the concept of psychological abuse has been particularly difficult
to define and measure, Podnieks et al. (1989) have concluded that it is
more useful to concentrate on the major manifestations of psychological abuse such as repeated insults or threats. Thus they have identified
an additional concept, of "chronic verbal aggression."

TABLE 14.1 Summary of Research Definitions of Elder Abuse and Neglect[1]

| Abuse | | | Neglect | |
Physical	Psychological	Material	Intentional	Unintentional
•physical assault (e.g., hitting, slapping, pushing, etc.) •sexual assault •medical maltreatment •physical restraint •physical coercion	•verbal and nonverbal abuse •name calling and ignoring •emotional abuse •emotional deprivation •mental cruelty •threatening and frightening elder •provocation of fear •infantalization •humiliation intimidation •isolation	•financial abuse •economic abuse •exploitation •misuse of money and property •theft of money and property •fraud	Intentionally or nonaccidentally withholding: •physical requirements (e.g., medicine, food, clothing, housing, environmental, etc.) •psychological requirements (e.g., social contact, emotional support, respect, etc.)	Unintentionally or accidentally withholding: •physical requirements (e.g., medicine, food, clothing, housing, environmental.) •psychological requirements (e.g., social contact, emotional support, respect, etc.)

NOTE: 1. Self-abuse and self-neglect are also referred to in the literature. However, they do not involve perpetrators and thus do not clearly fit in this paradigm.

Material abuse of the elderly is characterized by the intentional, illegal, or improper exploitation of the elder's material property or financial resources. This may involve theft, conversion of money, or use of funds without the elderly person's authority or consent (Douglass & Hickey, 1983; L. Phillips & Rempusheski, 1985; Shell, 1982; Stevenson, 1985; Valentine & Cash, 1986; Wolf, 1986). Recently Podnieks et al. (1989) have operationalized material abuse more broadly as attempts to persuade or influence elder persons to give up money and/or relinquish control over finances. Such broad definitions are more likely to measure the potential for this type of abuse rather than abuse itself, if it is assumed that the intent must be carried out, that is, exploitation must actually occur in order to be classified as "abuse."

In contrast to abuse, which is primarily active in nature, neglect is passive and can be divided into intentional and unintentional neglect. Intentional neglect refers to the conscious failure to fulfil a caretaking obligation. Intentional neglect refers to those situations in which a caregiver knowingly impinges on the elderly person's well-being by limiting or denying the fulfillment of basic needs (Block, 1983; Crouse et al., 1981; Valentine & Cash, 1986; Wolf et al., 1982). Unintentional neglect refers to situations in which the needs of the elder are unknown, not fully recognized, or are not dealt with appropriately by the caregiver (Block, 1983; Crouse et al., 1981; Valentine & Cash, 1986; Wolf et al., 1982). Such situations may result in lack of provision of food or health-related services or the elderly person being left alone, forgotten, or isolated (Douglass & Hickey, 1983; Podnieks, 1989; Wolf, 1986).

The taxonomy of elder abuse and neglect described in Table 14.1 incorporates most types found in the literature; however, the categories are not mutually exclusive or exhaustive. Violation of an elderly person's rights has also been cited as a distinctive form of elder abuse but has not been included in this table (Beck & Ferguson, 1981; Giordano & Giordano, 1984; Hall & Andrew, 1984; L. Phillips & Rempusheski, 1985; Valentine & Cash, 1986). We would suggest that if any form of abuse or neglect is experienced by the elderly, their rights have been violated.

It is important to note that the social research definitions of *elder abuse* and *neglect* provided above involve either acts of commission or omission on the part of the caregiver, who is often a person the older person loves, trusts, and is dependent upon for care and assistance. This limits the concept of elder abuse to acts involving caregivers and serves to distinguish elder abuse and neglect from criminal acts against the elderly that occur in a broader context. Acts such as physical assault, rape, and burglary committed by someone other than a caregiver would not normally be considered elder abuse although they do involve victimizing the elderly. In contrast, abuse may occur without the commission of a criminal act. For example, an elderly woman may willingly turn over all her pension checks to a family member in return for a minimal level of care (City of Toronto Mayor's Committee on Aging, 1984). However, if done willingly, this would not constitute a criminal act even though it could be exploitive.

In general, elder abuse and neglect may originate from two types of caregivers: (1) informal caregivers, and (2) formal caregivers. Informal caregivers include family members or close familial associates. Formal caregivers include professionals who work with the elderly, such as nurses, physicians, and home care providers. Elder abuse and neglect by professional or formal caregivers and abuse and neglect in institutional settings have only been recently addressed in the literature (Halamandaris, 1983; Podnieks, 1983; Solomon, 1983). Elder abuse and neglect by formal caregivers may fall into the same categories as that committed by informal caregivers (e.g., physical, psychological, and material abuse, intentional and unintentional neglect). The few articles addressing elder abuse and neglect in institutional settings tend to focus on material abuse, such as theft of patients' funds, medical care abuses (e.g., supplementing medical care support, charging costs unrelated to patient care, collecting for deceased or discharged patients) and fraudulent therapy and pharmaceutical charges (Halamandaris, 1983; Pepper, 1983; Stathopoulos, 1983).

It is also important to note at this juncture that caregiver abuse is not the whole story. There appears to be a category of independent elderly persons who are physically, psychologically, or financially abused by family members *who are not caregivers* (Pillemer & Finkelhor, 1988, 1989). That is, relatively well-functioning older persons who may have some responsibility for other relatives or who may have to interact with other relatives, are abused. Whether this is simply a matter of family violence (spouse abuse) or another unique manifestation of elder abuse remains to be debated.

The Legal Definition

In comparison with the social research definitions, the legal definitions of elder abuse are narrower in scope. This is the case because legal definitions are linked to criminal law and prosecution in the criminal justice system. However, legislative definitions are also problematic. If too general a definition is adopted, there is a danger that the legislative response will constitute unnecessary and unjustified intervention (Faulkner, 1982; Metcalf, 1986; Regan, 1981). Moreover, as Katz notes: "The sweep of some of the definitions is tantamount to legislating against unkindness to the elderly. It must be borne in mind that 'unreasonable or unrealistic laws serve neither the profession or the public'" (Katz, 1980, pp. 714-715).

Definitions of *abuse, neglect,* and *exploitation* vary significantly in the United States (Lee, 1986; Metcalf, 1986). Physical injury is always included in the definition of *abuse,* but only some states recognize the concept of emotional abuse (Metcalf, 1986). This may reflect the problems associated with defining and identifying emotional harm, as has been seen in the context of child welfare legislation (Katz, 1980; Sharpe, 1988). The U.S. legislation is most uniform in its definition of *exploitation,* which is generally defined as the illegal or inappropriate use of another's resources for one's own profit or advantage (Lee, 1986; Metcalf, 1986).

Some American jurisdictions have adopted a narrow definition of *abuse.* For example, the Minnesota legislation defines it as the intentional and nontherapeutic infliction of physical pain or injury, or any persistent course of conduct intended to produce mental or emotional distress (Ontario Ministry of the Attorney General, 1987).

In Canada, *abuse* is not defined concisely in the legislation. The Nova Scotia and New Brunswick statutes merely refer to adults who are victims of "physical abuse, sexual abuse, mental cruelty, or any combination thereof" (Gordon, Verdun-Jones, & MacDougall, 1986; Robertson, 1987). The Newfoundland statute is directed only at "neglected" adults, but is probably broad enough to include cases of abuse. None of the statutes make express reference to financial abuse.

Unlike existing Canadian adult protection legislation, the new law in Prince Edward Island (Adult Protection Act, 1988) provides a detailed definition in section (1) of abuse and neglect:

(a) "abuse" means offensive mistreatment, whether physical, sexual, mental, emotional, material or any combination thereof, that causes or is reasonably likely to cause the victim severe physical or psychological harm or significant material loss to his estate; . . .

(k) "neglect" means a lack of, or failure to provide, necessary care, aid, guidance or attention which causes, or is reasonably likely to cause, the victim severe physical or psychological harm or significant material loss to his estate.

It is significant that, as with the more recent enactments in the United States (such as in the District of Columbia), these definitions restrict the scope of the proposed legislation to cases of serious harm. They also include financial abuse, unlike existing Maritime legislation.

Incidence and Prevalence of Elder Abuse and Neglect

During the past 50 years, major demographic changes have inadvertently brought attention to the general problems and concerns of elderly persons, as well as to the specific issue of elder abuse. For example, life expectancy for both men and women has continued to increase since 1931. For men, the life expectancy has risen from 60 years of age in 1931 (Foot, 1982) to 71.9 years in 1980-1982 (Statistics Canada, 1984). Contrary to popular belief, the greatest gains in life expectancy have been made at the younger ages, especially in the first year of life (McDaniel, 1986). Since the 1970s, infant mortality, which is considered to be a chief indicator of improved longevity, has continued to decline.

As a result of increased life expectancy and population growth increases in general, there are growing numbers of individuals who are 60 years old or older, and the aging of the population continues to accelerate. For example, in 1983 the median age of the Canadian population was 30 years of age. It is projected that by 2006 the median age will be 41 years and will reach 48 years by 2031 (Statistics Canada, 1985). Not only has the number of individuals over 60 increased, the proportion of the population over 60 has also increased. According to McDaniel (1986), "it therefore seems realistic to anticipate that approximately one quarter of Canada's population in fifty years' time will be comprised of people over the age of 65" (p. 106). In actual numbers, this implies there will be 7 million older people in Canada by the first third of the 21st century (Statistics Canada, 1985).

The increase in the proportion of the population 65 years of age and older has led many to conclude that as a greater number of older persons become dependent on others for their care, there will be an increase in elder abuse (Montgomery & Borgatta, 1986). This hypothesis is based on the assumption that living with or being responsible for chronically ill elderly persons is extremely taxing on members of the family, thus leading to the increased probability of abuse occurring.

Unfortunately, both the public and the scientific community have been all too willing to accept claims concerning the "explosions" of elder abuse as well as the "tip of the iceberg" theories carried over from the early development of research in the child abuse area. This had led to a rapid growth in the scientific literature concerned with the detection, prevention, and intervention with the abused elderly—without reference to reliable statistics on the incidence or prevalence of elder abuse. Thus, as Montgomery and Borgatta (1986, p. 598) point out, "one could easily be led to believe that elder abuse exists, is growing, and that there is considerable knowledge about its causes and prevention."

Canadian Studies

Other than the studies in Manitoba (Shell, 1982), Nova Scotia (Province of Nova Scotia, 1986), and the recent cross-Canada survey by Podnieks et al., (1989), Canadian researchers have generally not attempted to estimate the incidence or prevalence of elder abuse and neglect in Canada. Shell (1982) conducted a limited exploratory study that involved interviewing a convenience sample of 105 professionals throughout the province of Manitoba. Although this study was successful in clearly demonstrating that elder abuse does occur in Manitoba, it is limited in its generalizability because of the small, nonrandom sample. According to the 105 professionals contacted, 540 incidents of elder abuse were experienced by 402 different people. Financial abuse (40.2%), psychological abuse (37.4%), and physical abuse (22.4%) were reported.

In 1982, the Nova Scotia Department of Social Services conducted a province-wide survey of elder abuse (Province of Nova Scotia, 1986). According to their findings, 137 (48.75%) of the total sample of 281 reported had been abused or neglected.

The most comprehensive Canadian study of the prevalence of elder abuse to date was conducted by Podnieks et al. (1989). This study consisted of a cross-Canadian telephone survey of 2,000 randomly chosen elderly persons living in private houses. The respondents were asked to provide information on whether they had been abused since the age of 65 years by family members, or other intimates, in the following four areas: (1) material abuse, (2) chronic verbal aggression, (3) physical violence, and (4) neglect. The results of the study indicate that material abuse was the most widespread form of maltreatment with 2.5% (25 per 1,000) of the sample reporting that someone had tried to persuade, cheat, or influence them in relation to finances. Chronic verbal aggression was the second most common form of abuse reported by 1.4% (14 per 1,000) of the sample. Physical violence was reported by 0.5% (5 per 1,000) of the respondents and neglect was the least common form of maltreatment with only 0.4% of the sample reporting it. Both physical abuse and chronic verbal aggression tended to be perpetrated by spouses, thus supporting the hypothesis that elder abuse tends to be spousal abuse grown old. Material abuse, in contrast, tended to be perpetrated by distant relatives or non relatives. Overall findings indicate that about 4% (40 per 1,000) of the elderly population has experienced some form of maltreatment since they passed their 65th birthday.

American Studies

Several American studies have attempted to identify the incidence of elder abuse, although their findings must also be interpreted cautiously in light of numerous methodological limitations. The estimated incidence rates range from 1% to 4.1%, which suggests that approximately one quarter of a million to one million of the national population are abused each year. For example, Gioglio and Blakemore (1983) interviewed a stratified, random sample of persons 65 years of age or older living in the community. Based on information collected from 342 respondents (88.3% response rate), their findings indicate that 1% of the respondents included in their survey were victims of some form of abuse.

In a more recent study, Pillemer and Finkelhor (1988) conducted a large-scale, stratified random survey, which involved interviews with 2,020 community-dwelling elderly persons in Boston regarding their experience of physical and verbal abuse and neglect. They found that 63 elderly persons had been maltreated, which translated into an overall rate of mistreatment of 32 elderly persons per 1,000, or 3.2%. More specifically, 40 experienced physical abuse (20 per 1,000), 26 verbal aggression (11 per 1,000) and 7 experienced neglect (4 per 1,000). Similarly, Crouse et al. (1981) and Pepper and Oakar (1981) estimate the incidence of elder abuse to be 4% of elderly respondents receiving informal care.

Most American studies report breakdowns of types of abuse and neglect instead of estimating overall incidence of abuse and neglect. For example, Lau and Kosberg (1979) reported that most cases of elder abuse seen at the Chronic Illness Center (i.e., 9.6%) involved physical abuse (75%), followed by psychological abuse (51%), material abuse (31%), and violation of rights (18%). Similarly, the Pennsylvania Department of Aging (1982) found that physical abuse was reported the most (44%), followed by psychological abuse (38%), material abuse (18%), and violation of rights (4%). In contrast, Gioglio and Blakemore (1983) reported that financial abuse occurred in 50% of all cases reported and physical abuse was the least reported form of mistreatment.

Throughout the 1970s, the United States' House and Senate Aging Committee on Long-Term Care, chaired by Senator Frank Moss, documented widespread abuse and fraud among nursing homes (Moss & Halamandaris, 1977). This study has "amply documented a variety of abuses in the nursing home industry. Of 23,000 nursing homes, more than half are below standard, only 5% are good, and few are exceptional" (Stathopoulos, 1983, p. 337). The Committee found that there was widespread fraud involving patients' personal funds. Thirty homes in six states were audited and each home had failed to safeguard patients' funds in at least one of several ways.

Based on a nationwide study, Doty and Sullivan (1983) stated that 7% of skilled nursing facilities/nursing homes ($N = 550$ facilities with 53,936 beds) are deficient in their care of elderly patients. They are deficient in that they fail to ensure that patients are free from physical and mental abuse and free from chemical or physical restraints except when authorized by a physician.

Legal Issues

Most jurisdictions in the United States, and several Canadian provinces, have responded to the problem of elder abuse by enacting special adult protection legislation, usually including a requirement of mandatory reporting. Before examining this type of legislation, it is important to consider the extent to which other existing laws afford protection to vulnerable adults in Canada.

General Legal Safeguards for Vulnerable Adults

Physical Abuse

The Canadian Criminal Code contains a number of provisions that (at least in theory) afford vulnerable adults protection from physical abuse, such as the provisions relating to assault and other offenses against the person. From a practical point of view, however, the criminal law is ineffective in protecting the victims of elder abuse. This is true of domestic violence in general. All too often, "practice falls sadly short of theory" (Law Reform Commission of Canada, 1984, p. 37). Victims of elder abuse are often unable or unwilling to complain to the police, and in many cases it is difficult to obtain the necessary evidence to prove the offense beyond reasonable doubt (Rozovsky & Rozovsky, 1987; Sharpe, 1988). Even if a criminal prosecution is brought, this will normally be of little assistance to the victim; prosecution focuses on punishing the offender rather than helping the victim (Metcalf, 1986; Sharpe, 1988).

Reliance on the criminal law may not only be ineffective, it may even make the situation worse. The victim may face retaliation from the abuser following a complaint to the police, and if the abuser is the victim's only means of support, imprisonment of the abuser may result in the victim having to be placed in institutional care (Metcalf, 1986).

Financial Abuse

Most instances of financial abuse and exploitation of the elderly constitute offenses under Canada's Criminal Code, such as theft, misuse of a power of attorney, breach of trust, forgery, fraud, and extortion. In addition to punishment such as imprisonment, the offender can be ordered to pay compensation to the victim. Some protection from financial abuse and exploitation is also afforded by the common law concepts of fraud, duress, undue influence, and unconscionability (Fridman, 1986; Waddams, 1984).

The protection offered by these laws is limited by the fact that they are reactive in nature. They either punish the wrongdoer or compensate the victim, but (other than having a possible deterrent effect) they do not prevent or detect financial abuse, nor are they intended to do so.

Elder Abuse in Institutions

For several years consumer and advocacy groups have been calling for tighter control and regulation of nursing homes and similar facilities (Gordon et al., 1986). These calls for reform are in part a response to the growing evidence of abuse and neglect of the elderly in institutions.

The Ontario Government has recently responded to these concerns by introducing amendments to the Nursing Homes Act. The Nursing Homes Amendment Act 1987 made a number of important changes to the regulation of these facilities. Two aspects of the 1987 Act stand out as particularly significant. First, the legislation introduces a mandatory reporting requirement in cases of abuse, neglect, or improper treatment of residents in nursing homes. Second, the Act establishes a Residents'

Bill of Rights, a concept common in several jurisdictions in the United States (Caldwell & Kapp, 1981; Opperman, 1981; N. Phillips, 1980). Section 1a of the Act lists 19 "rights" of residents that licensees of nursing homes must ensure are fully respected and promoted. These include: (1) the right to be treated with courtesy and respect and in a way that fully recognizes the resident's dignity and individuality; (2) the right to be free from mental and physical abuse; (3) the right to be properly sheltered, fed, clothed, groomed, and cared for in a manner consistent with his or her needs; and (4) the right to live in a safe and clean environment.

The concept of a resident's bill of rights has not escaped criticism. It has been suggested that it serves no meaningful purpose since many of the "rights" are vague and unenforceable (such as the right to be treated with courtesy and respect), and also that it is misleading in implying that the rights of residents are limited to those mentioned in the statutory list (Rozovsky, 1980; Rozovsky & Rozovsky, 1987).

Guardianship

In most Canadian provinces, guardianship legislation provides little help in dealing with elder abuse. The major problem is that the legislation tends to adopt an "all or nothing" approach, and does not provide for guardians with limited powers or for a limited period. Thus guardianship tends to conflict with the principle of the least restrictive alternative; in addition, it is not particularly well suited to respond to emergency situations.

Adult Protection Legislation

General Outline

Many jurisdictions in North America have introduced special adult protection legislation that is specifically designed as a response to elder abuse, and that creates considerable powers of investigation and intervention. Forty-three jurisdictions in the United States currently have adult protection legislation, including 38 with mandatory reporting requirements (Lee, 1986; Lewis, 1986).

Four Canadian provinces have enacted adult protection legislation. The first to do so was Newfoundland in 1973, followed by New Brunswick in 1980, Nova Scotia in 1985, and Prince Edward Island in 1988

(Bissett-Johnson, 1986; Gordon et al., 1986; Hughes, 1988; Poirier, 1988; Robertson, 1987).

As is true of most U.S. jurisdictions, the legislation in the Atlantic provinces is based on a child welfare model, and establishes extensive powers of investigation and intervention. For the purposes of a general overview, the Nova Scotia statute is a useful illustration. The Act imposes a duty on every person to report to the Minister of Social Services any information indicating that an adult is in need of protection. The Minister is given broad powers of investigation and assessment, including the power to have the adult examined by a physician. If the Minister is satisfied that there are reasonable and probable grounds to believe that the adult is in need of protection, an application may be made to the Family Court for a protective intervention order. In cases of immediate danger, the Minister can authorize the removal of the adult to a place of safety without a court order. If the court is satisfied that the adult is in need of protection, and is not mentally competent to decide whether to accept assistance or is refusing assistance because of duress, it can authorize the Minister to provide protective services (including placement in a facility). The court can also order any person who is a source of danger to the adult to leave the premises where the adult resides, and can prohibit or limit that person's contact with the adult (Bissett-Johnson, 1986; Gordon et al., 1986; Hughes, 1988; Poirier, 1988; Robertson, 1987).

Mandatory Reporting

Most states in the United States have a mandatory reporting requirement in their adult protection legislation. The legal obligation to report cases of elder abuse is usually imposed only on certain individuals, such as health care professionals, social workers, and the police, with the medical profession being the group most often required to report (Lee, 1986; Sloan, 1983). This appears to be based on the view that physicians will often be in the best position to observe, recognize, and report symptoms of suspected abuse (Kapp, 1982; Palinscar & Cobb, 1982). Lee (1986) suggests that if the duty to report is imposed on the public as a whole, this diminishes the effectiveness of the legislation, since there is a danger that "everybody's duty may easily become nobody's duty" (p. 740).

The reporting requirement in U.S. statutes is normally couched in terms such as "reasonable" or "probable" grounds for believing that an individual is the victim of abuse (Lee, 1986). For example, the District of Columbia legislation requires a report to be made where the individual has "substantial cause" to believe that a person is the victim of abuse or neglect and is in need of protective services (Lewis, 1986). In many U.S. jurisdictions lawyers are exempt from the mandatory reporting requirement, in recognition of the concept of solicitor-client privilege (Lee, 1986; Lewis, 1986). The legislation normally grants the individual immunity from civil and criminal liability in the event that the report is unfounded (Lee, 1986).

In Canada the introduction of mandatory reporting has been recommended by a number of writers (Bristow, 1987; Gordon et al., 1986) and by various committees and organizations, including the Ontario Advisory Council on Senior Citizens (1986), the Manitoba Council on Aging (Shell, 1982), and the Review of Advocacy for Vulnerable Adults in Ontario (Ontario Ministry of the Attorney General, 1987). The latter group viewed the absence of such legislation in Ontario as "startling" and recommended that its implementation be given the "highest possible priority" (p. 153).

Newfoundland and Nova Scotia both have mandatory reporting provisions in their adult protection legislation. Unlike many U.S. jurisdictions, the reporting requirement is not limited to specific groups or professionals. Every person who has information (whether or not it is confidential) indicating that an adult is in need of protection is required to report that information to the director or Minister. Immunity from liability is given to persons who report information, unless the report is made maliciously or without reasonable and probable cause (Gordon et al., 1986; Robertson, 1987).

New Brunswick does not have a mandatory reporting requirement, but its introduction is being actively considered (Gordon et al., 1986). The legislation in Prince Edward Island provides for voluntary, rather than mandatory, reporting. As is discussed above, recent amendments to Ontario's Nursing Homes Act have introduced mandatory reporting in respect of residents in those facilities.

Criticism

Many writers have questioned the wisdom of adult protection legislation, especially the concept of mandatory reporting. In particular, the following criticisms have been advanced. First, doubts have been raised as to the effectiveness of mandatory reporting. Studies in the United States indicate that the vast majority of reports of elder abuse and neglect are made on a voluntary basis by concerned citizens (Faulkner, 1982; Katz, 1980; Lee, 1986; Metcalf, 1986). Studies also indicate that many physicians are reluctant to report suspected cases of elder abuse (Kapp, 1982; Palincsar & Cobb, 1982). As Metcalf (1986) notes, if the effectiveness of mandatory reporting is in doubt, the intrusion on individual privacy is indefensible.

It has also been suggested that mandatory reporting is an inappropriate solution if the support services are lacking or inadequate (Faulkner, 1982; Katz, 1980; Lee, 1986; Shell, 1982). Without the necessary support services, mandatory reporting (even if effective) at best is nothing more than "case finding," and at worst is simply legislating for the sake of appearances (Faulkner, 1982; Lee, 1986).

Mandatory reporting may also have a negative impact on the doctor-patient relationship, undermining the concepts of trust and confidentiality that are essential to that relationship. This may result in the abused elder being discouraged from seeking medical assistance (Faulkner, 1982; Krauskopf & Burnett, 1983; Lee, 1986; Metcalf, 1986; Palincsar & Cobb, 1982).

It has also been suggested that mandatory reporting may reinforce and encourage ageism in society (Faulkner, 1982; Krauskopf & Burnett, 1983; Lee, 1986). Mandatory reporting is based on the premise that the victims of elder abuse are unable to seek help for themselves. Many critics question that premise and emphasize that one should not assume that older people will not seek assistance if it is available (Faulkner, 1982; Lee, 1986; Metcalf, 1986). Katz (1980) argues that, even if victims *are* reluctant to report elder abuse, it does not necessarily follow that others should be required to do so. She points out that the victim's reluctance may reflect a personal choice "that it is better to stay in a situation that is less than satisfactory than to suffer the consequences of professional intervention" (Katz, 1980, p. 711; see also Lee, 1986). Faulkner (1982) concludes that:

> The push for mandatory reporting therefore would appear to be a reflection of the attitude that old persons, like children, need more assistance and guidance, whether or not they know it or even want it. Policy planners and legislators should adopt, only with the greatest reluctance and demonstrated need, if at all, legislation which will further infantilize the older person. (p. 87)

Charter Implications

Adult protection legislation in the United States has been severely criticized for its lack of due process safeguards (Gordon et al., 1986; Kapp, 1983; Regan, 1981; Regan, 1985; Sloan, 1983). Regan and Sloan both describe the standards for intervention as "vague and conclusory," and note that there are serious procedural flaws in the laws of several States. The same criticisms have been leveled against the legislation in Canada. For example, Gordon et al. (1986) state that the Newfoundland legislation does nothing to protect fundamental rights and freedoms of the individual who is adjudged "neglected." Their criticism of the Nova Scotia legislation is even stronger. They note that the criteria for intervention are "vague in the extreme," and that there is a complete absence in the legislation of any due process rights, such as the right to legal representation.

The lack of due process safeguards is of particular concern in light of the Canadian Charter of Rights and Freedoms. Gordon et al. (1986) state that there can be little doubt that current adult protection legislation in Canada will have to be revised to comply with the Charter. Indeed, this is probably true of Canadian guardianship laws in general (Gordon et al., 1986; Gordon & Verdun-Jones, 1987; Hughes, 1988; Robertson, 1987; Savage & McKague, 1987). The extent to which adult protection legislation encroaches upon personal liberty and autonomy has been emphasized by many writers (Faulkner, 1982; Gordon et al., 1986; Hughes, 1988; Katz, 1980; Poirier, 1988). Clearly there is a need for proper due process protection and precise criteria if the legislation is to comply with the Charter.

Hughes (1988) suggests that the effect of the Charter is probably that any adult protection legislation must reflect the philosophy of the least restrictive alternative. She also states that compelling reasons would have to be present to justify the deprivation of a person's liberty and security pursuant to adult protection legislation.

Section 15(1) of the Charter is of particular concern in relation to protection legislation based on age per se, as opposed to mental or physical incapacity to protect or care for oneself. In order to comply with section 15(1), legislation would have to be based on proven vulnerability rather than on age.

Program and Service Issues

Service programs for adults have two primary characteristics: (1) actual or potential legal authority to provide substitute decision-making for the client, and (2) the administration and coordination of delivery of services to adults at risk (Regan, 1983). The legal authority of adult service programs may fall under protection acts (e.g., Florida, District of Columbia, Prince Edward Island), however, this is not always the case. For example, some adult services or services for the elderly may fall under hospital or nursing home legislation or may be established without legislative authority, as in the case of informal advocacy programs.

The general functions of programs include: (1) determination of policy goals and objectives, (2) assessment of client needs, (3) development of a comprehensive plan for service delivery, (4) arrangement for direct service delivery, (5) assessment of service delivery, and (6) evaluation and follow-up.

In this section, three general types of programs will be discussed. First, programs that fall under the adult protection approach similar to the child welfare model discussed above will be examined. Generally, these are statutory adult protection service programs that are mandated by adult protection legislation. Second, programs attached to the family violence model will be examined, and third, advocacy programs for the elderly will be discussed. Following the discussions of the adult protection, family violence, and advocacy programs, the client services available through these programs will be examined. It is important to note that, regardless of what approach is followed, similar services tend to be provided.

Adult Protection Programs

The adult protection approach is characterized by special legally mandated powers of investigation and intervention, and mandatory reporting. The intervention strategies associated with these programs may include the power of removal, and compulsory custody and services.

With the passage of adult protection legislation in the Atlantic provinces, protective services were delivered through the provincial departments of social services. For example, Nova Scotia established a specific program called Adult Protective Services to provide protection for adults (16 years of age and older) who were physically disabled and/or mentally infirm and therefore unable to care for themselves.

The recently passed Prince Edward Island legislation used the Nova Scotia Act as a model, but it does not include mandatory reporting. It contains a 68-step implementation plan that incorporates a multidisciplinary response to reported cases of elder abuse. It appears to be a very thorough approach intending to utilize as many different resources as are required in each particular case.

There are no specialized services for elderly victims of abuse or neglect in Prince Edward Island. However, two departments, Health and Social Services and Home Care and Support, are currently developing the Adult Protection Program. This program will involve coordinating already existing services, such as home care, nursing, occupational therapy, and homemaker services.

A review of the adult protection service programs in Canada and the United States indicates that the nature and organization of protective services may vary considerably among jurisdictions, depending on the legislation mandating the programs as well as the existing local resources (Hobbs, 1976; Quinn & Tomita, 1986; Zborowsky, 1985). Adult protection service programs combine a multitude of services requiring collaboration and cooperation among a number of agencies. In many cases, the adult protection service worker, who may be mandated by adult protection laws, must coordinate the agencies involved in direct service provision. The worker must follow established legal guidelines and criteria that often include: provisions for geriatric evaluations, voluntary protective services, involuntary court-ordered protective services; court hearing and petition procedures, mandatory reporting of abuse, and appeal mechanisms (Zborowsky, 1985). The clients served can be voluntary or involuntary, neglected or self-neglected, abused or abusive (Quinn & Tomita, 1986).

Much of the controversy surrounding adult protection service programs is a direct result of modeling them after child protection service programs (Crystal, 1986, 1987). The most significant issues appear to be: (1) the appropriateness of an enforcement-oriented approach to service provision, and (2) the inherent contradictions in the system that become evident through implementation. Both issues are discussed briefly below.

The legal intervention role is popular because it is argued that little can be done for the abused victim who refuses services, unless the practitioner wishes to place himself or herself at legal risk. It is also argued that the practitioner may lack the confidence and willingness to intervene without legal support. Opponents of legal intervention note that protection workers are "trigger happy" when it comes to petitioning for guardianship in order to place older persons in nursing homes (Quinn & Tomita, 1986). They argue that protective services serve to relieve caregiver stress, putting the caregiver ahead of the victim. Finally, they argue that legal intervention infantilizes the older person because he or she is treated the same way as children under child welfare legislation (Crystal, 1986; Pillemer, 1985).

The inherent contradictions of adult protection service programs have become evident with their implementation (Quinn & Tomita, 1986). In the first instance, the vagueness of the legislation and lack of protocols in some jurisdictions make the decision as to what constitutes abuse a difficult proposition. Second, balancing the right to protection and the right to privacy is a constant, if not impossible, struggle for the practitioner. Third, the adult protection worker is in an awkward position when it comes to divulging information to the rest of the team given the requirements for confidentiality. Last, the potential for conflict among service providers is high given the orientations of the different professions.

The Domestic Violence Programs

The domestic violence model has only recently been considered as an alternative to the child welfare model because it does not violate people's rights nor does it discriminate on the basis of age (Crouse et al., 1981; Crystal, 1987; Faulkner, 1982; Finkelhor & Pillemer, 1984; Pillemer, 1985).

The domestic violence model involves crisis intervention services, a strengthened role for the police, court orders for protection, emergency and second stage sheltering, support groups for the abused and the abuser, and the use of a whole range of health, social, and legal services. An integral component of domestic violence services is public education and education of the abused about their rights (Crouse et al., 1981).

To date, there are several individual and group programs for victims of elder abuse. The Victim's Services Agency in New York has instituted support and consciousness-raising groups for victims of elder abuse. A senior center in Winnipeg offers individual counseling for abused older people as do a few women's emergency shelters (Ghent, Da Silra, & Farren, 1985). Several states have special shelters for older abuse victims (Cabness, 1989) and several women's shelters do house older abused women (MacLeod, 1987). Most attempts at service delivery have been sporadic and have shown no evidence of coordination. The "newness" of the model for dealing with elder abuse may account for these observations.

The spouse abuse model is not without its critics (Beaudry, 1985: Schechter, 1982; Walker, 1984). There are problems with police response (McDonald, Chisholm, Peressini, & Smillie, 1986), with restraining orders (MacLeod, 1987), with shelters (Beaudry, 1985) and with follow-up services (Sample Survey and Data Bank, University of Regina, 1984). To illustrate, in one Canadian study, 42% of the women were still harassed by their abusers despite restraining orders. Police response was very low, sometimes nonexistent in emergencies, and follow-up services were not easily accessed because of transportation problems, access problems, and financial barriers (McDonald et al., 1986). The empirically substantiated flaws in the domestic abuse model need to be closely examined before transferring them to the elder abuse field.

Advocacy Programs

In the broadest sense, *advocacy* refers to those activities that involve speaking for or acting on behalf of an individual or group in order to ensure that their needs are met and their rights are respected (Ontario Ministry of the Attorney General, 1987). The advocacy approach recognizes that the older person is an adult in a potentially vulnerable position (Crouse et al., 1981; Hwalek, 1988).

In attempting to define advocacy, it is important to differentiate between legal and social advocacy, as well as between formal and informal advocacy. Legal advocacy is the most well-known type of advocacy and refers to the representation provided by a lawyer for a client in court. The concept of nonlegal advocacy or social advocacy means speaking or pleading on behalf of others by using nonlegalistic measures (Ontario Ministry of the Attorney General, 1987).

Formal advocacy is performed by individuals who are paid for providing advocacy services and may be mandated by legislation. Informal advocacy, in contrast, takes place on an unstructured and voluntary basis.

There are few American examples of advocacy that target elder abuse. First, the program proposed by the Illinois Department of Aging is one of the more sophisticated approaches in the United States. It is based on voluntary reporting, since it is considered to be the least restrictive response to elder abuse. Intervention is to be approached from a family systems perspective and any older person is to have access to an advocate regardless of income. Another example, the Consumer Advocate for Better Care in North Central Massachusetts, is an independent organization with a board of directors (mainly professionals) and 14 paid advocates for the elderly (Stathopoulos, 1983). Advocates monitor the quality of care in area nursing homes by visiting each of the nursing homes frequently, often unannounced and at varying times, including evenings and weekends.

Hooyman (1983) proposes the use of natural helping networks by professionals as a means to detect and prevent elder abuse. She reviews the existing gerontological programs that have been used to deal with other problems experienced by the elderly and makes a case for their use in responding to elder abuse. Support programs for families experiencing stress can easily incorporate information about elder abuse and can be used as a screening mechanism to detect abuse. Older people can be provided with information about elder abuse through almost any existing programs, such as self-growth, health, preretirement planning programs, leisure programs, and clubs. Volunteers in phone-a-friend, adopt-a-grandparent, friendly visiting, buddy systems, widow-to-widow, and neighborhood watch programs could be trained in the detection and reporting of elder abuse. Mail carriers, utility workers, and "handicab" personnel could also be trained in the detection. Professionals and paraprofessionals would also require training. The Council on Aging of Ottawa-Carleton has, for example, developed an elaborate educational model designed for organizers of information sessions explaining the nature of elder abuse to different types of audiences (Council on Aging of Ottawa-Carleton, 1988).

Review of Services

The preceding sections reviewed the three major types of programs, that is, adult protection, domestic violence, and advocacy programs, that currently respond to elder abuse. It is not useful to categorize the services by a similar dichotomy since at least two of the program approaches use the same services (adult protection and advocacy programs). The major criteria for choosing a particular service depends on the nature of the individual case and the resources available. Domestic violence programs have been rarely used by older persons so there are few services to evaluate.

The literature indicates that services attached to programs are mainly drawn from existing service systems designed to serve the general needs of the elderly. The only difference between the models appears to be who, if anybody, coordinates the services. For example, in adult protection programs it appears that the protection services worker coordinates services (Quinn & Tomita, 1986). In the advocacy approach, it appears that the advocate coordinates service delivery (Hwalek, 1988). Most service programs draw upon all forms of care from both the public and private sector and use various funding mechanisms to pay for these services.

In both Canada and the United States, the spectrum of services for older persons covers a wide variety of care needs. These services include community support services (homemakers, senior centers, "meals-on-wheels," etc.); multifacility or multifunction living and care complexes (senior citizens' housing), congregate or sheltered housing (foster homes, lodges); long-term care facilities (nursing homes and auxiliary hospitals); medical care (hospitals) and socio-medical care (day hospitals, respite care, adult day care) (Chappell, Strain, & Blandford, 1986). A continuum of care is implied in these services, ranging from integrative adjustment services (preretirement counseling, leisure activities, education) and supportive services (coordinated legal, medical, psychiatric, and social services) to specialized terminal-care facilities and services (Beattie, 1976; Chappell et al., 1986; Coward, 1979). In both Canada and the United States, the ultimate goal seems to be to use the least restrictive alternatives possible and to maintain older persons in their own homes (Kammerman, 1976).

The fundamental service issue is whether it is best to respond to elder abuse categorically, through legislation and programmatic solutions centered directly on the abuse problem, or whether it should be addressed by generic health and social services (Callahan, 1982, 1988; Crystal, 1986; Wolf, 1986). Presumably, those in favor of a specific response to elder abuse would argue that the hidden nature of the problem, its scope, and the lack of services (especially in rural areas) demand a specific categorical response. Wolf (1986) questions whether abuse services would be better located in age-segregated or integrated agencies, while Crystal (1986, 1987) speculates as to whether special abuse services are required at all.

A second consideration is whether elder abuse typically exists as a relatively self-contained problem that can be addressed on its own terms or whether it represents a single dimension of a more complex problem (Crystal, 1986; Douglass & Hickey, 1983). Experience with protective services suggests that abuse is only one component of a larger set of complicated problems. To focus only on the abuse dimension can unbalance a complex social, psychological, and economic equilibrium that has taken a lifetime to develop (Crystal, 1986). Furthermore, a singular focus on elder abuse creates an artificial split in the services already available to meet similar, related needs (Crystal, 1986).

The gerontological literature suggests that treatment interventions are more effective when delivered through those agencies that already serve the elderly (Zimberg, 1978). The workers in these agencies appear to be in the best position to recognize problems, they are familiar with services for the aged, they understand the complexities of the older person's problems, and the context is less stigmatizing for the older person.

Conclusion

Definition and Incidence of Elder Abuse

The definitions of elder abuse found in the family violence and gerontological literature are generally vague and imprecise. However, certain trends emerged from a review of the social definitions of elder abuse. First, these definitions tended to focus on physical abuse and both active and passive neglect. Second, there was some clouding of the differences between abuse and neglect. Third, the social research seemed to concentrate mainly on abuse or neglect that occurred in the home or domestic setting and was perpetrated by informal caregivers who are in a position of trust and authority, such as spouses or other family members.

The legal definitions of elder abuse in many American states are broader than the definitions used in social research since they recognize physical abuse, neglect, and exploitation (material abuse). Furthermore, the legal definitions of abuse tend to focus on all perpetrators as opposed to just by informal or formal caregivers. Definitions of neglect are more specific in the sense that they often identify the specific responsibilities of individual caregivers.

Incidence

Although a number of studies have been conducted on the incidence of elder abuse in both Canada and the United States, the results of these studies can, at best, be considered only rough estimates because of the many conceptional and methodological problems associated with these studies. The results of the studies vary considerably. Findings indicate that 1% to 4% of the elderly Canadian population and 2% to 4% of the elderly American population have experienced some form of abuse.

Legal Issues

General Legal Safeguards

There are a number of provisions in the Criminal Code that could afford vulnerable adults some protection from physical and emotional abuse. However, it is generally assumed that criminal law is ineffective in dealing with domestic abuse situations, including elder abuse, for the following reasons: (1) victims of abuse are often unable or unwilling to complain to police, (2) many incidents are difficult to prove beyond a reasonable doubt, and (3) victims who make complaints may suffer retaliation.

Both the Canadian Criminal Code and the provincial guardianship laws provide elderly persons with some protection from neglect by requiring those responsible to provide the necessities of life to elderly persons who cannot provide for themselves. The legislation, however, is not well-suited to those situations of elder abuse that call for an emergency response. In summary, it is apparent that existing laws are of limited utility in responding to the problem of physical abuse and neglect of the elderly.

In addition to Criminal Code sanctions against theft and fraud, the common law provides some protection against duress and undue influence in financial decision making. However, these laws tend to be reactive and focus on punishment of the wrongdoer. Some of the potential problems may be avoided by the granting of a power of attorney in advance of the elderly person becoming vulnerable to such pressures. On the other hand, the enduring power of attorney may easily be abused and exploited. Many safeguards have been developed in different jurisdictions to prevent misuse. However, these safeguards often conflict with the basic concept of providing individuals with a simple method of managing their financial affairs after they become incapacitated.

There are two basic legal responses to abuse of elderly persons in institutions; government regulation and tort law. Some jurisdictions, such as Ontario, have introduced mandatory reporting of abuse in nursing homes. In addition, some jurisdictions have established "rights" of residents. Both approaches, however, are of questionable effectiveness. Mandatory reporting presents many difficulties while "rights" are usually vague and thus unenforceable.

Adult Protection Legislation

Forty-three jurisdictions in the United States and four jurisdictions in Canada have enacted some type of adult protection legislation. This type of legislation has, to a large extent, been modeled after child welfare legislation. However, the similarities between child welfare issues and elder abuse are superficial and misleading. Thus the enactment of adult protection legislation has been characterized by much controversy and criticism.

First, intervention legislation that uses the criterion of age rather than incapacity to protect oneself from abuse has been labeled "ageist." Second, most jurisdictions with adult protection legislation in the United States and Canada have included a mandatory reporting requirement that may involve an intrusion on an individual's privacy (e.g., in the context of a doctor-patient relationship). Third, the most common characteristic of adult protection legislation is that it contains a wide range of powers of intervention including the power to remove individuals to institutions. However, there has been a recent trend in the United States to restrict this power, because of the lack of safeguards for due process.

While the aim of adult protection legislation may be laudable, the means adopted to achieve this end must impair as little as possible the rights and freedoms of the individual. The criteria for intervention must be precisely defined. They must be based on vulnerability rather than on age alone. Due process rights, such as the right to notice and the right to legal representation, must be respected. Above all, the legislation must truly reflect the principle of the least restrictive alternative if it is to withstand scrutiny under the Charter.

Program and Service Issues

The lack of information about the nature, extent, and outcomes of elder abuse has made it difficult to plan, implement, and evaluate effective social remedies (Crystal, 1987; Pillemer, 1985). Nevertheless, professional and political interest in elder abuse and the concomitant pressure to ameliorate the problem has spawned a wide variety of programs and services for elderly persons in need of protection.

Adult Protection Programs

The adult protection approach has been perceived as having the most potential for violating the rights of older persons. Mandatory reporting, investigation, and intervention can very quickly and easily override the rights of the older person, but so can police intervention, especially when police have the power to lay charges irrespective of the abused person's wishes. Reporting, whether it is mandatory or not, will still result in an investigation or an attempt at an investigation. In short, all adult protection programs are potentially intrusive. If there is to be a response to elder abuse, the scope and severity of the problem will have to be weighed against the degree to which rights are to be violated. Further, possible built-in safeguards should be considered.

Domestic Violence Programs

Domestic violence programs serve the general population and may not be well suited to meet the needs of the elderly. Neglect, for example, is a category of mistreatment that would not be served by domestic violence programs, since crisis intervention may not be comprehensive enough, and the effect of moving older persons into shelters may be negative.

Advocacy Programs

The effectiveness of informal advocacy in dealing with elder abuse is unknown. Again, there are descriptions of programs but no actual evaluations. Available findings point to three significant issues that should be considered when developing advocacy systems. First, the fragmentation of the current advocacy system should be taken into account in the development of an advocacy program for adult protection service delivery. Second, the focus of the advocacy approach should be considered. In some jurisdictions, the question of whether advocacy should include systemic as well as individual advocacy is a major issue. Last, although advocacy may appear to be nonintrusive, in practice it can be quite intrusive, especially if the advocates are immune from liability and not accountable. The temptation to forge ahead, contrary to the older person's wishes, could exist if the advocate is not held responsible in some way.

Service Issues

The service issues relevant to both adult protection and advocacy programs are: (1) what services should be provided, (2) who should be responsible for delivering these services, and (3) what type of organizational structure should be developed? It is evident from the literature that the services already available to older persons provide the resources used in response to elder abuse, regardless of which approach is utilized. In Canada, new or unique services are not necessarily required since the services already available to older persons provide the resources used in response to elder abuse. However, the variation in types and availability of services in different communities is a serious problem that must be addressed. Modification and coordination of already existing social services for the elderly to ensure their ready accessibility was found to be a better remedy than the establishment of a new set of services.

The organization patchwork of gerontological services, especially in the United States, has made coordination, collaboration, and follow-up somewhat difficult for practitioners operating under adult protection programs. The advocacy approach, with an advocate located outside the direct service delivery and case management systems, could provide an effective mechanism for calling on all types of service and ensuring their coordination and implementation from beginning to end. An advocate may also be in a better position to offer education to the public and to professionals, to identify gaps in the system and to respond to institutional abuse.

References

Beattie, W. M. (1976). Aging and the social services. In R. Binstock & E. Shanas (Eds.), *Handbook of aging and the social services* (pp. 619-642). New York: Van Nostrand Reinhold.

Beaudry, M. (1985). *Battered women.* Montreal: Black Rose Books.

Beck, C. M., & Ferguson, D. (1981). Aged abuse. *Journal of Gerontological Nursing, 7*(6), 333-336.

Bissett-Johnson, A. (1986). Domestic violence: A plethora of problems and precious few solutions. *Canadian Journal of Family Law, 5,* 253-276.

Block, M. R. (1983). Special problems and vulnerability of elderly women. In J. I. Kosberg (Ed.), *Abuse and maltreatment of the elderly: Causes and interventions* (pp. 220-233). Littleton, MA: PSG Publishing.

Bristow, E. (1987). *Family mediated abuse of non-institutionalized frail elderly men and women living in British Columbia.* Unpublished manuscript, Burnaby, British Columbia: Simon Fraser University, Gerontology Research Centre.

Cabness, J. (1989). The emergency shelter: A model for building the self-esteem of abused elders. *Journal of Elder Abuse and Neglect, 1*(2), 71-89.

Caldwell, J. M., & Kapp, M. B. (1981). The rights of nursing home patients: Possibilities and limitations of federal regulation. *Journal of Health Politics, Policy and Law, 6,* 40-48.

Callahan, J. J. (1982). Elder abuse programming: Will it help the elderly? *Urban and Social Change Review, 15,* 15-16.

Callahan, J. J. (1988). Elder abuse: Some questions for policymakers. *The Gerontologist, 28*(4), 115-121.

Chappell, N. L., Strain, L. A., & Blandford, A. A. (1986). *Aging and health care: A social perspective.* Toronto: Holt, Rinehart & Winston of Canada.

Chen, P. N., Bell, S., Dolinsky, D., Doyle, J., & Dunn, M. (1981). Elderly abuse in domestic settings: A pilot study. *Journal of Gerontological Social Work, 4*(1), 3-17.

City of Toronto Mayor's Committee on Aging. (1984). *Elder abuse: A shared problem.* Unpublished manuscript, City Hall, Toronto.

Council on Aging of Ottawa-Carleton. (1988). *Enhancing awareness of elder abuse: Three education models.* Unpublished manuscript, Council on Aging of Ottawa-Carleton, Ottawa.

Coward, R. T. (1979). Planning community services for the rural elderly: Implications for research. *The Gerontologist, 19,* 275-282.

Crouse, J. S., Cobb, D. C., Harris, B. B., Kopecky, F. J., & Poertner, J. (1981). *Abuse and neglect of the elderly in Illinois: Incidence and characteristics, legislation and policy recommendations.* Unpublished manuscript, Sangamon State University and Illinois Department of Aging, Springfield.

Crystal, S. (1986). Social policy and elder abuse. In K. A. Pillemer & R. S. Wolf (Eds.), *Elder abuse: Conflict in the family* (pp. 331-340). Dover, MA: Auburn.

Crystal, S. (1987). Elder abuse: The latest "crisis." *Public Interest, 88,* 55-66.

Doty, P., & Sullivan, E. W. (1983). Community involvement in combatting abuse, neglect, and mistreatment in nursing homes. *Milbank Memorial Fund Quarterly/Health and Society, 61,* 222-251.

Douglass, R. L., & Hickey, T. (1983). Domestic neglect and abuse of the elderly: Research findings and a systems perspective for social service delivery planning. In J. I. Kosberg (Ed.), *Abuse and maltreatment of the elderly: Causes and interventions* (pp. 115-133). Littleton, MA: PSG Publishing.

Douglass, R. L., Hickey, T., & Noel, C. (1980). *A study of maltreatment of the elderly and other vulnerable adults.* Final Report to U.S. Administration on Aging and the Michigan State Department of Social Services, Ann Arbor.

Faulkner, L. R. (1982). Mandating the reporting of suspected cases of elder abuse: An inappropriate, ineffective and ageist response to the abuse of older adults. *Family Law Quarterly, 16,* 69-91.

Finkelhor, D., & Pillemer, K. (1984). *Elder abuse: Its relationship to other forms of domestic violence.* Paper presented at The Second National Conference on Family Violence Research, Durham, NH.

Foot, D. K. (1982). *Canada's population outlook: Demographic futures and economic challenges.* Toronto: Lorimer.

Fridman, G. H. (1986). *The law of contract in Canada.* Toronto: Carswell.

Fulmer, T. (1982, May). Elder abuse detection and reporting. *Massachusetts Nurse,* pp. 10-12.

Ghent, W. R., Da Silra, N. P., & Farren, M. E. (1985). Family violence: Guidelines for recognition and management. *Canadian Medical Association Journal, 132,* 541-543.

Gioglio, G. R., & Blakemore, P. (1983). *Elder abuse in New Jersey: The knowledge and experience of abuse among older New Jerseyans.* Unpublished manuscript, Department of Human Services, Trenton, NJ.

Giordano, N. H., & Giordano, J. A. (1984). Elder abuse: A review of the literature, *Social Work, 29*(3), 232-236.

Gordon, R. M., & Verdun-Jones, S. N. (1987). The implications of the Canadian Charter of Rights and Freedoms for the law relating to guardianship and trusteeship. *International Journal of Law and Psychiatry, 10,* 21-34.

Gordon, R. M., Verdun-Jones, S. N., & MacDougall, D. J. (1986). *Standing in their shoes: Guardianship, trusteeship and the elderly Canadian.* Burnaby, British Columbia: Simon Fraser University, Criminology Research Centre.

Hageboeck, J., & Brandt, K. (1981). *Characteristics of elderly abuse.* Unpublished manuscript, Scott County, IA.

Halamandaris, V. J. (1983). Fraud and abuse in nursing homes. In J. I. Kosberg (Ed.), *Abuse and maltreatment of the elderly: Causes and interventions* (pp. 104-114). Littleton, MA: PSG Publishing.

Hall, P. A., & Andrew, S. R. (1984). *Minority elder maltreatment: Ethnicity, gender, age and poverty.* Unpublished manuscript, San Antonio, TX.

Hobbs, L. (1976). Adult protective services: A new program approach. *Public Welfare, 34*(3), 28-37.

Hooyman, N. R. (1983). Elder abuse and neglect: Community interventions. In J. I. Kosberg (Ed.), *Abuse and maltreatment of the elderly: Causes and interventions* (pp. 376-390). Littleton, MA: PSG Publishing.

Hudson, M. F. (1986). Elder mistreatment: Current research. In K. A. Pillemer & R. S. Wolf (Eds.) *Elder abuse: Conflict in the family* (pp. 125-166). Dover, MA: Auburn.

Hudson, M. F., & Johnson, T. F. (1986). Elder neglect and abuse: A review of the literature. *Annual Review of Gerontology and Geriatrics, 6,* 81-134.

Hughes, M. E. (1988). *Personal guardianship and the elderly in the Canadian common law provinces: An overview of the law and Charter implications.* Unpublished manuscript, The University of Calgary, Faculty of Law.

Hwalek, M. (1988). *Elder abuse: The Illinois Department of Aging's final report on the Demonstration Program Act.* Unpublished manuscript prepared for the Illinois Department of Aging.

Kammerman, S. B. (1976). Community services for the aged: The view from eight countries. *The Gerontologist, 16,* 529-537.

Kapp, M. B. (1982). Promoting the legal rights of older adults. *Journal of Legal Medicine, 3,* 367-412.

Kapp, M. B. (1983). Adult protective services: Convincing the patient to consent. *Law, Medicine and Health Care, 11,* 163-167.

Katz, K. D. (1980). Elder abuse. *Journal of Family Law, 18,* 695-722.

Krauskopf, J. M., & Burnett, M. E. (1983). The elderly person: When protection becomes abuse. *Trial, 19,* 61-67.

Lau, E., & Kosberg, J. I. (1979). Abuse of the elderly by informal care providers. *Aging,* (299-300), 10-15.

Law Reform Commission of Canada. (1984). *Working paper on assault.* Working Paper No. 38, Ottawa.

Lee, D. (1986). Mandatory reporting of elder abuse: A cheap but ineffective solution to the problem. *Fordham Urban Law Journal, 14,* 723-771.

Levenberg, J., Milan, J., Dolan, M., & Carpenter, P. (1983). Elder abuse in West Virginia: Extent and nature of the problem. In G. L. Schultz (Ed.), *Elder abuse in West Virginia: A policy analysis of system response.* Morgantown: West Virginia University.

Lewis, L. A. (1986). Towards eliminating the abuse, neglect, and exploitation of impaired adults: The District of Columbia Adult Protective Services Act of 1984. *Catholic University Law Review, 35,* 1193-1213.

Macleod, L. (1987). *Battered but not beaten . . . Preventing wife battering in Canada.* Ottawa: Canadian Advisory Council on the Status of Women.

McDaniel, S. A. (1986). *Canada's aging population.* Toronto: Butterworths.

McDonald, P. L., Chisholm, W., Peressini, T., & Smillie, T. (1986). *A review of a second stage shelter for battered women and children.* Ottawa: National Welfare Directorate.

McLaughlin, J. S., Nickell, J. P., & Gill, L. (1980). An epidemiological investigation of elder abuse in Southern Maine and New Hampshire. In *Elder abuse* (Publication No. 68-463) (pp. 111-147). U.S. House of Representatives Select Committee on Aging. Washington, DC: Government Printing Office.

Metcalf, C. A. (1986). A response to the problem of elder abuse: Florida's Revised Adult Protection Services Act. *Florida State University Law Review, 14,* 745-777.

Montgomery, R. J. V., & Borgatta, E. F. (1986). Possible theories and the development of scientific theory. *Research on Aging, 8*(4), 586-608.

Moss, F. E., & Halamandaris, V. J. (1977). *Too old, too sick, too bad: Nursing homes in America.* Germantown, MD: Aspen Systems.

O'Brien, J. G., Hudson, M. F., & Johnson, T. F. (1984). *Health care provider survey on elder abuse.* Unpublished manuscript, East Lansing, MI.

O'Malley, H., Segars, H., Perez, R., Mitchell, V., & Knuepfel, G. (1979). *Elder abuse in Massachusetts: A survey of professionals and paraprofessionals.* Unpublished manuscript, Legal Research and Services for the Elderly, Boston.

O'Malley, T. A., Everett, E. D., O'Malley, H. C., & Campion, E. W. (1983). Identifying and preventing family mediated abuse and neglect of elderly persons. *Annals of Internal Medicine, 90*(6), 998-1005.

Ontario Advisory Council on Senior Citizens. (1986). *A report on elder abuse.* Unpublished manuscript submitted to Honorable Ron van Horne, Minister for Senior Citizens Affairs.

Ontario Ministry of the Attorney General. (1987). *You've got a friend: A review of advocacy in Ontario.* Report of the Review of Advocacy for Vulnerable Adults. Toronto: Queen's Printer.

Opperman, D. S. (1981). Michigan's Bill of Rights for nursing home residents. *Wayne Law Review, 27,* 1203-1227.

Palincsar, J., & Cobb, D. C. (1982). The physician's role in detecting and reporting elder abuse. *Journal of Legal Medicine, 3,* 413-441.

Pedrick-Cornell, C., & Gelles, R. J. (1982). Elder abuse: The status of current knowledge. *Family Relations, 31*(3), 457-465.

Pennsylvania Department of Aging. (1982). *Elder abuse in Pennsylvania.* Unpublished manuscript, Bureau of Advocacy, Harrisburg.

Pepper, C. D. (1983). Frauds against the elderly. In J. I. Kosberg (Ed.), *Abuse and maltreatment of the elderly: Causes and interventions* (pp. 68-83). Littleton, MA: PSG Publishing.

Pepper, C. D., & Oakar, M. R. (1981). Elder abuse: An examination of a hidden problem (Publication No. 97-277). U.S. House of Representatives Select Committee on Aging. Washington, DC: Government Printing Office.

Phillips, L. R., & Rempusheski, V. F. (1985). A decision-making model for diagnosing and intervening in elder abuse and neglect. *Nursing Research, 34,* 134-139.

Phillips, L. R., & Rempusheski, V. F. (1986). Making decisions about elder abuse. *Social Casework, 67*(3), 131-140.

Phillips, N. M. (1980). Ohio's Bill of Rights for nursing home patients. *University of Dayton Law Review, 5,* 507-525.

Pillemer, K. A. (1985). *Domestic violence against the elderly.* Unpublished manuscript prepared for the Surgeon General's Workshop on Violence and Public Health, Leesberg, VA. Durham: University of New Hampshire, Family Violence Research Program and Department of Sociology.

Pillemer, K. A., & Finkelhor, D. (1988). The prevalence of elder abuse: A random sample survey. *The Gerontologist, 28*(1), 51-57.

Pillemer, K. A., & Finkelhor, D. (1989). Causes of elder abuse: Caregiver stress versus problem relatives. *American Journal of Orthopsychiatry, 59*(2), 179-187.

Podnieks, E. (1983). Abuse of the elderly. *The Canadian Nurse, 79*(5), 34-35.

Podnieks, E. (1985). Elder abuse: It's time we did something about it. *The Canadian Nurse, 81*(11), 36-39.

Podnieks, E. (1989). *Abuse of the elderly: When caregivers cease to care.* Prepared for the National Clearinghouse on Family Violence. Ottawa: Minister of Supply and Services.

Podnieks, E., Pillemer, K., Nicholson, J. P., Shillington, T., & Frizzell, A. (1989). *National survey on abuse of the elderly in Canada: Preliminary findings.* Toronto: Ryerson Polytechnical Institute, Office of Research and Innovation.

Poirier, D. (1988). Models of intervention for the guardianship and protection of elderly persons in Canada. In M. E. Hughes & E. D. Pask (Eds.), *National themes in family law* (pp. 157-178). Toronto: Carswell.

Province of Nova Scotia. (1986). *Elder abuse: Everyone's concern.* Unpublished manuscript, Senior Citizens Secretariat, Halifax, Nova Scotia.

Quinn, M. J., & Tomita, S. K. (1986). *Elder abuse and neglect: Causes, diagnosis, and intervention strategies.* New York: Springer.

Regan, J. J. (1981). Protecting the elderly: The new paternalism. *Hastings Law Journal, 32,* 1111-1132.

Regan, J. J. (1983). Protective services for the elderly: Benefit or threat. In J. I. Kosberg (Ed.), *Abuse and maltreatment of the elderly: Causes and interventions* (pp. 279-291). Littleton, MA: PSG Publishing.

Regan, J. J. (1985). Process and context: Hidden factors in health care decisions for the elderly. *Law, Medicine and Health Care, 13,* 151-152.

Robertson, G. B. (1987). *Mental disability and the law in Canada.* Toronto: Carswell.

Rozovsky, L. E. (1980). *The Canadian patient's book of rights.* Toronto: Doubleday Canada.

Rozovsky, L. E., & Rozovsky, F. A. (1987). Why the patient's Bill of Rights is not a good thing. *Health Care,* 38.

Sample Survey and Data Bank. (1984). *Silence: Description report of a follow-up study of abused women using a shelter.* Regina, Saskatchewan: University of Regina.

Savage, H., & McKague, C. (1987). *Mental health law in Canada.* Toronto: Butterworths.

Schechter, S. (1982). *Women and male violence.* Boston: South End Press.

Sharpe, G. S. (1988). The protection of elderly mentally incompetent individuals who are victims of abuse. In B. Schlesinger & R. Schlesinger (Eds.), *Abuse of the elderly: Issues and annotated bibliography* (pp. 64-74). Toronto: University of Toronto Press.

Shell, D. J. (1982). *Protection of the elderly: A study of elder abuse.* Unpublished manuscript, Manitoba Council on Aging, Winnipeg.

Sloan, I. J. (1983). *The law and legislation of elderly abuse.* Dobbs Ferry, NY: Oceana.

Solomon, K. (1983). Victimization by health professionals and the psychologic response of the elderly. In J. I. Kosberg (Ed.), *Abuse and maltreatment of the elderly: Causes and interventions* (pp. 150-171). Littleton, MA: PSG Publishing.

Stathopoulos, P. A. (1983). Consumer advocacy and abuse of elders in nursing homes. In J. I. Kosberg (Ed.), *Abuse and maltreatment of the elderly: Causes and interventions (pp. 335-354). Littleton, MA: PSG Publishing.*

Statistics Canada. (1984). *Current demographic analysis: Report on the demographic situation in Canada in 1983* (Catalogue No. 91-209E Annual) [Prepared by J. Dumas]. Ottawa: Minister of Supply and Services.

Statistics Canada. (1985). *Population projections for Canada, provinces and territories, 1984-2006* (Catalogue No. 91-520). Ottawa: Minister of Supply and Services.

Stevenson, C. (1985). *Family abuse of the elderly in Alberta.* Unpublished manuscript prepared for the Senior Citizens Bureau, Alberta Social Services and Community Health.

Valentine, D., & Cash, T. (1986). A definitional discussion of elder mistreatment. *Journal of Gerontological Social Work, 9*(3), 17-28.

Waddams, S. M. (1984). *The law of contracts.* Toronto: Canada Law Book.

Walker, L. E. (1984). *The battered woman syndrome.* New York: Springer.

Wolf, R. S. (1986). Major findings from three model projects on elderly abuse. In K. A. Pillemer & R. S. Wolf (Eds.), *Elder abuse: Conflict in the family* (pp. 218-238). Dover, MA: Auburn.

Wolf, R. S., Strugnell, C. P., & Godkin, M. A. (1982). *Preliminary findings from three model projects on elder abuse.* Worcester: University of Massachusetts Medical Center, Center on Aging.

Zborowsky, E. (1985). Developments in protective services: A challenge for social workers. *Journal of Gerontological Social Work, 8,* 71-83.

Zimberg, S. (1978). Treatment of the elderly alcoholic in the community and in an institutional setting. *Addictive Diseases, 3*(3), 417-427.

Statutes

Adult Protection Act, Statutes of Nova Scotia 1985, c. 2, as amended.

Adult Protection Act, Statutes of Prince Edward Island 1988, c. 6, as amended.

Charter of Rights and Freedoms, being Part I of the Constitution Act, 1982, being Schedule B of the Canada Act 1982, Statutes of Canada 1980-81-82, c. 11, as amended.

Nursing Homes Amendment Act 1987, Statutes of Ontario 1987, c. 20.

Nursing Homes Act, Revised Statutes of Ontario, c. 320, as amended.

Index

About the Editors

Ray DeV. Peters is Professor of Psychology at Queen's University in Kingston, Ontario, and is Research Director of the Better Beginnings, Better Futures Project, a large, multisite longitudinal study in Ontario on the prevention of mental health problems in young children from birth to seven years of age. He was a Visiting Scientist with the Oregon Social Learning Center in 1979-1980, and with the Mental Health Division of the World Health Organization in Geneva, Switzerland in 1986-1987. His primary research interests are in the areas of children's mental health and developmental psychology. Since 1982 he has served on the executive committee of the Banff International Conference on Behavioural Science.

Robert J. McMahon is Associate Professor in the Department of Psychology at the University of Washington in Seattle and the Director of the Child Clinical Psychology program. His primary research and clinical interests concern the assessment, treatment, and prevention of child conduct disorders. Much of his research has been focused on the development, evaluation, and application of social learning-based family interventions for dealing with young children's conduct problems. He is the author (with Rex Forehand) of *Helping the Noncompliant Child: A Clinician's Guide to Parent Training* (1981) and of more than 40 scientific articles, chapters, and reviews. He is currently a co-investigator on a large, multisite collaborative study on the prevention of conduct disorders in school-age children, and has served as a member of the executive committee of the Banff International Conference on Behavioural Science since 1982.

Vernon L. Quinsey received his Ph.D. in experimental psychology from the University of Massachusetts at Amherst in 1970. For 15 years he was the Director of Research at the Mental Health Centre in Penetanguishene, Ontario where most of his research dealt with maximum security psychiatric patients. He is currently Professor and Coordinator of Forensic/Correctional Studies in the Psychology Department at Queen's University. His research interests include the prediction of violent behavior, the assessment and treatment of sex offenders, institutional violence, and evolutionary influences on sexual and aggressive behaviors.